RESEARCH WITH THE LOCUS OF CONTROL CONSTRUCT

Volume 3

Extensions and Limitations

RESEARCH WITH THE LOCUS OF CONTROL CONSTRUCT

Volume 3

Extensions and Limitations

EDITED BY

Herbert M. Lefcourt

Department of Psychology
University of Waterloo
Waterloo, Ontario, Canada

FRANCIS CLOSE HALL
LEARNING CENTRE
UNIVERSITY OF GLOUCESTERSHIRE
Swindon Road
Cheltenham GL50 4AZ
Tel: 01242 532913

1984

ACADEMIC PRESS, INC.

(*Harcourt Brace Jovanovich, Publishers*)
Orlando   San Diego   San Francisco   New York   London
Toronto   Montreal   Sydney   Tokyo   São Paulo

ACADEMIC PRESS, INC.
Orlando, Florida 32887

United Kingdom Edition published by
ACADEMIC PRESS, INC. (LONDON) LTD.
24/28 Oval Road, London NW1 7DX

Library of Congress Cataloging in Publication Data

Main entry under title:

Research with the locus of control construct.

   Includes bibliographical references and index.
   Contents: v. 1. Assessment methods. 2. Developments and social problems -- v. 3. Extensions and
limitations.
   1. Control (Psychology) 2. Psychology, Applied.
I. Lefcourt, Herbert M. [DNLM: Internal-external
control. BF 632.5 R432 1981]
BF611.R47   155.2'32   81-7876
ISBN 0-12-443203-4

PRINTED IN THE UNITED STATES OF AMERICA

84 85 86 87   9 8 7 6 5 4 3 2 1

CONTENTS

1

INTRODUCTION

Herbert M. Lefcourt

I

APPLICATIONS OF LOCUS
OF CONTROL RESEARCH

II

LIMITATIONS IN LOCUS
OF CONTROL RESEARCH

5

AN ATTRIBUTION ANALYSIS OF THE LOCUS
OF CONTROL CONSTRUCT AND THE TRENT
ATTRIBUTION PROFILE

Paul T. P. Wong and Catherine F. Sproule

6

PARTICIPATORY CONTROL AND THE CHRONIC-ILLNESS
ADJUSTMENT PROCESS

David W. Reid

7

EPILOGUE
Herbert M. Lefcourt

LIST OF CONTRIBUTORS

Numbers in parentheses indicate the pages on which the authors' contributions begin.

Kirk R. Blankstein (73), Department of Psychology, Erindale College, University of Toronto, Mississauga, Ontario L5L 1C6, Canada

James A. Dyal (209), Department of Psychology, University of Waterloo, Waterloo, Ontario, N2L 3G1, Canada

Herbert M. Lefcourt (1, 391), Department of Psychology, University of Waterloo, Waterloo, Ontario, N2L 3G1, Canada

Gordon E. O'Brien (7), School of Social Sciences, The Flinders University of South Australia, Bedford Park, South Australia 5042

David W. Reid (361), Department of Psychology, York University, Downsview, Ontario M3J 1P3, Canada

Catherine F. Sproule (309), Department of Psychology, Trent University, Peterborough, Ontario K9J 7B8, Canada

Paul T. P. Wong (309), Department of Psychology, Trent University, Peterborough, Ontario K9J 7B8, Canada

PREFACE

Part I of this volume contains three lengthy chapters that describe in detail the large number of investigations that have been conducted in each of three psychological domains: industrial psychology, psychophysiology, and cross-cultural psychology. In each of these chapters the authors have reviewed the overabundant literature, attempting to sort out real contributions from the usual repetitive, methodologically weak, and inconclusive studies. In each domain, there are tempting findings that beg for replication and extension. At the same time, much of the literature reviewed can leave psychologists with the sense that psychology is still an infant science. The difficulties encountered in research are of such magnitude that one wonders if clear results are ever attainable.

The last two chapters examine the question of the circumstances under which locus of control is a useful construct. Thus the term *limitations* is added to that of *extensions* in this volume's subtitle. As the construct is applied to research, such as that pertaining to health and the recovery from illness, we begin to learn in what cases the construct is inappropriate in its simple unidimensional form or under what circumstances the presumably "better" internality bodes ill for the individual.

This volume, therefore, presents both (1) the extensions of use of the locus of control construct into areas far removed from the purview of the construct's originators and (2) the limitations of that usage that data have revealed.

These chapters, we hope, will not discourage would-be investigators, but will alert them to the errors that can stem from overextension of conceptual tools and from poor definition of intentions and hypotheses. Clear conceptual and methodological approaches to the study of any problem are rare and must be cherished when they are found. But the muddling through that comprises the core of much research must be accepted as the more common endeavor. If clarification and highlighting of difficulties can help others muddle through, then we will feel that these chapters have served their purpose well.

RESEARCH WITH THE LOCUS OF CONTROL CONSTRUCT
Volume 3
Extensions and Limitations

1

Herbert M. Lefcourt

INTRODUCTION

In this third and final volume of the *Research with the Locus of Control Construct* series we turn our attention to a set of applications in which the locus of control variable has been used to examine particular spheres of interest. In each case there has been some conceptual justification for making use of the locus of control variable in that area.

The chapter by Gordon O'Brien examines the literature linking locus of control to various aspects of work and retirement. Because work settings provide so much opportunity for assessment—from absenteeism to ratings of efficiency, competence, and role attainments—they seem most appropriate areas in which social learning variables could be used. That is, when feedback is clear, as is the case with wages or promotions, expectancy and value variables should be powerful predictors of responses to success or failure at attaining those goals. Indeed, a number of years ago executives' illnesses were predicted successfully from knowledge of whether or not they had been bypassed for promotions (French & Kahn, 1962). Dashed hopes and disbelief in one's efficacy proved demoralizing and debilitating for these middle-level executives. O'Brien does not report conclusive evidence linking locus of control with work-relevant variables, though he does discuss some studies that offer compelling data in support of that linkage. It becomes clear in this literature that there is much unevenness among the studies, as one might expect with field studies in general. However, since those early findings linking an internal locus of control with union membership (Seeman, 1966) and with recovery from business failures

RESEARCH WITH THE LOCUS
OF CONTROL CONSTRUCT (Vol. 3.)
Extensions and Limitations

following a natural catastrophe (Anderson, 1977), it has been difficult not to believe that locus of control can be a valuable variable for predicting behavior in work settings.

The chapter by Kirk Blankstein was long overdue. Investigators concerned with biofeedback and the management of bodily processes have been making use of locus of control variables for over a decade and have been speaking about self-control in terms that are similar to those used in describing locus of control. Though several researchers have found relationships between locus of control and the learning of control over certain physiological processes (acceleration of heart rate, for example), there have been few attempts to conceptualize the meanings and ramifications of those relationships. Perhaps this is due to the fact that for most investigators of these processes, locus of control was rarely of more than peripheral interest, albeit an interesting low-level correlate of physiological processes. Though primarily interested in such processes, Blankstein has had a more persistent interest in the locus of control literature than most of his fellow psychologists concerned with biofeedback and physiological control, which acounts for the lengthy and cogent review of the literature included in this volume. In a sense, his chapter can stand alone as a review of the way psychologists have tried to link molar variables, as are found in personality literature, with more molecular variables, such as those pertinent to physiological processes, with all of the foibles, oversights, and plain errors that commonly plague such attempts.

If Blankstein's extensive review reveals many of the flaws and failings in linking molar with molecular processes, Jim Dyal's chapter can be seen as its equivalent in drawing our attention to the weaknesses in much of the cross-cultural research that so often seems to be influenced more by convenience and ease than it is by theoretical constructions. Because so many of the studies cited by Dyal offer little more than atheoretical comparisons, one can be led to wonder if cross-cultural psychology has anything to offer investigators concerned with the functioning of personality. It is not until Dyal describes attempts to examine the function of variables like locus of control in different cultures that the reader's hopes become more sanguine regarding cross-cultural research. Though a great number of studies have been reported, as Dyal notes, most have led to no substantial conclusions, partly because they are devoid of information about the cultures being compared and bereft of theorizing that would help to account for the translation of a given culture's mores into the personal perceptions assessed by personality scales. Captivating models of cross-cultural research, represented in John Berry's work (Berry & Annis, 1974) with field dependence, have not been adapted by researchers concerned with locus of control and cultural differences.

The second part of this volume comprises two chapters, which, like the final chapters by deCharms and McKinney in the first volume, help to clarify the locus of control construct by positing limits and conditions in which it functions. Both the chapter by Paul Wong and Catherine Sproule and the one by Dave Reid raise arguments against considering internality as a stable optimal state and externality as always being a deficiency or negative state. As Gurin, Gurin, Lao, and Beattie (1969) contended over a decade ago, the maintenance of an internal locus of control could be highly detrimental for persons deprived of opportunities for success. Given continuous failure, persons who regard all outcomes as due to their own efforts would eventually have to regard themselves as inept rather than as victims of injustice. Such depressive conclusions, in turn, should lead to less initiative than would a tendency to blame an oppressor or other external causes. This kind of concern has led some investigators to speak of *real* control as opposed to *perceived* control, and it has led others to assess more specific attributions for success versus failure, for stable versus unstable characteristics, and so on.

Wong and Sproule provide an example of the latter approach. The Trent Attribution Profile, originally published in 1978 (Wong, Watters, & Sproule, 1978), like the Multidimensional–Multiattributional Causality Scale (MMCS—see Lefcourt, von Baeyer, Ware, & Cox, 1979) described in the first volume, creates subsets of attributions such that one can speak in more specific terms than internal–external. These attempts at specificity are welcome, but it should be noted that the use of more specific attributions has yet to produce the kinds of findings that have been obtainable by those who have relied on the more general dimension of internal–external control.

In Reid's chapter we come again to the issue of when internal control is optimal and when it is not. Certain quandaries of life just have to be accepted (the argument would go), and the sense of efficacy is at best irrelevant under such circumstances. Though Reid's examples cause one to pause and reconsider assumptions regarding the benefits of an internal control orientation, the effects of such writings should be to encourage more investigators to consider interactive models such as were described in the chapters by Sandler, Reese, Spencer, and Harpin (1983) and Lefcourt (1983) in Volume II. In the literature reviewed in those chapters it became clear that persons characterized as internals performed or acted well in certain conditions and poorly in others, and that externals often revealed diametrically opposite predilections.

Thus the assumption that internality is always a positive asset and externality always a deficit is obviously an overstatement and incorrect. The more differentiated conceptions of locus of control advocated by so many of the writers in these volumes seem essential if sense is to be made of the many discrepancies from predictions in which internals have been expected to fare more adequately but in fact have suffered more than have their external counterparts.

References

Anderson, C. R. Locus of control, coping behaviors and performance in a stress setting: A longitudinal study. *Journal of Applied Psychology*, 1977, *62*, 446–451.

Berry, J. W., & Annis, R. C. Ecology, culture and psychological differentiation. *International Journal of Psychology*, 1974, *9*, 173–193.

French, J. R. P., Jr., & Kahn, R. L. A programmatic approach to studying the industrial environment and mental health. *Journal of Social Issues*, 1962, *18*, 1–48.

Gurin, P., Gurin, G., Lao, R. C., & Beattie, M. Internal–external control in the motivational dynamics of Negro youth. *Journal of Social Issues*, 1969, *25*, 29–53.

Lefcourt, H. M. *Locus of control: Current trends in theory and research*. Hillsdale, NJ: Lawrence Erlbaum, 1982.

Lefcourt, H. M. The locus of control as a moderator: Stress. In H. M. Lefcourt (Ed.) *Research with the locus of control construct* (Vol. 2). New York: Academic Press, 1983.

Lefcourt, H. M., von Baeyer, C. L., Ware, E. E., & Cox, D. J. The Multidimensional–Multiattributional Causality Scale: The development of a goal-specific locus of control scale. *Canadian Journal of Behavioral Science*, 1979, *11*, 286–304.

Sandler, I., Reese, F., Spencer, L., Harpin, P. Person × environment interaction and locus of control: Laboratory, therapy and classroom studies. In H. M. Lefcourt (Ed.) *Research with the locus of control construct* (Vol. 2). New York: Academic Press, 1983.

Seeman, M. Alienation, membership and political knowledge. *Public Opinion Quarterly*, 1966, *30*, 353–367.

Wong, P. T. P., Watters, D. A., & Sproule, C. F. Initial validity and reliability of the Trent Attribution Profile as a measure of attribution schema and locus of control. *Educational and Psychological Measurement*, 1978, *38*, 1129–1134.

I

APPLICATIONS OF
LOCUS OF CONTROL
RESEARCH

2

Gordon E. O'Brien

LOCUS OF CONTROL, WORK, AND RETIREMENT

Introduction

A large part of a person's life is spent working. Hence it is reasonable to expect that work tasks, together with the organizational structure in which they are performed, should have a considerable effect on a person's expectations and personality. Conversely, individual expectancies and personality may determine behaviors that lead to changes in organizational processes and structures. However, relatively little research is available that is relevant to understanding the interplay between work and personality. Most research studies in organizational psychology have been concerned with work motivation and organizational effectiveness. This chapter aims to integrate and assess what is known about the relationship between work activities and one personality variable—locus of control. (*Locus of control* is a concept that refers to a generalized expectancy about the extent to which reinforcements are under internal or external control. Persons characterized as internal believe that reinforcements are determined largely by personal effort, ability, and initiative, whereas persons classified as external believe that reinforcements are determined largely by other people, social structures, luck, or fate. The extent to which a person believes that he or she is internally or externally controlled has commonly been measured using Rotter's Internal–External Control Scale (Rotter's I–E Scale; Rotter, 1966).)

This scale has been used by most researchers who have studied the

RESEARCH WITH THE LOCUS
OF CONTROL CONSTRUCT (Vol. 3.)
Extensions and Limitations

relationship between work and locus of control. However, a number of studies have used modified versions of this scale or alternative scales. This review examines the effect of locus of control upon work choices, work performance, and work attitudes. It also considers studies that are relevant to understanding how work structures can determine an employee's locus of control. The scope of the review extends to studies that examine the relationship between work and nonwork activities. Hence, relationships between locus of control and leisure, unemployment, and retirement are also assessed.

A considerable number of studies on work and locus of control have appeared since the publication of Rotter's scale. The most popular type of study has examined employee behavior as a consequence of locus of control. This literature has been examined in a recent review (Spector, 1982). However, there is little overlap between Spector's article and the present chapter, as Spector was more concerned with developing a theoretical model. His review presents a number of testable hypotheses about the relation between locus of control scores and measures of organizational behavior. As these hypotheses are derived from a summary of the research findings, their usefulness is dependent on the soundness of the research on which they are based. The hypotheses are also used to make recommendations about the appropriate strategies to use in selecting internals and externals. Consequently, these recommendations cannot be accepted until the literature on locus of control and work organizations is critically examined. The main purpose of this chapter is to review critically the published studies dealing with the direct effects of locus of control variables on work and on nonwork behavior. Second, studies about the effect of employment and unemployment on locus of control are considered. The analysis of both kinds of study is partially integrated by some specific theories about the reciprocal effects of locus of control and work structures. Finally, the adequacy of Rotter's scale for measuring generalized expectancies about the locus of control is assessed. Despite the proliferation of locus of control scales, it is maintained that the general internal–external locus of control construct has not been properly measured.

Occupational Choice and Career Planning

The studies that have examined occupational choice and career planning as a function of an individual's locus of control generally have been concerned not with testing a theory of career development but rather with identifying simple associations between locus of control and activities associated with planning and choosing a career. There are exceptions, but most of the studies ignore Rotter's (1975) warning that locus of control is likely to be most useful as a construct when it is embedded in a theory that includes both situational and personality variables. The typical prediction is that internals will expend more effort than externals in planning their careers and will choose occupations that allow them to make use of personal skills and initiative. These differences are likely to be greatest in situations where there are opportunities for career planning. The actual occupations chosen by internals and externals are also likely to depend on the jobs and careers available to them at the time of choice.

Some studies have shown indirect support for this view. Using a nationwide United States sample, Valecha (1972) found that internals sought jobs with greater autonomy than did externals and also that internals reported receiving more educational training related to progress on their jobs than did externals.[1] However, these relationships held only for the White subsample; locus of control was unrelated to job choice and reported training for the Black subsample. This difference between Whites and Blacks could be due to the fact that Whites typically have greater opportunities for job mobility than Blacks. If this were the case, then it seems inappropriate for Valecha to conclude that the locus of control scale has better validity for Whites than for Blacks. The construct simply has been shown to vary in its association with reported career activities as a function of racial background, which would be expected if opportunities for job mobility and career planning differed significantly for Whites and Blacks. The results of this study need to be qualified further because information about job choice and job-related training was obtained by self-reports, which could have been affected by locus of control itself. Internals may be more likely than externals to perceive their career activities as goal oriented. Hence it would have been desirable to have independent and objective information about job choices and training activities related to job choice.

Other studies, using smaller samples, have also reported that internals and externals differ in job choices and career preparation. With female undergraduates, Maracek and Frasch (1977) reported that externals engaged in less career planning, had less commitment in their

[1]Valecha used an 11-item version of Rotter's I–E Scale. Items selected were considered to be more general, adult oriented, and work related. The format also required respondents to rate their degree of agreement with the chosen alternative on a 1–4 scale so that total scores ranged from 11 to 44. With a sample of 56 students, Valecha and Ostrom (1974) reported a correlation of .69 between the original and the modified Rotter scale.

careers, and reported that they would feel more discomfort than internals in violating gender-role stereotypes. Burlin (1976) found similar results with teenage girls. Internals were more likely to choose innovative ideal-occupations than externals. *Innovative occupations* were defined as those in which less than 30% of the occupants were women. When the 14–16-year-old girls were asked what occupations they would actually follow, however, there was no significant difference between internals and externals.

These two studies suggest that young women who are internally oriented are more likely to choose nontraditional occupations as ideal choices than are externals. However, control orientation has little effect on actual choices, and this could be due to the perception that females' job opportunities are relatively limited. These studies do not provide information about the amount of effort subjects expended in making vocational choices. On the basis of earlier research on locus of control (Joe, 1971; Lefcourt, 1976; Phares, 1976; Rotter, 1966), internals would be expected to exert more effort and to try to use more information in order to obtain career goals. One study relevant to this expectation was conducted by Gable, Thompson, and Glanstein (1976), who examined the vocational maturity of college women. Vocational maturity was measured using Crites's Career Maturity Inventory (Crites, 1971). This inventory measures involvement in the process of vocational choice. It was found that vocational maturity of college women was unrelated to whether they chose traditional or nontraditional female occupations. Maturity scores were greater for internals than for externals, and locus of control interacted with vocational choice as a predictor of maturity. For internals, vocational maturity was greater for those making nontraditional than for those making traditional choices. The opposite was true for externals: The vocational maturity of those making traditional choices was greater than for those making nontraditional choices.

The authors interpret their findings using the results of an earlier study by Liberty, Burnstein, and Moulton (1966), who found that males low in their concern with environmental mastery tended to prefer occupations with high prestige to occupations that provided opportunities to exercise competence. Gable *et al.* concluded that external college-women seek prestigious occupations after immature efforts at vocational choice. This interpretation is unconvincing, for several reasons. First, Liberty *et al.* used Strodtbeck's Value Achievement Scale (Strodtbeck, 1958, pp. 138–195) to measure mastery, which is correlated only weakly with Rotter's I–E Scale ($r = -.26$). Second, the Liberty *et al.* study did not distinguish clearly between prestigious and competence-demanding occupations, and a correlation of .90 was found between prestige and competence level. Third, Gable et al. actually report that nontraditional female occupations have higher occupational prestige. As no differences were reported between internals and externals in their type of vocational choices, it is difficult to see why externals should be labeled *prestige seekers*. The results could be interpreted as suggesting that those externals who do not spend much time making decisions about careers choose nontraditional occupations that are higher in prestige and skill level. Other externals spend more time on career planning, become aware of the difficulty in attaining certain occupations, and then settle for an occupation that is accessible to them. In this sense they may be more realistic and display greater vocational maturity. Hence the results of this study do not justify the conclusions that attempt to label all externals prestige seekers and vocationally immature.

One problem with assessing the contribution of locus of control to vocational decisions is that most studies have not considered the role of scholastic ability in determining both vocational decisions and locus of control. The differences between internal and external subjects may be due to differences in their ability. One study that did examine the joint influence of ability and locus of control on vocational plans was by Taylor (1982). Scores were obtained on Rotter's locus of control score, on fear of success (Zuckerman & Allison, 1976), and on ability (American College Test composite scores) for a mixed gender sample of 201 psychology undergraduates. Vocational decision was measured using the Career Decision Scale (Osipow, Carney, Winer, Yanico, & Koschier, 1980). Vocationally undecided students were found to be more external in locus of control, more fearful of success, and had lower ability scores than decided students. When the sample was split into high- and low-ability groups, locus of control was not a predictor of vocational indecision for lower-ability students but remained a significant predictor for high-ability students. This form of analysis is not appropriate for assessing the interaction between ability and locus of control (Arnold, 1982), although it does show that the strength of the association between locus of control and vocational indecision varies with ability. Taylor interprets the result as being due to high-ability externals believing that the actual career one chooses is in part due to chance. However, it is possible that these external students, whose ability levels may provide the basis for a large variety of career paths, actually were more undecided because they had a more realistic assessment of the structural factors that could determine whether or not they were going to be able to pursue various careers. Internals could have responded to vocational questions more in terms of their ideal choices whereas externals may have realized that the pursuit of ideal choices has to be tempered by labor market trends, costs of training, and personal obligations to their family and close friends. However, the study does show that locus of control can predict vocational indecision even when ability is controlled. The reasons why high-ability externals are more indecisive than high-ability internals has yet to be established.

The studies reported thus far do not investigate the extent to which reported job choices are actually followed by behavior consistent with the choice. It could be argued that the most direct and valid way of examining vocational choices is to examine the characteristics of those who have committed themselves to a particular career by job application or by choice of training. One study used this strategy (Wertheim, Widom, & Wortzel, 1978). The authors examined the personality and social–demographic correlates of choice of training in four professional occupations: two traditional male professions (law and management) and two traditional female professions (education and social work). Locus of control did not differ significantly across students in the four different training programs. The relevance of this study for understanding locus of control as a determinant of choice seems limited. No good reasons were given for expecting locus of control to be associated with choice of training. All courses required a great deal of skill utilization and effort, and information was not provided about accessibility of training. Even if significant differences in locus of control had been found, the results would have been difficult to interpret. In addition, the study was cross-sectional, and locus of control was measured after choice of training. Hence the locus of control scores might have been affected by the experience of professional training.

The studies reviewed here assumed that work is an important and highly valued component of a person's life. This may not be the case. One study did investigate the role of work importance as a contributor, with locus of control, to career planning. Greenhaus and Sklarew (1981) predicted a positive correlation between work salience and career exploration; *work salience* was defined as the importance of work in a person's life. These investigators also predicted that the relationship between work salience and career exploration would be stronger for internals than for externals. Career exploration was assessed using a list of 15 activities, 6 of which dealt with self-oriented exploration (such as taking aptitude tests) and 9 with work-related exploration (such as reading career handbooks or seeking advice about career opportunities). Undergraduates were asked to indicate the activities in which they had engaged. The interaction between work salience and locus of control on career exploration was analyzed using a moderated multiple-regression procedure. Locus of control was not related significantly to either work or self-exploration activities, and the relationship between work salience and career exploration was similar for internals and externals. For all subjects, work-role salience was related positively to participation in self-related and work-related exploration.

Career planning of those already in occupations also has been examined. Thornton (1978) measured the locus of control of secretaries before they started a 1-day career-planning workshop. Four months later they were sent a questionnaire that asked them to record career-planning activities they had undertaken since the workshop. It was found that internals reported more actions undertaken to further career goals than did externals. Thornton noted that the significance of this finding is limited because no attempts were made to verify self-reports. In addition, no attempt was made to describe the work environments the secretaries had experienced previously. It is possible that the internals could have come from organizations that encouraged career development, whereas the externals did not.

One study did use a behavioral, rather than a self-report, measure of career-planning. Giles (1977) investigated the relationship between locus of control and volunteering for job enrichment, using a sample of female factory-workers. Locus of control did not predict volunteering behavior for the total sample. However, internals who were dissatisfied with their jobs were more likely to volunteer for job enrichment than were externals.

The importance of the organizational environment as a determinant of the relationship between locus of control and career planning was recognized by Hammer and Vardi (1981) in their study of non-supervisory employees in industrial organizations. They predicted that locus of control would influence career self-management if the organization allowed employees to exercise initiative. However, if job mobility opportunities were limited by situational factors, locus of control would be a poor predictor of career planning. Two situational factors were assumed to affect career self-management: organizational policy on career mobility and the nature of the technology. Career effort, career planning, and career attainment were examined as functions of two levels of company policy (facilitating versus constraining personnel policy), two levels of technology (routine versus complex), and three levels of locus of control (low, moderate, and high).

Although reported self-initiation of mobility was higher in facilitating than in constraining organizations, there was no significant interaction between locus of control and company policy as determinants of self-initiated mobility. However, internals reported higher self-initiated mobility than did externals. Locus of control did not have a direct or interactive effect on reported effort toward job mobility or on the use of career strategies, such as telling the supervisor about a desire to move to another job.

Hammer and Vardi concluded that internals played a more active role in their career progress when they worked in facilitating organizations. This appears to be overstating the results. The only one of the three measures of career management to show a significant result was a measure of self-reported self-initiation of job moves. No attempt was made to verify these self-reports, and hence it is possible that this result was due to biased perceptions by internals and externals. The overall significance of the results, however, can be questioned seriously due to the types of organizations used. It was stated that the facilitating organization was 100% unionized and that the union had a seniority clause in its job contracts. If seniority was a major criterion for job promotion and mobility, it is doubtful that the organization encouraged advancement on the basis of skill, effort, and training. This interpretation is supported by the finding that there was no difference between internals and externals in the degree to which they saw personalistic factors (e.g., skills, competence) or external factors (e.g., seniority) as determining job mobility. It is also consistent with the conclusion that "organizational practices and policies regarding job mobility dominate completely over locus of control in determining perceptions of mobility requirements" (Hammer & Vardi, 1981, p. 26).

A number of conclusions can be drawn from these studies on occupational choice and career planning.

1. Internals are more likely than externals to choose jobs that have higher skill requirements and provide greater personal autonomy. However, this appears to apply to choices of ideal occupations. When internals and externals are asked about their actual or realistic choices, they display few differences. Actual choices are probably constrained by situational factors, such as social pressures and the accessibility of various jobs. It is possible that actual job choices are determined jointly by locus of control and situational factors, but further research is needed for this to be demonstrated.

2. Internals sometimes report more effort than do externals in career planning. It appears that the extent of the difference between internals and externals is determined by the degree to which their organizational environment encourages and provides opportunities for career development. Evidence suggests that internals are more likely

to report greater career planning than externals if they are in organizations where career advancement is possible and the criteria for advancement are related to personal motivation and skill. Further research is needed before this hypothesis can be considered to have been supported.

3. Nearly all research studies use self-reports as measures of occupational choice and planning. Hence the results may not extend to objective choices and objectively measured planning behavior. Another qualification that needs to be made is that results from various studies may differ because of the use of different locus of control scales. The use of different scales is not necessarily unsound, but interpretations are difficult when no information is provided about the degree of correspondence between revised scales and one or more commonly used locus of control scales.[2]

Occupational Attainment and Job Performance

Occupational Attainment

A number of cross-sectional studies have found that internal employees tend to attain higher occupations than externals (Hammer & Vardi, 1981; Harvey, 1971; Pandey & Tewary, 1979; Ryckman & Malikioski, 1974; Valecha, 1972). The immediate question raised by these results is the direction of causality. Do internals achieve higher occupational attainment than externals, or is locus of control a consequence of occupational attainment, or do both processes occur simultaneously? Without longitudinal evidence or some method of inferring reciprocal causation from correlational data, it is not possible to infer either that locus of control contributes to occupational attainment or that occupational attainment contributes to locus of control. Only Andrisani and Nestel (1976) and Andrisani, Applebaum, Koppel, and Miljus (1978) appear to have examined this question using longitudinal data. In the earlier report, the first aim was to assess the extent to which locus of control affected occupational attainment independently of education,

[2]Valecha (1972) used a modified 11-item version of Rotter's I–E Scale (Rotter, 1966). This modified version was also used by Wertheim, Widom, and Wortzel (1978); Burlin (1976); and Greenhaus and Sklarew (1981). Maracek and Frasch (1977) used the Adult Nowicki–Strickland Internal–External scale (Nowicki & Duke, 1974). A modified version of the Rotter scale was used by Thorton (1978), who cited Robinson and Shaver (1973) as the source. Gable *et al.* (1976) used the MacDonald–Tseng (1971) internal–external scale. Finally, Hammer and Vardi (1981) adopted a 14-item version of the Rotter scale. Items they considered irrelevant to an industrial population (e.g., educational and political items) were excluded.

age, and demographic variables. The second aim was to examine the stability of locus of control over a 2-year period (1969–1971) and to establish the extent to which changes in occupational attainment predicted changes in locus of control.

The sample was a large representative group of United States male employees in the age range of 45–59 years. Locus of control was measured with an 11-item version of Rotter's (1966) I–E Scale.[3] Occupational attainment was measured by Duncan's (1971) Index of Socioeconomic Status. Respondents reported their occupations, which were then rated using the index.

The relationship between locus of control in 1969 and occupational attainment in 1971 was examined by multiple regression; other predictors included occupational attainment in 1969, hourly earnings in 1969 and 1971, and change in occupational attainment from 1969 to 1971. The analyses showed that, in 1969, internals had higher-status occupations and earned more money. Locus of control in 1969 was also related significantly to 1971 earnings and occupational attainment, even when 1969 measures were included in the regression equation. Andrisani and Nestel (1976) suggested that internals experience more favorable employment circumstances than do externals. What this means is unclear. The results did not support the prediction that locus of control would affect changes in occupational attainment. The beta coefficients for change in occupational attainment (1969–1971) and change in hourly earnings (1969–1971) were not significant. Hence the evidence reported shows that locus of control predicts future occupational attainment significantly, even when present occupational attainment is controlled. However, locus of control does not significantly predict change in occupational attainment. This is puzzling, and the authors do not elaborate on their finding.

Later analyses of the same data did show, however, that locus of control was related to subsequent change in occupational attainment and annual earnings (Andrisani, 1978). This result was obtained when

[3]In a later report (Andrisani, 1978, chap. 4), it was stated that the items were selected on the basis of Gurin, Gurin, Lao, and Beattie's (1969) factor analysis of the Rotter scale. Actually, this factor analysis included 16 items added to the 23 Rotter items. Andrisani did use only the Rotter items, however. He also elaborated the forced-choice format by requiring respondents to rate the degree to which the chosen item reflected their opinion. The responses were rated 1–4 and the final locus of control score ranged from 11 to 44. In a footnote, Andrisani and Nestel (1976) stated that a pretest showed that this method produced "nearly identical measures" with those obtained using Rotter's I–E Scale. If this means that the ordering of scores was nearly identical and analyses give similar results regardless of scale used, then it is puzzling why the original scale was not retained.

only items loading on a personal control factor were used. The set of predictors in the regression equation was not the same as the predictors reported in the earlier analyses, suggesting that the results obtained are sensitive to the sample used, the locus of control scale, and the set of predictors used in the regression.

The schematic summary of later analyses is shown in Table 2.1. These results show that changes in occupational attainment were related significantly to locus of control for all three of the White samples but unrelated to locus of control for two of the three Black samples. Andrisani (1978) argues that this is due to structural impediments to job mobility for Blacks.

Another study examined the effect of locus of control on future occupational characteristics (O'Brien, in press). This cross-sectional study was based on a large cluster sample of employees in an Australian city and used two-stage least-squares analysis (James & Singh, 1978) to establish the extent of reciprocal causation between locus of control and job attributes. The results partly supported the prediction that locus of control, as measured by Rotter's scale, determined the amount of skill utilization and influence in an employee's job, as well as the amount

TABLE 2.1

Association between Locus of Control and Subsequent Change in Occupational Attainment and Annual Earnings—Multiple Regression Analyses[a]

	Sample					
	Men				Women	
	Young		Mature		Mature	
Change	White	Black	White	Black	White	Black
In annual earnings	NS[b]	NS	S[b]	S	NS	NS
In occupational attainment	S	S	S	NS	S	NS

[a] A personal control scale derived from Rotter's scale was used. Other predictors in the regression were education, training, health, urbanization of region, and geographical area. The sign of the beta coefficients indicated that employees with low scores on personal control (internal) were more likely to have increased their occupational attainment and earnings than were employees with high scores on personal control (external). This table was constructed from results reported by Andrisan (1978).

[b] NS = nonsignificant beta coefficient. S = significant beta coefficient.

of income earned. *Skill utilization* was defined as the degree of match between employee skills and skills required by the job. *Influence* was defined as the degree of say or control the employee had over various aspects of the job (e.g., tasks done, design of workplace, work organization, pay). This study is described in more detail in the section on alienation and powerlessness. The results could not be attributed to the effect of locus of control on perceptions of these job attributes, as these attributes were estimated, using regression analysis, from measures of occupational status, organizational level, and employee education. For the total sample, the results showed that employees with a relatively low locus of control score (internal) were more likely than high scorers (external) to have obtained jobs that were higher on skill utilization, influence, and income. When the sample was split on the basis of gender and marital status, it was found that the effect of locus of control on skill utilization and influence was significant only for married males and single females. For the effect of locus of control on income, the results were significant only for single males and single females. The analyses were repeated with a personal control scale obtained by factor analysis (O'Brien & Kabanoff, 1981), but the pattern of results was practically identical.

The results of this study are reasonably consistent with those obtained by Andrisani. However, they do provide additional information about the actual attributes of the jobs that attract individuals who have an internal locus of control. It appears that internals tend to gravitate toward jobs that allow them greater opportunities for using their skills and exercising influence. Whether or not internals actually obtain such jobs appears to depend on job-relevant abilities and structural opportunities for job mobility. Locus of control does not predict job attributes or occupational attainment when mobility is likely to be restricted (e.g., among Blacks and married women).

The next question concerns why internals rather than externals should obtain jobs with high skill-utilization and occupational status. Three separate, but not mutually exclusive, explanations are considered in the following subsections. First, internals could show greater job mobility than externals because of the nature of their career planning and job choice. Second, they could acquire such jobs because they perform better than externals through greater effort and work motivation, thus increasing their likelihood of promotion. A third and related explanation is that internals are more likely to be promoted than externals because they choose task behaviors that approximate more closely the behaviors required for optimal job performance. This also implies that internals perform better on the job than do externals.

Explanations of Occupational Attainment

CAREER CHOICE AND PLANNING

It is possible that internals actually choose and plan to get jobs that are higher in skill utilization, autonomy, and income than do externals. However, the evidence reviewed in the previous section is inconclusive on this question. Before this explanation can be supported, it is necessary to examine studies that provide objective information about job choices and career planning. The large majority of studies have used self-report measures for these variables, and hence it is not known whether differences in career choices correspond to actual choices or simply reflect perceptions and attributions of individuals varying in locus of control.

JOB PERFORMANCE

The majority of studies that have examined the direct relationship between an employee's locus of control and job performance have reported that internals perform better than externals[4] (Table 2.2). However, a considerable number of studies show no significant difference in performance. Those that do show significant relationships generally used ratings of instructor performance that had not previously been validated against objective performance. Hence it is possible that raters were using their own theories about the personal qualities and behavior needed for success on the job. In addition, many of these studies did not establish the fact that task-relevant abilities and personal attributes were equivalent for internals and externals. In one study where ability was controlled statistically (Lied & Pritchard, 1976), the relationship between locus of control and performance became insignificant. In another, when ability was measured by preexperimental performance, internals performed better on quantity but not on quality measures (Mimnaugh & O'Brien, 1981). Many studies did not attempt to measure the interaction between situational differences and locus of control. Where situational differences were varied, the interaction effects were inconsistent. Ruble (1976) found that internals performed better in participative decision groups than directive leader groups, whereas externals performed better in directive leader groups than in participative groups. The overall difference in performance was insignificant, but

---

[4]The general significance of the results could have been assessed using the formulas reviewed by Rosenthal (1978). However, the use of these methods requires that the designs and measures are adequate for testing the hypotheses being assessed. For the studies listed in Table 2.2, this assumption is not justified.

TABLE 2.2
Summary of Results of Studies Examining the Relationship between Locus of Control and Work Performance[a]

Researchers	Subjects	Assessment of situational equivalence	Control for ability or other personal attributes	Situational moderators measured	Task	Performance measure	Results
				EXPERIMENTAL STUDIES			
Dossett, Latham, & Mitchell (1979)	60 Female clerks	Yes	Random assignment	Assigned vs. participative goals Knowledge of results	Arithmetic problems presented on 35mm slides	Number of problems solved	No direct or interactive effect of I-E control
Mimnaugh & O'Brien (1981)	50 Job applicants for computer training; 31 male, 19 female	Yes	Random assignment	Clear vs. unclear feedback Positive vs. negative feedback	Sort computer card data	Number of cards sorted (quantity); accuracy of sorting (quality)	Internals performed better than externals on quantity ($F = 8.43$, $df = 1, 31$, $p < .01$) No difference on quality No interactions with type of feedback

Study	Sample			Condition	Task	Dependent variable	Results
Ruble (1976)	64 Students in management; sex composition not stated	Yes	No	Self-planning vs. leader directed	Number assembly in groups of three	Number of correct assemblies	No direct effect of I-E control. Internal groups performed best under self-planning (SIG). External groups performed best under leader direction (Not SIG) I-E—planning structure interaction significant ($F = 5.50$, $df = 1,12$, $p < .05$)
Weiss & Sherman (1973)	41 Male undergraduates	Yes	No	Prior failure on task	Solve mazes	Time spent on a maze after failure on a previous maze	I-E unrelated to pretest performance. ($r = .04$) I-E correlated with effort after failure ($r = .38$, $p < .05$).
Yukl & Latham (1978)	41 Female typists	No	No	Participative goal setting vs. assigned goals	Typing	Number of lines typed	No relationship between I-E and performance improvement in either participative ($r = .06$, $n = 20$) or assigned goal condition ($r = .19$, $n = 21$)

(continued)

TABLE 2.2 (continued)

LONGITUDINAL STUDIES

Anderson (1977)	90 Managers of small businesses; sex composition not stated	No	No	No	Management of business after flood	Ratings of business performance by credit agency	Time 1 I-E (8 months after flood) correlated −.21 ($p < .05$) with Time 2 performance ($2\frac{1}{2}$ years after flood). Internals performed better
Durand & Shea (1974)	29 Black owners or managers of small businesses; 22 males, 7 females	No	No	No	Management of small business	Ratings by interviewers	Business activity, 18 months after completion of I-E, of internals superior to that of externals ($U = 65.5$, $M_1 = 14$, $M_2 = 15$, $p < .05$)

22

CROSS-SECTIONAL STUDIES

Anderson & Schneier (1978)	125 Business students; 84 male, 41 female	Partly; group organization unknown	No	No	Business class exercises	Instructors' ratings of exercises	Internal leaders of small groups more effective than external leaders ($t = 2.26$, $p < .05$, $n = 19$) Internally led groups more effective than externally led groups ($t = 1.76$, $p < .05$, $n = 19$).
Broedling (1975)	207 Naval officers and enlisted men	No	No	No	Variety of naval jobs	Supervisor and peer ratings of effort and quality of work	Internals tended to be superior on ratings of effort and performance: I–E-supervisor effort—$r = -.20$ ($p < .01$) I–E-supervisor performance—$r = -.19$ ($p < .01$) I–E-peer effort—$r = -.15$ I–E-peer performance—$r = -.17$ ($p < .01$)

(continued)

TABLE 2.2 (continued)

| Heisler (1974) | 175 Government administrators, "mostly male" | No | Age; education; tenure | Rewards skill determined vs. chance determined (perceptions) | Administrative jobs | Scale of personal effectiveness based on self-reports | Internals had higher personal effectiveness. I–E-effectiveness $r = -.22$ ($p < .01$), with age, education, and tenure partialed out. $r = -.27$ in skill-determined reward situations ($p < .01$). $r = -.08$ in chance-determined reward situations. |

| Keller & Holland (1978) | 256 Employees in professional occupations, 89% male | No | 6 personality variables education age | No | Professional jobs— various | Peer rating of value of employee as a source of innovative and administrative information. | Zero-order correlations between I–E and ratings significant; internals superior; innovativeness $r = .15$ ($p < .05$) Administrative communications, $r = -.11$; ($p < .05$). However, I–E beta coefficient nonsignificant when other personality variables, age, and education are included in multiple regression equation. |

(continued)

TABLE 2.2 (continued)

Lied & Pritchard (1976)	146 Airforce technical trainees; 5 females, 141 males	No	Ability	No	Technical training tasks	Self- and instructor ratings of effort; derived effort performance corrected for ability	Internals superior on ratings of effort I-E-self-rating—$r = -.33$, $n = 74$ ($p < .01$) I-E-instructor rating—$r = -.24$ ($p < .01$) I-E-derived effort—$r = -.15$, n.s.
Majumder, McDonald, & Greever (1977)	90 Rehabilitation counselors; 66 male, 24 female	No	Age	No	Rehabilitation counselor job	Supervisor ratings of performance as counselor	Internals rated more effective; $r = .37$ (age partialed out), $n = 90$ ($p < .01$).
Organ (1975)	180 Graduate students; 80% male, 20% female	Yes	Ability; extraversion	No	Class quizzes	Performance on quizzes; final exam performance	I-E not related to quiz or exam performance when ability and extraversion are controlled Internals showed greater rate of initial improvement on quizzes than did externals.

Pandey & Tewary (1979)	44 Applicants for business loans, gender unknown	No	Age	No	Assessment interview	Ratings of business potential by interviewers	Selected applicants had more internal scores than those rejected [$F = 4.16$, $df = 1,140$, $p < .05$].
Szilagyi, Sims, & Keller (1976)	1161 Medical center employees; 80% female	No	No	Role conflict & role ambiguity (perceived)	Performance of administrative, professional, clerical, and service jobs	Supervisor ratings	I–E-performance ratings non-significant ($r = -.06$). Still not significant when role ambiguity and role conflict are partialed out
Tseng (1970)	140 Vocational rehabilitation clients; 95 male, 45 female	No	No	No	Vocational training tasks	Instructor rating	Ratings of work quality and class success not significantly different for internals and externals

[a] All studies used Rotter's I–E locus of control scale (Rotter, 1966), except Yukl and Latham (1978), who used a 14-item version of the scale. Racial composition of subjects, if known, is specified.

the difference between internals in the two conditions was significant, although the same was not true for externals. Unfortunately, comparisons of the performances of internals and externals within conditions was not reported. The study did illustrate how locus of control, in interaction with structure, could be a stronger predictor of performance than structure itself. The main effect of condition accounted for 2% of variance in productivity, whereas the interaction between locus of control and the planning condition accounted for 22% of the variance.

Other studies show that internals' performance is slightly higher than externals' when perceived role conflict is partialed out (Szilagyi, Sims, & Keller, 1976). The relationship between internal–external control and performance was found to be significant in situations where all subjects perceived rewards to be based on skill; internals were superior to externals (Heisler, 1974). There was no significant difference in performance, however, when the situation was perceived as one where rewards were based on chance. In another study, neither the sign nor the clarity of feedback had differential effects on internals and externals (Mimnaugh & O'Brien, 1981). Two studies found no differential effect of assigned or participative goals on performance (Dossett, Latham, & Mitchell, 1979; Yukl & Latham, 1978).

Differences in studies could be due to a number of factors, including the following:

1. *Situational factors.* In some studies, the performance of internals and externals could have been affected systematically by differences in their situations. In addition, the failure of some studies to measure situational factors precluded estimation of locus of control–situational interactions.

2. *Valence differences.* Many studies did not establish that the value or attractiveness of performance outcomes was equivalent for internals and externals.

3. *Ability.* Some studies found that significant differences between internals and externals disappeared when ability was controlled for. Hence studies that failed to measure ability might be interpreted as showing different ability distributions among internals and externals.

4. *Use of performance ratings.* Although ratings are more often associated significantly with objective performance when both types of performance measures are used, the degree of correspondence is often low. In a recent review, Landy and Farr (1980) reported that ratings are affected by many types of systematic and random error. Some stud-

ies have shown that personality factors can affect ratings of performance. No study appears to have been performed on the accuracy of performance ratings as a function of rater locus of control and the locus of control of ratees. However, one study showed that locus of control of the rater affects ratings of leadership behavior (Lord, Phillips, & Rush, 1980). Hence it is not possible to say whether locus of control definitely affects the performance rating process. Nevertheless, it seems possible that raters could estimate performance not on the basis of objective attainment but on the basis of exhibited behavior and attitudes of internals and externals. The rater might believe, sometimes erroneously, that goal-directed, inquisitive, and persistent behavior leads to high performance. If such behaviors are then observed in the internally oriented employee, the rater may award him or her a higher performance rating than is objectively justified.

Despite these difficulties of interpretation, some generalizations are possible. Locus of control accounts for a small percentage of the variance in performance measures (the direct effect is generally less than 10%). When interaction between locus of control and structure is estimated, the percentage of variance accounted for is increased. Internals tend to be rated by supervisors as higher on performance than externals. However, the results do not allow one to infer actual performance differences, as the ratings could be due to an interaction between the public presentation of internals and externals with raters' stereotypes of the better-performing employee. The results could also be attributable to systematic differences in the abilities of internals and externals and in the job structures in which they are found.

It is still plausible that real performance differences exist between internals and externals. For this to be substantiated, it is necessary to show that internals are either more motivated than externals or that internals generally use behavioral strategies that are more similar to optimal performance behaviors than are the strategies used by externals.

Expectancy models of effort and performance. To the extent that high motivation induces greater effort, internals might be expected to perform better than externals in situations where effort makes a difference. Some researchers have tried to show, using expectancy theory, that the predicted effort of internals is greater than the predicted effort of externals. In organizational psychology, the typical expectancy model for predicting job effort is a composite of Vroom's (1964) effort and valence models. The general model, as stated by Mitchell (1974), is

$$W = E \sum_{j=1}^{n} [I_{ij} \, V_j] \qquad (1)$$

where W is the predicted effort, E is the expectancy that effort is associated with performance levels, I_{ij} the instrumentality of performance for the attainment of outcomes, V_j the valence of job outcomes, and n the number of outcomes.

The model has received moderate support, in that correlations between W and measures of effort (rated by supervisor or self) or performance have been statistically significant. However, the correlations indicate that predicted effort can account for at most 25% of the variance in rated effort or performance. Typically, the percentage of variance accounted for is between 10% and 15%. There are three reasons for these results: First, the model omits ability measures; second, task and structural variables may prevent intended effort from being realized in performance; and third, the model may be applicable only to those individuals who tend to see performance outcomes as being related to their personal effort.

This third qualification has been the justification for a number of studies that attempted to establish the effect of locus of control on effort toward performance expectancies and instrumentality expectancies. The effort-to-performance expectancy is the expectancy that effort is associated with performance levels, whereas instrumentality is the expectancy that performance is instrumental in attaining valued outcomes or reinforcements. Following Lawler (1971), it was expected that internals would have higher values of performance and reward expectancies than would externals. Internals, defined as individuals who attribute the attainment of valued outcomes to their personal efforts and abilities, were more likely to perceive that effort was related to performance and that performance was related to valued outcomes or reinforcements. Externals are more likely to perceive performance and its rewards as contingent on factors other than personal effort and performance. The studies testing these predictions are summarized in Table 2.3. All of the correlations between locus of control and performance expectancies, and locus of control and reward expectancies, are negative. However, the association is not as strong as might be expected. The percentage of variance accounted for is never greater than 16%. This partly accounts for the small relationship between locus of control and performance (Table 2.2). Even for situations where the relationship between effort and performance is high, the predicted effort (and thus performance) of internals should not be expected to be much greater than that of externals.

TABLE 2.3
Correlations between Locus of Control and Components of the Expectancy Model of Work Effect [a]

Study	Subjects n	Effort → performance expectancy (E)	Performance → reward expectancy (I)	Valence outcomes (V)	Effort (force) $(= E \cdot \times \Sigma(I \times V))$
Broedling (1975)	207 Naval officers and enlisted men.	-.28**	NA	-.27**	-.38**
Evans (1974)	86 Business students	8%	6.4%	NA[b]	5.2%
Lawler (1971)	Managers, number unknown	Verbal report that I-E was related to E	Verbal report that I-E was related to I	NA	NA
Lied & Pritchard (1976)	146 Airforce technical trainees	-.40**	-.20*	-.15	-.42**
Mimnaugh & O'Brien (1981)	50 Computer job applicants	-.13	-.14	-.09	-.20
Szilagyi & Sims (1975)	53 Administrative, 249 professional, 132 technical, 227 clerical, 312 service personnel.	-.07	-.39**	NA	NA
		-.16**	-.25**	NA	NA
		-.02	-.20*	NA	NA
		-.25**	-.24**	NA	NA
		-.15*	-.21**	NA	NA
Weiss & Sherman (1973)	41 Undergraduates	-.15	-.03	NA	NA

[a] Numbers are correlations, except Evans (1974), who reported percentage of variance in expectancies accounted for by locus of control.
[b] NA = not reported.
* p < .05.
** p < .01.

The results also show a slight tendency for externals to see performance-related outcomes as less desirable than do internals. This suggests that further research on work motivation could examine the desired outcomes of internals and externals. Externals may have different sets of desired outcomes, and hence their performances, compared to internals, might improve or even be superior if reinforcements appropriate to them were found.

It is possible that the expectancy formulation might not be the most appropriate for incorporating a generalized expectancy such as locus of control. Although it appears consistent with Rotter's (1954) general social learning formulation,

$$NP = f(\text{FM, NV}), \tag{2}$$

where need potential (NP) is a function of expectancies that behaviors will lead to reinforcements (Freedom of Movement: FM) and the value (need value: NV) of the reinforcements, it is not necessarily consistent with a version that includes general problem-solving expectancies. If, for example, locus of control as measured by I/E was replaced by a scale that measured general expectancies that effort led to performance (GE_E) and general expectancies that performance led to rewards (GE_I), then a possible model is

$$W = (E \times GE_E) \sum (I \times GE_I \times V). \tag{3}$$

Certainly, none of the studies in the job expectancy literature has explored such models.[5] Rather, they have concentrated on a simple approach that has investigated the direct association between locus of control and expectancies or locus of control and performance. Even this more complex Equation (3) neglects ability and structural variables. It seems that further research is needed to incorporate locus of control into more complex models if it is to improve the prediction of job performance and also demonstrate the conditions under which the generalized expectancy (locus of control) component is an important contributor to performance. Such a model could have a number of components, including effort, ability, and objective opportunities for personal control.

It is possible to explore a multiplicative model of the general form described by Shiflett (1979).

[5]Some research suggests that such equations should include a culture factor as the distribution of locus of control among employees who vary across cultures (Reitz & Groff, 1974) and across ethnic groups within the same culture (O'Brien & Kabanoff, 1981). However, this may be necessary only if locus of control has different relationships with other work motivation variables in different cultures. So far, this has not been shown (Reitz & Jewell, 1979).

$$P = [T] [R] \tag{4}$$

where P is the individual performance, T the matrix of situational constraints affecting the utilization of resources (transformers), and R the matrix of task-relevant resources of an individual. Going beyond Shiflett's formulation, which lacks a specific theory of resources and transformers, R could be represented by a column vector

$$R = \begin{bmatrix} W \\ a \end{bmatrix}. \tag{5}$$

The W entry is an individual's predicted effort

$$W = (E \times GE_E) \sum (I \times GE_I \times V), \tag{3}$$

and a is a measure of an individual's task-relevant ability.
T can be represented by a row vector

$$T = [sp]. \tag{6}$$

where s is a measure of job opportunities for skill utilization—a measure of personal control derived from job content (O'Brien, 1980, 1982a; O'Brien & Dowling, 1980)—and p is a measure of the objective potential influence of the individual within the group structure—a measure of personal control derived from the job context (O'Brien, Biglan, & Penna, 1972).

If all measures W, a, s, and p, had the range $0 \rightarrow 1$, then

$$P = [sp] \begin{bmatrix} W \\ a \end{bmatrix}. \tag{7}$$

With matrix multiplication, then

$$P = (s \times W) + (p \times a). \tag{8}$$

This is only one possible combination of variables. The main reason for introducing it is to suggest ways in which locus of control can be combined with motivational, ability, and situational variables. Such a model seems required if theories of individual performance are to account for substantially more than 15% of the variance in measured performance.

Task behavior. An alternative approach for understanding the relationship between locus of control and performance in work contexts is to examine the task behavior of internals and externals. The prediction of individual performance would start from knowledge of the required set (or alternative sets) of behaviors for performance of a specific type of task in a specific type of organizational structure. An internal individual could be expected to perform better than an external individual if his or her task behavior more closely resembled the ideal set of behaviors. Some studies have noted rather crude differences in the task behavior of internals and externals. When compared to externals, internals use behavioral rather than emotional responses to stress (Anderson, 1977; Anderson, Hellriegel, & Slocum, 1977), display less structuring behavior in groups (Durand & Nord, 1976), comply less with leaders (Cravens & Worchel, 1977), and show more work-group cooperation, self-reliance, courtesy, and compliance with rules (Tseng, 1970). However, such behaviors have not been related systematically to individual performance. A major difficulty of this approach is that it must await reasonably supported theories about the relationship between task behavior and performance in work organizations that vary in task type and structure. Such theories, however, are not available; most theories have advanced a so-called black box model that predicts performance outputs from individual (and occasionally structural) inputs without considering intervening behavior. It is possible that the performance of an individual might, for example, be a function of the extent to which the individual is resistant to external influences. If this were so, then it could be predicted that internals would be better in situations requiring resistance to influence, given that some research has shown that internals are less affected by external influence sources than are externals (Lefcourt, 1976). Externals, on the other hand, might be more effective than internals in situations requiring more responsiveness to influence communications. The one study that reported superior performances by externals was by Bigoness (1976), who studied the effects of locus of control and alternative styles of third-party intervention on bargaining behavior. Externals were found to be better than internals at resolving issues. This finding is consistent with data that show that externals perform in accord with directions and are more highly responsive than are internals to external task definitions (Lefcourt, 1976).

Work Structures, Affective Responses, and Powerlessness

Previous sections considered locus of control as a predictor of career choice, occupational attainment, and job performance. In this section studies are reviewed that consider the relationship between locus of control, affective states, and employee job-involvement. Most of these treat locus of control as an antecedent of stress reactions, job satisfaction, and job involvement. However another set of studies have also considered locus of control as a consequence of organizational structures. These studies are also reviewed as well as the small number of studies that have analyzed the reciprocal causal relationships between locus of control and organizational variables.

Work Stress

Most of the studies that have considered locus of control in relation to stress reactions in work settings have viewed stress as a reaction to imposed restrictions on goal-directed behavior. The main hypothesis is that internal employees experience less stress than external employees when exposed to the same work stressors. This prediction is deduced by assuming that internals are more likely than externals to engage in behavior that changes a stressful situation in a manner that facilitates the achievement of valued goals. This explanation assumes, although it does not state explicitly, that the situation is amenable to change and that internals have freedom of movement within the situation. Three types of stressors have been considered: economic loss, role ambiguity or role conflict, and the incidence of so-called disturbing life and work events.

ECONOMIC LOSS

Anderson (1977) and Anderson et al. (1977) described the effects of a flood on the behavior and performance of 90 owner–managers of small businesses. The objective measure of stress was the ratio between total monetary loss and total assets. Experienced stress was measured using Kerle and Bialek's (1958) Subjective Stress Scale. The first measure of subjective stress was made 8 months after the flood. At this time the managers were also asked in an interview to describe their responses to the flood, and these were categorized using Kahn, Wolfe, Quinn, Snoek, and Rosenthal's (1964) classification of coping behaviors. Two classes of behavior were identified. The first set of behaviors were those directed at the objective task situation, and the second set included emotional or anxiety responses to the flood.

The correlation between objective and perceived stress was significant but small ($r = .23$, $p < .05$). Perceived stress was related only slightly to the number of business days lost ($r = .28$, $p < .01$). However, the correlation between the manager's locus of control scores on Rotter's Scale and perceived stress was much higher ($r = .61$, $p < .01$). Locus of control scores also correlated $-.54$ ($p < .01$) with task-directed coping behaviors, which, in turn, correlated $.49$ ($p < .01$) with rated performance of the managers. Organizational performance was measured using ratings made by a credit agency. These ratings comprised financial strength, credit data, and strength of personnel resources. However, regression analysis indicated that locus of control was not related directly to these ratings of performance. Additional data were collected 2 years later, and changes in performance and locus of control were estimated. In this second phase, locus of control was related to performance but appeared to account for only 4% of the variance in performance.

In order to estimate the relationships between change in performance and change in locus of control, difference scores for each variable were obtained and then correlated. The dynamic correlation was $-.44$, $p < .01$, suggesting that improvements in performance were associated with increased internality and decrements in performance were associated with increased externality. In an attempt to establish the direction of causality, cross-lagged correlations were obtained. The correlation between locus of control at time T_1 and performance at time T_2 was $-.22$. The correlation between performance at time T_1 and locus of control at time T_2 was $-.14$. Both of these correlations were insignificant. The significance of the difference between correlations should have been calculated, but this was not reported. Anderson (1977) interpreted the results as

> showing a dynamic and reciprocal relationship such that locus of control orientation influences performance (primarily through the choice of task versus emotional coping behavior) and that performance, in turn, operates as a feedback mechanism and influences future locus of control orientation [p. 450].

The study also is interpreted as showing that externals experienced more stress than internals because they engaged in less task-directed behavior. Thus they would be less likely to improve their performance and reduce the effects of economic loss.

Although this study is one of the few to use longitudinal data and provide objective measures of stress and performance, the interpretation is not entirely consistent with the results, for a number of reasons. First, the low correspondence between perceived and objective stress at the time of the initial measurements suggests that reports of stress were more affected by locus of control than by the objective situation. Externals may be more predisposed to identify external constraints on their behavior than internals, who might seek to deny or repress limitations on their own behavior. Initially, there were no significant relationships between locus of control and performance, so it is not possible to argue that internals reported less stress because they had made greater progress toward reducing the effects of economic loss. It is possible, however, that internals were busier than externals and that this high level of activity might have been useful in alleviating stress. It could also have meant that internals thought less about the loss and also reassured themselves that task activity would eventually reduce the effects of their losses. Without objective measures of behavior, however, these interpretations cannot be tested.

Second, it is possible that internals did engage in more task-related activity than externals, but this was attributable to greater opportunities for acting. This explanation could be evaluated only if there were objective measures of the behavioral options available to both internals and externals.

Third, reported behaviors of internals and externals were related only weakly to performance measures. The relationships were insignificant at T_1 and very small at T_2. Therefore it seems rather unlikely that these small differences in performance were sufficient to account for the large differences in the objective stress measures. Internals' reduced stress perceptions are thus more likely to be related to their perceptions of their performance and predisposition to deny limitations on their personal control.

Fourth, the cross-lagged correlation method was used incorrectly. Significant differences in cross-lagged correlations were not reported, and hence the direction of causality between locus of control and performance is indeterminate. Even if the difference were significant, the results could not be used to make a causal inference; Rogasa (1980) showed that unequal cross-lagged correlations are consistent with either absence of causal effects or equal or unequal causal effects.

Despite these difficulties, the study does raise a number of hypotheses about the relationships among stressors, perceived stress, and locus of control. The most important questions concern why internals and externals report different stress levels in response to the same situation. In order to evaluate the degree to which stress is determined by objective factors, coping behavior, or cognitive style, it is essential that future studies examine the objective behavioral opportunities afforded to internals and externals and their actual as well as self-reported behavior.

ROLE AMBIGUITY AND ROLE CONFLICT

In a work organization, the formal organizational structure and the content of jobs may be sources of stress for employees. A minimum requirement for studies seeking to establish the relationships between these situational variables and stress is to measure aspects of the situation and stress reactions independently. Then it becomes possible to establish the extent to which situational factors have uniform effects on individuals and the extent to which personality factors, such as locus of control, moderate the stress reactions. Unfortunately, the value of many studies is limited because only locus of control and stress reactions are measured. Gemmill and Heisler (1972) reported a positive correlation ($r = .31$, $p < .05$, $n = 133$) between job strain and locus of control with a sample of North American managers, Kyriacou and Sutcliffe (1979) reported a positive correlation of ($r = .36$, $p < .05$), $n = 130$) with a sample of United Kingdom teachers. Although these results are similar, we can only propose a variety of possible explanations. Internals may have reported less stress because they were placed in situations of less stress. They also might have experienced less stress because they changed the environmental determinants of stress. Internals may be more likely to deny constraints on their behavior, whereas externals may exaggerate environmental constraints. Another possibility is that internals do not act to change environmental stressors but act in a manner that allows them to accept external stressors. For example, the managers and teachers who were internal might have concentrated on task activities that, although absorbing, did not change the structural work content. They might have also developed a belief system that allowed them to tolerate stress to a greater extent than is the case among externals. For example, internals might have developed a career plan that made stress meaningful to them. Simple catchphrases like "out of stress comes progress and change" or "acceptance of stress is a test that I have to pass in order to achieve career goals" might be stronger beliefs among internals than among externals. Hence future studies should examine alternative theories about the possible determinants of stress reactions in internals and externals.

The earliest study on role ambiguity was that by Korman (1971), who predicted that environmental ambiguity at colleges would be related negatively to satisfaction for internals but not for externals. This hypothesis can be justified by assuming that internals find ambiguous work settings impeding their efforts to exert personal control over their task activities. With undergraduates Korman claimed limited support for this prediction, but actually only one of three different samples confirmed the expected relationship between environmental ambiguity and locus of control. No measures of behavior were obtained. A similar hypothesis was tested by Organ and Greene (1974a) with senior scientists and engineers employed by a large manufacturer of electronics equipment. They predicted, following Rotter (1966), that internals would be more alert than externals to those aspects of the environment that provided useful information for future behavior. Therefore internals should be more frustrated and dissatisfied in a work situation that does not provide clear information about their expected job behavior. Such situations would be those high in role ambiguity. This was measured by asking respondents to complete Rizzo, House, and Lirtzman's (1970) Role Ambiguity Scale. The correlation between role ambiguity and work satisfaction was negative for both internals ($r = -.29$, $p < .01$) and externals ($r = -.19$, $p < .05$). Externals were less satisfied than internals with their work and the organization even when role ambiguity was statistically controlled. Externals tended to report more role ambiguity than did internals ($r = .42$, $p < .01$).

Organ and Greene interpreted their results as suggesting that role ambiguity is aversive to those who are frustrated in the active attempt to secure job-related information—internals. This interpretation seems premature, given the following:

1. No test of the significance of the difference between role ambiguity and satisfaction correlations is given, and the difference is small and unlikely to be significant.
2. No observations of behavior of internals and externals were made.
3. No attempt was made to examine the extent to which self-reported role ambiguity was determined by the cognitive style of internals and externals or by differences in objective or independently measured role ambiguity.
4. The Rizzo et al. scales for role ambiguity and role conflict have poor validity as measures of role structure (Tracy & Johnson, 1981).

Similar criticisms could be made of three other cross-sectional studies that examined the relationships among role ambiguity, locus of control, and satisfaction. One study with middle- and lower-level managers found a significant interaction between locus of control and role ambiguity measured by the Rizzo et al. scale (Abdel-Halim, 1980). Under low ambiguity conditions, internals and externals did not differ on satisfaction. However, externals were less satisfied than internals under conditions of high role ambiguity. These findings are not consistent with those obtained from a study of supermarket managers (Batlis, 1980). In this study, Rotter's mean I–E was not a significant moderator of the relation between role ambiguity, role conflict and job satisfaction. Another study with middle managers found that the same measure of role ambiguity was associated with job tension for externals but not for internals (Keenan & McBain, 1979). Neither study examined the extent to which a manager's objective job structure varied with locus of control and tension.

As far as the role of ambiguity studies are concerned, the results are not clear. Unfortunately, the designs and measures were inappropriate for testing hypotheses about the effects of situational factors and locus of control, because either situational factors were not measured or they were measured by self-reports that were not validated against objective measures. Researchers have been more ready to report associations between variables than to examine the extent to which their preferred causal explanations are consistent with their observations. The problem is not one inherent to only correlational research. With a large number of relevant variables measured, it is possible to examine the extent to which causal explanations are consistent with the data. This is not the strongest method of confirming causal models, but, if used properly, it can at least allow the researcher to evaluate the relative probabilities for the confirmation of competing models. For the studies reviewed in this section, even this modest task is not possible.

STRESSFUL LIFE EVENTS

Although the explanations of the results are still lacking, the studies discussed previously show that externals report greater levels of stress than do internals. This suggests that externals might also display higher levels of illness; numerous studies have shown an association between stress experiences and various forms of physical and psychological illness (Dohrenwend & Dohrenwend, 1974, 1978; Gunderson & Rahe, 1974). The role of personality factors as a moderator of the effects of stressful life events on illness was investigated by Kobasa (1979). She studied two groups of middle- and upper-level business executives in the United States who reported that they had experienced a high degree of life stress in the previous 3 years. An adaptation of the Holmes and Rahe (1967) Schedule of Recent Life Events was used to measure stress. This schedule assigns numbers to life events in proportion to their estimated stress effects and includes events such as death of a spouse, divorce, or traffic violations. To this Kobasa added 15 work-related events, such as geographical transfer of work location. Illness was measured with the Seriousness of Illness Survey (Wyler, Masuda, & Holmes, 1968, 1970). From a total sample of 837, 86 were selected who reported a large number of stressful life events and a high level of illness. Another group, composed of 75 subjects, was selected that reported a large number of stressful life events but also a low level of illness. Subjects in the category of high life stress were discarded if they reported that illness preceded stressful events. Presumably, then, those in the comparison groups included some for whom illness and life stressors were contemporaneous and some who reported illness as occurring subsequent to stressors. All executives had been asked to report, by month and year, which of a list of stressful life events and illnesses they had experienced in the past 3 years. Executives were also asked to complete a set of 18 personality tests, including Rotter's I–E Scale.

Cross-validated discriminant analysis yielded a cluster of personality variables that discriminated between the high- and low-illness groups. The main variables distinguishing the two groups were Nihilism, Locus of Control, Alienation from Self, and Vegetativeness. Nihilism was measured by a scale from the Alienation Test (Maddi, Kobasa, & Hoover, 1978) and measured the extent to which a person was able to find meaning in stressful life events. Alienation from Self was also measured using the same test and was meant to measure personal commitment to individual goals. The Vegetative scale, also from the Alienation Test, measured the extent to which the respondent sought stimulation from the environment. These variables Kobasa subsumed under the construct of *psychological hardiness*. A hardy individual was defined as having a strong "commitment to self, an attitude of vigorousness toward the environment, a sense of meaningfulness and an internal locus of control" (Kobasa, 1979, p. 1).

The hardy individual, it was assumed, reduces stress through coping behaviors, either through cognitive activity, such as evaluating a stressful life event in terms of a general life plan, or behavioral activity designed to minimize the stress. Thus a hardy and internally controlled business executive faced with a job transfer will be more likely to construe the effects of the transfer as being dependent on how he handles it. Unlike the externally controlled executive, he does not see himself as the victim of a threatening change but as "an active determinant of the consequences it brings about." The nonhardy and external-oriented executive will be more likely to remain a passive victim of the stressful life event and experience prolonged stress that will, by some unknown physiological mechanism, produce physical illness.

This is a plausible interpretation of the results, but it needs to be substantiated by further research on the behavior of internals and externals under stress. More research is also needed on the physiological effects of perceived stress. Kobasa acknowledges that simpler interpretations of the results are possible. In terms of Mechanic's (1976) concept of illness behavior, it is possible that the high-stress–high-illness groups may not have been in worse health, but merely wanted to act sick and thereby withdraw from an uncomfortable life situation. This alternative explanation could have been examined if some objective measures of illnesses, such as visits to physicians, had been collected.

Another explanation, mentioned earlier, refers to the possibility that internals underreport illnesses and/or externals overreport illnesses. Kobasa dismissed the possibility of great distortion in reports of illnesses. She argued that subjects are unlikely to misreport major symptoms like heart attacks, hypertension, and cancer. This seems debatable, considering that such symptoms could be threatening to individuals who place high value on personal control. Repressing or denying their occurrence could reduce threat. Actually there is substantial evidence that individuals are not very accurate in reporting past illnesses; this is a function of time, age, and seriousness of the illness (Daughety, 1979). In general, self-reports underestimate illnesses when these are checked independently through physician and hospital records. This might lead one to conclude that Kobasa's measures of illnesses are actually conservative and hence the true relationships between stress and health are likely to be stronger. Unfortunately, this view cannot be sustained, because Kobasa's groups were not representative and there still remains the possibility that the reports of illness were systematically distorted by internals and externals.

It may still be possible that locus of control affects stress reports and, at the same time, that externals experience higher objective stress. This is suggested by a study with dentists by Brousseau and Mallinger (1981), who found that externals experienced higher physiological stress than internals. Physiological stress was measured by a summary health index formed from blood pressure readings and electrocardiogram recordings. The results of this study, however, are not entirely consistent with Kobasa's interpretations. Although locus of control was related to physiological stress, there was no significant correlation between locus of control and perceived stress. Surprisingly, neither was there a significant correlation between perceived stress and physiological measures of stress. The perceived stress measure used nine Likert-type items designed to assess perceptions of stress involved in dealing with patients. The difference in the locus of control–reported stress relationships that are found in these studies may be due to differences in the type of scale used. Had the life-event type of measure been given to the sample of dentists, it might have been related to objective stress and locus of control. Obviously, more research is needed to establish the relationship between locus of control and various types of stress measures. A final difficulty with Kobasa's study is that locus of control measures were taken after illness and stress had occurred. Hence it is possible that locus of control scores may not have been the same prior to stress and illness, and explanations based on stability of personality measures may not be tenable.[6] There is no strong evidence to show that such changes could occur, although the study by Wolfe (1972) suggested that job-related stress could affect locus of control, and the results reported by O'Brien (1981b) with retirees are consistent with a causal model that predicts that the locus of control of male retirees is determined by stress states.

In summary, this section on locus of control and perceptions of stress has suggested that situational factors such as economic loss, work role structure, and certain life events can determine stress responses. Many studies have reported that individuals with an external locus of control report higher stress than internals. For the samples considered, however, there is no evidence that perceptions of stress correspond to physiological or behavioral measures of stress. An important unanswered question is what role locus of control plays in distorting responses to stress questions. Even if locus of control did not affect responses to stress scales, the reasons for externals reporting higher stress are still to be established. Most studies fail to measure objective stress factors, the objective degree of structure in jobs, or the behavior of internals and externals subsequent to the onset of stressors. It is not realistic to advocate strong experimental designs in work settings, but it is desirable that future research measure objective situational variables and behaviors so that alternate explanations can be examined using multivariate procedures.

Job Satisfaction

A number of studies report that internal individuals are more satisfied with their jobs than are externals (Duffy, Shiflett, & Downey, 1977; Gemmill & Heisler, 1972; Kimmons & Greenhaus, 1976; King, Murray,

[6]Some attempt to deal with this problem was made in a longitudinal study in which measures of reported life stress, illness, and locus of control were administered three times over a period of 5 years (Kobasa, Maddi, & Kahn, 1982). When initial measures of illness were used as covariates in an analysis of subsequent reported illness, it was found that later illness was related significantly to hardiness but not to stressful life events. The hardy, internally controlled managers reported less illness than did those who lacked hardiness and had an external orientation. The interaction between stress and hardiness just failed to reach statistical significance ($p = .05$). The study does show that reported illness is related to hardiness at a given time, even when reported illness is corrected for past illness experiences. However, it still leaves unanswered the question of the relationship between locus of control and self-reports of illness and life stress. The study, unfortunately, also raises another problem. No effect of life stress was found on reported illness when analyses used a prospective estimate of both hardiness and stressful life events. This result appears inconsistent with the interpretation of the results of the earlier study (Kobasa, 1979).

& Atkinson, 1982; Mitchell, Smyser, & Weed, 1975; Organ & Greene, 1974a, 1974b).[7] The authors generally try to explain that, in equivalent job situations, externals feel they have less control over work reinforcements than internals and hence less satisfaction than internals. Unfortunately, all of these studies rely on a simple negative correlation or beta coefficient without establishing whether the job situations are equivalent. In addition, job attributes that are known to be important predictors of job satisfaction were not controlled. Organ and Greene (1974a) did show that the correlation between locus of control and work satisfaction was still significant when role ambiguity was partialed out. However, the sign of the correlation changed, indicating that externals tended to report higher satisfaction than internals. In a reanalysis of the same data Organ and Greene reported that locus of control had a direct effect on job satisfaction as well as an indirect effect via perceptions of the purposefulness of work-related behavior (Organ & Greene, 1974b). Internals tended to be more satisfied and perceived greater purposefulness. This analysis has been criticized by Griffin (1977), who showed that the causal model most consistent with these data specified no association between locus of control and job satisfaction.

When the satisfaction of internals and externals is measured after work on objectively identical tasks and work structures, no differences in work satisfaction are found (Mimnaugh & O'Brien, 1981; Ruble, 1976). Results consistent with this finding have been found in cross-sectional studies where situational variables were controlled statistically. Sims and Szilagyi (1976) found that locus of control was not a significant moderator of the relationship between work satisfaction and perceived job characteristics (variety, autonomy, feedback, task identity, dealing with others). Similarly, O'Brien (1982) found that locus of control was not a significant predictor of job satisfaction when perceived job attributes, desired job attributes, age, income, and education were controlled statistically.

[7]One study has reported that internals are less satisfied with coworkers than externals (Dailey, 1978). The value of this study is limited by the use of a two-item satisfaction scale and the neglect of situational factors that could determine the relationship between scores on the 11-item version of the Rotter scale and coworker satisfaction. The author explains the result by stating that social cues of warmth and satisfaction are more important to externals than to internals. This appears unconvincing as this could lead externals to express greater dissatisfaction, especially if coworkers do not display warmth. This has been reported in one study where externals had lower satisfaction with inconsiderate leaders than with leaders who were relatively considerate (Abdel-Halim, 1981). Leader evaluations made by internals were unrelated to their perceptions of leader consideration.

Job Involvement

Kimmons and Greenhaus (1976) and Runyon (1973) claim that internals are more job involved than externals. Both studies used Lodahl and Kejner's (1965) scale of job involvement. This scale attempts to measure the importance of work to an employee's "total self-image" or the extent to which an employee identifies psychologically with work. Although an association between locus of control and a measure of job involvement was reported in these studies, on two grounds their design was unsuitable for inferring higher job involvement among internals compared to externals. First, the validity of the job involvement measure has been questioned (Kanungo, 1979). Second, jobs may differ in attributes such as autonomy, skill level, variety, and challenge. Differences in job involvement may be a function of differences in these attributes and not differences in locus of control. There is some evidence that involvement in the job is related significantly to job challenge, autonomy, and variety (Sekaran & Mowday, 1981). Hence internals may report greater job involvement than externals because their jobs have higher levels of these attributes. In order to infer that internals are more involved in their jobs than externals, it becomes necessary to control for potential differences in job attributes.

Runyon (1973) argued that internals are more likely to be more job involved than externals because they have internalized the Protestant work ethic. This argument appears tautological, but it does seem plausible to expect that internals value work more than externals because they believe it provides opportunities for obtaining rewards through the exercise of skills and personal autonomy. It may be true that internals are more involved in their work than externals, but this hypothesis has yet to be tested in a study with a suitable design and a valid measure of job involvement.

Alienation and Powerlessness

The early writings of Karl Marx have provided many social scientists with a framework for investigating the subjective responses of employees to work structures in capitalist economies (Marx, 1844).[8] The

---

[8]Connections to Marx's writings are tenuous. Marx did write imprecisely about the alienation of labor in terms of the cognitions and behavior generated in employees who worked for wages in industries where tasks were segmented and the employee was on the bottom of a hierarchical power structure. It appears that recent psychological research on alienation has distorted many Marxian concepts so that the results have little direct relation to Marx's theory of alienation. This can be seen easily by the neglect of

literature largely discusses the relationships between job attributes and alienation (Blauner, 1964; Kanungo, 1979, 1981; Seeman, 1959, 1971; Tudor, 1972). Alienation is considered a general and relatively enduring set of beliefs about personal powerlessness, social isolation, and the meaningfulness of social activity. Thus powerlessness is considered one component of alienation. Employees are powerless to the extent that they perceive they have little influence over work reinforcements. According to some writers, they are powerless in Rotter's sense, in that they have a generalized expectancy that they have little control over work and nonwork reinforcements.

A few studies are relevant to understanding how work structures can induce powerlessness or an external locus of control. Nearly all of them describe jobs on a single global job dimension. This has the advantage of simplicity, but it does not provide much information about the relative importance of different job attributes as predictors of powerlessness. One series of studies showed that the substantive complexity of a job was a significant predictor of employee fatalism and employee valuation of self-direction (Kohn & Schooler, 1973, 1978; Miller, Schooler, Kohn, & Miller, 1979). Substantive complexity appeared to be a composite of job challenge, autonomy, skill level, and variety. Seeman (1971) reported insignificant correlations between Rotter's locus of control scale and a measure of work alienation. The latter was a composite measure of job attributes, and the 7-item scale contained measures referring to influence, skill level, and variety.

Andrisani and Nestel (1976) showed that changes in occupational attainment were related to changes in locus of control as was discussed previously. The results suggested that increases in occupational attainment, as measured by changes in occupational status (Duncan, 1971), were associated with increased internality. The authors also suggested that decreases in occupational attainment were associated with increased externality.

Some of these findings were also found in a more recent study of labor market experience and locus of control. Frantz (1980) used a national United States sample of young males who were contacted in both 1968 and 1971. It was found that labor market success in private-sector jobs enhanced feelings of internal control during the transition from school to work. However, one result appears inconsistent with that ob-

---

critical variables, such as the ownership of the means of production and the distribution of power and profits within work structures. A thorough description and analysis of Marx's theory of personality and social structure is given in Venable (1975).

tained by Andrisani and Nestel (1976). Getting a job in the public sector and progressing in it led to increases in externality. Franz suggests that public-sector employees may experience more bureaucratic restrictions, use less skills, and receive lower wages than employees in private-sector jobs.

None of these studies was able to identify the job attributes that determined locus of control. High-status jobs, complex jobs, and private–public sector jobs can differ on many dimensions, including level of skill, work influence, variety, interaction, pressure, task identity, income, amount of feedback, and opportunity to use skills. In order to understand why certain jobs are likely to induce an external locus of control, it is necessary to develop a theory about job attributes and the way these attributes might be related to locus of control. In a recent study with a large cluster sample of employees in a medium-sized Australian city, it was predicted that the most important job attributes determining locus of control were skill utilization, influence, and income (O'Brien, 1981c). Skill utilization was defined as the degree of match between employee skills and skills required by the job. Influence denoted the amount of say an employee had over various aspects of the job, including work organization, jobs allocated, and design of workplace. It was hypothesized that perception of low skill utilization and influence by employees would, over a reasonable period of time, induce a higher locus of control score as measured by Rotter's I–E Scale. This was because skill utilization and influence were major determinants of intrinsic job reward–job satisfaction. Hence employees who perceived their jobs to have low skill utilization and influence would come to expect that their own efforts were not instrumental in obtaining intrinsic rewards. It was assumed that the actual experience of skill use and autonomy is regularly required to maintain a belief in personal control.

Income is an extrinsic reward for work, and it was predicted that employees who perceived their income to be relatively low despite their efforts would come to believe that they had limited power in obtaining this reward. It was assumed that specific expectations about the extent to which personal effort could lead to intrinsic and extrinsic job rewards would result in general expectations about locus of control because of the importance of work activity to self-identity and because work for full-time employees is, in terms of time spent, a major life activity.

It was also recognized that locus of control could affect perceptions of job attributes either via job choice or because internals and externals perceive the same situation differently. The two hypotheses about the direction of causality could not be evaluated by simple correlations obtained from cross-sectional studies. Longitudinal data were desirable but were not available for the sample. In order to estimate the direction of causality, two-stage least-squares analysis was used (James & Singh, 1978). In order to use this technique it was necessary to have a theoretical model with external or exogenous variables predicting locus of control (Y_1) and job attributes (Y_i). It was predicted that locus of control would be significantly predicted by age (X_1), physical health (X_2), leisure quality (X_3), and education (X_4). Prior studies established that this was a reasonable expectation (Kabanoff, 1980; Kabanoff & O'Brien, 1980; O'Brien, 1981; O'Brien & Kabanoff, 1981). The job attributes were assumed to be determined by occupational status (X_5), occupational level (X_6), organizational size (X_7), and education (X_4).

The causal model is shown in Figure 2.1. Estimates of locus of control ($\hat{Y}_1$) and job attributes ($\hat{Y}_i$) were obtained by regressing Y_1 and Y_i separately onto all predictors $X_1 \rightarrow X_7$. The second-stage equations were then used to estimate causal effects. The effect of locus of control on job attributes were estimated by the beta coefficient, β_{i1}, in the equations

$$Y_i = \beta_{i1}\,\hat{Y}_1 + \beta_{i4}\,X_4 + \beta_{i5}\,X_5 + \beta_{i6}\,X_6 + \beta_{i7}\,X_7, \qquad (9)$$

while the effects of job attributes on locus of control were estimated by the beta coefficient, β_{1i}, in the equations

$$Y_1 = \beta_{1i}\,\hat{Y}_i + \beta_{11}\,X_1 + \beta_{12}\,X_2 + \beta_{13}\,X_3 + \beta_{14}\,X_4 \qquad (10)$$

Results showed that for the total sample of 1383 employees, locus of control was related reciprocally to skill utilization, influence, and income. Thus support was obtained for the hypothesis that skill utilization, influence, and income determined locus of control, as well as the

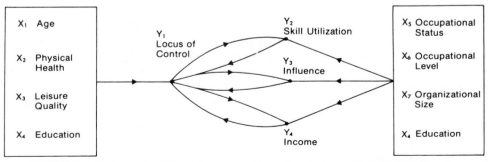

FIGURE 2.1. *Reciprocal relationships among locus of control and job skill-utilization, influence, and income.*

hypothesis that locus of control determined skill utilization, influence, and income. Reasonable confidence that the results could be generalized to actual and not just perceived job attributes was engendered because the second-stage equations (Equation 10) used measures of job attributes that were estimated by relatively objective variables (occupational status, occupational level, organizational size, and education). However, further research is still needed on the correspondence between perceived and objective job attributes.

When the sample was split on the basis of gender and marital status, it was found that reciprocal causation held only for married males. The restriction of the effects of skill utilization and income to the locus of control of married men could be due only to

1. higher job tenure of married men than other groups (the longer an employee is in a job, the greater the effect of the job on locus of control), or
2. the greater value placed by married men on work and its rewards.

The results suggest a complex relationship between locus of control and job attributes. However, there was relative weakness in the direct reciprocal relationships. The percentage of variance in locus of control accounted for by job attributes was less than 10. This suggests that the effects of work on locus of control are significant but not great. Further research is needed to plot the interdependence among perceived job attributes, objective job attributes, and locus of control.

At present the thesis that low skill utilization, low autonomy, and low income produce employees with a relatively external locus of control is not well supported. There appears to be a small, significant effect, but the magnitude of this effect is not great. It is possible that locus of control is determined largely by socialization processes in the family and at school. Part of this socialization process could lead individuals, on entering the workforce, to choose occupations with control structures that are largely congruent with their own personal control structures. If this were so, small effects between work structures and locus of control would be expected. Other factors that could account partly for the observed low associations are employee social activities and organizational decision processes. It is possible that an employee's locus of control is more affected by his or her close personal relationships in nonwork groups. In addition, organizations may, to an unknown degree, induce perceptions of personal control through using participatory decision structures that require employees to express their views about work organization without granting them a great deal of influence in shaping their own job and work organizations.

Occupational Discrimination

Some studies have examined the effect of occupational discrimination upon locus of control. Discrimination occurs when job selection and promotion is based on factors other than individual merit. Some earlier studies (Andrisani, 1978; Frantz, 1980; Gurin, Gurin, Lao and Beattie, 1969) suggested that racial difference in locus of control could be due to occupational discrimination. These studies did not attempt to measure discrimination, so were unable to establish the relative effects of occupational experience, initial locus of control, and discrimination upon observed locus of control scores. A recent study, using a large national sample of United States employees, did measure these variables in order to establish the effects of discrimination upon locus of control (Becker & Krzystofiak, 1982). Using regression analysis, the criterion was locus of control in 1971. Locus of control was measured using the same instrument as that used by Andrisani and Nestel (1976). The predictors were locus of control in 1968, occupational attainment, education, socio-economic status and awareness of discrimination. The results showed that blacks who were victims of discrimination were significantly more external than blacks who did not experience discrimination. Those blacks who were aware of racial discrimination in the workforce but did not report experiencing it themselves were not significantly different from whites in locus of control. This study does provide stronger evidence than previous studies on the relationship between discrimination and locus of control. One weakness of the study however is that retrospective self-report measures of discrimination were used. Thus, to an unknown extent, perceived discrimination may be attributable to changes in locus of control.

Work and Nonwork

Some studies have examined how persons differing in locus of control might also differ in their reactions to situations that occur after cessation of work. The cessation of work may be either temporary or permanent. It is temporary when periods of work alternate with periods of leisure or nonwork activities. One study was identified that considered how leisure activities were determined jointly by work experiences and locus of control. The remaining studies reviewed and examined the activities and experiences of employees after a relatively permanent cessation of work. These studies reported reactions to either long-term unemployment or retirement.

Leisure

Kabanoff and O'Brien (1980) found that locus of control was a significant moderator of the relationship between work and leisure attributes. Previous research showed that internals were more active, alert, and directive in attempting to control and manipulate their environment than were externals (Lefcourt, 1976; Phares, 1976). Consequently, it was predicted that internals who experienced poor-quality jobs (low personal influence, skill utilization, and variety) would be more likely than externals to compensate for these deficiencies by actively seeking out leisure activities high in influence, skill utilization, and variety. This process was termed *supplemental compensation*. Externals, by contrast, were predicted to show *reactive compensation*. If they held jobs high in perceived influence and skill utilization, they would be found to experience incongruence between job requirements and their control orientations. In unstructured situations or simply leisure time, they might choose activities low on skill utilization and influence.

Information about job and leisure attributes was obtained from interviews with a cluster sample of 1383 employees in a medium-sized Australian city. Locus of control was measured using Rotter's Scale. Perceived job attributes were obtained using reliable scales that measured skill utilization, influence, variety, pressure, and amount of personal interaction. Respondents described their frequent leisure activities by selecting from a list of 93 items. These leisure pursuits were then rated independently on the same dimensions as were used for measuring job attributes.

Kabanoff and O'Brien (1980) found that the leisure activity of internals had significantly higher skill utilization, influence, pressure, and variety than did that of externals. This tended to support the prediction that individuals, in an unstructured situation, would choose activities congruent with the control orientation. For the total sample, there was no significant relationship between work and leisure attributes. For each task attribute, four groups were formed that defined different work–leisure patterns (low work–low leisure; low work–high leisure; high work–low leisure; high work–high leisure). Discriminant function analysis was used to identify the personal characteristics that differentiated between individuals in the four groups. Personal characteristics included work orientation, age, education, income, gender, marital status, and locus of control. The results were complex but generally supported the expectation that internals were more likely than externals to exhibit the low work quality–high leisure quality pattern (supplemental compensation). Externals were more likely than internals to exhibit the reactive compensation pattern (high work quality–low leisure quality).

These results, then, show that locus of control is a significant predictor of leisure attributes. They also show that the pattern of work and leisure attributes chosen by an employee is determined partly by his or her locus of control.

Unemployment

Individuals who value work as a means of gaining intrinsic and extrinsic rewards might be expected to become more externally controlled as a result of unemployment, because (a) they are deprived of the opportunity for using effort and skills as a means of obtaining personal job satisfaction (intrinsic reward) and income (extrinsic reward); (b) they probably had no say in the cessation of their employment or, if school dropouts, they had little choice among employment opportunities; and (c) they are likely to receive unemployment or welfare benefits, further noncontingent rewards. Thus it could be predicted that unemployed persons become more external with the passage of time and also that, in general, the unemployed would have more external orientations than those who are employed. Only a few studies have examined these hypotheses using scales for measuring locus of control. With a United States sample, Searls, Braucht, and Miskimins (1974) found that those who were chronically unemployed were significantly more external than a sample of warehouse employees. (Chronically unemployed persons were defined as individuals with a history of vocational failure who show no recent attempts to find employment.) The employed and unemployed groups also differed on measures of work values and personality. This study did not report whether locus of control differences were found when these other variables were controlled statistically.

Another cross-sectional study compared representative samples of employed and unemployed in an Australian city (O'Brien & Kabanoff, 1979, 1981). This study also found that unemployed individuals—those out of work and actively looking for work—were more external on Rotter's I–E Scale than employed workers. The difference was still significant when age, education, health, work values, leisure quality, home involvement, and life satisfaction were controlled statistically.

The O'Brien and Kabanoff (1979, 1981) studies are useful in establishing differences between those working and those not working, but they do not allow inferences about the direction of causality. It is logically possible for an external control orientation to contribute to an inability to find work and some evidence is available to support this hypothesis (Becker & Hills, 1981).

Greater confidence in employment status as a determinant of locus of control is obtained from longitudinal studies. Using a United States sample, Parnes and King (1977) compared men who had reported job loss within a 2-year period with a matched group of employed men. The two groups were not significantly different on Rotter's I–E Scale before job loss occurred. Two years later, those who had become unemployed were significantly more external. The only other longitudinal study identified used an Australian sample of school dropouts and compared those who found employment with those who were unemployed (Tiggemann & Winefield, 1980). Initial measures of locus of control were given before the students had quit school, and subsequent measures were obtained 7 months later. Those who were unemployed showed no significant difference in locus of control from those who were employed at either measurement point.

The apparent difference in results between these two studies could be attributable to a number of factors, including differences in prior employment status, work motivation, time unemployed, alternate leisure activities, social support, and the general availability of work. This latter variable might be particularly important for future studies. At the time of the Australian study, youth unemployment was 21%. When unemployment is as high as this, it is easier for the unemployed to attribute their failure to find work to the social system and not to themselves. Although this would be an external attribution, it might help individuals to maintain a belief in personal control. It is possible for them to believe they could achieve work rewards by their own effort if work was available. Future research is needed to show how changes in locus of control are affected by changes in employment status. Such research should be longitudinal and include repeated measures of work opportunities, work values, nonwork activities such as leisure, and causal attributions for work status.

Unemployment studies also offer a fruitful area for investigating the relationship between locus of control and personality functioning. Previous reviews (Lefcourt, 1976; Phares, 1976) showed significant relationships among locus of control, anxiety, and various measures of social adjustment. Unemployment has also been shown to contribute to personal inadequacy and social deviance (Dooley & Catalano, 1980), and hence it is possible that locus of control expectancies could be an important variable in understanding individual differences in reactions to unemployment.

Retirement

Some writers have suggested that elderly people become more external in orientation because they are at a stage of life when personal and environmental changes that restrict personal autonomy are likely to increase (Butler & Lewis, 1973). Failing physical health, financial insecurity, death of friends, and loss of work opportunities are some of the factors that might contribute to increases on Rotter's locus of control scale. However, cross-sectional studies generally do not show a steady increase in externality with age. With United States samples, some studies reported an increase in internal orientation up to 50 years of age (Bradley & Webb, 1976; Penk, 1969). However, this result was not found in a study by Staats (1975). With an Australian sample, it was found that locus of control scores were highest for persons in the 15–19-year age range (i.e., they were highest in external orientation). Scores then declined steadily (up to the early 60s) (O'Brien & Kabanoff, 1981). The locus of control of people over 60 years rose, but the mean score was comparable to those in the 25–44-year range. One study examined age differences in locus of control, using Levenson's (1972) scales for belief in internality, powerful others, and chance (Ryckman & Malikioski, 1975). With a sample of 38 adults whose age ranged from 21 to 79 years, there was a significant relationship between age and both belief in powerful others and belief in chance. Those in their fifties were most likely to believe that their lives were controlled by powerful others, while the oldest groups reported that powerful others had relatively small effects on their lives. Belief in the operation of chance forces was lowest among those in their thirties and forties. No evidence was found to support the view that elderly people feel less personal control than those in younger age-groups. Hence present evidence does not warrant the conclusion that people necessarily become more externally oriented as age increases.

This does not mean that events associated with old age and retirement do not help to determine locus of control. It is likely that the effect of these events depends on the initial locus of control of people who are entering the retirement phase, as well as the magnitude and frequency of stressful life events.

Few studies have investigated the determinants of locus of control in old age. Felton and Kahana (1974) found that institutionalization lowered perceptions of personal control in the aged. In an experimental study (Krantz & Stone, 1978), no differences in locus of control were found between young and old women, but age was a significant moderator of the relationship between locus of control and reactions to failure experiences. Older subjects who were external were most affected by failure at problem solving. They performed worse than younger externals when confronted with a new problem situation after failure. Aged internals performed better than young internals. This evidence suggests that aging may not affect locus of control scores, but it might magnify the importance of locus of control as a predictor of stress adaptation.

A number of studies have shown that locus of control is associated with personal adjustment in old age (Kuypers, 1971; Palmore & Luikart, 1972), with externals displaying poorer adjustment than internals. More recently, Reid, Haas, and Hawkings (1977) found that the relationship between locus of control and life satisfaction among the elderly was stronger for males than females. Some recent correlational and longitudinal studies have used a new index to predict adjustment of the elderly (Reid & Ziegler, 1981). This index, called the Desired Control measure is obtained by multiplying corresponding items on a Desire scale and an Expectancy scale. Items on the Desire scale measure the attractiveness or valence of various activities and reinforcements. These were constructed after analyzing responses from a survey with elderly people who lived either in institutions or in their own homes. The expectancy items require the respondent to indicate the extent to which these activities or reinforcements are obtainable. The score on each Desire item is multiplied by the score on the parallel Expectancy item. The cross-products are then summed to obtain a total Desired Control score. High scorers on Desired Control are better adjusted, contented, and satisfied with their lives than are those who have low scores. Although the authors see their approach as a revision and extension of Rotter's social learning approach it seems to abandon the concept of a generalized locus of control expectancy. The Expectancy items are discussed as if they were perceptions of objective attributes of the environment. However, no information is provided about the accuracy of these perceptions or the extent to which the responses might be affected by generalized beliefs about locus of control. This neglect is understandable, given the authors' assessment of Rotter's locus of control scale. Nevertheless, the theoretical and practical implications of the Desired Control scale are dependent on the degree to which the reinforcement expectancies are based on accurate perceptions and generalized beliefs about control.

Studies on locus of control and adjustment generally have not advanced a causal model for predicting the joint effects of health, personal stress, and locus of control on the adjustment of aged and retired people. It is possible, for example, that an observed relationship between locus of control and life satisfaction would disappear if state of health was controlled for. One recent study (O'Brien, 1981b) examined a causal model that predicted that the antecedents of locus of control for retirees were health, mental strain, and the degree of skill utilization experienced in their preretirement occupation. It was predicted that retirees would be more external if they had experienced poor health, high mental strain, and low occupational skill utilization. The latter variable was included, as it was argued that prolonged experience with jobs that allowed an employee little opportunity to use valued skills would induce a general belief that personal efforts and abilities had little relation to the acquisition of intrinsic and extrinsic rewards. Some evidence for this hypothesis for employed samples (O'Brien, 1980, in press) was discussed earlier. The O'Brien study also predicted that satisfaction with life in retirement would be a function of locus of control and the three antecedents of locus of control. The complete model expressed in path form, showing the two-stage model with life satisfaction as the dependent variable, is illustrated in Figure 2.2.

A large representative sample of retirees in an Australian city were interviewed. During the interview they were given Rotter's I–E Scale and were asked to check, from a large list of common physical and mental symptoms, those they had experienced during the previous year. These symptoms were then used to obtain ratings of physical health and mental strain. Skill utilization was measured not by asking retirees to describe their previous jobs, but rather asking them to name their occupation, if any, prior to retirement. Previous studies with a large employed sample (O'Brien & Dowling, 1980; O'Brien, Dowling, & Kabanoff, 1978) provided mean skill utilization scores for a large range of occupations, and retiree's prior job skill utilization was assigned using this information. Hence it is unlikely that estimates of skill utilization were distorted by locus of control.

Adjustment to retirement was measured using a life satisfaction scale (Quinn & Shepard, 1974), and separate scales measured satisfaction with activities, finance, people, and health (Smith, Kendall, & Hulin, 1969). Using partial correlations, it was found that locus of control was associated negatively with most measures of adjustment when health and mental strain were controlled. The magnitude of the association was greater for males than for females. Using path analysis the consistency of the data with the causal model was examined. The re-

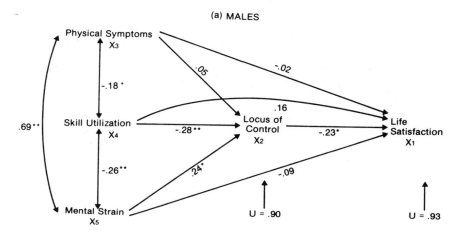

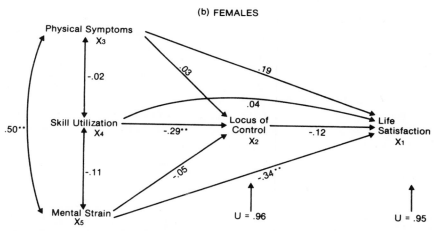

FIGURE 2.2. *Expected relationships among mental strain, physical health, pre-retirement job skill utilization, and locus of control for male and female retirees. Numbers on lines with one-way arrows are beta coefficients.* *p < .05. **p < .01.

sults are shown in Figure 2.2 for males and females. Generally, the model was not well supported. However, the predicted relationship between previous work skill utilization and locus of control of retirees was supported. Obviously, a number of variables contribute to locus of control and life satisfaction that are not identified. The study was also limited, in that it was cross-sectional and used self-report measures of health, mental strain, and adjustment. However, these results and those of a related study (O'Brien, 1981a) suggest that better studies, using longitudinal designs, should consider the role of work experiences as determinants of retiree adjustment. It appears that work experiences might directly affect health, financial status, and leisure activities of retirees. Work experiences could also have an indirect effect on retirement adjustment via locus of control. Retirees who have adopted a more external orientation as a result of working at jobs low on skill utilization appear to have a lowered capacity for enjoying retirement in comparison to internal retirees who have had prior occupations that allowed high skill utilization.

Conclusions

Future Research

This review has shown that employees' locus of control can, in certain situations, be a significant predictor of their career choices, occupational attainment, job performance, and attitudes toward work. The relationships are reciprocal to some extent, as work structures can determine employees' locus of control. The nature of these relationships must be qualified because of the magnitude of the relationships and the incompleteness of the evidence. Analyses of published studies show that the strength of the association between locus of control and work variables is generally quite weak. This is due partly to the neglect or inadequate measurement of situational variables. Personality variables, such as locus of control, are likely to have greater explanatory power in situations where an individual has a fair amount of discretion or freedom of movement. Most work situations allow little freedom of movement for employees who are constrained by formal power, communication, and task structures. Hence there are few opportunities for personality characteristics to affect job behavior and performance.

Unfortunately, the results of many studies are amenable to different interpretations. This appears attributable to a desire on the part of researchers to find results that are consistent with a single hypothesis. It would be preferable for studies to seek to evaluate alternative hypotheses. Reported differences in the behaviors, attitudes, and expectancies of internals and externals can be attributed easily to unknown differences in the work situations encountered by internals and externals. Furthermore, there may be systematic differences in the abilities and work values of internals and externals in many of the studies examined. The results certainly do not justify the recommendations about personnel selection that were made in a recent review of studies dealing with locus of control and organizational behavior (Spector, 1982). This review concluded that internals were most suited to work groups where they could exercise initiative and avoid compliance with authority. By contrast, externals should be assigned to groups where high compliance with authority was required and initiative was not required. These conclusions preceded more specific recommendations that externals should be assigned to assembly-line jobs and battlefield operations.[9] Such recommendations are unjustified and potentially discriminatory for externals with high ability, realism, and initiative.

Future research on locus of control in work organizations should endeavor to derive hypotheses from theories about the interaction between locus of control and situational variables. These hypotheses should be tested with designs that include measures of (a) situational structure, (b) abilities, (c) work values, (d) objective measures of performance and behavior, and (e) multiple classifications of locus of control.

Situational structure. Two kinds of situational variables are relevant. First there should be objective measures of organizational structure. These measures should allow the researcher to estimate the degree to which the employee has access to job information and opportunities for personal autonomy. The structural variables likely to be most important are communication, power, task allocation, and task precedence relationships. The second kind of situational variable is job content. Whether or not a task allows the employee opportunities for skill utilization and personal control is likely to be important for understanding the responses of employees who vary in locus of control.

Few studies have used objective measures of situational structure. Some have used employee perceptions of structure as indicators of objective structure. The validity of this procedure has yet to be demonstrated. The degree of correspondence between objective and perceived structures is unlikely to be very high when measured across a range of objective structures. Comprehensive theories are likely to require the measurement of both objective and perceived structures.

Abilities. This variable is likely to be most important in studies that assess the effects of locus of control on occupational attainment, job performance, and work motivation. The relationship between locus of

---

[9]"Tasks that require close coordination of many people generally require directive styles. Thus, assembly line work where individual workers' tasks are highly independent, and battlefield operations where precise carrying out of orders is essential, would be most appropriate for externals who are more suited for directive supervision" (Spector, 1982, p. 494).

control and achievement variables is best assessed when abilities are measured and used as statistical controls.

Work values. No studies have examined the possibility that extreme scorers on the locus of control scale might attribute different meanings to work outcomes. Some studies suggest that the attractiveness or valence of work outcomes varies with locus of control. It is possible, then, that some of the observed differences in work behavior and performance between internals and externals might be attributable to differences in work valences and not differences in effort–performance–reward expectancies.

Objective measures of performance and behavior. Unless objective measures of performance and behavior are obtained, it is not possible to establish the extent to which perceived measures reflect objective differences or the selective perceptions of raters and ratees who vary on locus of control.

Multiple classifications of locus of control. It is possible that a great deal of information could be lost in studies that classify individuals as internals or externals on the basis of a median split. This procedure not only creates difficulties in comparing studies where the median varies, it also prevents analysis of the characteristics of those who have intermediate scores. The literature has been concerned with identifying relatively consistent behaviors of those who are extreme on locus of control scales. Intermediate scorers may have more flexibility in their behavior, and it is logically possible that this group is superior in occupational attainment, performance, and adjustment to stress.

These criticisms and comments also apply to research on unemployment and retirement. In these areas, the construct of locus of control has been shown to be useful in understanding both the psychological consequences of unemployment and the reactions of elderly people to retirement. For retirees, the construct also has been shown to have value for understanding how previous work experiences can affect reactions to retirement.

Research in the area of work and retirement has produced no new measures to assess locus of control in specific situations. Most studies have used Rotter's I–E Scale. A few have used subscales derived from factor analyses of the total scale. However, results indicate that there are only very small differences in observed relationships when a personal control factor scale and the total Rotter scale is used. The main difficulty in constructing locus of control scales for work contexts appears to be due to the necessity for distinguishing between measures of perceived influence and control orientation. Measures of perceived influence are used frequently to assess situational influence (e.g., Hackman & Oldham, 1975; O'Brien, 1982a; O'Brien & Stevens, 1981). These perceptions are likely to reflect partly an individual's control orientation that is assumed to be general and stable over time. However, perceptions of influence and control are also likely to reflect specific and temporary sources of objective influence (O'Brien, 1982b; Roberts & Glick, 1981). If work-specific measures of locus of control are developed for conceptual clarity, they should be independent of measures of perceived influence.

Realists, Internals, and Externals

Finally, some comments can be made about the adequacy of the Rotter scale for measuring a generalized expectancy about locus of control. The Rotter scale is meant to measure a generalized expectancy about the extent to which valued reinforcements are controlled by personal or external factors. It was not meant to provide a typology that classifies individuals as internally controlled or externally controlled but rather a single dimension for measuring a range of general control expectations. Although a large number of studies have now shown that the scale is not unidimensional (Abrahamson, Schludermann & Schludermann, 1973; Cherlin & Bourque, 1974; Collins, 1974; Dixon, McKee & McRae, 1976; Duffy, Shiflett & Downey, 1977; Garza & Widlak, 1977; Gurin, Gurin, Lao & Beattie, 1969; Levenson, 1974; Mirels, 1970; O'Brien & Kabanoff, 1981; Reid & Ware, 1973; Watson, 1981; Zuckerman & Gerbasi, 1977), this does not necessarily mean that the construct of locus of control is imprecise. A reasonable inference, however, is that the scale is not an adequate operational definition of the construct. Factor analyses have identified a variety of factors depending on the size and characteristics of the sample. Most of these studies have not considered the degree to which the factor solution adopted fits the data but a recent analysis of these studies (Watson, 1981) concludes that only a two factor solution is justified. The typical labelling for these two factors is general personal control and belief in system control. Situation-free items tend to load on the personal control factor and items about political situations tend to load on the system control factor. The existence of these separate factors have led some researchers to conclude that the search for generalized control expectancies is misguided and should be abandoned. Instead, they argue, there should be separate scales measuring situation-specific control orientations.

The development of situation-specific measures of locus of control may be desirable and is indeed advocated by Rotter (1975), but they will no longer be measures of generalized expectancies. The factor analyses of the scale do not justify the abandonment of the general construct of locus of control but rather indicate that the scale does not measure the construct adequately. This is due to a number of reasons. First, it does not tap a sufficient range of situations. A generalized expectancy should be one that is measured on the basis of responses to a range of situations that are commonly experienced by the respondent. At this point it might be pointed out that Rotter originally used the term *generalized expectancies* to refer to expectancies that are generalized from a specific situation to a set of situations perceived as related or similar (Rotter, 1966). Whether or not they apply to a given situation, strictly, depends on a person's past experiences and his or her perception of the similarity between a particular situation and situations previously experienced. However, Rotter also contrasts generalized expectancies with specific expectancies in a manner that does not refer to the process of generalization, but rather to an expectancy that applies to a wide range of common situations. This latter usage is the one adopted here.

Inspection of the items on the Rotter scale, as well as results of factor analyses, show that the situations tapped are small in number and concentrate on educational and political situations. For an adult, a number of salient situations are entirely omitted. There are few items referring to work, leisure, home, and interpersonal situations. If a person is to be classified as internal or external, his or her responses should be consistent across a range of situations.

The second main problem is that the scale does not allow a distinction to be made between those who accurately describe their social situations and those who have distorted perceptions of objective situations. Thus, many individuals may be labeled external when they do not have a generalized belief in external control of reinforcement, but rather accurately describe the social situations they experience. This point is also made by Wong and Sproule (Chapter 5, present volume). A number of other authors have also suggested that external in locus of control scores may be attributable to individual shifts toward realistic perceptions (Gorman, Jones & Holman, 1980; O'Brien & Kabanoff, 1981; Lange & Tiggeman, 1980). There appear to be two possible ways of overcoming this problem. One way is to construct a scale that does not mention any specific situation. This would not be the best alternative, as it would be difficult to estimate the extent to which the response could be attributed to a generalized expectancy or to the respondent's experience of control in current situations. A preferred alternative is to ask an individual to indicate the determinant of valued reinforcements in situations where the source of personal outcomes is known. There are three main sources—personal, structural and joint personal–structural.

On the basis of research or experience, three types of situations would be identified. The personal situation would be one where it is known that personal factors largely determine a specified personal outcome. An example would be a work situation where an individual works alone. Performance outcomes are largely self-determined and are not affected by machine or people demands. A structural situation at work would be one where the operation of personal effort and skill is minimized by machine demands and directive supervision. A mixed situation could be a semi-autonomous work group where an individual's performance is partly determined by personal effort and skill and partly by the effort and skill of co-workers.

Within each task domain (educational, work, leisure, home, interpersonal, political), these three types of situations could be described and the individual asked to identify which type of factor would determine the attainment of the valued outcome. The response alternatives would tap four alternative determinants of the outcome—self, nonself factors (e.g., people, machines, physical conditions), a joint self–other factor, and chance. If these responses are labeled respectively internal (I), external (E), mixed (M) and chance (C), then it is possible to identify three main types of respondents (see Table 2.4). The extreme internally controlled individual would choose internal factors across all three types of situations. One response would be accurate but the other two could be distortions. The extreme externally controlled individual would make an accurate assessment of the structural situation but have distorted judgments about the other two. The realistic type makes accurate choices for all three situations. Other response patterns are possible but the table identifies the major locus of control orien-

TABLE 2.4
Possible Control Response Patterns to Different Situations[a]

	Objective determinants of personal outcomes		
Response pattern	Personal	Structural	Mixed personal–structural
Internal	I	I	I
Realistic	I	E	M
External	E or C	E or C	E or C

[a] I = Internal response; E = External response; C = Chance response; M = Mixed response.

tations. Very extreme scorers on the Rotter scale would probably be the designated internal and external respondents. The internals would be what Wong and Sproule (Chapter 5, present volume) have called ideal-istic–optimistic controllers. They overestimate their own capability to control and underestimate the strength of external constraints. The ex-ternals are the unrealistic, pessimistic controllers who underestimate their capacity to control and overestimate the strength of external con-straints. The Rotter scale does not allow the identification of the real-istic respondents, although they may be those with scores in the middle range.

The realistic mode of response, however, does not necessarily cor-respond to Wong and Sproule's *bilocals*, who are defined as those who perceive and desire control from both internal and external loci. The way in which these bilocals are identified does not guarantee that they make realistic assessments about the determinants of personal behav-ior. The items on the Trent Attribution Profile (TAP) used to identify control orientations, refer to undefined situations and it is not possible to assess whether respondents are making realistic judgements. This is a problem shared with others who have defined separate scales (Lef-court, 1981; Lefcourt, Von Baeyer, Ware & Cox, 1979; Levenson, 1972, 1981; Reid & Ware, 1973, 1974; Paulhus & Christie, 1981).

This formulation of locus of control does not require the formula-tion of separate scales, and retains the construct of a generalized ex-pectancy for locus of control. This construct appears to have been abandoned by most current writers. If scales were constructed in the manner described then it would be possible to identify four major re-sponse patterns.

Internals ─────── Realists ⟨ Externals (Structuralists) / Externals (Fatalists)

Internals and externals both have distorted views of the nature of social reality. Structuralistic externals overestimated the role of struc-tural determinants of behavior (e.g., power and task structures), whereas the fatalistic externals are unrealistic in seeing most outcomes as de-pendent on luck, fate, or chance, and underestimate the role of personal and structural factors.

If such a scale were developed then it could provide more detailed information about the relationship between employee behavior and lo-cus of control. It could also lead to some redirection in organizational theory. Spector (1982) has maintained, and he is probably correct, that organizational psychologists have assumed that productivity is highest when employees believe in self-determination and the possibility of attaining desired reinforcements through personal effort. Such beliefs, if held rigidly, define what has been called an *unrealistic internal*. It may well be a dysfunctional belief for an employee in cooperative situations with strong power, task, and economic restraints. Most organizations have such structural features, and productive adaptive behavior may only occur when an individual has sufficient objectivity to distinguish between courses of action that allow self-determined effort and courses of action that must be followed when fixed rules govern the distribution of persons, positions, and tasks.

References

Abdel-Halim, A. A. Effects of person–job compatibility on managerial reactions to role ambiguity. *Organizational Behavior and Human Performance*, 1980, *26*, 193–211.

Abdel-Halim, A. A. Personality and task moderators of subordinate responses to perceived leader behavior. *Human Relations*, 1981, *34*, 73–88.

Abrahamson, D., Schludermann, S., & Schludermann, E. Replication of dimensions of locus of control. *Journal of Consulting and Clinical Psychology*, 1973, *41*, 320.

Anderson, C. R. Locus of control, coping behaviors, and performance in a stress setting: A longitudinal study. *Journal of Applied Psychology*, 1977, *62*, 446–451.

Anderson, C. R., Hellriegel, D., & Slocum, J. W. Managerial response to environmentally induced stress. *Academy of Management Journal*, 1977, *201*, 260–272.

Anderson, C. R., & Schneier, C. E. Locus of control, leader behavior, and leader performance among management students. *Academy of Management Journal*, 1978, *21*, 690–698.

Andrisani, P. J. Internal–external attitudes, personal initiative, and labor market experience. In P. J. Andrisani, E. Applebaum, R. Koppel, & R. C. Miljus (Eds.), *Work attitudes and labor market experience*. New York: Praeger, 1978.

Andrisani, P. J., Applebaum, E., Koppel, R., & Miljus, R. C. *Work attitudes and labor market experience*. New York: Praeger, 1978.

Andrisani, P. J., & Nestel, G. Internal–external control as a contributor to and outcome of work experience. *Journal of Applied Psychology*, 1976, *61*, 156–165.

Arnold, H. J. Moderator variables: A clarification of conceptual, analytic, and psychometric issues. *Organizational Behavior and Human Performance*, 1982, *29*, 143–174.

Batlis, N. C. Job involvement and locus of control as moderators of role-perception/individual outcome relationships. *Psychological Reports*, 1980, *46*, 111–119.

Becker, B. & Hills, S. M. Youth attitudes and adult labor market activity. *Industrial Relations*, 1981, *20*, 60–70.

Becker, B. E. & Krzystofiak, F. J. The influence of labor market discrimination on locus of control. *Journal of Vocational Behavior*, 1982, *21*, 60–70.

Bigoness, W. J. Effects of locus of control and style of third-party intervention upon bargaining behavior. *Journal of Applied Psychology*, 1976, *61*, 305–312.

Blauner, R. *Alienation and freedom: The factory worker and his industry*. Chicago: University of Chicago Press, 1964.

Bradley, R. H., & Webb, R. Age-related differences in locus of control orientation in three behavior domains. *Human Development*, 1976, *19*, 49–55.

Broedling, L. A. Relationships of internal–external control to work motivation and performance in an expectancy model. *Journal of Applied Psychology*, 1975, *60*, 65–70.

Brousseau, K. R., & Mallinger, M. A. Internal–external locus of control, perceived occupational stress, and cardiovascular health. *Journal of Occupational Behavior*, 1981, *2*, 65–71.

Burlin, F. Locus of control and female occupational aspiration. *Journal of Counseling Psychology*, 1976, *23*, 126–129.

Butler, R. N., & Lewis, M. I. *Aging and mental health*. St. Louis: Mosby, 1973.

Cherlin, A. & Bourque, L. B. Dimensionality and reliability of the Rotter I–E Scale. *Sociometry*, 1974, *37*, 565–582.

Collins, B. E. Four separate components of the Rotter I–E scale: Belief in a difficult world, a just world, a predictable world, and a politically responsive world. *Journal of Personality and Social Psychology*, 1974, *29*, 381–391.

Cravens, R. W. & Worchel, P. The differential effects of rewarding and coercive leaders on group members differing in locus of control. *Journal of Personality*, 1977, *45*, 150–168.

Crites, J. O. The maturity of vocational attitudes in adolescence. *APGA Inquiry Series*, No. 2. Washington: American Personnel and Guidance Association, 1971.

Dailey, R. C. Relationship between locus of control, perceived group cohesiveness, and satisfaction with co-workers. *Psychological Reports*, 1978, *42*, 311–316.

Daughety, V. S. Illness conditions. In R. Andersen, *et al.* (Eds.), *Total survey error: Applications to improve health surveys*. San Francisco: Jossey-Bass, 1979.

Dixon, D. N., McKee, C. S. & McRae, B. C. Dimensionality of three adult, objective locus of control scores. *Journal of Personality Assessment*, 1976, *40*, 310–319.

Dohrenwend, B. S., & Dohrenwend, B. P. (Eds.), *Stressful life events: Their nature and effects*. New York: Wiley, 1974.

Dohrenwend, B. S., & Dohrenwend, B. P. Some issues in research on stressful life events. *Journal of Nervous and Mental Disease*, 1978, *166*, 7–15.

Dooley, D., & Catalano, R. Economic change as a cause of behavioral disorder. *Psychological Bulletin*, 1980, *87*, 450–468.

Dossett, D. L., Latham, G. P., & Mitchell, T. R. The effects of assigned versus participatively set goals, knowledge of results and individual differences when goal difficulty is held constant. *Journal of Applied Psychology*, 1979, *64*, 291–298.

Duffy, P. J., Shiflett, S., & Downey, R. G. Locus of control: Dimensionality and predictability using Likert scales. *Journal of Applied Psychology*, 1977, *62*, 214–219.

Duncan, O. D. A socioeconomic index for all occupations. In A. J. Reiso, O. D. Duncan, P. Hatt, & C. North (Eds.), *Occupations and social status*. New York: Free Press, 1971.

Durand, D. E., & Nord, W. R. Perceived leader behavior as a function of personality characteristics of supervisors and subordinates. *Academy of Management Journal*, 1976, *19*, 427–438.

Durand, D. E., & Shea, D. Entrepreneurial activity as a function of achievement motivation and reinforcement control. *Journal of Psychology*, 1974, *88*, 57–63.

Evans, M. G. Extensions of a path-goal theory of motivation. *Journal of Applied Psychology*, 1974, *59*, 172–178.

Felton, B., & Kahana, E. Adjustment and situationally-bound locus of control among institutionalized aged. *Journal of Gerontology*, 1974, *27*, 295–301.

Frantz, R. S. The effect of early labor market experience upon internal–external locus of control among young male workers. *Journal of Youth and Adolescence*, 1980, *9*, 203–210.

Gable, R. K., Thompson, D. L., & Glanstein, P. J. Perceptions of personal control and conformity of vocational choices as correlates of vocational development. *Journal of Vocational Behavior*, 1976, *8*, 259–267.

Garza, R. T., & Widlak, F. W. The validity of locus of control dimensions for Chicano populations. *Journal of Personality Assessment*, 1977, *41*, 635–643.

Gemmill, G. R., & Heisler, W. J. Fatalism as a factor in managerial job satisfaction, job strain, and mobility. *Personnel Psychology*, 1972, *25*, 241–250.

Giles, W. F. Volunteering for job enrichment: A test of expectancy theory predictions. *Personnel Psychology*, 1977, *30*, 427–435.

Gorman, P., Jones, L., & Holman, I. Generalizing American locus of control norms to Australian populations: A warning. *Australian Psychologist*, 1980, *15*, 125–127.

Greenhaus, J. H., & Sklarew, N. D. Some sources and consequences of career exploration. *Journal of Vocational Behavior*, 1981, *18*, 1–12.

Griffin, L. J. Causal modeling of psychological success in work organizations. *Academy of Management Journal*, 1977, *20*, 6–33.

Gunderson, E., & Rahe, R. (Eds.). *Life stress and illness*. Springfield, IL: Thomas, 1974.

Gurin, P., Gurin, G., Lao, R. C., & Beattie, M. Internal–external control in the motivational dynamics of Negro youth. *Journal of Social Issues*, 1969, *25*, 25–53.

Hackman, J. R., & Oldham, G. R. Development of the Job Diagnostic Survey. *Journal of Applied Psychology*, 1975, *60*, 159–170.

Hammer, J. H., & Vardi, Y. Locus of control and career self-management among non-supervisory employees in industrial settings. *Journal of Vocational Behavior*, 1981, *18*, 13–29.

Harvey, J. M. Locus of control shift in administrators. *Perceptual and Motor Skills*, 1971, *33*, 980–982.

Heisler, W. J. A performance correlate of personal control beliefs in an organizational context. *Journal of Applied Psychology*, 1974, *59*, 504–506.

Holmes, T. H., & Rahe, R. H. The social readjustment rating scale. *Journal of Psychosomatic Research*, 1967, *11*, 213–218.

James, L. R., & Singh, B. K. An introduction to the logic, assumptions, and basic analytic procedures of two-stage least squares. *Psychological Bulletin*, 1978, *85*, 1104–1122.

Joe, V. C. Review of the internal–external control construct as a personality variable. *Psychological Reports*, 1971, *28*, 619–640.

Kabanoff, B. Work and non-work: A review of models, methods and findings. *Psychological Bulletin*, 1980, *88*, 60–77.

Kabanoff, B., & O'Brien, G. E. Work and leisure: A task attributes analysis. *Journal of Applied Psychology*, 1980, *65*, 595–609.

Kahn, R. L., Wolfe, D. M., Quinn, R. P., Snoek, J. D., & Rosenthal, R. A. *Organizational stress: Studies in role conflict and role ambiguity*. New York: Wiley, 1964.

Kanungo, R. N. The concepts of alienation and involvement revisited. *Psychological Bulletin*, 1979, *86*, 119–138.

Kanungo, R. N. Work alienation and involvement: Problems and prospects. *International Review of Applied Psychology*, 1981, *30*, 1–15.

Keenan, A., & McBain, G. D. M. Effects of Type A behavior, intolerance of ambiguity, and locus of control on the relationship between role stress and work-related outcomes. *Journal of Occupational Psychology*, 1979, *52*, 277–285.

Keller, R. T., & Holland, W. E. Individual characteristics of innovativeness and communication in research and development organizations. *Journal of Applied Psychology*, 1978, *63*, 759–762.

Kerle, H. H., & Bialek, H. M. Construction, validation, and application of a subjective stress scale (Staff Memorandum). Monterey, CA: U.S. Army Leadership Unit, 1958.

Kimmons, G., & Greenhaus, J. H. Relationship between locus of control and reactions to job characteristics. *Psychological Reports*, 1976, *39*, 815–820.

King, M., Murray, M. A. & Atkinson, T. Background, personality, job characteristics, and satisfaction with work in a national sample. *Human Relations*, 1982, *35*, 119–133.

Kobasa, S. C. Stressful life events, personality, and health: An inquiry into hardiness. *Journal of Personality and Social Psychology*, 1979, *37*, 1–11.

Kobasa, S. C., Maddi, A. R., & Kahn, S. Hardiness and health: A prospective study. *Journal of Personality and Social Psychology*, 1982, *42*, 168–177.

Kohn, M. L., & Schooler, C. Occupational experience and psychological functioning: An assessment of reciprocal effects. *American Sociological Review*, 1973, *28*, 97–118.

Kohn, M. L., & Schooler, C. The reciprocal effects of the substantive complexity of work and intellectual flexibility: A longitudinal assessment. *American Journal of Sociology*, 1978, *84*, 24–52.

Korman, A. K. Environmental ambiguity and locus of control as interactive influences on satisfaction. *Journal of Applied Psychology*, 1971, *55*, 339–342.

Krantz, D. S., & Stone, V. Locus of control and the effects of success and failure in young and community-residing aged women. *Journal of Personality*, 1978, *46*, 536–551.

Kuypers, J. A. Internal–external locus of control and ego functioning correlates in the elderly. *Gerontologist*, 1971, *12*, 168–173.

Kyriacou, C., & Sutcliffe, J. A note on teacher stress and locus of control. *Journal of Occupational Psychology*, 1979, *52*, 227–228.

Landy, F. J., & Farr, J. L. Performance rating. *Psychological Bulletin*, 1980, *87*, 72–107.

Lange, R., & Tiggeman, M. Changes within the Australian population to more external control beliefs. *Australian Psychologist*, 1980, *15*, 495–497.

Lawler, E. E. *Pay and organizational effectiveness: A psychological view.* New York: McGraw-Hill, 1971.

Lefcourt, H. M. *Locus of control: Current trends in theory and research.* New York: Wiley, 1976.

Lefcourt, H. M. The construction and development of the multidimensional-multiattributional causality scales. In Lefcourt, H. (Ed.). *Research with the locus of control construct* (Vol. 1). New York, Academic Press, 1981.

Lefcourt, H. M., Von Baeyer, C. L., Ware, E. E. & Cox, D. J. The multidimensional-multiattributional causality scale: The development of a goal specific locus of control scale. *Canadian Journal of Behavioural Science*, 1979, *11*, 286–304.

Levenson, H. Distinctions within the concept of internal–external controls: Development of a new scale. *Proceedings of the 80th Annual Convention of the American Psychological Association*, 1972, 261–262.

Levenson, H. Activism and powerful others: Distinctions within the concept of internal–external control. *Journal of Personality Assessment*, 1974, *38*, 377–383.

Levenson, H. Differentiating among internality, powerful others, and chance. In Lefcourt, H. (Ed.). *Research with the locus of control construct* (Vol. 1). New York, Academic Press, 1981.

Liberty, P. C., Burnstein, E., & Moulton, P. W. Concern with mastery and occupational attraction. *Journal of Personality*, 1966, *34*, 105–107.

Lied, T. R., & Pritchard, R. D. Relationships between personality variables and components of the expectancy-valence model. *Journal of Applied Psychology*, 1976, *61*, 463–467.

Lodahl, T. M., & Kejner, M. The definition and measurement of job involvement. *Journal of Applied Psychology*, 1965, *49*, 24–33.

Lord, R. G., Phillips, J. S., & Rush, M. C. Effects of sex and personality on perceptions of emergent leadership, influence, and social power. *Journal of Applied Psychology*, 1980, *65*, 176–182.

MacDonald, A. P., & Tseng, M. S. *Dimensions of internal versus external control revisited: Toward the development of a measure of generalized expectancy.* Unpublished manuscript, Rehabilitation Research and Training Center, West Virginia University, 1971.

Maddi, S. R., Kobasa, S. C., & Hoover, M. *The Alienation Test: A structured measure of a multidimensional subjective state.* Unpublished manuscript, 1978 (cited in Kobasa, 1979).

Majumder, R. K., MacDonald, A. P., & Greever, K. B. A study of rehabilitation counselors: Locus of control and attitudes toward the poor. *Journal of Counseling Psychology*, 1977, *24*, 137–141.

Maracek, J., & Frasch, C. Locus of control and college women's role expectations. *Journal of Counseling Psychology*, 1977, *24*, 132–136.

Marx, K. *Economic and philosophic manuscripts of 1844.* Moscow: Progress Publishers, 1977.

Mechanic, D. Stress illness and illness behavior. *Journal of Human Stress*, 1976, *2*, 2–6.

Miller, J., Schooler, C., Kohn, M., & Miller, K. Women and work: The psychological effects of occupational conditions. *American Journal of Sociology*, 1979, *85*, 66–94.

Mimnaugh, C. M., & O'Brien, G. E. *The effects of feedback and locus of control on performance and job satisfaction.* Unpublished manuscript, Flinders University, 1981.

Mirels, H. L. Dimensions of internal versus external control. *Journal of Consulting and Clinical Psychology*, 1970, *34*, 226–228.

Mitchell, T. J. Expectancy models of job satisfaction, occupational preference and effort: A theoretical, methodological, and empirical appraisal. *Psychological Bulletin*, 1974, *81*, 1053–1077.

Mitchell, T. R., Smyser, C. M., & Weed, S. E. Locus of control: Supervision and work satisfaction. *Academy of Management Journal*, 1975, *18*, 623–631.

Nowicki, S., & Duke, M. P. A locus of control scale for noncollege as well as college adults. *Journal of Personality Assessment*, 1974, *38*, 136–137.

O'Brien, G. E. The centrality of skill utilization for job design. In K. Duncan, M. Gruneberg, & D. Wallis (Eds.), *Changes in working life.* Chichester: Wiley, 1980.

O'Brien, G. E. Leisure attributes and retirement satisfaction. *Journal of Applied Psychology*, 1981, *66*, 371–384. (a)

O'Brien, G. E. Locus of control, previous occupation, and satisfaction with retirement. *Australian Journal of Psychology*, 1981, *33*, 305–318. (b)

O'Brien, G. E. The relative contribution of perceived skill utilization and other perceived job attributes to the prediction of job satisfaction: A cross- validation study. *Human Relations*, 1982, *35*, 219–237. (a)

O'Brien, G. E. Evaluation of the job characteristics theory of work attitudes and performance. *Australian Journal of Psychology*, 1982, *34*, 383–401. (b)

O'Brien, G. E. Reciprocal effects between locus of control and job attributes. *Australian Journal of Psychology*, in press.

O'Brien, G. E., Biglan, A., & Penna, J. Measurement of the distribution of potential influence and participation in groups and organizations. *Journal of Applied Psychology*, 1972, *56*, 11–18.

O'Brien, G. E., & Dowling, P. The effects of congruency between perceived and desired job attributes upon job satisfaction. *Journal of Occupational Psychology*, 1980, *53*, 121–130.

O'Brien, G. E., Dowling, P., & Kabanoff, B. *Work, health and leisure* (Working Paper 28). National Institute of Labour Studies, Flinders University, 1978.

O'Brien, G. E., & Kabanoff, B. Comparison of unemployed and employed workers on work values, locus of control and health variables. *Australian Psychologist*, 1979, *14*, 143–154.

O'Brien, G. E., & Kabanoff, B. Australian norms and factor analyses of Rotter's Internal–External Control Scale. *Australian Psychologist*, 1981, *16*, 184–202.

O'Brien, G. E., & Stevens, L. The relationship between perceived influence and job satisfaction among assembly line employees. *Journal of Industrial Relations*, 1981, *23*, 33–48.

Organ, D. W. Extraversion, locus of control, and individual differences in conditionability in organizations. *Journal of Applied Psychology*, 1975, *60*, 401–404.

Organ, D. W., & Greene, C. N. Role ambiguity, locus of control, and work satisfaction. *Journal of Applied Psychology*, 1974, *59*, 101–102. (a)

Organ, D. W., & Greene, C. N. The perceived purposefulness of job behavior: Antecedents and consequences. *Academy of Management Journal*, 1974, *17*, 69–78. (b)

Osipow, S. H., Carney, C. G., Winer, J. L., Yanico, B., & Koschier, M. *The career decision scale.* (3rd Rev.) Columbus, Ohio, Marathon Consulting and Press, 1980.

Palmore, E., & Luikart, C. Health and social factors related to life satisfaction. *Journal of Health and Social Behavior*, 1972, *13*, 68–80.

Pandey, J., & Tewary, N. B. Locus of control and achievement values of entrepreneurs. *Journal of Occupational Psychology*, 1979, *52*, 107–111.

Parnes, H. S., & King, R. Middle-aged job losers. *Industrial Gerontology*, 1977, *4*, 77–95.

Paulhus, D. & Christie, R. Spheres of control: An interactionist approach to assessment of perceived control. In Lefcourt, H. (Ed.). *Research with the locus of control construct* (Vol. 1). New York, Academic Press, 1981.

Penk, W. E. Age changes and correlations of internal–external locus of control. *Psychological Reports*, 1969, *25*, 859.

Phares, E. J. *Locus of control in personality.* Morristown, NJ: General Learning Press, 1976.

Quinn, R., & Shepard, L. *The 1972–1973 quality of employment survey.* Ann Arbor: Survey Research Center, University of Michigan, 1974.

Reid, D., Haas, G., & Hawkings, D. Locus of desired control and positive self-concepts of the elderly. *Journal of Gerontology*, 1977, *32*, 441–450.

Reid, D. W. & Ware, E. E. Multidimensionality of internal-external control: implications for past and future research. *Canadian Journal of Behavioural Science*, 1973, *5*, 264–271.

Reid, D. W. & Ware, E. E. Multidimensionality of internal-external control: Addition of a third dimension and non-distinction of self versus others. *Canadian Journal of Behavioural Science.* 1974, *6*, 131–142.

Reid, D. W. & Zeigler, M. The Desired Control measure and adjustment among the elderly. In H. M. Lefcourt (Ed.). *Research with the locus of control construct* (Vol. 1). New York, Academic Press, 1981.

Reitz, H. J., & Groff, G. K. Economic development and belief in locus of control among factory workers in four countries. *Journal of Cross-Cultural Psychology*, 1974, *5*, 344–355.

Reitz, H. J., & Jewell, L. N. Sex, locus of control, and job involvement: A six-country investigation. *Academy of Management Journal*, 1979, *22*, 72–80.

Rizzo, J. R., House, R. J., & Lirtzman, S. I. Role conflict and ambiguity in complex organizations. *Administrative Science Quarterly*, 1970, *15*, 150–163.

Roberts, K. H., & Glick, W. The job characteristics approach to task design: A critical view. *Journal of Applied Psychology*, 1981, *66*, 193–217.

Robinson, J. P., & Shaver, P. R. *Measures of social psychological attitudes*. Ann Arbor, MI: Institute for Social Research, 1973.

Rogasa, D. A critique of cross-lagged correlation. *Psychological Bulletin*, 1980, *88*, 245–158.

Rosenthal, R. Combining results of independent studies. *Psychological Bulletin*, 1978, *85*, 185–193.

Rotter, J. B. *Social learning and clinical psychology*. Englewood Cliffs, NJ: Prentice-Hall, 1954.

Rotter, J. B. Generalized expectancies for internal versus external control of reinforcement. *Psychological Monographs*, 1966, *80*, (1, whole No. 609).

Rotter, J. B. Some properties and misconceptions related to the construct of internal versus external control of reinforcement. *Journal of Consulting and Clinical Psychology*, 1975, *43*, 56–67.

Ruble, T. L. Effects of one's locus of control and the opportunity to participate in planning. *Organizational Behavior and Human Performance*, 1976, *16*, 63–73.

Runyon, K. E. Some interactions between personality variables and management styles. *Journal of Applied Psychology*, 1973, *57*, 288–294.

Ryckman, R. M., & Malikioski, M. Differences in locus of control orientation for members of selected occupations. *Psychological Reports*, 1974, *34*, 1224–1226.

Ryckman, R. M., & Malikioski, M. Relationship between locus of control and chronological age. *Psychological Reports*, 1975, *36*, 655–658.

Searls, D. J., Braucht, G. N., & Miskimins, R. W. Work values of the chronically unemployed. *Journal of Applied Psychology*, 1974, *59*, 93–95.

Seeman, M. On the meaning of alienation. *American Sociological Review*, 1959, *24*, 783–791.

Seeman, M. The urban alienations: Some dubious theses from Marx to Marcuse. *Journal of Personality and Social Psychology*, 1971, *19*, 135–143.

Sekaran, U., & Mowday, R. T. A cross-cultural analysis of the influence of individual and job characteristics on job involvement. *International Review of Applied Psychology*, 1981, *30*, 51–63.

Shiflett, S. Toward a general model of small group productivity. *Psychological Bulletin*, 1979, *86*, 67–79.

Sims, H. P., & Szilagyi, A. D. Job characteristic relationships: Individual and structural moderators. *Organizational Behavior and Human Performance*, 1976, *17*, 211–230.

Smith, P., Kendall, L., & Hulin, C. *The measurement of satisfaction in work and retirement*. Chicago: Rand McNally, 1969.

Spector, P. E. Behavior in organizations as a function of employee's locus of control. *Psychological Bulletin*, 1982, *91*, 482–497.

Staats, S. Internal versus external locus of control for three age groups. *International Journal of Aging and Human Development*, 1975, *5*, 7–10.

Strodtbeck, R. L. Family interaction, values, and achievement. In D. C. McClelland, A. L. Baldwin, U. Bronfenbrenner, & F. L. Strodtbeck (Eds.), *Talent and society*. Princeton: Van Nostrand, 1958.

Szilagyi, A. D., & Sims, H. P. Locus of control and expectancies across multiple occupational levels. *Journal of Applied Psychology*, 1975, *60*, 638–640.

Szilagyi, A. D., Sims, H. P., & Keller, R. T. Role dynamics, locus of control, and employee attitudes and behavior. *Academy of Management Journal*, 1976, *19*, 259–276.

Taylor, K. M. An investigation of vocational indecision in college students: Correlates and moderators. *Journal of Vocational Behavior*, 1982, *21*, 318–329.

Thornton, G. C. Differential effects of career planning on internals and externals. *Personnel Psychology*, 1978, *31*, 471–476.

Tiggemann, M., & Winefield, A. H. Some psychological effects of unemployment in school leavers. *Australian Journal of Social Issues*, 1980, *15*, 269–276.

Tracy, L., & Johnson, T. W. What do the role conflict and role ambiguity scales measure? *Journal of Applied Psychology*, 1981, *66*, 464–469.

Tseng, M. S. Locus of control as a determinant of job proficiency, employability, and training satisfaction of vocational rehabilitation clients. *Journal of Counseling Psychology*, 1970, *17*, 487–491.

Tudor, B. A specification of relationships between job complexity and powerlessness. *American Sociological Review*, 1972, *37*, 596–604.

Valecha, A. G. K. Construct validation of internal–external locus of control of reinforcement related to work-related variables. *Proceedings of the 80th Annual Convention of the American Psychological Association*, 1972, *7*, 455–456.

Valecha, A. G. K., & Ostrom, T. M. An abbreviated measure of internal–external locus of control. *Journal of Personality Assessment*, 1974, *38*, 369–376.

Venable, V. *Human nature: The Marxian view*. Gloucester, Mass. Peter Smith, 1975. (Originally published by Alfred A. Knopf, 1945).

Vroom, V. H. *Work and motivation*. New York: Wiley, 1964.

Watson, J. M. A note on the dimensionality of the Rotter Locus of Control Scale. *Australian Journal of Psychology*, 1981, *33*, 319–330.

Weiss, H., & Sherman, J. Internal–external control as a predictor of task effort and satisfaction subsequent to failure. *Journal of Applied Psychology*, 1973, *57*, 132–136.

Wertheim, E. G., Widom, C. S., & Wortzel, L. H. Multivariate analysis of male and female professional career choice correlates. *Journal of Applied Psychology*, 1978, *63*, 234–242.

Wolfe, R. N. Effects of economic threat on anomie and perceived locus of control. *Journal of Social Psychology*, 1972, *86*, 233–240.

Wyler, A. R., Masuda, M., & Holmes, T. H. Seriousness of illness rating scale. *Journal of Psychosomatic Research*, 1968, *11*, 363–375.

Wyler, A. R., Masuda, M., & Holmes, T. H. Seriousness of illness rating scale: Reproducibility. *Journal of Psychosomatic Research*, 1970, *14*, 59–64.

Yukl, G. A., & Latham, G. P. Interrelationships among employee participation, individual differences, goal difficulty, goal acceptance, goal instrumentality, and performance. *Personnel Psychology*, 1978, *31*, 305–323.

Zuckerman, M., & Allison, S. N. An objective measure of fear of success: Construction and validation. *Journal of Personality Assessment*, 1976, *40*, 422–430.

3

Kirk R. Blankstein

PSYCHOPHYSIOLOGY AND PERCEIVED LOCUS OF CONTROL: CRITICAL REVIEW, THEORETICAL SPECULATION, AND RESEARCH DIRECTIONS

Introduction

> A Brazilian Indian condemned and sentenced by a so-called medicine man is helpless against his own emotional response to this pronouncement—and dies within hours. In Africa a young Negro unknowingly eats the inviolably banned wild hen. On discovery of his "crime" he trembles, is overcome by fear and dies in twenty-four hours. In New Zealand a Maori woman eats fruit that she only later learns has come from a taboo place. Her chief has been profaned. By noon the next day she is dead [Basedow, 1925, cited in Richter, 1957, p. 191].

The well-known physiologist Walter Cannon studied these and other reports of such "voodoo" deaths and concluded that they merit serious scientific investigation (Cannon, 1942). Drawing on his experimental work on the emotions of rage and fear in cats, Cannon proposed that an individual whose autonomic nervous system is maintained in a highly aroused state, with little opportunity for effective action to reduce the tension, may indeed die. Cannon argued that under such extreme autonomic arousal, certain vital bodily organs can be irreparably damaged, and death is actually brought about by severe fright.

Much additional anecdotal evidence suggests that the actual or perceived lack of control or a sense of helplessness can lead to dramatic negative psychological and physiological consequences. For example, Bettleheim's (1960) descriptions of the "Muselmänner" or walking corpses in Nazi concentration camps represent another instance in

RESEARCH WITH THE LOCUS
OF CONTROL CONSTRUCT (Vol. 3.)
Extensions and Limitations

which an apparent feeling of having lost control over an aversive life situation led to apathy and withdrawal and often culminated in death due to no known cause.

Lefcourt (1973) witnessed a dramatic example of sudden death in an institutional setting. A female psychiatric patient who had been mute and withdrawn for nearly 10 years but in excellent medical health was temporarily shifted from a unit known as the chronic, "hopeless" floor to an exit ward from which patients typically anticipated rapid discharge. Shortly after the move, necessitated by unit redecoration, she became socially responsive, ceased being mute, and actually became gregarious. When the redecorations were completed she was returned to her previous unit. Lefcourt described the impact of her loss of control as follows:

> Within a week after she had been returned to the "hopeless" unit, this patient, who like the legendary Snow White had been aroused from a living torpor, collapsed and died. The subsequent autopsy revealed no pathology of note and it was whimsically suggested at the time that the patient had died of despair [Lefcourt, 1973, p. 422].

Seligman (1975) has documented other apparent instances of sudden death in both humans and animals due to "uncontrollability" of a stressful environment. The term was coined by Richter (1957) to describe the phenomenon in wild rats. He found that if the fierce and vigorous *Rattus norwegicus* was placed in a large vat of warm water from which there was no escape, the rat would swim for about 60 hours before drowning as a result of exhaustion. However, when he first held these rats in his hand until they stopped struggling and then put them in the water, Richter found that the rats swam around excitedly for a few minutes, then suddenly sank to the bottom and drowned. When restraint was combined with trimming of the rats' whiskers (a primary sensory organ), all rats tested died suddenly. Richter argued that being held, having the whiskers trimmed, and being placed in the vat of water from which escape was impossible instilled in the animals a sense of hopelessness. Richter also demonstrated that sudden death could be prevented by showing *Rattus norwegicus* that escape was possible.

What was the physiological condition of the wild rats during sudden death? In the most common forms of mammalian death, tachycardia occurs prior to death (sympathetic death) as increased heart rate and blood pressure speed blood to the extremities. Presumably such emergency sympathetic activation occurred during the initial period when the rats were thrashing around. However, in Richter's wild rats the heart slowed prior to death, and autopsy showed the heart was engorged with blood (parasympathetic death). When Richter treated some of his rats with the parasympathetic (and cholinergic) blocking agent atropine, death was prevented in a small but significant number of the rats. Richter concluded that death was caused by "giving up the struggle."

In other research, rats trained to make an avoidance response to electric shocks were found to experience substantially reduced physiological disturbance relative to yoked-control rats that had no available avoidance response, even though both groups received the same degree of shocks (see Weiss, 1971; Weiss, Stone, & Harrell, 1970). Weiss et al. (1970) demonstrated that in addition to the weight loss, increase in gastric secretion, and ulceration rate in rats exposed to uncontrollable stress, the level of norepinephrine (the basic adrenergic transmitter substance) in the brain decreases, and suggested that norepinephrine depletion may be an explanation for helplessness. Seligman (1975, p. 70) cited Thomas's argument that Seligman's learned helplessness phenomenon (in cats at least) may be explained by the cholinergic action of the septum, since blocking it with atropine eliminated helplessness.

Unknown variables make it difficult to interpret the sudden death phenomenon among humans, despite research with rats and cats. However, it seems clear from these examples that control (or noncontrol—helplessness or hopelessness) in aversive situations has important physiological consequences for the organism. It also seems clear that dispositional differences in the belief in control or noncontrol must be related to these outcomes. Not everyone dies as a consequence of the voodoo curse. People did survive the Nazi death camps. Sadly, many psychiatric patients live to an old age in so-called hopeless wards. There were even individual differences in the behavior of Richter's wild rats: Some lasted a relatively long time in the water before giving up; and a few died in the investigator's hands, before being placed in the water.

Consistent with the foregoing anecdotal data with human subjects and early animal research, it should not be surprising that individual differences in perceived control as measured by Rotter's (1966) Internal–External (I–E) Locus of Control Scale and related measures are related to physiological changes and disease processes and, under some circumstances, can even predict the ultimate index of physiological disregulation: death. For example, in relation to disease processes, we can ask whether internals are less likely than externals to suffer from cardiovascular disease. The evidence is quite sketchy. However, the results of two research investigations suggest that this may be the case. Naditch (1974) examined the records of over 400 Black American adults who suffered from essential hypertension. Group members who reported high life discontent and who also perceived that events in their lives were beyond personal control had a significantly higher percentage of hypertension (46%) than any of the other groups (mean of 21%). The group of persons designated as highly content by self-report and who perceived events as controllable had a hypertension rate of only 7%. Given that high blood pressure is thought to be a risk factor for heart attack and stroke, these findings suggest a possible relationship between the perception of control as measured by internal–external locus of control and cardiovascular disease.

More compelling data come from an investigation conducted by Cromwell, Butterfield, Brayfield, and Curry (1977). These investigators studied 229 cardiac patients and a group of 80 medical patient controls. Although the coronary patients as a group were significantly more external than the medical controls, and the specifics of treatment had differential impact on patients varying in internal–external beliefs, of major import are the findings that locus of control predicted many of the ongoing physiological and biochemical indexes that were monitored during the patients' stay in the hospital. Internality was linked to better prognostic ratings: lower sedimentation rates, lower serum glutamic oxalacetic transaminase levels, lower lactate dehydrogenase levels, and lower cholesterol. Furthermore, internals had lower peak temperatures during intensive care and left the coronary intensive care unit and the hospital sooner than did externals. Cromwell and his colleagues also reported a near-significant relationship among treatment congruence, personal expectancies, and long- term effects. Congruence of expectancies and remedial conditions appeared to enhance responses to treatment. Thus none of the patients in conditions where I–E beliefs and degree of participation in treatment were congruent either returned to the hospital following discharge or died within 3 months.

These findings are subject to alternative interpretations, and it is difficult to establish the cause–effect relationship. However, at the very least they suggest a relationship between I–E and physiological changes among ill persons. In her review of this and related literature, Strickland (1979, p. 226) posed the critical questions:

Would these findings result only from the social and personal characteristics associated with internal expectancies, such as beliefs in control, attempts to master one's destiny, achievement striving, and so on? Or are these results also occurring as a function of more basic physiological responding that we do not yet understand very well? Do people stay healthy because they engage in appropriate health maintenance behaviors of which they are fully aware, or do individuals also reduce the risk of heart attack because at some level below awareness, they have developed appropriate and adaptive bodily responses to stress?

In this chapter I review research that has examined the relationship between individual differences in perceived control and measures of central and peripheral (autonomic and somatic) physiological activity in human beings. Consistent with the theme of this volume, the emphasis is on Rotter's social learning theoretical approach and, in particular, the locus of control construct. The reader will quickly discover that very little research exists that is directly relevant to disease processes and that there is not a single study on locus of control, physiological processes, and sudden death. However, we can expect to find data relevant to differences in basic physiological responding, and we try to determine whether or not differences in perceived control modulate physiological reactions to stressful situations. Internals differ cognitively and behaviorally from externals on many tasks and in many life situations (see Lefcourt, 1976, 1982; Phares, 1976). Are there differences in psychophysiological functioning consistent with these differences? Since the available literature is limited in many areas and the studies are not of uniform quality, I describe many of the experiments in some detail. I also engage in theoretical speculation and make some suggestions for future research.

Psychophysiology: Measurement, Perspectives, and Methodological Concerns

Psychophysiology involves the relatively unobtrusive (noninvasive) measurement of human physiology under varying psychological conditions. It can be defined best as a perspective or strategy for studying behavior and experience: "Its subject matter is the subject matter of all psychology. The psychophysiologist hopes to bring new insights into old problems by seeing man as a biological being" (Hassett, 1978, p. 5).[1]

Presumably measures of physiological activity, together with behavioral and self-report data, provide a more complete picture of individuals who vary in perceived control. Of course, to be of use to the personality and social psychological researcher, the addition of physiological measurement should provide information that could not be obtained as efficiently and effectively using other procedures. Elliott (1974) made the point quite simply when he stated that we hope to learn something from recording physiological activity that would otherwise

---

[1] For a scholarly discussion of definitional issues and the ways in which they affect empirical basic research and applied practice, see Furedy (1983).

escape us. This is often the case, as is illustrated rather elegantly in a statement by Gantt (1960, p. 290): "Though the observed actions of men hide their real thoughts and feelings, these are revealed by the observation of their hearts." In effect, he was saying that we can objectify cognitive and behavioral processes by assessing cardiovascular activity. It may in fact be found that physiological differences between internals and externals parallel differences in overt motor behavior and verbal responses, but this relationship cannot always be expected. This position follows that of Shapiro and Schwartz (1970), who state:

> Physiological, overt behavioral, verbal, and subjective responses are most simply considered multiple concurrent responses functionally related to environmental conditions but not necessarily to each other. . . . There may be varying degrees of integration of the different responses depending upon prior experience and learning and possible constitutional factors [p. 104].

Our hope in employing psychophysiological measures and research strategies is not simply to enumerate the psychophysiological correlates of locus of control behavior, even though that is important. Rather, the hope is to use psychophysiological data and theories to elucidate the processes further that underlie the different behavior patterns found in persons who differ in perceived control.

Measurement of Physiological Activity

The multichannel physiological recorder (polygraph) is the standard piece of equipment in psychophysiology laboratories. Advances made in the design and construction of polygraphs, sometimes backed up by an FM multichannel tape recorder or an A–D (analogue to digital) converter and a digital tape recorder and, most recently, the microcomputer and minicomputer (e.g., Marshall–Goodell, Gormezano, Scandrett, & Cacioppo, 1981) allow the investigator to record and analyze multiple central, autonomic, and peripheral somatic nervous activity simultaneously. The types of physiological activity commonly measured as electrical signals include the electroencephalogram (EEG) and event-related brain potentials; pupillography (measures of changes in pupil size); eye movements or electroculography (EOG); eye blinks; salivation; cardiac activity, including the electrocardiogram (EKG), heart rate, diastolic and systolic blood pressure, and vasomotor activity; respiration; peristaltic activity of the stomach and gut; temperature of internal and external body sites; gross and fine motor activity; and electrodermal measures of sweat gland activity (skin conductance and skin potential). Sometimes the sophisticated researcher also employs biochemical measures. In recording physiological activity there is an important distinction to be made between *tonic* measurements of activity over a relatively extended period of time (such as the number of heartbeats in one minute) and *phasic* measurements of short-term adjustments in the immediate situation (for example, the rate for each of five successive beats of the heart). This activity can be measured under basal or resting conditions as well as in response to stimulation.

Investigators typically focus on several of these physiological measures but usually not all of them. Physiological measures are, of course, all under the control of the nervous system. Although the nervous system is highly integrated, for the sake of convenience the various measures can be seen as controlled primarily by one or another subdivision of this system. Many of the responses of interest are controlled by the autonomic nervous system (ANS), which is subdivided into the parasympathetic nervous system (PNS), the innervation mechanisms, which are dominant when the individual is at rest; and the sympathetic nervous system (SNS), which is dominant in situations requiring mobilization of energy. Historically, perhaps because of interest in the physiological bases of emotion, there has been an emphasis on recording ANS activity. Many early researchers focused on measures of electrodermal activity as indexes of fear, emotion, or arousal. Although these measures are still popular, in recent years there has been increased emphasis on the assessment of cardiovascular activity (e.g., Obrist, 1981)—especially heart rate—and workers have attempted to derive noninvasive measures of sympathetic activity (e.g., T-wave amplitude and the carotid dP/dt). The ANS is part of the peripheral nervous system; EMG and electroculographic and respiratory measures are taken frequently to assess the somatic subdivision of this system. Other recent emphasis has been on renewed interest in the measurement of central nervous system (CNS) activity. Over the past 15 years there has been a surge of research using brain measures, in part due to the application of computer technology to the study of brain processes, especially to specific stimuli (see Andreassi, 1980). Many psychophysiologists are investing heavily in attempts to determine the functional role of the P300 component of the human average-evoked potential in information processing (Pritchard, 1981). Furthermore, Beatty (1982) argues that changes in CNS activity systematically related to cognitive processing can be extracted from task-evoked pupillary responses. These developments are consistent with the cognitive trend in psychology and emphasis on a more complete system perspective of the nervous system.

Some Principles and Theoretical Perspectives

The technical problems of physiological measurement may be great, but they are not insurmountable. Interpretation of the data derived from these measures is another matter. As Averill and Opton (1968, p. 268) pointed out, "physiological reactions do not come with psychological labels attached, such as 'fear' or 'anger.'" Although psychophysiology as a field does not have an all-inclusive conceptual framework (Andreassi, 1980), a number of concepts or principles have relevance for the integration and interpretation of experimental findings. The major principles of psychophysiology include the law of initial values (similar to the familiar ceiling effect often observed in the use of rating scales), autonomic balance, activation or arousal, stimulus–response specificity, individual response specificity, cardiac–somatic coupling, adaptation and rebound, and orienting and defensive responses. Some principles are partly contradictory. It is also important to realize that the data base for some of these concepts and even the concepts themselves are changing rapidly. The interested reader can obtain more information in several excellent primers of psychophysiology (e.g., Andreassi, 1980; Hassett, 1978; Stern, Ray, & Davis, 1980; Sternbach, 1966). At this point I want to focus on the current status of a few of these principles and on some recent developments that have important implications for the understanding of earlier publications on locus of control and physiological processes and for the design of new psychophysiological studies of individual differences in perceived control.

In early research many theorists (e.g., Duffy, 1957, 1962; Lindsley, 1952; Malmo, 1959) supported the theory of a unidimensional physiological activation continuum and the hypothesis of an inverted U-shaped curve relating level of activation and performance on various tasks. Although these ideas do account for the data from many experiments and have received support in terms of a hypothesized physiological mechanism—the reticular activating system (RAS)—they are probably too simplistic. Activation or arousal theory has been criticized by Lacey (1967) and others. First, Lacey suggested that there are at least three different forms of arousal: cortical, autonomic, and behavioral. Each is very complex, not a simple continuum, and one form of arousal cannot always be used as a valid measure of another form of arousal. Second, specific stimulus situations bring about certain *patterns* of responding, not just an increase or decrease in a unidimensional activation continuum (principle of stimulus–response specificity) which he termed *directional fractionation*: the idea that different fractions of the total physiological response pattern may respond in opposite directions.

In the earliest studies, Lacey (1959) demonstrated that for most people, a task like solving a mental arithmetic problem led to a classical arousal reaction in which both heart rate and skin conductance increased. The same people, when listening to a series of tones, showed heart rate decreases along with skin conductance increases—thus an example of directional fractionation. As more tasks were discovered to show similar patterns, Lacey and his colleagues (Lacey, 1967; Lacey & Lacey, 1974; Lacey, Kagan, Lacey, & Moss, 1963) went on to argue that *environmental rejection* (in stressful situations or situations requiring attention to internal events—thinking) leads to phasic heart rate increases, while *environmental intake* (attention to external events) leads to phasic heart rate decreases.

Similar patterns have been observed in Western investigations of the Russian neurophysiologist Sokolov's (e.g., 1965) theories of the so-called orientation or orienting (OR) and defense (DR) reflexes. In contrast to much of the research derived from Lacey's hypotheses, which employ complex as well as simple stimuli, research derived from Sokolov's model emphasizes differences in habituation to strings of discrete, simple stimuli such as tones or lights. The orienting response is the group of reactions (especially physiological reactions) that usually occur to novel stimuli (the "what is it" response). The defensive response occurs in response to intense, potentially painful stimulation. Orienting responses habituate rapidly, whereas the DR habituates very slowly. Graham and Clifton (1966) suggested that the OR is accompanied by heart rate deceleration, while heart rate acceleration represents a DR to stimuli of prepain intensity. This suggestion has received some empirical support (e.g., Raskin, Kotses, & Bever, 1969).

According to Sokolov, the biological significance of the OR is that it prepares the organism to deal with novel stimuli. Once the person determines that the stimulus poses no threat, there is no reason to prepare to deal with it, and the response habituates. The DR protects the individual from the possible dangers of intense stimulation. Its function is (apparently) to limit the effect on the body of intense stimuli. Thus there seems to be a correspondence with the Laceys' "intake rejection" hypothesis. Namely, it appears that heart rate deceleration is associated with stimulus intake and the OR, whereas heart rate acceleration accompanies stimulus rejection and the DR. Direct tests of the Lacey hypothesis have yielded mixed results (see reviews and critiques by Carroll & Anastasiades, 1978; Elliott, 1972; Hahn, 1973), and there are conceptual and methodological problems with Sokolov's OR–DR concept (see Furedy & Arabian, 1979; Lang, Rice, & Sternbach, 1972). However, research has indicated support for stimulus or situational specificity—that is, a consistent pattern of physiological responses will occur in a given situation, and different physiological variables will show different directions of response.

The theoretical mechanisms of these response patterns and their adaptive or behavioral significance are still matters of considerable controversy. The Laceys contend that cardiovascular changes *cause* changes in brain function. They argue that changes in heart rate and blood pressure can influence cortical activity and thereby affect sensitivity to stimuli (such as in a reaction-time task). Neurophysiological evidence from animal studies and psychophysiological data have prompted the Laceys (e.g., Lacey & Lacey, 1974; 1978) to propose that decreases in cardiovascular activity are sensed by baroreceptors in the carotid and aortic arteries, resulting in decreased afferent feedback to cortical areas, thus causing increased cortical activity and facilitating sensorimotor performance and attentional processes. In one study, Lacey and Lacey (1970) reported a relationship among a measure of brain activity (CNV), heart rate deceleration, and reaction-time efficiency. According to their formulation, increased cardiovascular activity decreases efficiency in the same types of activities because increased afferent feedback from the same baroreceptors inhibits cortical and subcortical activity.

The Lacey hypothesis has been attacked vigorously by Obrist (1976), who is skeptical about the ultimate value of concentrating on small, transient responses (although some of the Laceys' earlier work focused on tonic changes). Obrist went so far as to term the phasic HR effect "biologically trivial." His theory of cardiac–somatic coupling (e.g., Obrist, 1976, 1981) stresses more traditional and commonsense notions of cardiovascular function—namely, heart rate increases to supply more blood to tissues that need it. He presents impressive data from a series of animal and human studies to show that heart rate and muscle activity frequently covary directly. In Obrist's view, heart rate and somatic activity do not cause each other; rather, they are concomitant changes produced by the same CNS mechanism. The body is simply wired in such a way that heart rate and EMG measures ordinarily change together. Thus in Obrist's view, heart rate slows when a person attends to the environment, such as in a reaction-time task, because the individual is sitting quietly. When a person tries to solve a mental arithmetic problem, heart rate increases because muscles are tensed.

Recently, Obrist (Obrist, 1976, 1981) argued that, depending on circumstances, an organism has at its disposal two means of coping with a situation that is perceived to be significant to its survival or wellbeing. One occurs when recourse to action does not appear to be a viable strategy and the individual feels helpless (passive coping). When the organism has little control over the environment, such as when a person in a classical conditioning paradigm receives periodic electric shocks regardless of his or her actions, the heart, according to Obrist, is under the control of the vagus nerve of the parasympathetic nervous system and cardiac–somatic coupling occurs. Thus in passive coping, heart rate provides an index of bodily activity. A second set of circumstances occurs when some event or covert act is anticipated to result in effective coping (active coping). In active coping, for example, when a person can avoid the shock by pressing a button, the cardiac response seems to be under sympathetic nervous system control and large-magnitude tonic heart rate increases are observed that do not directly reflect somatic responses. Thus we have a situation of cardiac–somatic uncoupling. Obrist makes the case that the relationship between cardiovascular activity and coping is understandable from an evolutionary perspective. He asks whether active coping is influential in the etiology of hypertension, given that the anticipatory mobilization response persists only in certain individuals. Obrist (1981) has many reservations and questions about his theory, and the verdict is not in on either the Lacey or the Obrist view.

In summary, the concepts of orienting and defense, the intake–rejection hypothesis, and the active–passive coping distinction, reflect the kinds of biologically based categories of psychological events that are useful in helping researchers to understand individual differences in perceived control. Whatever one's theoretical position, it seems clear that patterns of physiological response are directly implicated in attentional and adaptive processes.

By examining the relationship between locus of control and performance on various tasks and in different situations while physiological activity is monitored, we hope to achieve new insights and greater understanding about the role of perceived control in human experience and behavior. These tasks and situations can include those examined in more traditional locus of control and general psychological research, but they also include those that are more unique to the psychophysiology laboratory. One such task would be to self-regulate physiological processes under various conditions, a possibility that has generated considerable excitement and controversy in the past 20 years. Even on this task, the principles and concepts of psychophysiology, in conjunction with other psychological constructs and theories, may help us to understand differences between persons who vary in perceived control. Thus in addition to their empirical usefulness, psychophysiological techniques and concepts may help to provide a sounder theoretical foundation for the locus of control construct.

Methodological Considerations

A number of methodological considerations arise in attempts to investigate the relationship between a personality variable such as locus of control and physiological activity. Some of these are general to research in personality and psychophysiology (e.g., Averill & Opton, 1968; Christie & Todd 1975) and some are specific to the study of a particular stimulus situation or psychophysiological paradigm, such as habituation (see O'Gorman, 1977). Problems of the design of the investigation and the measurement of locus of control would belong to the former category, whereas the conditions under which physiological activity is studied and the method of quantifying responses belong to the latter. A few issues are presented here in order to alert the reader to some of the possible sources of confounding and interpretative confusion in the results of the studies to be reviewed. This section draws heavily from O'Gorman's (1977) scholarly discussion, although I have adapted his presentation to a discussion of perceived control.

PROBABILITY OF FINDING A LOCUS OF CONTROL–
PHYSIOLOGICAL PROCESSES RELATIONSHIP

Conceptual difficulties in the measurement of generalized expectancies for control have been discussed throughout these volumes. It is appropriate to be reminded here of Lefcourt's (1972, p. 2) warning that "when research is presented focusing on locus of control as a sole predictor of a given set of criteria, it necessarily represents a limited approach to the prediction of these criteria, such that high magnitude relationships should not be anticipated." The relationship between locus of control as measured by one of the existing instruments and differences in physiological activity is not likely to be strong. Where a relationship does exist, coefficients of the order of .3 to .4 might be anticipated, above the so-called noise level for random relationships among personality variables (Lykken, 1968) and within the typical range of personality coefficients (Mischel, 1968). If this expectation is correct, factors that reduce the magnitude of correlation, such as unreliability of measurement, and factors that reduce the power of statistical tests, such as sample size, become crucial.

Cohen (1970) illustrated that a sample of 60 subjects is required where a correlation is computed for two continuously distributed variables using a sample of unselected subjects, and if the true population correlation is .3, in order to have better than a 50% chance of demonstrating a significant departure from 0 correlation. Feldt (1961) argued that a more powerful strategy than correlation of continuous variables is the selection of subjects with extreme scores on one variable so as to form contrasting groups, and the comparison of scores on the second variable between the two groups. Although Lefcourt (1981) and Rotter (1975) eschew the tendency to view locus of control as a trait or typology, use of the contrasting-groups design seems most appropriate at this time, especially if steps are taken to separate the defensive externals from congruent externals (see Phares, 1976; Rotter, 1975) and a group in the moderate (bilocal) range (see Wong & Sproule, this volume) is included.

Although the contrasting-groups design does not allow determination of the true strength of the relationship between I–E and physiological activity in the population, it does establish relationships. However, unreliability of measurement will attenuate relationships; and although Rotter's I–E Scale, the assessment device most commonly used, and several of the derivative scales are quite reliable, reliability should be examined for the sample being studied, given that groups formed on the basis of extreme scores can fail to show extreme scores on a second testing.

It is also appropriate to reiterate here Lefcourt's (1981) point that it is a mistake to identify the control construct with a particular scale (such as Rotter's) and that in many research studies scales have been misapplied. The point is illustrated eloquently and dramatically in the following quotation: Asking a dying person how he or she thinks school grades are assigned will not provide much help in predicting how that person will respond to the stress of the dying process" (Lefcourt, 1981, p. 2). Investigators should employ a scale that is consistent with the question they are asking, and under some circumstances create a new device for their specific application. Some subscales, factors, or goal-specific measures may be more predictive of psychophysiological processes, whereas other measures may not be predictive at any level. Instruments that tap personal or self-control may be especially appropriate. Mirels's (1970) factor of "felt mastery over the cause of one's life" is one example, although the scale is composed of very few items. The scales developed by Nowicki and his colleagues (Nowicki & Duke, 1974; Nowicki & Strickland, 1973) focus much more than Rotter's scale on aspects of personal control, especially in social interactions. Scales or subscales that focus specifically on self-control (e.g., Reid & Ware's [1974] Belief in Self-Control; Rosenbaum's [1980a] Self-Control Schedule) have rarely been used in psychophysiological investigations. A test designed specifically to predict perceived control over physiological activity and internal bodily processes could be extremely useful. This recommendation was probably first made by Cox, Freundlich, and

Meyer in 1975: "an instrument constructed to measure perception of intrapersonal self-control, specifically on a physiological dimension would have a greater predictive value" (p. 897), and more recently by Carlson (1982). The only extant scale to even mention physiological activity at the item level is Rosenbaum's (1980a) measure.

Despite the fact that a specific measure of perceived physiological control might lead to significant increments in the prediction of physiological response to diverse situations, stimuli, and tasks, it is important to examine the predictive utility of Rotter's I–E Scale and other existing measures in order to relate information about perceived control and physiological activity to the large body of empirical data on generalized expectancy measures.

ASSESSMENT OF PHYSIOLOGICAL ACTIVITY

The previous discussion of physiological response patterning and the theoretical ideas of the adaptive or biological significance of patterns should have convinced readers of the wisdom of recording multiple physiological measures. As Hassett (1978, p. 148) stated, "psychophysiology would have a dismal future indeed if every one of its variables were telling the same simple tale." Obviously, a window on the nervous system cannot be obtained, but most psychophysiologists would agree that as many different physiological systems as possible should be sampled. Ideally, measures of central and peripheral somatic and autonomic nervous system activity are recorded. Unfortunately, many investigators are victims of the classic indicant fallacy and mistakenly believe that a single physiological index will bear meaningful results. However, patterns of physiological activity in the context of an understanding of the organism's transactions with the environment are common in modern psychophysiological research. Furthermore, the concept of individual response specificity also requires the sampling of multiple physiological systems to assure a valid assessment. As Lacey, Bateman, and Van Lehn (1953) indicated, an individual subject may have an idiosyncratic pattern of responding that is emitted to numerous environmental stimuli, and within this pattern one particular system may reliably show a maximal response to various stimuli. Thus some persons may show maximum reactivity in their heart rate, others in their blood pressure, yet others in their electrodermal activity (see Roessler & Engel, 1977). Although these patterns do not predict the responses of all subjects, when only one response is measured (and this response has not been predetermined for each subject [see Averill & Opton, 1968, p. 270]), it is possibly a reactive response for some subjects and a relatively nonreactive response for others. Thus, concepts of stimulus and individual response patterning suggest that the probability is slight that one particular response can be maximally sensitive when measured across different stimuli in several subjects. Concurrent measurement of numerous physiological responses should be a guiding principal of sound psychophysiological research.

The number and kind of response systems chosen for study will depend on various factors, some of which are entirely practical (see Claridge, 1970). Certain autonomic responses (e.g., pupil response) are more difficult, or more expensive, to measure than others. Others, such as salivary flow, are relatively insensitive and unsuitable for continuous recording or investigation of subtle variations in arousal. Another practical consideration is the physical restriction placed on the subject due to multiple recordings from numerous electrodes. A subject who is too wired up may find it difficult, if not impossible, to carry out some psychological tasks that may form an additional part of the investigation. Furthermore, a particular measure may be particularly disruptive to the person. Most psychophysiologists agree that measurement should be as unobtrusive as possible. Given this commitment to studying the psychobiology of human functioning with the least possible interference, the investigator should select among comparable measures that measure which is least obtrusive and disturbing to the subject. For example, there is currently a controversy in the literature over whether the carotid dP/dt or amplitude of the EKG T-wave is the best index of beta adrenergic (sympathetic) influences on the myocardium (see Obrist, 1981, p. 183–194). These are both noninvasive measurements; however, the carotid dP/dt is probably much more disruptive to the subject who is not even permitted to swallow during the recording (see Heslegrave & Furedy, 1980).

From a theoretical perspective, the investigator needs to consider the relevant research on response patterning under different stimulus conditions and situations and select measures that are relevant to the questions being asked. For example. Heslegrave and Furedy (1979) compared the sensitivities of heart rate and T-wave amplitude for detecting cognitive and anticipatory stress. They concluded that T-wave amplitude was a more sensitive index of cognitive stress associated with the performance of a mathematical task, whereas heart rate was a more sensitive index of anticipatory stress associated with the anticipation of a noxious event (noise stimulus). Although these findings need to be replicated and extended to different intensities of stressors and different types of tasks, the study illustrates my point. An investigator might conclude that there are no differences between individuals who differ in perceived control if heart rate only is measured in response to a cognitive task when a possibly more sensitive measure, such as T-wave amplitude, might lead to the conclusion of significant differences.

Even within a single system different measures *may* have different psychological significance, and the researcher needs to decide whether or not to measure more than one component. For example, Kilpatrick (1972) reported that a task presented as an IQ test elicited increases in the level of skin conductance without corresponding changes in non-specific activity. However, when Kilpatrick presented the same test as a measure of brain damage, both measures increased. This finding is consistent with other evidence that nonspecific electrodermal activity increases under emotional stress, while level changes reflect both emotional and cognitive problem-solving demands. Thus "even at the level of the sweat glands, biologically based distinctions can be made that emphasize the importance of focusing attention on response-patterning" (Hassett, 1978, p. 44).

COMMENT ON EXPERIMENTER–SUBJECT–
SITUATION INTERACTION

The psychophysiologist must worry about or control a large number of factors that are known to influence (or potentially influence) physiological activity in addition to the psychobiologically relevant events or stimuli of concern in a particular experiment. These factors may serve to moderate relationships with a personality construct such as locus of control. Thus it is generally accepted that the testing environment must be controlled as to temperature, pressure, and humidity, and sound-treated and illuminated at a constant level within and between testing sessions (see Wenger & Cullen, 1972). The existence of circadian, seasonal, and other cyclical variations in the physical and chemical properties of the internal environment also presents a methodolgical problem of some importance for the measurement of individual differences in physiological activity and reactivity (see Wenger & Cullen, 1972). These different cycles may interact with each other and also with individual differences. Subjects must also be habituated to the laboratory environment because the unfamiliarity of the laboratory and equipment may elicit psychophysiological reactions, and these reactions may represent the result of an interaction between previous experience and personality characteristics. Christie and Todd (1975) gave the following example of a hypothetical interaction: "The sight of a multi-channel pen recorder purring away in the laboratory might well elicit quite different responses in a stable, extraverted engineer, to those of a neurotic introverted classicist" (p. 63). Such differences might well occur as a function of perceived control.

Characteristics of the subject, possibly independent of I–E classification, that have been suggested as sources of bias are gender, age, need for approval, method of recruitment for the study, and life history factors (e.g., previous experience in similar studies, willingness of the subject to participate in the study, use of drugs, sleep deprivation, anticipation of academic examinations) (see O'Gorman, 1977). In addition, Orne (1966) argued that the subject perceives the totality of cues from the experimental environment and generates a hypothesis concerning the nature of the experimenter's aim that significantly determines the subject's behavior. Orne labels the sum total of such cues the "demand characteristics" of the experimental situation. Kallman and Feuerstein (1977) assumed that physiological responses are not very susceptible to voluntary distortion from demand characteristics and expectancies, given that "volitional control of bodily responses is not as readily apparent in the physiological response mode as in the self-report and behavioral channels" (p. 358). However, subject control of overt motor or cognitive activity could have indirect effects on physiological activity.

Characteristics of the experimenter that have been suggested as important are the gender and race of the experimenter in relation to that of the subject, experimenter's interpersonal response to the subject, and the expectancy the experimenter has about the outcome of the study. These factors may interact with subject factors, including dispositional differences, and the situation of the experiment.

An example of expectancy effects in psychophysiological research: Locus of control of the experimenter and the subject. Clarke, Michie, Andreasen, Viney, and Rosenthal (1976) examined the role of experimenters' expectancies on the outcome of a psychophysiological experiment. They monitered an electroencephalogram and an electromyogram (EMG) during presentation of a tendon tap that elicited a phasic stretch reflex. Experimenters were given the expectation that one set of tendon taps would be heavy, resulting in large contractions of the subject's responding muscle, whereas another set of taps would be light, resulting in smaller contractions of the subject's muscle. In fact, tap intensity was kept constant. The experimenter sat beside and within view of the subject during the course of the experiment and was given a rating task to complete that directed attention toward the subject prior to each stimulus presentation. An intriguing and, for present purposes, important aspect of this study was that the investigators also examined the relationship between observed experimenter expectancy effects and both the subject's and the experimenter's generalized expectancies of perceived locus of control as measured by Rotter's I–E Scale. Given that those whose perceived locus of control is internal tend to be more alert to environmental cues, they more than externals might be influenced as subjects by subtle cues conveying the experimenter's expectations. As experimenters, internals are expected to be more controlling, confident, and alert to cues from the subject to aid in control of the subject.

The clearest evidence for an experimenter expectancy effect was shown in the data for EEG alpha amplitude in the 1-second periods immediately prior to an immediately following stimulus presentation. When the experimenter expected the stimulus intensity to be high, subjects' alpha amplitude was lower (indicating alertness) than when the experimenter expected intensity to be low. EEG alpha was more biased in the direction of experimenter expectation when both experimenters and subjects were similar in their I–E scores. These biasing effects were found early in the experimental session, when subjects or their experimenters scored as internally controlled. EMG measures increased or decreased in the direction of the experimenter's expectation when subjects were internally controlled, but there was a reversal of the direction of the experimenter's expectations with subjects who scored as externally controlled so that no significant experimenter expectancy effect was observed. Clarke *et al.* hypothesized that internals responded to subtle cues emitted by the experimenters, whereas the externally controlled subjects were continually aroused because the experimenter was present in the room. They speculated that the mechanism for the observed effect was greater attentiveness on the part of experimenters and subjects to one another's facial expressions and body movements just before and after the presentation of the stimulus.

Clearly, further research is needed to elucidate the interaction of experimenter expectancy effects and the generalized expectancies of perceived locus of control. However, the implications of these results for the conduct of research are also clear: Since unintentional social influence can occur in psychophysiological experiments and these effects may interact with perceived locus of control of both the experimenter and the subject, investigators should evaluate perceived control orientation in their experimenters and, if the mechanism of the effect is as proposed by Clarke *et al.*, isolate experimenter and subject during the course of an experiment.

Summary

Familiarity with the principles of psychophysiology, issues of measurement, and methodological problems associated with conducting research in which physiological variables are employed as dependent measures will assist the reader in evaluating critically research conducted to date on the relationship between perceived control and physiological processes. The reader, it is hoped, will be encouraged to design and conduct new psychophysiological studies in this area but be discouraged from conducting the kinds of studies that serve only to muddy the waters.

Psychophysiology and Locus of Control

Despite the fact that Rotter's 1966 monograph has been cited almost 3000 times since its publication (Current Contents, February 1, 1982) very little of the research action has employed central and peripheral physiological measures, and it was several years before the first reports of significance were published (e.g., Houston, 1972; Ray & Lamb, 1974). There has been, however, an increase in such research in the past decade. In order to place this increased activity in the context of the body of locus of control research, I examined the frequency of empirical research and theoretical papers in which I–E and physiological processes were measured or discussed, relative to the total frequency of I–E citations in *Psychological Abstracts* for the years 1980 and 1981. Including doctoral dissertations, there were 473 locus of control citations. Only 26 citations, or roughly 5.5%, involved psychophysiological processes. Several of these citations were only loosely related to physiological measurement, many of them were unpublished doctoral dissertations, and, as can be seen, most of the empirical research relates to the prediction of biofeedback effects. Is this research inactivity perhaps a reflection of lack of interest on the part of psychophysiologists in relating dispositional personality constructs to peripheral, physiological processes? No. There is a long history of extensive psychophysiological research that has attempted to examine the relationship between personality variables and physiological activity. (Compare reviews by Eysenck, 1967; Gale, 1973; O'Gorman, 1977; Stern & Janes, 1973; Stern & Plapp, 1969). O'Gorman reviewed studies up to 1976 of the relationship between psychometrically defined dimensions of personality and individual differences in habituation of EEG and autonomic responses in nonclinical populations. In this one area he was able to find 46 studies; however, not a single study employed the locus of control measure.

Admittedly, studies of the relationship between physiological processes and personality do not often produce consistent and positive results. In fact, Koriat, Averill, and Malmstrom (1973) characterized relationships between personality dimensions and indexes of response habituation as "will-o-the-wisps", when they are observed more likely due to Type 1 errors in statistical decision making than to any true relationship. With reference to the general literature as of 1969, Stern and Plapp (1969, p. 227) stated that "although the search for invariant relationships between physiological parameters is a quest for gold, unfortunately, to date, the principal product has been chalcopyrite, or fool's gold." Gale, Coles, Kline, and Penfold (1971, p. 533) took a somewhat different point of view:

> The psychophysiology of individual differences is replete with first-rate questions and second-rate answers. It is reasonable to ask whether different personality groups differ also in terms of physiological reactivity. Unfortunately, this question is rarely asked properly.

Gale *et al.* outlined 21 possible sources of experimental error in studies of the relationship between EEG and personality.

Researchers interested in the psychophysiology of individual differences in perceived control have asked a number of questions, and some of these are first-rate. The following are a few of the questions that have been asked, or are suggested by the theoretical and empirical literature:

1. Are there differences in physiological activity between persons who differ in generalized perceptions of control under baseline or resting conditions? Do externals show an autonomic imbalance in the direction of relative sympathetic dominance at rest? Do externals seem to be overaroused on specific physiological measures? Do internals and externals show differential patterns of adaptation to the experimental environment?

2. Do internals and externals differ at a psychophysiological level in attention to environmental events? Are differences in performance on complex cognitive tasks reflected in different patterns or levels of physiological responding? Do internals show relatively greater heart rate deceleration (environmental intake) on tasks that require attention to external stimuli? When stimulation is not in accord with past experiences, do internals respond more to the change? Do internals show more rapid OR habituation to nonsignificant or irrelevant stimuli? Are

they more responsive to stimuli that have signal value? On tasks that require the active manipulation of symbolic material, do internals, relative to externals, show a pattern of physiological responding consistent with the Laceys' notion of rejection of stimuli disruptive of performance? Are internals more involved with these tasks? How do instructions and task characteristics affect these relationships?

3. Are internals' greater efforts at attaining mastery over their environment reflected in differential ability to self-regulate the internal physiological environment? When appropriately instructed and/or given external feedback of internal physiological processes, are internal-oriented persons better able to control these bodily proceses, such as heart rate? How are observed differences mediated? Do psychophysiological principles contribute to an understanding of reported differences and the mediation process? How do these effects interact with situational and expectancy manipulations? Is relative performance affected by success or failure on a prior task? Do the effects generalize or transfer to other situations?

4. Are there differences between internals and externals in responsiveness to relaxation and meditation procedures, such as progressive muscle relaxation or transcendental meditation? Are some relaxation techniques or strategies more appropriate for internals and others more relevant to externals?

5. Do psychophysiological interventions lead to changes in generalized perceptions of control? Do changes, if observed, interact with individual differences in locus of control? Are such changes predicted by changes in physiological activity?

6. Is there any evidence that internals show more adaptive physiological functioning during stressful or aversive stimulation? Or do they show superior coping at a cognitive or behavioral level but at significant physiological cost? Do physiological differences interact with the actual or perceived controllability of the aversive situation? How do internals and externals react physiologically to helplessness training? What is the relation of the Type A coronary-prone behavior pattern to locus of control?

7. Are there effects on physiological behavior that contribute to an understanding of differences between internals and externals during social interactions?

The knowledgeable reader can probably think of many additional first-rate questions that psychophysiological principles and techniques could help answer. In the subsequent sections I examine the attempts to answer some of the preceding questions and try to determine whether or not the answers are better than second-rate.

Autonomic Balance and Resting Levels

Most psychophysiological research on personality differences evaluates the reactivity of defined groups to psychobiologically relevant stimuli. However, differences in baseline or resting levels are sometimes reported (see Stern & Janes, 1973). It seems unlikely that individuals who differ in some enduring way in perceived control will differ in baseline physiology as a consequence of a defect in some physiological regulatory mechanism (see Alexander, 1972). Averill and Opton (1968, p. 285) stated their pessimism about the possibility of reducing personality constructs to underlying physiological mechanisms: "It appears unlikely that normal variations in personality are greatly dependent upon gross constitutional differences in physiological functioning." Nonetheless, it is possible to speculate that there may be resting-level differences between internal and external-oriented persons, not so much due to constitutional differences (which would be difficult to test for) but as a consequence of long-term experiences.

When does the sense of personal control emerge? How can we explain the development of individual differences in perceived control? Peterson (1980) summarized what is known about the development of, and changes in, perceived control and concluded that it develops early in life, differs as a function of early child-rearing experiences, and increases throughout the life span until deterioration in personal control occurs among the aged. Although longitudinal studies of these stages have not been conducted, it seems probable that locus of control is relatively stable for many persons.

Might long-term differences in perceived control be reflected in differences in resting physiology? Strickland (1978) reviewed research suggesting that beliefs about internal versus external control are related in significant ways to health-related behaviors. Internals are more likely to assume responsibility for their health and "appear to maintain their physical well-being and to guard against accidents and disease to a greater extent than individuals who hold external expectancies" (p. 114). As one specific example, Sonstroem and Walker (1973) found internal college males to hold more positive attitudes toward physical exercise and cardiovascular fitness than did externals. These internal students were also more likely to participate in voluntary exercise. Furthermore, extensive research on the relationship between externality and the reporting of psychological and emotional difficulties, although subject to alternative interpretations (see Strickland, 1978), is consistent with the findings in the physical health area. These findings may have implications for asserting a relationship between locus of control and resting physiological states.

Although this is speculative, generalized expectancies for internal–

external locus of control, when of relatively long duration, may have a significant impact on the resting physiology of the person. This possibility is difficult to assess because the critical time frame is probably many years and longitudinal research is difficult. Furthermore, although investigations of adults (usually college students) may assume considerable stability on the locus of control dimension, this is rarely assessed in individual studies, even over short intervals. The impact of locus of control on physiological processes at rest could be quite general or specific to a particular system (e.g., cardiovascular). Before examining specific studies, I consider the possibility that generalized impact on the resting physiology might be reflected in the balance of the subsystems of the autonomic nervous system.

LOCUS OF CONTROL AND AUTONOMIC BALANCE?

In 1939, Marion Wenger began a long series of studies among children and adults to investigate the ways in which people differ in ANS functioning under resting conditions (see Wenger & Cullen, 1972, for a summary). Simply, Wenger hoped to develop a single index (the $\overline{A}$ score) of relative activation in the antagonistic subsystems of the ANS by combining information from many different physiological measures. Measures used included salivary output, several measures of electrodermal activity, heart rate, systolic and diastolic blood pressure, finger temperature, sublingual temperature, respiration period, and pupillary diameter. Information was combined into a single, reasonably reliable, weighted average representing a person's overall level of *apparent* sympathetic or parasympathetic dominance (autonomic balance). It appears that various disease and psychiatric conditions can be differentiated from the control reference group by these $\overline{A}$ scores. Anxious subjects, for example, give evidence of sympathetic dominance in the resting state.

More recently, Porges (1976) called attention to the possible link between ANS balance and CNS neurotransmitter biochemistry; that is, inhibitory activity of the CNS neurotransmitter, acetylcholine, may be reflected in the PNS, whereas the excitatory CNS effects of the catecholamines may be reflected in the SNS. He proposed a new method for assessing autonomic balance that is physiologically simple (although mathematically complex). It involves measuring the degree of shared variance between resting heart rate and respiratory patterns (reflected in an index called *weighted coherence*[2] score). Quantifying the respiratory influence on heart rate gives a measure of relative parasympathetic–sympathetic activation—a high degree of shared variance (high weighted coherence[2] score) reflects high parasympathetic influence.

We can hypothesize that there is a direct relationship between generalized control expectancies and autonomic balance, as assessed by either the Wenger or Porges approach. Alternatively, the I–E dimension may serve as a moderator of more established relationships, such as between anxiety and autonomic balance. Mandler (1966) suggested that the feeling of not being in control is a central characteristic of all views of anxiety, and there appears to be a strong relationship between externality and a variety of measures of anxiety. It would thus be predicted that externality is related to relative sympathetic dominance (or alternatively that internals show relative parasympathetic dominance) in resting physiological activity. Although Porges has stated that his model is most relevant to understanding behavior pathologies, most of Wenger's studies have involved some measures of personality. Unfortunately, Wenger reported no results in detail and did not examine generalized control expectancies, and other laboratories have not followed up on this line of research. However, Harrell (1979) did report that 7 of 10 males with high coherence[2] scores (i.e., high parasympathetic influence) were classified as internal on locus of control on the basis of a median split of a sample of 20 subjects.

Both the Wenger and Porges approaches to autonomic balance reflect greater sophistication than measurement of a single physiological system. Unfortunately, what little data are available on the issue of resting-level differences between internals and externals come mainly from studies in which a single physiological measure (or only a few measures) is reported. Furthermore, in a majority of cases, the establishment of the baseline was inadequate.

RESTING LEVELS OF SPECIFIC PHYSIOLOGICAL MEASURES

Matus (1974) suggested that personality dimensions may be related to specific physiological responses rather than to global responses. He recorded EMG activity from the frontalis and from the right forearm muscles in male subjects under resting conditions. He found a relationship between resting frontalis EMG and introversion–extraversion, but this was not significant with forearm EMG levels. Field independence–dependence was related to resting forearm EMG but not significantly correlated for frontalis EMG. Differences would not have been detected if only one measure of muscle activity had been recorded.

A study by Notarius and Levenson (1979) indicates the importance of multiple measures across physiological systems. These investigators sought to determine the relationship between facial displays of emotion and physiological reactivity to stress, and also to explore personality correlates of expressive tendencies, including locus of control. They preselected 23 natural inhibitors (persons who show little or no facial responsivity to an emotional situation) and 22 natural expressers (people who show high levels of facial responsivity). An interesting pattern of differences in physiological activity emerged during a 4-minute pre-stimulus baseline—natural expressers displayed a significantly faster heart rate, whereas natural inhibitors displayed a higher skin conductance level. The two groups did not differ in respiration rate. These baseline differences were unexpected in subjects "who had just entered the laboratory and who were told only to monitor a 'voltmeter'" (p. 1208). Further, in conjunction with observed group differences in physiological reactivity, these differences led to a tentative interpretation that expressive tendency may be associated with differences in individual physiological response stereotypy.

These two studies illustrate several important points about the assessment of baseline physiological activity. First, they show the utility of multiple physiological assessment both across and within physiological systems. In Matus's study, the different indexes of EMG activity provided different information about the relationship between muscle activity and personality dimensions. Had Notarius and Levenson measured heart rate only, they might have concluded that natural expressers were more aroused than natural inhibitors, and the opposite if skin conductance level alone had been recorded. Instead, they found a different pattern of resting physiological activity that would have been missed with a single measure. Second, the circumstances of the resting assessment were dramatically different. Matus instructed his subjects to relax in a reclining chair and recorded muscle activity for 20 minutes for three sessions. Presumably, his subjects had become habituated to the experimental environment, laboratory personnel, and procedures. Notarius and Levenson's baseline was only 4 minutes long and should probably be identified as an anticipatory threat period: Subjects observed a voltmeter, ostensibly an indication of voltage flowing through the body, and were instructed to signal the experimenter if the numbers 9999 flashed as a warning that internal voltage was dangerously high and that a strong shock could result. In fairness to Notarius and Levenson, they suggested that the observed differences may have reflected "the operation of differential appraisal from the moment the subjects entered the laboratory" (p. 1209). However, the differences between the two studies point up the fact that we should not assume that measures reflect baseline or resting levels just because an experimenter designates periods as such.

It is necessary to assess resting or baseline activity in subjects who are accustomed to the laboratory. Otherwise, differences between groups might reflect individual differences in appraisal processes with respect to the emotional significance of the laboratory situation (positive or negative) or the subjects' attempts to process cognitively what is going to transpire subsequently. Thus baseline data might reflect responses to the novelty of the situation, apprehension about the situation in general or about the stimuli to be presented, or excitement in anticipation of working on a demanding task. Clearly it would be difficult to expect a subject to relax, despite instructions to do so, when he or she has just signed a consent form agreeing to get "zapped" later on in the experiment! All instructions given to the subjects before the baseline period are important and should be specified. Although it is typically recommended that subjects be thoroughly adapted to the measurement situation before baseline data are collected (e.g., Christie & Todd, 1975; Epstein, 1976), in practice this is rarely assessed. In fact, Lang (1971) indicated that adaptation is seldom a smooth and steady decline in rate or magnitude of response. Some authorities (e.g., Epstein, 1976) thus argued that a standard introductory session or sessions should be designed to produce baselines. Furthermore, most studies use an inadequate time for assessment of both average and variability.

In one of the few studies of psychophysiological adaptation, Lichstein, Sallis, Hill, and Young (1981) charted the course and magnitude of physiological adaptation in 20 undergraduate volunteers during three 30-minute sessions. Subjects were told (in truth) that the purpose of the study was to evaluate physiological changes when people rest peacefully. Under these conditions, the authors found that 7, 13, and 13 minutes of adaptation were required for skin resistance level, frontalis EMG, and EKG, respectively. They also found that (a) high arousal levels in any of these measures at the session's outset resulted in relatively longer adaptation times; (b) EMG showed strongest variance across sessions; and (c) females required longer adaptation periods than males in skin resistance level and EKG. Both Matus (1974) and Notarius and Levenson (1979) employed undergraduate males as subjects. Would the same differences be found with subjects who are female and/or older? Finally, although the sample size in the Notarius and Levenson study was probably adequate, the sample employed by Matus was probably inadequate for the correlational design. Regardless, the point is that we should take the size of the research sample into account when interpreting differences or null effects in studies of baseline physiological activity.

With these points in mind, we can now examine the relevant literature on the relationship between perceived control and specific measures of physiological activity and the patterns (if any) among measures. When I began reviewing the available literature, I became excited about the results of several investigations that seemed to indicate that differences in perceived control are reflected in resting physiological activity. Table 3.1 presents a listing of studies in which resting physiology was identified to be different between locus of control groups. All of these studies employed Rotter's I–E Scale. As is obvious from inspection of Table 3.1, the intuitive hypothesis that an internal locus of control would be reflected in a lower level of arousal or more adaptive pattern of physiological activity would have to be rejected on the basis of any box score evaluation. However, let us examine the specifics of these studies and place them in the context of the available information from other studies.

Smith (1973) was the first to report on resting activity in relation to I–E. In a nonpsychiatric sample, he found a significant correlation between resting frontalis EMG levels and external locus of control $(r = .41, p < .05)$. However, he also found significant correlations with anxiety and neuroticism, and he failed to report the relationships among the several measures or to partial out the effects of the different personality variables. The EMG data were averaged over two 20-minute sessions held in the same week and probably represented a reasonable assessment of resting levels. Although these results are consistent with a theoretical expectation of greater relaxation in the internally controlled person, enthusiasm should be tempered by the fact that the re-

TABLE 3.1
Locus of Control and Resting Level Differences[a]

Externals higher arousal	Internals higher arousal
Smith (1973)	
frontalis EMG $(r = .41)$	
DeGood & Valle (1975)	Fotopoulos et al. (1975)[b]
% time alpha $(r = -.41)$	hand temperature
Lang et al. (1975)	Lang et al. (1975)
respiration (nonpatients)	heart rate (nonpatients)
heart rate (patients; final session)	Fotopoulos & Binegar (1976)[c]
	EMG
	Ollendick & Murphy (1977)
	heart rate

[a] Differences were not found in 11 studies.
[b] Unpublished.
[c] Abstract only.

sults are based on a small, nonhomogeneous sample of male ($n = 9$) and female ($n = 11$) persons.

Fotopoulos and Binegar (1976) also assessed potential differences in physiological base levels as a function of locus of control. They preselected 24 internal males and 24 external males and measured EMG, EEG alpha and beta, and skin temperature during a 20-minute baseline. In contrast to Smith, they found that internal controllers had significantly higher resting EMG levels. No other significant differences in baseline physiology were observed. Evaluation of this study is difficult on the basis of the brief abstract of their work; however, it appears that subjects had received instructions about a subsequent biofeedback task that may have influenced the results.

In another study, Fotopoulos, Cook, and Larsen (1975) examined the relationship between locus of control and baseline skin temperature in 32 male and 32 female university students selected because they were extreme internals or externals in a sample of over 500 potential subjects. They reasoned that if physiological activity is related to perceived control, then evaluation of persons at the extremes should maximize chances of observing the relationship. The experimenter was blind to I–E scores that were reassessed in the first session. Skin temperature was recorded from the preferred hand, and forearm EMG activity was measured to control for movement artifact. In two sessions subjects were requested to sit quietly until a stabilization criterion of less than 0.25F° change in two minutes. This strategy is consistent with the recommendation by Lichstein et al. (1981) that researchers employ individual adaptation periods. Unfortunately, the authors did not report time to stabilization. However, it was reported that skin temperature was significantly higher for subjects with an external locus of control during the first session baseline. Skin temperature was also higher for males than for females. External subjects showed little change between session baselines, whereas internal subjects showed a marked increase in skin temperature, presumably a reflection of relaxation (see Kappes & Michaud, 1978).

Thus in both unpublished studies by Fotopoulos and her colleagues, the data presented suggest higher arousal in internally controlled persons. De Good and Valle (1975) reported EEG data that are more consistent with the muscle activity results of Smith. De Good and Valle correlated both eyes-open and eyes-closed percentage time resting alpha (alpha density) with a variety of objective personality measures in 40 undergraduate and graduate male volunteers for a supposed brain wave control experiment. The Rotter scale was one of several measures assumed to correlate with greater alpha density. Midline occipital alpha (8–13 Hz) was recorded as the accumulated time a digital counting circuit was activated. Subjects were instructed simply to sit comfortably and minimize movement. After a 5-minute adaptation period, four 2-minute blocks of resting-level EEG were obtained, two samples with eyes open and two with eyes closed, and the second set of samples was used in the data analysis. Pearson product-moment correlations between the resting-level alpha density and the various personality measures revealed that the largest and most consistent of the predicted relationships (eyes closed) were found with Locus of Control ($r = -.41$, $p < .01$) and the Personality Research Form (PRF)scale of Endurance ($r = +.54$). Resting alpha was also positively related to PRF scales of Dominance, Exhibition, and Achievement. The authors did not report on the intercorrelations among the scales related to alpha density but concluded that resting alpha is related to "self-confidence, expressiveness, ambition, and feelings of control over the significant events that affect one's life" (p. 627).

On the basis of scores on Rotter's scale, Ollendick and Murphy (1977) selected 18 female internals (M I–E = 6.2; SD = 1.3) and 18 female externals (M I–E = 15.0; SD = 1.4) from a research pool of 250 undergraduates. The subjects participated in a study of muscular and cognitive relaxation. They were instructed that it was designed to learn more about clinical techniques used "to reduce worries and concerns," and further that the investigators were especially interested in subjects' physiological heart rate response. Following these preliminary instructions and attachment of a heart rate transducer, subjects were asked to sit quietly for a 10-minute period. The last minute of this adaptation period was evaluated. Although internals were significantly lower in trait anxiety and state anxiety assessed at the end of the baseline, internals were significantly higher in heart rate than externals (Ms = 84.9 and 79.4 bpm, respectively).

Finally, Lang, Troyer, Twentyman, and Gatchel (1975) reported some significant relationships between locus of control and baseline physiological activity in a study of heart rate modification training with 30 male ischemic heart disease patients and 20 healthy males, age matched to the controls. Resting levels of respiration and heart rate were assessed during 3-minute baselines prior to heart rate slowing and speeding trials in each of three sessions and correlated with scores on Rotter's I–E Scale. In the patient group (M age = 58.0 years; M I–E = 7.0) there was a trend for slower heart rates in internal-oriented subjects, although the correlation was significant only for the third session. However, the more external oriented nonpatients (M age = 60.6 years; M I–E = 8.5) tended to have relatively slower heart rates (significant during the first two sessions) and, paradoxically, significantly faster respiration. It is difficult to become too excited about these results given that the relatively small sample of males was not preselected on the basis of I–E scores. However, they point to the possibility that relationships between perceived control and resting physiology might emerge if investigators would look beyond young, healthy college students. Perhaps the perception of control is related to some of the biological changes that occur with increasing age (see Schulz, 1982).

Are these the only studies that examined the relationship between generalized control expectancies and resting physiology? Although a few studies either did not include baselines as part of the basic methodology or did not report them (e.g., Harrell, 1980; Hurley, 1980; Kappes & Michaud, 1978; Vogt, 1975; Wagner, Bourgeois, Levenson, & Denton, 1974), some form of baseline assessment was reported in most studies. Of these studies, many used an inadequate time sample or suffered in some other way (such as not specifying instructions given to the subjects). Nonetheless, at least 11 studies reported that there were no statistically significant differences in resting activity between internals and externals, and some of these must be considered adequate tests of relationship, at least for specific measures in samples of female and male college students. Several investigators reported null effects for single measures, including heart rate (e.g., Gatchel, 1975a, 1975b; Ray, 1974), frontalis EMG (e.g., Carlson & Feld, 1978; Stern & Berrenberg, 1977), occipital alpha (e.g., Goesling, May, Lavond, Barnes, & Carreira, 1974), and level of skin potential (Volow, Erwin, & Cipolat, 1979). Several studies employed multiple physiological measures. For example, Blankstein and Egner (1977) analyzed heart rate, respiration rate, frequency of eye blinking, and level of skin conductance during the last minute of a 10-minute adaptation period. They reported that there were no differences between male locus of control groups. These subjects had spent approximately one-half hour in the laboratory prior to the adaptation period. Lobstein, Webb, and Edholm (1979) gave male and female subjects 20 minutes to acclimatize to the laboratory environment. Following instructions they received a 2-minute quiet period. Heart rate, heart rate variability, skin conductance level, and spontaneous fluctuations were not different between groups. It is unfortunate that no other published study has reported on spontaneous electrodermal activity given the assumed relationships between nonspecific activity and attention or alertness (see Raskin, 1973) and locus of control and attentional processes (see the foregoing section entitled "Some Principles and Theoretical Perspectives"). However, Katkin (personal communication, 1982) found no relationship between spontaneous activity and Rotter's I–E

Scale in large-sample investigations. Although Fotopoulos and Binegar (1976) reported that EMG levels were higher in internally oriented males, there were no differences in EEG alpha and beta and skin temperature measures.

Carlson (1977) found no differences for frontalis EMG and finger temperature. It is unfortunate that he did not record additional physiological measures because his study is important on at least two counts. First, subjects were administered two baseline sessions of 20 minutes before they received specific instructions about a subsequent session task (biofeedback) and thus were probably reasonably well-adapted to the laboratory environment. Second, integral average EMG levels for successive minutes in each of the two baseline sessions were subjected to analysis (between-subject factors were locus of control orientation, ethnicity, and gender). Thus not only the "end game" but the differential rate of EMG adaptation was assessed. Although it is not clear from the report, there were presumably no significant interactions involving the I–E factor. Other studies employed relatively long adaptation periods or multiple baseline assessment; unfortunately, the results of any analyses were not reported. For example, Logsdon, Bourgeois, and Levenson (1978) devoted an initial 30-minute session to adaptation but did not report the effects on heart rate. Stoffer et al. (1979) employed an 8-minute pretest baseline in 14 biweekly sessions during which temperature and blood pressure were monitored. Lundberg and Frankenhaeuser (1978) used the last session of a three-session study to determine baseline values. Subjects relaxed for about 60 minutes in a quiet and comfortable office, reading magazines and listening to the radio. Telemetered heart rate was recorded for the entire session and catecholamine and cortisol excretion collected from urine samples at the end of the period. Presumably, there were no differences as a function of perceived control. However, unless investigators report the results of analyses, or say that they did them, it cannot be assumed that statistical analyses were conducted. Although DeGood (1975) did not report an analysis, presentation of the means suggests that internals and externals did not differ during baseline for both systolic and diastolic blood pressure. However, consistent with the finding reported by Ollendick and Murphy (1977), inspection of McCanne and Lotsof's (1980) presentation of results suggests that resting heart rate after approximately 10 minutes of rest was possibly higher (about 4 beats per minute) in internal subjects relative to the external group. Inspection of the means suggests no apparent between-groups differences in EEG alpha and EMG in the Clarke et al. (1976) study and EEG alpha in an unpublished report by Jamieson and Dreger (1976). Unfortunately, in many studies means and standard deviations are not presented for baseline data. In all, 32 studies failed to report analyses of baseline or resting levels of physiological activity.

SUMMARY AND EVALUATION

Although a few studies have reported significant differences between external- and internal-oriented individuals in specific physiological measures, there is no consistent pattern to the results. Some studies reported higher values; others reported lower values (sometimes in the context of no differences on other measures). The only study suggestive of a difference in physiological patterning was that of Lang et al. (1975) on a small sample of older nonpatients: Correlational data suggested faster respiration and slower heart rate in more external individuals. The significance of this difference is not immediately clear, and the study should be replicated with a larger sample of carefully selected male and female subjects. Even among the few studies that found significant differences there is contradiction: Smith (1973) reported higher EMG levels in externals; Fotopoulos and Binegar (1976) found the opposite result. Given that a majority of studies reported no significant differences, any suggestion that a higher (or lower) level of arousal or sterotypic pattern of physiological activity characterizes the resting behavior of the internal- or external-oriented person seems premature. It is probably equally premature to conclude on the basis of currently available evidence that no differences exist.

What is needed are evaluations of large samples of males and females at various ages who are carefully selected with respect to locus of control orientation. Furthermore, multiple physiological parameters should be measured over relatively long periods in subjects who are well-adapted to the laboratory environment and who do not anticipate a subsequent demanding or aversive task or stimulus. This strategy would allow a clearer evaluation of intrinsic physiological characteristics of individuals who differ in perceived control. In this context it would be of interest to determine whether carefully selected chronic internals and externals differ in autonomic balance. Possible differences in physiological activity during initial adaptation periods should also be examined more carefully. Such assessments may provide further insights into how internals and externals react to the laboratory environment or anticipate being presented with various experimental stimuli or tasks. Tentatively, I conclude that the repeated failure to obtain consistent differences between internal and external subjects in baseline assessments supports a view that generalized locus of control expectancies are likely to be most important when subjects are responding to stimulation or are actively involved in various tasks.

Attention and Cognitive Processes

Lefcourt (1972) argued that greater attention to all types of cues is found in internal subjects provided these cues are relevant and can be utilized to resolve uncertainty. In fact, there is quite extensive support, from investigations that have used a wide range of dependent measures, for the contention that persons at the extreme internal end of the I–E continuum attend more actively and selectively to environmental events than do extreme externals. This evidence comes from studies of perceptual sensitivity, attention, and information-seeking behavior. For example, internals are more ready than externals to search for and use information necessary for the successful handling of experimental tasks—that is, they attend more to task-relevant cues (e.g., Davis & Phares, 1967; Lefcourt & Wine, 1969; Lefcourt, Gronnerud, & McDonald, 1973). Lefcourt et al. (1973) suggested that internals resist external manipulation due to greater cognitive activity. Further, internals are more likely to refer to inner standards when they judge external (especially social) demands, and Lefcourt et al. hypothesized that "this 'referral' could consist of an internal verbal dialogue, a more extensive information processing that includes more comparisons with past experiences" (p. 162). Wolk and DuCette (1974) conducted a study of intentional performance and incidental learning and concluded that internals were more perceptually sensitive than externals and that they had "more active attentional processes and more intensive efficient structuring of environmental stimuli" (p. 100).

Most of these studies have employed complex and cognitively loaded indexes of attention, such as incidental learning or number of eye contacts with an interviewer. With respect to psychophysiological processes, Berggren, Öhman, and Fredrikson (1977, p. 708) suggested that "it would be of interest to study the reported attention differences on a more basic level as a first step in the delineation of the psychological processes involved." We therefore first examine recent studies that compared orienting and habituation to simple stimuli in individuals who differed in perceived control.

ORIENTING AND HABITUATION

Psychophysiologists have generally accepted the orientation response to a new, significant, or unexpected stimulus and its subsequent habituation as a basic mechanism of attention (see Raskin, 1973). The

OR may be defined as a tonic or phasic response that is most conveniently indicated by such peripheral autonomic activity as heart rate or vasomotor or electrodermal responses. When the stimulation is presented repeatedly without significant consequences, or in Sokolov's terms a "neuronal model" of the stimulus is built up in the cortex, the OR will gradually subside or habituate. According to Sokolov (e.g., 1965), the model encodes all of the properties of the stimulus such as intensity, temporal, and qualitative characteristics, and when the model completely matches the stimulus input, the OR shows complete habituation.

The OR and rate of habituation to simple stimuli, such as lights and tones, have been frequent dependent measures in psychophysiological investigations, and a great deal of research in the 1970s was directed toward testing predictions from Sokolov's model and other models of the physiological changes underlying habituation (e.g., Groves & Thompson, 1970; Lynn, 1966). Studies of perceived control in relation to the OR and habituation should provide information about differences in the attentional processes of internals and externals. It might be predicted that internals would show larger magnitude ORs and slower habituation to relevant or significant stimuli and smaller ORs and faster habituation to nonsignificant or irrelevant stimuli. Put another way, if externals showed large magnitude ORs and/or slow habituation to irrelevant stimuli, it would be an indication that attention capacity is misused. Internals should turn off more quickly to recurring nonsignificant cues.

Several recent studies have tested these hypotheses. I present these studies in some detail because, as will be apparent to the reader, experiments designed to ask the same or similar questions appear to yield very different answers. In an initial study, Berggren *et al.* (1977) tested the hypothesis that internals, because of better control over attention processes, would show more rapid habituation of the electrodermal OR than externals. Berggren *et al.* selected 21 externals and 21 internals from the upper and lower thirds of the distribution of I–E scores of 200 college student respondents. Their measure of generalized expectancy, an extension of Mirels's (1970) first factor, contained 26 items referring to experienced personal control over important events. Subjects were exposed to a recurring tone of moderate intensity while skin conductance was measured. The 20 4-second duration stimuli were presented at an intensity of 80 decibels (1000 Hz) with a mean interstimulus interval of 30 seconds, and skin conductance was measured directly as the maximum change in conductance initiated 1–4 seconds after stimulus onset. Berggren *et al.* used the number of trials to reach a habituation criterion of three successive zero responses as their primary dependent variable, and reported that the external group took significantly more trials to habituate than did the internal group. This difference was reliable for both genders, although there were only six males in each locus of control group. They also investigated changes in responding across trials by converting the number of responses in successive trial blocks to a response probability score. More responses were elicited by the stimuli in the external than in the internal group; however, response frequency did not change differentially over the blocks of stimuli. Analyses of response amplitude and spontaneous fluctuations prior to each stimulus did not differentiate between groups.

These results, in conjunction with the replicated findings of the nonsignal condition of a second experiment, suggest that externals respond at a higher rate and for a longer time to nonsignal stimuli. Although the groups did not differ in amplitude of response across trials, the investigators did not test to determine whether or not the groups differed in initial ORs. The first trials are of interest because the largest ORs have been reported during initial exposure to stimuli (Graham & Clifton, 1966), although it has been argued that data relating to the initial response should be interpreted with caution (e.g., Lader & Wing, 1966). Although the authors took the fact that the differences in habituation were not accompanied by clear differences in spontaneous responses as an indication that the groups did not differ in "activation," they did not report possible differences in tonic skin conductance level either at rest or as a function of stimulus repetition. Berggren et al. suggested that more conclusive data on this point could be obtained by comparing externals and internals in heart-rate-orienting response, since in this response modality differences between attention and activation or arousal effects are assessed more easily (Graham, 1973).

This possibility was pursued by Lobstein et al. (1979), who examined both heart rate and electrodermal activity in internals and externals who listened to a series of 15 1000 Hz tones at pseudo random intervals (mean = 35 seconds). The intensity of the stimuli at 85 db was comparable to the intensity employed by Berggren et al. (1977), although the 1-second duration exposure was much shorter. Subjects were not preselected but rather were assigned to groups on the basis of a median split of responses to the adult version of the Nowicki–Duke I–E scale (Nowicki & Duke, 1974). Further, half of the subjects completed the locus of control scale *after* the session, and the possibility that responses to the scale were influenced by subjects' appraisal of the experimental session must be considered. Equal numbers of males and females were assigned to the internal and external groups (20 subjects per group). In addition to analyses of variance (ANOVA) of responses by the two groups, product-moment correlations were calculated for the total sample. In contrast to Berggren *et al.* (1977), Lobstein and his associates did not find a difference in trials to habituation in the skin conductance response. In fact, although they did not test for a groups × trials interaction on the amplitude measure, the response to the initial stimulus did not differ between groups on amplitude, latency, and recovery half-time irrespective of analysis across I–E classification or by correlation; however, 12 of the 40 subjects showed no response to the first stimulus (proportion among internals and externals did not differ). Furthermore, there were no differences in tonic level change from the minute preceding the first stimulus to the last stimulus. The results for heart rate, although not clear-cut, did suggest a difference due to locus of control. Heart rate responses were derived from the poststimulus beats expressed as deviations from the mean value of the 10 prestimulus beats, and were defined as the minimum value in beats 1 to 5 poststimulus (deceleration) and maximum value in beats 1 to 6 (acceleration), both scores expressed as deviations from the prestimulus mean value. Although this derivation of the cardiac response is relatively common in the literature (e.g., Koriat, *et al.*, 1973), it is based on the assumption that the cardiac response is a biphasic deceleration–acceleration. Although the authors presented a figure illustrating the phasic cardiac response (12 consecutive cardiac cycles) suggesting that internals showed more deceleration to stimulus 1, the results of the analysis were not reported. Nonetheless, the ANOVA on the deceleration index for the first stimulus was significant (M deceleration: Internals = -8.1 bpm; Externals = -3.4 bpm), although this finding was not confirmed in the correlational analysis. Furthermore, the ANOVA across the I–E classification was significant for the change in deceleration from stimulus 1 to stimulus 15, which was interpreted as suggesting that the deceleration shown by internals to the first trial became attenuated or habituated. In contrast, the change index for the acceleration component was significantly negatively correlated with I–E ($r = -.38$), which suggests habituation of the accelerative component in internals. Consistent with the electrodermal data, there were no differences in tonic heart rate. I interpret these results to mean that internals tend to show greater initial deceleration to the tone and subsequent habituation, whereas external-oriented persons were relatively unresponsive throughout the series.

McCanne and Lotsof (1980) also examined heart rate and electrodermal activity but chose a visual orienting task. They tested 24 males and 24 females who were assigned to locus of control groups on the basis of a median split for each gender of scores on the Rotter scale. This type of subject selection is suspect to some degree because in some cases the same scores lead to the internal designation for females but the external grouping for males. Subjects viewed eight blue or red slides (illumination level unspecified) for 5 seconds at intertrial intervals of 10–20 seconds. McCanne and Lotsof did not assess a trials-to-criterion index of habituation, although analysis of the amplitude of the electrodermal response was nonsignificant with respect to a locus of control main effect and interaction with trials. Nonparametric tests suggested that externals were more likely to exhibit electrodermal activity during the first trial of stimulus presentation. The amplitude of first trial response apparently was not analyzed. Furthermore, there was a significant decrease in the number of externals exhibiting electrodermal activity over trials, but no significant change was noted for the internals. The analyses of heart rate data showed more significant effects, although some investigators may consider the method of scoring, and hence the interpretation of results, suspect. The unit of analysis was the raw beat-by-beat change in heart rate for the heart beat associated with stimulus onset and the five successive beats. The overall analysis indicated a significant I–E × heart beat interaction (but not an interaction with trials that would usually be taken as an indication of differential habituation). Neuman–Keuls tests indicated no significant difference between heart beats for internals but significant deceleration for externals (beats +1 and +2 poststimulus onset). Simple effects tests indicated that internals displayed significantly higher heart rates than externals during the +1 and +2 beats. The results were comparable for an analysis of the cardiac response to the first stimulus only. McCanne and Lotsof concluded that "externals manifested a deceleration in heart rate in response to the [first] stimulus, whereas Internals displayed an acceleration in heart rate" (p. 140). However, before we attach too much significance to these findings, it should be noted that there is an apparent four-beat difference in the initial values of internals (M = approximately 73.5 bpm) and externals (approximately 69.5 bpm). It is possible that the response patterns would differ and very probable that the simple effects analyses would be reduced to insignificance if based on changes from a sample of prestimulus beats. For purposes of discussion let us assume that the effects are reliable.

Although the OR and its habituation is usually indexed by peripheral autonomic measures, EEG and somatic measures are also components of the OR (see Lynn, 1966). In an attempt to relate individual differences in perceived control to physiological habituation, Dale, Anderson, DeGood, and Blankstein (1979) recorded indexes of heart rate, skin potential, finger temperature, EEG alpha, and frontalis EMG from 69 undergraduate volunteers during a series of eight tones presented approximately 1 minute apart. In analyses of the 10 extreme internals and 10 extreme externals, there were no significant group effects or interactions with stimulus repetition in separate univariate or multivariate analyses. Correlational analysis on all subjects using a habituation index of the first four and last four trials again indicated no relationship to Rotter I–E scores. Although some significant results were obtained with other personality measures (e.g., anxiety, field dependence), it was concluded that there were no consistent relationships between the individual difference variables and physiological habituation. It is possible that the stimuli (66 db, 500 Hz for .5 seconds) were not salient enough (see Raskin et al., 1969). Alternatively, the assessment of I–E may not have been reliable, given that the Rotter and other measures were completed after several laboratory sessions that included a biofeedback treatment.

How should we interpret the conflicting findings from these four studies of orienting and habituation in relation to perceived control? Certainly the results are not clear-cut. With respect to initial orienting, the Lobstein et al. (1979) study suggests relatively greater cardiac deceleration in internals, whereas the McCanne and Lotsof (1980) study reveals a pattern of acceleration–deceleration in internals and deceleration–acceleration in the five-beat response during stimulation, with more reliable electrodermal responding in the internals. McCanne and Lotsof discounted the possibility that the acceleration in the internals represented a defensive response (given the innocuousness of the visual stimulus employed) and hypothesized that it may reflect a cognitive response. It is also possible that the response represented a so-called startle response to the slide onset (see Graham & Clifton, 1966). In any event, internals quickly became habituated to this response. Lobstein et al., following Lazarus's (1966) suggestion that subjects who believe they have control over the environment should perceive less threat (and thus be less anxious) in a threatening situation than subjects who tend to believe they are helpless, interpreted their results as indicating less anxiety-like responding and more information seeking on the part of internals. McCanne and Lotsof concluded that externals were more attentive to the stimulus than were internals. The change in cardiac response from the first to the last tone suggests more rapid habituation in internals, whereas the electrodermal data presented by Berggren et al. (1977) indicated clearly that externals continue to orient to a nonsignal stimulus for a longer time than do internals. In my opinion, these data should be given an attention interpretation, considering the stimulus intensities employed were well below those that have been shown empirically to elicit the DR and the responses habituated relatively quickly, in contrast to the DR that does not habituate or habituates slowly (see Raskin et al., 1969). We are thus left with the puzzle of results suggesting more attention to initial stimuli in internals, more attention in externals, or no differences. The only relatively clear finding seems to be the slower rate of habituation in externals.

What is the adaptive significance of the results obtained? The OR is presumed to alert the body and prepare it to deal with a new or unexpected stimulus. Both McCanne and Lotsof and Berggren et al. informed subjects that they would be viewing visual stimuli or hearing tones and that no voluntary responses were required of them, clearly a case of irrelevant cues or meaningless stimuli. Depending on the subjects' interpretation or appraisal of the situation, one might predict any of the results obtained.[2] Thus the internal subject may wish to decide for himself or herself that the stimulus is innocuous and attend more closely to the stimulus or take the experimenter at his word and ignore the stimulus. Lobstein et al.'s instructions were most specific: "This part of the experiment is about relaxation. Please just sit here and relax but keep awake. You will hear occasional 'pips' through these headphones but these don't mean anything, so just ignore them" (p. 14). Since even in this context internals showed significant cardiac deceleration relative to externals, I am inclined to conclude that internals are more alert and attentive to the initial presentations of most stimuli. This is not to say that internals tend to mistrust statements from significant others, but rather that they rely on their own internal appraisal of events (which may be automatic, unconscious, or outside awareness in most situations). However, when there is no adaptive significance to repeated orienting, the response quickly habituates in internals, but externals continue to respond, suggesting poor attentional control. It would be of interest to assess subjects' expectations about the significance of the stimuli to be presented. Furthermore, since the occurrence of ORs and resistance to habituation are strongly influenced by the instructions given to subjects (e.g., Iacono & Lykken, 1983; Maltzman & Raskin, 1965), the ambiguity of the situation and relevance of the stimuli could be manipulated via instructions (e.g., "These stimuli may or may not be relevant to performance on a subsequent task"; or "Pay

---

[2]Iacono and Lykken (1983, p. 72) also argued that "the vague instructions common to habituation studies invite subjects to decide for themselves how to attend to the stimuli."

close attention to these stimuli because we will be asking you some questions about them later on"; or "Try to ignore these stimuli because we want to see how relaxed you can become during the presentation of extraneous noise").

Another way to assess differences in attention between internals and externals is to introduce a discrepant stimulus. According to Sokolov's model, any alteration in stimulus quality, intensity, or temporal characteristics provides conditions for reinstatement of the OR. Graham (1973) thoroughly reviewed that literature, finding that recovery of ORs as a result of stimulus alteration is a useful technique for assessing discriminative and attentional capacities. Lobstein et al. (1979) pursued this possibility by presenting three additional stimuli that continued with identical characteristics as the first series of tones, except that the pitch was changed to 500 Hz. They hypothesized that "an unexpected change in stimulus characteristics of this sort, which contradicts an expected pattern and possibly heralds a significant change in the environment, may elicit differential responses from internal and external subjects" (p. 13). The results provided relatively strong support for the hypothesis: In response to the reorienting stimulus internals showed significantly greater deceleration in cardiac rate, reliably smaller acceleration, relatively smaller amplitude and longer latency skin conductance response, and significantly faster recovery half-time. The most reliable finding was the sustained cardiac deceleration in internals, which was significant in both analyses across the I–E classification and correlation. The recovery time result is consistent with the heart rate effect, in that skin conductance recovery time seems to relate to information intake (shorter recovery time) and defensive aspects (longer recovery time) of a situation (see Edelberg, 1972). Taken together, these results lead to the conclusion that internals attend more to the reorienting stimulus and, possibly, that externals are more aroused by it. The latter possibility would be better tested using more intense stimuli, perhaps at the borderline between stimuli that typically elicit an OR or DR. Additional studies of perceptual disparity responses may reveal further information about the attentional and arousing components of a situation in individuals who differ in generalized perceptions of control.

Yet another way to investigate attention to relevant versus irrelevant cues is to attach *signal value* to a stimulus or series of stimuli. Signal value is usually established by instructing subjects to perform a response or task whenever a particular event occurs. This is exactly what Berggren et al. (1977) did in a second experiment. They tested four groups of 17 subjects, with gender balanced between groups. The groups of extreme internals and externals were selected from a sample of 203 students. Subjects in a nonsignal condition received typical habituation instructions; subjects in a signal condition were instructed to respond as quickly as possible by pressing a microswitch at the offset of each tone. The habituation series was identical to that employed in the first study, except that there were 10 additional tones.

The main finding of interest in analysis of the trials to habituation criterion measure was the significant interaction between I–E groups and signal value. Although the groups did not differ in the signal condition, internals significantly slowed their speed of habituation in the signal as compared to the nonsignal condition, whereas the externals did not differentiate the tone situations. Analyses of the other dependent measures were not significant, as was found in Experiment 1. Unfortunately, Berggren et al. did not conduct separate analyses of the initial stimuli. However, the data from both studies do support their hypothesis of poor attentional control in externals:

> External subjects keep attending to irrelevant events and do not seem to differentiate between relevant and irrelevant cues. Internals, on the other hand, stop responding to irrelevant cues quite quickly, and they differentiate sharply between relevant and irrelevant cues [p. 14].

This line of research needs to be followed up. Although Berggren et al. did not find differences between internals and externals in the signals condition only, such differences might emerge if the information value of the signal stimuli were somehow made more salient—for example, by making presentation of an aversive stimulus contingent on a slow response to tone offset. Bernstein (1969) believes that the OR is not an automatic accompaniment to perceptible stimulus novelty. In his two-stage model, stimulus change represents the first stage and signal value of the information represents the second stage. He proposed that ORs will follow stimulus change only if the person judges the stimuli to be of some significance. Possibly with stimuli of increased signal value (relevance) more clear-cut differences between internals and externals would be obtained. It seems plausible that the criterion for the significance of signals may shift depending on the subjects' expectations and on the requirements of the situation (Bernstein, 1973).

COMPLEX COGNITIVE TASKS

The preceding discussion focused on tasks where orienting or attention to the external environment or stimulus events is most important. Although the theoretical perspective was that of orienting and habituation theory, the tasks emphasized perceptual activities (e.g., attention to visual or auditory stimuli) that require intake of environmental stimuli (Lacey, 1959). The cardiac deceleration (and other physiological responses) are assumed to reflect attentional processes and (possibly) facilitate performance. But what about the more complex cognitive activities in which increases in tonic heart rate or phasic cardiac accelerations are presumed to be associated with attempts to exclude or reject those stimuli that would be disruptive to the performance of some cognitive function and with mental elaboration, as during the solution of a problem such as mental arithmetic? In a subsequent section we examine differences between internals and externals in situations where the task or task situation was intended to be stressful or provoke an emotional reaction. Here I want to focus on differences between internals' and externals' problem-solving and cognitive activity and the psychophysiological data that may provide further information about physiological differences between the groups. Presumably, the increases in heart rate associated with tasks requiring internal manipulation of symbolic material, first reported by the Laceys (e.g., Lacey, 1967; Lacey et al., 1963) and since confirmed by other investigators, may differ as a function of locus of control.

Unfortunately, although this kind of study seems to represent an obvious application of psychophysiological theory and research to the understanding of individual differences in perceived control, and there are numerous model studies in the literature, I was able to find only a single locus of control investigation. Runcie, Graham, and Shelton (1978) examined the relationship between I–E and the cardiac response to reaction time, mental arithmetic, and time-estimation tasks. The first experiment utilized a simple reaction-time and a mental arithmetic task that afforded an opportunity to focus both externally (reaction signal) and internally (mental calculations). The pattern of cardiac responding on both tasks has been reasonably well-established. Subjects participated in both tasks with the order counterbalanced across subjects. In the fixed foreperiod simple reaction-time task, the warning signal was onset of a light followed at a fixed interval (4 seconds) by light offset, which was the signal for release of a telegraph key. Subjects were instructed to respond as quickly as possible. The mental arithmetic task required subjects to add by threes, as quickly as possible, for a 4-second period. The onset of a trial was signaled by the presentation of a two-digit number on a display panel. Twenty trials were given on each task, with an average intertrial interval of 60 seconds. The second-by-second heart rate (3 seconds prior to, 4 seconds during, and 3 seconds following the critical interval) across the 20 trials was compared for the locus of control groups. Although the tasks reliably influenced the cardiac reaction, in neither case was the locus of control main effect significant, nor did it reach significance in any interactions. Actual performance on the task was not reported, nor were tonic levels of activity during the task evaluated. The authors were hoping to find (quite incorrectly, in my opinion) faster reaction times and greater cardiac deceleration in externals as opposed to internals. This hypothesis was based on a finding by Ray (1974), which suggested a predisposition of external subjects to attend to objects in the external environment during a biofeedback task (see the following section on biofeedback and self-regulation).

Consistent with the previous discussion, I would expect greater deceleration during the fixed foreperiod reaction-time task among internals. It was also anticipated, consistent with my own expectations, that internals would show more cardiac acceleration during mental performance. The investigators were required to conclude that "the assumption that the locus of control variable is related to physiological styles of responding on tasks where attentional requirements differ was not confirmed" (p. 1203).

Several methodological shortcomings, however, preclude rejection of the hypotheses pending further investigation. Although it is possible that physiological differences on these tasks—especially the cognitive tasks—do not exist, the study can be criticized on the basis of subject selection and sample size. Gender of subjects was not specified, and it is not clear whether subjects were selected as extreme scorers on Rotter's I–E scale. More important, the relatively small sample size ($N = 10$ per I–E group) is probably inadequate for research of this type. While the pattern of cardiac response was as expected (cardiac deceleration to the reaction-time signal and acceleration while performing mental arithmetic), the tasks should be modified in subsequent research. The reaction-time task could be modified to employ a longer fixed foreperiod (e.g., 8 seconds) in order to allow more complete development of the deceleration response, or the use of "catch" trials (see Lacey & Lacey, 1974). Furthermore, the mental arithmetic task was quite easy and probably required little mental elaboration (see Lacey & Lacey, 1974, p. 541). More complex arithmetic tasks, as well as other types of problem-solving and learning tasks, should be employed in the future. It is possible, as Runcie et al. (1978) stated, that "the performance requirements during RT and mental arithmetic tasks are so clear and pervasive that individual cognitive differences are overridden" (p. 1203). However, I concur with their conclusion that "mediational differences may emerge in tasks that allow more individuality in their solution" (p. 1204).

Lacey and Lacey (1974) have pointed out that responses on these tasks are not invariant but are affected by many factors, "among them the obvious one that 'identical' tasks are not necessarily identically perceived nor identically performed by all subjects" (p. 545). The question is, are these differences related to locus of control?

Runcie et al. conducted a second experiment with a larger sample of subjects (N = 20 per group) and a broader range of I–E beliefs. The experiment required the use of feedback information to improve performance in a time-estimation task. Such tasks also require cognitive work or attention to internal events ("counting" strategies), and consistent with the Laceys' formulation, time estimation is associated with more rapid heart rate (Johnson & May, 1969). Subjects were required to estimate in seconds the time during which a light remained on (M duration = 15 seconds; SD = 3 seconds). If a subject estimated correctly, he or she was told "correct"; if incorrectly, the error magnitude and whether he or she overestimated or underestimated. Heart rate for each of the 10 trials was divided into five periods tapping different points in the time sequence.

A significant locus of control group × periods interaction indicated that the I–E groups responded differentially on the task. Both groups showed similar heart rates during pre and early periods, with the external group then showing deceleration relative to the internals. Internals were superior in time estimation, although the groups did not differ in rate of improvement as a result of feedback. Runcie et al. speculated that the heart rate differences between locus of control groups were due to differences in perception of the task along a skill-chance dimension. Thus internals expended increased effort (task involvement) in their attempt to modify counting rhythms where feedback information resulted in increased heart rate and generally better estimation. Externals were assumed to perceive the task as a chance task, with the consequence that "less heart rate effort is expended in modifying estimation on the basis of feedback and less heart-rate acceleration as a function of relatively less effort" (p. 1206). It would be interesting to obtain self-reports of situational expectancies and effort on the task in a replication that varied the feedback variable, such that half the subjects in each group received feedback but the remainder did not. Since the applicability of generalized expectancy is particularly evident when the task is either ambiguous or very difficult (e.g., Wolk & DuCette, 1974), it may be necessary to manipulate task characteristics and instructions in order to determine the relationship between physiological and performance differences between internals and externals.

Runcie *et al.* (1978) initiated an important line of research that should be followed up. In subsequent studies additional physiological measures should be employed, including measures of cortical-evoked responses.

SUMMARY AND EVALUATION

Although the issues are far from settled, the reviewed studies on orienting and habituation suggest an interpretation of more adaptive orienting in internals and poorer attentional control in externals. Results of studies that employed discrepant stimuli and stimuli with signal value are at least consistent with the hypotheses from the I–E literature that internals attend more actively and selectively to *relevant* cues. This conclusion is not supported by the single study that employed a Lacey-type reaction-time task; however, more research is obviously called for. The results are also less clear-cut with respect to physiological activity during more complex cognitive tasks that are assumed to require mental elaboration and rejection of extraneous external stimuli. Here again, the appropriate studies have not been conducted. Although some of the findings are encouraging and these research directions should be pursued, investigators interested in addressing the questions of psychophysiological differences between internals and externals in attention and cognitive processes should attend more actively and selectively to both the locus of control and psychophysiological research literatures in order to refine their hypotheses, develop appropriate experimental designs, and select physiological measures that are likely to detect differences between individuals who differ in the generalized expectancy for locus of control. Physiological measures should also be related to performance and self-report measures.

From a psychophysiological perspective it would be of interest to compare internal and external subjects in other situations to which orienting and habituation and intake-rejection have been related in a meaningful way (see Berggren *et al.*, 1977). Possibilities could include the development of sleep during monotonous stimulation (e.g., Bohlin, 1971), discriminative conditioning (e.g., Öhman & Bohlin, 1973), semantic conditioning (e.g., Raskin, 1969), and even more complex learning and memory tasks (see Craik & Blankstein, 1975).

Research on *vigilance* (e.g., Krupski, Raskin, & Bakan, 1971; Mackworth, 1969; Siddle, 1972) suggests another area of possible interaction. The term "vigilance" was used by Mackworth (1957) and others to describe the situation in which a person must detect and respond to randomly occurring and infrequent signals over an extended period. Sanders, Holcomb, Fray, and Owens (1976) hypothesized that the internal person's search for mastery would probably help him or her to perform better, relative to the external person, on such a task. They evaluated the performance of extreme internals and externals who were required to perform a watch-keeping task on a visual display for one hour. The internal subjects showed almost no decrement in performance, whereas externals exhibited a significant decrement. The pattern of errors also suggested that endurance and persistence were characteristic of an internally controlled person on this task. Although Sanders et al. did not record physiological measures, in a psychophysiological investigation of vigilance Krupski et al. (1971) found that subjects who produced larger-amplitude skin conductance responses when they detected a signal produced fewer detection responses in the absence of signals. They concluded that subjects who produced large-amplitude skin conductance responses manifested higher levels of attention and, therefore, better vigilance performance.

Other investigators have argued that higher levels of arousal and frequent nonspecific activity prior to the occurrence of a signal are associated with better performance in the vigilance situation. The high levels of skin conductance may reflect motivational factors. Since motivation appears to be generally higher among subjects scoring internally—particularly that associated with avoidance of failure (e.g., McGhee & Crandall, 1968)—measures of tonic and phasic physiological activity, in conjunction with behavioral and self-report measures, may contribute to our understanding of the psychological differences between internals and externals on a continuous monitoring task.

Biofeedback and Self-Regulation of Physiological Processes

In the past 15 years an extensive literature has developed concerning the operant conditioning or "biofeedback" control of central, somatic, and ANS functioning (see Yates, 1980). The basic principle of biofeedback is quite simple: Feedback of internal physiological states, typically outside of awareness, makes learning to control these bodily processes possible, especially if feedback for very small changes is given (operant principle of shaping). Feedback may be given in the form of verbal and/or nonverbal reinforcement of desired responses, although more typically the person is given instructions about the desired response and digital or analogue feedback in the form of auditory stimuli or visual displays that reflect ongoing physiological activity. The final goal is self-regulation of the bodily response. A number of studies have demonstrated that some people can regulate these internal processes prior to a feedback manipulation.[3]

Early research focused on demonstrations of the phenomenon and attempted to determine its specificity relative to mediation issues. A second wave of laboratory research addressed methodological and parametric issues, such as the effects of knowledge of feedback contingencies, various feedback parameters, and the effects of extended training. A parallel literature began to explore the clinical application of the techniques. From the beginning one fact was very clear: Individuals differ markedly in the extent to which they demonstrate bodily control. This point was expressed metaphorically by Miller (1978, p. 385): "Just as athletic skills differ in the population with some stars being able to accomplish incredible feats, so most experimenters report considerable individual differences among subjects in the ability to learn to control visceral responses." A current emphasis of both laboratory and clinical research asks what individual characteristics differentiate people who differ in the ability to regulate internal bodily processes. Toward this end investigators have examined the role of dispositional variables, including locus of control. In fact, much of the extant literature on the relationship between perceived control and physiological processes has examined I–E as a predictor of individual differences in self-regulation of physiological activity.

In his 1976 review, Phares concluded that "the most basic characteristic of internal individuals appears to be their greater efforts at coping with or attaining mastery over their environments. This is the most elemental deduction that could be made from the nature of the I–E variable" (p. 78). He also stated that "perhaps related to internals' feelings that they can control the environment is the feeling that they can control themselves" (p. 68). The basic assumption of many investigators who have related I–E to physiological control, with or without biofeedback, is that the potential of the internal-oriented person for exercising self-control extends to manipulation of the internal physiological environment.

---

[3]In many studies, biofeedback is only one component of a total treatment package that also includes experimenter–subject or therapist–patient interactions, relaxation instructions or other specific instructions about how to control the target response, and expectancy or placebo manipulations. It is still unknown to what extent biofeedback is a necessary and/or sufficient part of the treatment package (see Hatch, 1982; Simkins, 1982). Furedy and Riley (1982, p. 82) proposed a narrow definition of *biofeedback* as a phenomenon that occurs "if and only if it is the contingent signal ('feedback') from a biological function that has led to the increase of control of that function."

In this section I review the literature on the relationship between locus of control and self-regulation of heart rate, muscle activity, and other physiological variables from the p⸱ rspectives of several models of perceived control, psychophysiological principles, and the current biofeedback literature. The interested reader is referred to Carlson's (1982) excellent review for another perspective on many of the studies reviewed here.

HEART RATE

The first study to report a relationship between I–E control and physiological regulation in a biofeedback context was a dissertation presented by Fotopoulos at the meetings of the Biofeedback Research Society (Fotopoulos, 1970a, 1970b). Although never published, her report that internals are better able to increase heart rate in response to instructions directly or indirectly prompted a relatively large number of published studies. These studies are summarized in Table 3.2.

The first published study, by Ray and Lamb (1974), initiated a controversy that is not yet fully resolved. In a brief threephase, single-session study, internals and externals were instructed to increase and decrease heart rate under conditions with and without feedback of heart rate. Ray and Lamb also reported that internals performed more consistently at increasing heart rate. However, external subjects were reported to be more consistent at decreasing heart rate. These findings did not hold for the magnitude of heart rate control. Furthermore, the addition of feedback did not add to the effects, although it should be pointed out that exposure to feedback was minimal in this study.

In a second study, Ray (1974) more than doubled the sample size. The procedures were virtually identical to those employed by Ray and Lamb, except that an awareness condition was added and the final no-feedback trials were deleted. In the awareness condition, half of the subjects received 200 beats of analogue feedback and were instructed to associate changes in the display with internal heart rate sensations. Subjects in the nonawareness condition were instructed to remain calm so that physiological level would stabilize. Although the awareness training had no effect, Ray and Lamb's findings were replicated: Internal subjects were better at complying with the instruction to increase heart rate and externals performed best at the decrease task, and this relationship held for both consistency and magnitude measures. Inspection of the means suggests that the decrease effect was due to performance on the feedback trials; unfortunately, statistical breakdown of the interaction was not reported.

The finding that internals performed relatively better at increasing heart rate is consistent with expectations from the I–E literature. However, the replicated finding that externals were better able to decrease heart rate is contrary to intuitive notions about I–E differences in self-control behavior. Why should externals be superior at decreasing heart rate when theory and past research would predict that, if any effect occurred, internals would demonstrate superior performance? Ray (1974) offered an intriguing explanation based on the Laceys' work on directional fractionation. Ray's subjects reported on the strategies they used to control heart rate. The external group reported that they "looked at objects in the room" more during the decrease heart rate task than during the increase task, whereas internals tended not to use this strategy on either task. Moreover, this response was significantly negatively correlated with correct performance on the heart rate increase task and significantly positively correlated on the heart rate decrease task.

Perhaps differences in the degree of attention to the external environment mediate the I–E/heart-rate-slowing relationship? Given that attention to, or the acceptance of, the environment (intake) leads to decreased heart rate, and that externals reported attending more to the external environment, the differences in heart rate control may be a consequence of this differential attention. This speculation influenced many investigators who came to expect that externals are not only superior at decreasing heart rate but are also more attentive in general (e.g., Lobstein et al., 1979; McCanne & Lotsoff, 1980).

Gatchel (1975a, 1975b) conducted two studies in which he employed multiple sessions in order to give subjects more exposure to the task (see Table 3.2). Gatchel wanted to determine whether Ray's findings reflected significant differences between internals and externals in learning heart rate control per se or were simply a reflection of differences between the groups in initial physiological response to a novel task. In one study (Gatchel, 1975a) extreme internal and external subjects were assigned to either a speeding or a slowing condition. This study did not employ feedback; subjects were simply instructed to control heart rate on cue as follows: "Decreasing (Increasing) your heart rate is possible if you concentrate on your heart and try very hard to make your heart go slower (faster)" (p. 635). In the initial session, Gatchel reported that internals were better able to increase their heart rate; however, consistent with Ray's studies, externals were more successful at the slowing task. In the second training session these differences diminished to statistical nonsignificance.

Similar results were found in the second study (Gatchel, 1975b), which employed analogue visual feedback. In this study, subjects first

TABLE 3.2
Summary of Studies of Locus of Control and Self-Regulation of Heart Rate[a]

Study	I–E measure	Number, gender, and selection of subjects	Baseline	Treatment
Fotopoulos (1970a)	Rotter	16M, 16F, median split (internals $M = 5.8$) (externals $M = 15.7$)	7 min	1.(a) Unaware of success (nonreinforced group) (b) Aware of success (reinforced group) Phases: (increase) (1) No feedback (thinking) (2) Information feedback (oscilloscope) (3) External stimulus (metronome) Order of (1) and (2) counterbalanced
Ray & Lamb (1974)	Rotter	8M internals 7M externals (M & SD not reported ? preselected	100 beats preceding each phase	1. Phases: (1) No feedback (2) Feedback (light panel on R–R Interval) (3) No feedback Each phase = 4 trial pairs (increase, decrease) each 50 interbeat intervals (IBIs) (order counterbalanced)
Ray (1974)	Rotter	20M internals ($M = 6$) 20M externals ($M = 16$) Selected from larger sample (N unspecified)	100 beats preceding each phase	1. Phases: (1) Awareness training (half of subjects) (2) No feedfack (3) Feedback

TABLE 3.2 (Continued)

Treatment duration	Dependent measures	Results [b]	Comment
2 3-min. trials, interspersed by 3-min. pause period, for each phase (total = 18 min; increase only)	1. HR ("peak" method) (baseline used as covariate)	Internals better able to increase heart rate than externals without feedback; no difference with feedback	Different mean baselines Baseline inordinately high Feedback display difficult
12 50-IBI trial pairs (total = approx. 12–14 min. per direction ?)	1. No. of IBIs in correct direction relative to prephase baseline. 2. Magnitude of HR change (relative to prephase baseline). 3. Respiration. 4. Open-ended strategy questionnaire. 5. Affect questionnaire.	1. Internals best at increasing; externals best at decreasing; no difference due to feedback 2. No significant effects 3,4,5. No I–E differences reported	Baseline data not reported Simple effects analyses of interaction not reported
Same as Ray & Lamb (1974) (total = 8–10 min per direction ?)	1,2. as above; 3 absolute difference. 4. Strategy questionnaire and performance estimate. 5. Affect (4,5 followed each trial pair).	1,2. Internals best at increasing, externals best at decreasing ? Feedback effects No awareness effects 4. Externals "looked at objects in room" (decrease) (significantly correlated with increase, decrease heart rate)	Brief intervention Decrease effect appears to be due to feedback only

(continued)

TABLE 3.2 (*Continued*)

Study	I–E measure	Number, gender, and selection of subjects	Baseline	Treatment
Gatchel (1975a)	Rotter	8M, 8F internals 8M, 8F externals (*M*s and *SD* not reported) Upper and lower 20% of distribution of potential subjects (*N* unspecified)	3-min. pre 1-min. "time out" between trials	No feedback—instructions only 1,2. (a) Speeding (b) Slowing
Gatchel (1975b)	Rotter	15M internals (*M* = 5) 15M externals (*M* = 16) Median split I–E completed at *end* of training sessions	2 tracking task sessions of baseline preceding each training session not specified	1. Selection session followed by 2,3. Tracking task (habituation) session 4,5. HR speeding session 6,7. HR slowing session (order randomized within blocks of two) Each session = 15 min. analogue feedback plus 5 min. transfer
Blankstein & Egner (1977)	Rotter	19M internals (*M* = 6.6) 19M externals (*M* = 14) Median split	10-min. pre 1-min. pretrial baselines prior to each trial	1. 4 series of HR control trials Each series = block of 5 raised trials and block of 5 lower trials (order counterbalanced) Feedback (beat-by-beat meter) during first 3 series. No feedback generalization on last series.

TABLE 3.2 (*Continued*)

Treatment duration	Dependent measures	Results [b]	Comment
10 1-min. trials 2 sessions (total = 20 min.)	1. HR relative to pre-experiment base-line	Speeding: Internals better on Session 1 only Slowing: Externals better on Session 1 only	Slowing probably inflated Small N
15 min. feedback and 5 min. transfer per session (total = 40 min. per direction)	1. HR relative to initial base for each session (median r-r)	As in Gatchel (1975a), slowing and speed-ing analyzed sep-arately	Slowing probably inflated Did not report ef-fects of feedback versus no-feedback
15 min. feedback & 5 min. generalization (total = 20 min. per direction)	1. HR relative to run-ning pretrial base-line 2. Respiration 3. Eye blinks 4. Skin conductance level 5. Self-rating scale (10-pt.) 6. Strategy Question-naire	1. Internals better able to raise HR; consistent improve-ment across series including no-feed-back (see text) 2–6 No interaction with I–E	

(*continued*)

TABLE 3.2 (*Continued*)

Study	I–E measure	Number, gender, and selection of subjects	Baseline	Treatment
Schneider et al. (1978)	Rotter	12M internals (*M* = 3.2) 12 M externals (*M* = 13.8) Selected from upper and lower quartiles of distribution of 48 potential subjects	5-min. pre 2-min. rest between blocks	1. Selection session 2,3. HR control—Each session = 2 blocks increase–decrease trials (order randomized) each block = 15 1-min. HR control trials Trials 1–4 and 12–15 = no feedback Trials 5–11 = continuous meter feedback 15-sec. rest between trials; 2-min rest between blocks
Levenson & Ditto (1981)	Rotter	Data from 3 experiments combined 74M, 28F—no preselection. Correlation and multivariate regression analyses on I–E plus ANOVA on 18 most internal (*M* = 5) and 18 most external (*M* = 16). ? gender confounded	50 beats	Experiments I and II (single session: 12 trials: 50 beat pretrial baseline, 6 decrease and 6 increase trials (order counterbalanced), 120 beats of attempted HR control, and 1-min. rest period Trials 1–4 = no feedback Trials 5–12 = beat-by-beat feedback Experiment III (2 sessions): 1. 6 trials (50 heart beat baseline, 120 beats of attempted HR control without feedback). Order counterbalanced: 3 HR decrease and 3 HR increase 2. 12 trials as in Session 1 with feedback

TABLE 3.2 (*Continued*)

Treatment duration	Dependent measures	Results [b]	Comment
8 min. no-feedback 7 min. feedback per session (total = 30 min. per direction)	1. HR relative to pre-block rest	Internals best at speeding HR during feedback portion of Session 1 and during first no-feedback and feedback portion of Session 2 (no difference on transfer) Internals' performance improved over sessions	
Experiments I and II: 240 beats no-feedback, 480 beats feedback (total = 720 per direction) Experiment III: 480 beats no-feedback, Session 1 720 beats feedback, Session 2 (assuming resting HR of 75 bpm total = 9.6 min. for Experiments I and II (6.4 min. feedback); 16 min. for Experiment III (9.6 min. feedback)	1. Criterion correct IBIs relative to baseline means (magnitude not reported) 2. Respiration 3. General Somatic activity (ACT) 4. Strategy Questionnaire	No effects due to I–E	Brief intervention

(*continued*)

TABLE 3.2 (*Continued*)

Study	I–E measure	Number, gender, and selection of subjects	Baseline	Treatment
Lodgsdon et al. (1978)	Levenson	12M internals 12M externals (divided on basis of Internal Scale scores) Median split ? unselected Scale administered 1 month previously Ms and SDs not reported Readministered at end of Session 4	10 min.	Sessions (5–30 min.) 1. Adaptation session 2,3. Bogus "electrorheographic" feedback (a) Success (false visual feedback indicating success on task) (b) Failure (false visual feedback indicating no control) (c) Control 4,5. Actual analogue HR feedback. Each treatment session = 10 min. baseline; 3 5-min. trials (2-min. rest between trials) Subjects told to either increase or decrease "electrorheographic" output (Sessions 2–3) or HR (4–5) (order counterbalanced by session)

TABLE 3.2 (*Continued*)

Treatment duration	Dependent measures	Results[b]	Comment
Actual feedback during sessions 4,5 (15 min. total per direction)	1. HR relative to pre-session baseline (HR sampled every 15 sec.)	Significant main effect of order on increase trials: Subjects who increased second actually decreased HR Only decrease task analyzed further No significant effects using Internal and Powerful Others scales Significant Conditions × I–E interaction when Chance scale used No differences between high and low Chance groups in control condition High Chance failure (helplessness) decreased HR more than low Chance Low Chance success decreased HR more than high Chance	Small *N* Selection of subjects not clear Decrease effects may be overestimated Baselines not reported No test for no-feedback

[a] *Studies by Bell and Schwartz (1973), Lang et al. (1975), and Friedman et al. (1980) are discussed in text. Unless otherwise specified, control is bidirectional. F = female, M = male; M = mean; SD = standard deviation; HR = heart rate.*

[b] *Effects for locus of control only.*

participated in two tracking task sessions designed to habituate subjects to the laboratory environment and feedback display. They then received four sessions of heart rate training. Each successive block of two sessions consisted of one speeding and one slowing session (order randomly determined). A session included 15 minutes of feedback training followed by a 5-minute transfer trial. Once again, Gatchel reported that internal subjects displayed greater speeding performance than externals and externals displayed greater slowing performance than internals in the first session. However, these differences also disappeared in second speeding and slowing sessions.

Gatchel concluded that locus of control influences heart rate control performance only during the early stages of training. He too resorted to the Laceys' intake-rejection hypothesis to explain the initial differences in heart rate control. Thus "externals may approach the control task with a set prompting a heart-rate deceleratory tendency. . . . Internal locus of control subjects may . . . approach the task with a set which . . . prompts more speeding" (Gatchel, 1975a, p. 637). The externals' set of accepting or orienting to environmental stimuli and the accompanying decrease in heart rate was proposed as the mechanism for superior heart rate slowing (and inferior speeding) by externals, given that the physiological (cardiac) consequences of the orienting set should aid slowing performance and work against attempts to speed heart rate. Internal-oriented persons by contrast perhaps engage in internal cognitive elaboration that has the opposite effects. Gatchel further speculated that habituation of the heart rate deceleratory component of the orienting set (externals) and the heart rate acceleratory component of the cognitive elaboration set (internals) may account for the diminution in the strength of the relationship over sessions. These speculations are interesting, but they await validation.

Blankstein and Egner (1977) adopted a slightly different theoretical perspective on the alleged interaction between I–E and direction of cardiac control. We were also critical of previous studies on methodological grounds. We accepted Ray's psychophysiological explanation for the personality group differences in his studies (and possibly in Gatchel's) but argued on the basis of the I–E literature that internals should be superior at both speeding and slowing (or at the very least, not inferior to externals). We suggested that Ray's findings of more successful decrease performance by externals "may simply reflect the externals' failure to attend to the task of lowering HR and simultaneous attention to task-irrelevant cognitive cues" (Blankstein & Egner, 1977, p. 293). In Ray's studies the lighting level and characteristics of the physical environment were not specified, nor is it clear that subjects were instructed to pay attention to a display (as is typical in biofeedback studies). We speculated that if the lumination level was relatively bright and the environment relatively rich in potentially distracting stimuli, and if attention deployment was not controlled by instructions, then external subjects might show better control of heart rate slowing initially as an artifactual consequence of the testing environment. We also speculated that Ray's feedback system may not have been optimally effective. Finally, we proposed that training time was inadequate to test for effects of the locus of control constuct on ability to lower heart rate (combined feedback and no-feedback training in Ray's 1974 study probably averaged about 5 minutes). Although very rapid acquisition of heart rate speeding is typical, heart rate slowing tends to develop more gradually (e.g., Lang & Twentyman, 1974).

Finally, Blankstein, Zimmerman, and Egner (1976) and McCanne and Sandman (1975) previously demonstrated that the practice of computing heart rate changes relative to preexperiment or presession baseline usually yields artifactual effects because tonic heart rate typically declines throughout a session. Thus use of an initial baseline to assess control tends to overestimate the magnitude of heart rate decrease effects and to underestimate increase effects. Although no-treatment control groups are preferred, Blankstein et al. recommended the practice of computing heart rate changes relative to pretrial resting levels (running baseline).

Blankstein and Egner (1977) employed an initial adaptation period and determined baselines prior to each trial. The experimental chamber was dimly illuminated, and subjects were instructed to pay attention to the display panel. Subjects received continuous visual feedback of cardiac rate (relative to median pretrial rate) during three series of trials, followed by a no-feedback transfer series. During each series, subjects attempted to raise heart rate on five trials and to lower it on five trials (order counterbalanced). Subjects were further instructed to raise or lower heart rate "using purely mental means." Internals were superior at raising heart rate during the first series and improved consistently across subsequent series, attaining maximum increases during the no-feedback generalization series. By contrast, there were no significant differences between groups on heart rate decrease trials.

We concluded that externals are not better able to decrease heart rate and hypothesized that internals would possibly demonstrate superiority at slowing heart rate with more extended training. Although assessment of somatic activity indicated an influence of the instruction and feedback contingency on both respiration and blink rate (but not skin conductance), these variables were not differentially influenced by locus of control. The eye blink data suggested greater attention to the display by both groups during attempts to lower heart rate. Moreover, in contrast to Ray's (1974) and Gatchel's (1975a) hypotheses, analyses of questionnaire data failed to reveal any differences in cognitive strategies. These results were essentially replicated by Schneider and his colleagues (Schneider, Sobol, Herrman, & Cousins, 1978); however, they employed additional trials over two sessions. Internals, relative to externals, were better able to increase heart rate and showed improved performance with feedback. Neither group was able to lower heart rate significantly.

How do we reconcile these findings with the diminishing differences reported by Gatchel in his multisession studies? Contrary to the hypothesis that cognitive or attentional sets habituated, it seems more probable that tonic heart rate habituated throughout the sessions. Since Gatchel assessed change relative to the presession baseline, heart rate increase effects may have been underestimated. Inspection of the presented means indicates that the absolute magnitude of heart rate control on increase and decrease sessions combined is approximately two beats greater in the second session and that there is very little difference between the I–E groups. Although there were no initial differences in heart rate base level, Gatchel did not report final levels. It is possible that the groups habituated at different rates, which would not be reflected in the change scores employed.

Matters are further complicated by research reported by Logsdon et al. (1978). Their subjects were first divided into high and low internals on the basis of a median split on Levenson's (1973) Internal Scale and then randomly assigned in equal numbers to one of three conditions for pretreatment (see Table 3.2). Subjects in the success condition received false visual biofeedback (actually a mean heart rate) to give the impression of success on a bogus preliminary task ("electrorheography"). In the failure condition, subjects received false feedback indicating that they had no control over the task and were doing poorly. This procedure was intended to induce learned helplessness (see Seligman, 1975). The control group received identical instructions without feedback. Following a 30-minute baseline session, subjects received two sessions with the preliminary task and then two sessions of actual beat-by-beat heart rate feedback. During the rest periods of the preliminary task sessions, the experimenter gave verbal feedback appropriate to the subjects' experimental condition.

Preliminary analyses indicated an effect due to order of presentation on increase trials: Those who increased second actually decreased heart rate when instructed to increase it (relative to presession baseline). Analyses of increase trials were not reported further, nor were analyses of actual heart rate during the preliminary task. Analysis of the three 5-minute feedback trials for the heart rate decrease condition failed to reveal any differences using the Internal and Powerful Others scales. However, analysis on the basis of Chance scores revealed a significant locus of control × conditions interaction. It was concluded that the high Chance subjects in the failure (helplessness) condition were able to decrease heart rate significantly more than low Chance subjects (in both the failure and success conditions). Conversely, in the success condition low Chance subjects were better than high Chance subjects (and low Chance subjects in the failure condition). There were no significant differences between high and low Chance subjects in the control condition. A hypothesis that subjects in the learned helplessness condition would score lower on the postmanipulation Internal Scale was not supported.

Logsdon et al. (1978) argued that these results add validity to Levenson's multidimensional approach, given that "the rather striking differences between the groups" may have gone undetected using a traditional scale. Although there was no independent validity check on the manipulation (except for failure to find effects on the generalized I–E measures), the authors concluded:

> The present results suggest that certain kinds of feedback (success or failure) in the early stages of biofeedback treatment can enhance the ability of individuals with different locus of control orientations (low and high Chance) to decrease their heart rates [p. 541].

Logsdon et al. explained these results by invoking the concept of learned helplessness; that is, the idea that failure on a cognitive task produces interference in learning a different cognitive task. They cited Phares's (1971) report that externals tend to devalue a task after failing it because they do not take responsibility for the failure themselves but attribute it to other causes, whereas internals attribute failure to themselves and are (presumably) unable to devalue it. Although not stated at the outset, it was clear from Logsdon et al.'s discussion (and the original selection of subjects) that the investigators predicted that high internals would not be as affected by the learned helplessness manipulation as the low internals. It was suggested that the failure to confirm this hypothesis was possibly due to the inclusion of defensive externals in the low internal group.

Although this study represents an interesting strategy for revealing the relationship between locus of control and self-regulation of cardiac rate, the many methodological shortcomings preclude attaching any significance to the results. The sample size was inadequate ($N = 4$ per subgroup of each condition); the feedback procedure is probably less than optimal (videocamera monitoring of the polygraph record); the heart rate sampling procedure may not be reliable; and, finally and most important, the results were probably contaminated because running baselines were not employed. Although an adaptation baseline session, presession baselines, and rests between trials were employed, the data were not reported (and possibly not analyzed). Given the history of relatively large-magnitude heart rate increases and small decreases reported by most researchers in this field, the findings of Logsdon *et al.*'s study must be regarded as atypical and probably artifactual until replicated.

Inspection of Table 3.2 reveals that not all studies reported significant relationships between locus of control orientation and heart rate control. In a recent study, Levenson and Ditto (1981) examined the relationship between individual differences in ability to control heart rate with feedback and differences in self-reported cognitive strategies, personality variables (including Rotter's I–E Scale), physiological variables, and auxiliary variables such as weight and smoking. Data were combined from three experiments that used essentially the same methodology ($N = 102$). Using a measure of correct interbeat intervals as the index of subjects' ability to control heart rate on feedback trials, locus of control did not predict ability to increase or decrease heart rate in correlational analyses including all subjects, ANOVAs (possibly confounded by gender) using the 18 most internal ($M = 5$) and 18 most external ($M = 16$) scoring subjects, and multivariate regression analyses in which I–E was included with trait and state anxiety and added to changes in general somatic activity and respiration intercycle interval in the regression formula. Levenson and Ditto concluded that their results "generally argue against the importance of these personality dimensions in ability to control HR" (p. 97). On a more positive note, they suggested that

a conceptually sound indirect relationship may exist which explains the occasional significant relationships found between personality constructs and ability to control HR. As a hypothetical example, a finding that "impulsive" individuals are better able to increase HR than "repressed" individuals makes little conceptual sense. However, if "impulsive" subjects are found to be more physically active during attempted HR increase (compared to "repressed" subjects) despite instructions to remain still, then a more understandable, indirect mediational linkage between the personality construct and HR control can be made [p. 98].

Levenson and Ditto's conclusion must be qualified because they employed an initial baseline to evaluate changes in heart rate and also because subjects received very little exposure to the feedback. Furthermore, although the notion of presenting feedback in so-called heart time (each trial consisted of 120 beats of attempted heart rate control) is novel, individual differences in tonic heart rate could have significant impact on real time on the task. Furthermore, while successful slowing would increase time on the task, successful speeding could penalize the subject because real time on the task would decrease.

These reservations notwithstanding, Levenson and Ditto's data indicate that the relationship, if one truly exists, between I–E and cardiac control is not particularly strong. Their point about mediation is very important. Although they did not report their exact instructions to subjects, it is usual in these studies to request that subjects attempt to control heart rate without moving, tensing muscles, or changing their breathing rate. Yet their analyses indicated quite clearly that in addition to the strong relationship between ability to control heart rate without feedback (initially) and ability to control heart rate with feedback, the best heart rate controllers evidenced the most somatic parallelism on control trials. Perhaps internals make more efficient and effective use of this strategy; or, alternatively, when somatic and respiratory activity is more constrained by instructions or otherwise, it is the internal locus of control subjects who are able to make effective use of alternative strategies. Unfortunately, few attempts have been made to examine these possibilities; no study of the I–E cardiac control relationship has employed adequate somatic restraints and few studies have included and analyzed measures of somatic variables.

Levenson and Ditto (1981) are not the only investigators who looked for but failed to find a relationship between I–E and cardiac control. Bell and Schwartz (1973) reported that scores on Rotter's scale were not correlated with self-control of heart rate in 20 male college students. Lang et al. (1975) found that the Rotter scale did not yield consistent correlations with heart rate control performance in 20 older normals and 30 patients with heart disease. The highest value was obtained for patients during a third slowing session ($r = .40$, $p < .07$). The I–E scale was filled out after the final session. Friedman, Cleveland, and Baer (1980) also reported that locus of control was uncorrelated with heart rate speeding and slowing in patient groups ($N = 10$).

One other study merits examination. Glass and Levy (1982) were interested in the effects of subjects' perceptions of achieved control on a biofeedback task. The study did not deal with actual biofeedback training or changes in physiological parameters, but rather focused on the cognitive aspects of self-control. It was hypothesized that the mere perception of control, whether veridical or not, may interact with the specific effects of biofeedback in determining the pattern of subjective and physiological changes. The experiment was quite complex and not all of the details will be presented here. In a 2 × 2 × 2 factorial design, the independent variables of source of perceived control (heart rate self-control task versus externally controlled due to physiological response to color of room illumination), level of efficacy (effective heart rate change versus no change), and direction of suggested change (increase versus decrease in heart rate) were manipulated by varying the instructions and visual meter (false heart rate) feedback given to subjects. In addition, Rotter's I–E Scale was administered to determine whether I–E scores would interact with effects of perceived control.

In fact, there were no differences in major results with I–E as a covariate; however, several results are relevant to the present discussion. Thus subjects did not react uniformly to situations structured to allow for the possibility of self-control. Perceived effective self-control, compared to ineffective self-control, led to a more positive mood, stronger causal attributions to effort and less to task difficulty, and increased expectations for future effective self-control on a similar task. Although the authors cannot rule out the possibility that effects were influenced by actual physiological changes, the results support the importance of cognitive factors in biofeedback training. They hypothesized, after Bandura (1977), that self-efficacy expectations play a role in the mediation of situations of both actual and perceived physiological change, concluding:

> Future research in biofeedback and self-control must, therefore, include better controls in order to distinguish the contributions of perceived control and a sense of personal power from those of actual psychophysiological control [p. 102].

This analysis suggests that investigators should make explicit assessments of attributions (skill, effort, luck, and difficulty), interest (reinforcement value), and efficacy and outcome expectations in order to determine the role such variables play in the mediational linkage between I–E and heart rate control.

ELECTROMYOGRAPHIC (EMG) CONTROL

Studies that examined the relationship between generalized locus of control and the effectiveness of EMG training procedures are summarized in Table 3.3. The first such study was a brief report by Vogt (1975). Although there were no differences between groups in mean EMG levels in response to instructions to tense or relax muscles, Vogt suggested that subsequent self-estimates of success predicted actual

EMG levels, but only in external subjects. Although the correlations were only marginally significant, he speculated that "individuals with an external locus of control orientation were more sensitive to or aware of the proprioceptive feedback from the muscle groups during the taped instruction sessions than were internal subjects" (p. 978). Evaluation of Vogt's study is difficult on the basis of the brief report. Although his data are not consistent with those that followed, the study points to the potential utility of assessing subjects' cognitions about performance on the task.

Locus of control has since been related to EMG training with bio-feedback in a number of unpublished and published papers. Among these, a 1976 study presented by Reinking and his colleagues (Reinking, 1976) appeared to be quite sound methodologically, although it was never published. Reinking examined the impact of two dimensions (locus of control and trait anxiety) hypothesized to influence the acquisition of reduced EMG levels as a consequence of biofeedback training. A large number of subjects were assigned to six groups (internal and external control nested within high, moderate, and low anxiety) and were administered ten 30-minute EMG relaxation training sessions (auditory feedback of frontalis EMG potentials). The training sessions occurred between two pre- and posttest no-feedback EMG recording sessions. All groups reduced their EMG levels across sessions, as assessed by analysis of pre–post training change scores. Furthermore, the internal-oriented subjects, irrespective of level of trait anxiety, lowered their EMG scores significantly more than did externals as a function of the feedback training. Anxiety also influenced the acquisition of EMG relaxation in a linear fashion, with high anxious subjects performing the best. Moreover, the interaction effect between the two individual difference variables was also reported to be significant: Internal–high-anxiety subjects acquired EMG control far more rapidly than any other group (and the other groups did not differ from each other).

The alert reader will notice one important difference between this study of EMG training and the previously discussed heart rate control studies. In research on EMG relaxation training, which has enjoyed widespread clinical use (see Tarler-Benlolo, 1978), subjects are typically exposed to many more training sessions (although these sessions often employ progressive deep muscle relaxation in addition to EMG bio-feedback). Given that most of these studies focus on EMG relaxation and sometimes employ groups (e.g., high anxious) who may potentially differ in initial levels and/or rate of adaptation, it is important to conduct careful baselines (see Dale, Anderson, Klions, Tane, & Blankstein, 1979) and, preferably, to employ no-treatment control procedures.

TABLE 3.3
Summary of Studies of Locus of Control and Self-Regulation of EMG Activity [a]

Study	I–E measure	Number, gender, and selection of subjects	Baseline	Treatment
Vogt (1975)	Rotter	12 F Internals (0–8) 12 F Externals (11–12) 83 volunteers	Unspecified	Instructions for bidirectional muscle control (tense and relax) Details unspecified
Reinking [b] (1976)	Rotter	120 subjects assigned to 6 groups in 3 (high, moderate, low anxiety) × 2 (internal versus external control design (Ms and SDs not presented)	30-min. pretraining no-feedback Training session baseline not specified	1,11. Pre/posttest no-feedback 2–10. 30-min. EMG relaxation training

TABLE 3.3 (*Continued*)

Treatment duration	Dependent measures	Results [b]	Comment
Unspecified	1. Raw EMG (forearm) 2. Performance estimates (scale not specified)	1. No significant differences in muscle control 2. Nonsignificant correlations of EMG and performance estimates for internals; negative correlations between EMGs and relaxing ($r = -.54, p < .07$) and tensing muscle control ($r = -.50, p < .10$) for externals	Unclear brief report
10 30-min. feedback sessions (total = 300 min.)	1. Pre–posttraining change in frontalis EMG	1. Internals lowered EMG significantly more than externals; internal–high anxiety group showed best acquisition rate	? training sessions Baseline not specified

(*continued*)

TABLE 3.3 (Continued)

Study	I–E measure	Number, gender, and selection of subjects	Baseline	Treatment
Carlson (1977)	Nowicki–Strickland (adult)	12M, 12F internals ($M = 3.2$) 12M, 12F externals ($M = 16.1$) ? selected from larger sample (two replications)	2 20-min. pretraining "relaxation" baselines (eyes closed) No training session baselines (5-min. from seating of subject)	1,2. Baseline 3–10. Training (a) Feedback group—instructed to lower pitch of feedback tone (continuous analogue) (b) Control group—instructed that (constant) tone should aid relaxation
Carlson & Feld (1978)	Nowicki–Strickland (adult)	28M internals ($M = 3.7$) 28M externals ($M = 14.9$) ? selected from larger sample	As in Carlson (1977)	As in Carlson (1977), except only 6 training sessions and feedback and control conditions subdivided into incentive and no-incentive groups Incentive = bonus points contingent on EMG performance Included 2 posttraining (no-tone/no-feedback) sessions

TABLE 3.3 (*Continued*)

Treatment duration	Dependent measures	Results[b]	Comment
8 20-min. feedback sessions (2 per wk.) (total = 160 min.)	1. Integral average EMG levels (end of each min.), converted to proportion of M for corresponding periods of baseline sessions 2. Finger temperature (? as with EMG) 3. Pre–post I–E changes 4. Postexperiment questionnaire	1. Feedback subjects acquired lower EMG potentials than controls, and internals in feedback condition performed best; no consistent differences in control conditions 2. No significant effects 3. Shift in internal direction by externals in feedback condition; not correlated with EMG change 4. Internal–feedback subjects less relaxed than external–feedback and internal–control subjects; no differences in perceived control and strategies	No posttraining no-feedback condition ? active versus passive set
6 20-min. feedback sessions (total = 160 min.)	1. Integral average EMG levels 2. Pre–post I–E change	1. No significant I–E effects in training stage. Externals in incentive–feedback condition increased (relative to externals in no-incentive–feedback conditions) during posttraining stage 2. Shift in I–E scores in internal direction for external subjects in incentive–feedback condition; not correlated with EMG levels	

(*continued*)

TABLE 3.3 (*Continued*)

Study	I–E measure	Number, gender, and selection of subjects	Baseline	Treatment
Carlson & Feld (1981)	Nowicki–Strickland (adult)	12M, 12F internals (M = 3.8) 12M, 12F externals (M = 15.4)	As in Carlson (1977)	1,2. Baseline (no treatment) 3–5. Pretreatment (fictitious "blood pressure control" task) plus cognitive task (a) Success (false feedback and success instructions) (b) Failure (false feedback and no-control instructions (c) Control (no specific task) 6. Self-control relaxation 7–10. Test. True EMG feedback and instructions to reduce tension levels through relaxation

TABLE 3.3 (*Continued*)

Treatment duration	Dependent measures	Results [b]	Comment
4 20-min. feedback sessions (total = 80 min.)	1. Integral average EMG levels 2. Performance in Progressive Matrices (end of 5) 3. Postexperiment questionnaire	1, 2, 3. No significant I–E effects.	Small N

(*continued*)

TABLE 3.3 (*Continued*)

Study	I–E measure	Number, gender, and selection of subjects	Baseline	Treatment
Russell *et al.* (1982)	Nowicki–Strickland (adult)	16 internals (> 28) 16 externals (< 20) Sex unspecified Selected from 226 undergraduates	3-min. pre-session	1. Relaxation with auditory proportional EMG feedback 2. (a) Positive Expectancy Instructions (b) Negative Expectancy Instructions Each session = baseline trial and 7 feedback trials (3-min. trial, 59 sec. ITI, 30 sec. running baseline)
R.H. Carlson *et al.* (1982)	Health Locus of Control Scale	40 subjects assigned to 4 groups in 2 (high versus low Health Locus of Control) × 2 (high versus low "Health" value) design Selected from 300 undergraduates; gender mixed (predominately female)	5-min. pre-training (eyes closed)	1,2. 15-min. EMG relaxation training (auditory relaxation instructions plus continuous auditory feedback) followed by 5-min. "posttraining" period

TABLE 3.3 (Continued)

Treatment duration	Dependent measures	Results [b]	Comment
7 3-min. trials/session (total = 42 min.)	1. Frontalis EMG (integrated) 2. Respiration 3. Finger pulse 4. Subjective relaxation 5. Postsession questionnaire	1. Session 1: No differences. Session 2: Positive Expectancy: internal higher EMG levels; Negative Expectancy: no differences. External–positive subjects differ from external–negative. 2, 3. No significant effects (externals higher pretrial respiration rates in Session 2). 4. Externals reported less anxiety. 5. No differences. Higher anxiety in positive expectancy condition.	Baseline inadequate. Baseline affect treatment evaluation.
2 15-min. feedback sessions (total = 30 min.)	1. Pre/post training change in integrated frontalis EMG	1. Internals showed greater EMG reductions at low health value; externals showed greater EMG reductions at high health value	? positive expectancy Initial levels not reported Changes during training not reported

[a] Effect for locus of control only. Unless otherwise specified, control is in decrease direction (EMG relaxation). F = female, M = Male, M = mean; SD = standard deviation.
[b] Unpublished.

Carlson conducted much of the research in the area of I–E and EMG biofeedback and, although his findings are not always consistent from study to study, his program of research is commendable for the creative effort to untangle and determine the limits of the I–E/EMG control relationship by exploring more complex relationships suggested by Rotter's social learning theory and related models of perceived control. It is important to note that Carlson and his colleagues have employed the Adult Nowicki–Strickland Internal–External Control Scale (Nowicki & Strickland, 1973) to select internal and external locus of control groups. This scale emphasizes control over the individual's immediate environment, rather than less direct social or political factors.

In the first study, Carlson (1977) examined differences between internals and externals in a frontal EMG relaxation task. During two baseline sessions, subjects were instructed to relax with eyes closed while muscle tension was monitored. Beginning in the third session, half of the subjects were provided with continuous analogue auditory feedback. Control subjects were provided with a constant tone of fixed frequency. Feedback subjects were told that "the pitch of the tone would vary as a function of their level of relaxation and that their task was now to attempt to lower the pitch as much as possible" (p. 262). Control subjects were told that the constant low tone "should help in relaxation." Both groups received eight 20-minute training sessions, and EMG levels were expressed as proportions of baseline levels. Carlson reported that internal subjects in the feedback condition lowered their tension levels significantly faster and to a lower level than did subjects who perceived themselves to be externally controlled. The I–E groups differed neither during the baseline sessions nor in the control condition.

From these findings Carlson concluded that generalized control expectancies are likely to be important only when persons are task-involved—that is, "locus of control is not relevant to bodily self-regulation as a static dimension of personality but rather as a construct that conveniently summarizes a set of factors that may determine whether a person will successfully manipulate bodily processes when required" (p. 269). Reflecting on the 1977 study, Carlson (1982) stated that several measures of trait anxiety were administered; however, they failed to interact significantly with I–E in determining rate of EMG learning.

I find the results for the comparison between feedback and control conditions and Carlson's conclusion somewhat problematic. Did the subjects differ in their set toward the task? The description of instructions to subjects in the different conditions (actual instructions were not reported) suggests that subjects in both conditions were given a passive set toward the task ("attend to the tone and let it carry . . . to low levels of relaxation" (p. 263); however, it appears that feedback subjects were explicitly or implicitly led to try actively to lower EMG levels, whereas subjects in the control condition simply closed their eyes and relaxed. This speculation may be supported by the assertion that internal subjects in the feedback condition reported the least relaxation. Carlson stated that this "suggests the rather paradoxical conclusion that in their efforts to perform well in a frontal muscle relaxation task, internally oriented people may actually sacrifice their subjective state of relaxation" (p. 270). In some of the heart rate control studies, internals were better able to speed heart rate on instructions without cardiac feedback. Would it not be expected that internals could relax more effectively if motivated to do so, at least early in training? In fact, the higher EMG levels of the external subjects relative to the internal subjects were significant in the second and third training sessions. Although Carlson attributed these effects to chance, it is possible that they reflected real differences between internals and externals. It would be of interest in future studies to compare groups that are instructed to try actively to relax, with and without feedback, with groups whose members simply sit quietly throughout the training sessions. This design would more adequately assess the rate of learning or acquisition with or without feedback, relative to the changes that occur without an active intervention.

Carlson did not employ a baseline at the beginning of each session, so it is impossible to determine how much of the effects observed are related to changes in tonic levels across the multiple sessions or due to adaptation within each session. In a subsequent study (Carlson & Feld, 1978) it was reported that the general downward trend in EMG levels occurs for the most part during the first half of each session. A final posttraining baseline would permit an assessment of changes, unrelated to control efforts, from the beginning to the end of the study. It is also unfortunate that portions of each session were not devoted to attempted relaxation in the absence of feedback in order to assess true self-control of EMG levels (perhaps with eyes open).

A second study from this laboratory (Carlson & Feld, 1978) tested subjects under essentially the same conditions used by Carlson (1977) except for the manipulation of an "incentive" (see Table 3.3). Half of the subjects in the feedback condition were told that a small number of bonus points (3 in addition to 10 given noncontingently) in their introductory psychology course would be given contingent on successful reductions in EMG levels from session to session. At the end of each session, subjects were informed whether or not they had attained a lower muscle tension level and, therefore, whether or not an additional half-point had been earned. (It should be noted that this manipulation included knowledge of results plus reinforcement for results.) It is not made clear, but apparently subjects in the no-incentive conditions did not receive the information about their progress. The remaining subjects in the feedback condition were instructed that points would be given solely on the basis of reliable attendance at experimental sessions. Control subjects were similarly assigned to incentive conditions, but control subjects in the contingent conditions were actually yoked to contingent-incentive feedback subjects. In this study Carlson and Feld also included two posttraining sessions during which the tones were not presented.

Although subjects in the feedback groups reduced their frontal EMG levels relative to the pretraining baselines and to the control groups, the incentive did not affect performance in the feedback conditions, although it appeared to facilitate lower EMG levels in the control condition (interpreted as a general motivational effect). None of the changes in EMG levels of any of the groups from training to posttraining was significant. However, only the no-incentive feedback group remained significantly different from pretraining baselines.

It is difficult to know how to interpret these posttraining baseline comparisons. Does it mean that subjects can transfer control from feedback to no-feedback conditions? Or does the posttraining assessment reflect adaptation in tonic EMG activity, suggesting that there really are not treatment effects relative to a shifting baseline? These questions may be irrelevant to present purposes given that there weren't any significant locus of control effects. The authors stated that there was some reason to expect an attenuation of the I–E effect when the incentive was used if the bonus points could be regarded as a social cue, since task performances are facilitated in externals by the presence of social cues (see Lefcourt, 1976). Although the reader may question the hypothesis that bonus points represent significant social cues, the fact that no differences between EMG levels of internals and externals were found in the no-incentive feedback condition is especially problematic, given that this condition was almost an exact replication of the procedures used by Carlson (1977). Carlson and Feld concluded that some (unspecified) variable in their study modified the influence of locus of control expectancies. Differences between the two studies include: (a) males only in the Carlson and Feld study compared to equal numbers of males and females in the original study; (b) fewer subjects in the feedback–no-incentive conditions of the 1978 study (14 males versus 24 males and females in Carlson's study); and (c) two fewer training sessions in Carlson and Feld's study.

Carlson and Feld speculated on the possibility that the incentive, whether response-contingent or not, acted as a social cue that had greater facilitation effects on external relative to internal subjects. Irrespective of the reason for the failure to find an I–E effect, these results suggest that the basic locus of control effect is not as robust as originally thought. Carlson (1979, Experiment 3) reported preliminary data suggesting that the fundamental internal–external difference in EMG relaxation training can be replicated; however, the effect may be very sensitive to external manipulations. Perhaps, as Phares (1976) suggested, generalized I–E is most applicable in ambiguous and unstructured tasks in which situational determinants of performance are relatively weak. It would be very useful in subsequent research if experimenters would assess "situation-specific expectancy" and the reinforcement value of the task. As Carlson (1979, p. 128) pointed out, "when reinforcers and the means to attain them are well defined, generalized locus of control orientation may become largely irrelevant." Situation-specific expectancies should have more impact when situational cues and instructions are very explicit and as the person gains more specific experience in the situation.

Recent research by Carlson and others has focused on the role of the immediate situation and expectancies in the EMG biofeedback environment. As was the case with Levenson and her colleagues and Glass and Levy (1982) for heart rate control, Carlson is now examining other concepts relevant to perceived control such as learned helplessness, attributions, and reactance. In a study on the effects of expectancies concerning the controllability of outcomes in a biofeedback task, Carlson and Feld (1981) modified the standard learned helplessness procedure and tested for effects on frontal EMG training. Extreme internally and externally oriented subjects were randomly assigned in equal numbers to each of six cells defined by groups and gender. Frontal EMG responses were measured throughout baseline (no treatment), pretreatment, and test sessions (see Table 3.3). In the pretreatment stage, two groups were given instructions and prerecorded feedback on a fictitious blood pressure control task. The failure group was given false feedback and end-of-session information that the subject had not done well relative to others (e.g., "Gee, I'm sorry, but you didn't do a very good job. Most people do better than that."). The success group received false feedback and instructions that conveyed that blood pressure had been successfully controlled. A control group was given no specific task at this stage. During a subsequent self-control stage, all subjects were instructed to attempt to relax as much as possible, particularly the muscles in the facial region. Finally, all subjects attempted to reduce frontal muscle tension levels while being assisted with true EMG feedback for four sessions (test stage).

Although Carlson and Feld assigned equal numbers of extreme internal and external subjects to each pretreatment condition, they did not report that they conducted any analyses of the EMG data on the basis of the generalized control factor, although some nonsignificant I–E/performance relationships were reported. At any rate, the sample sizes were so small (8 internals and 8 externals per pretreatment condition) and the situational factors so salient that significant interactions were probably precluded. However, they did report a number of interesting findings relevant to our understanding of the influence of situational expectancies in the biofeedback setting. Although the pretreatment did not affect performance on an unrelated cognitive task (Raven's Progressive Matrices), and there were no differences during the single session without EMG feedback, in the final EMG feedback session the failure pretreatment group showed more rapid acquisition of frontal muscle relaxation than did the success and control groups. The latter groups did not differ significantly from each other. Other results of interest include the following: During the pretreatment stage, frontal EMG levels were elevated in the failure pretreatment and control groups; and in the pretreatment stage, the failure group reported less control, more difficulty, and more frustration relative to the success group. Performance was attributed by both groups to internal factors (ability and effort) rather than to luck or task difficulty. Although generalized locus of control expectancies were not found to be affected by the pretreatment, possible changes in I–E as a consequence of veridical feedback training were not assessed.

The pattern of these results supports Carlson and Feld's conclusion that expectancies specific to the false feedback pretreatment subsequently influenced performance with veridical feedback; however, the direction of the effects—that is, facilitation of frontal EMG training due to the prior failure experience—requires explanation. The results are consistent with but not directly predicted by social learning theory notions of situation-specific expectancies (see Phares, 1976). Nor are they consistent with predictions from models of learned helplessness, despite the apparent similarity to the learned helplessness paradigm (see Abramson et al., 1978; Miller & Norman, 1979).

However, the data are consistent with the results of several studies that have obtained a reversal of the helplessness effect and that can be explained according to Wortman and Brehm's (1975) reactance theory.

As applied to the present study, Carlson and Feld (1981) speculated that failure subjects "expected to have bodily control in the subsequent frontal EMG task" (p. 88). Carlson and Feld concluded that the situational expectancies were prepotent in this experiment and unrelated to generalized expectancies concerning control over behavior outcomes. It would be interesting, however, to replicate this study with much larger samples of internals and externals to determine whether or not generalized I–E does interact with situational expectancies at different phases of treatment. It is still tempting to predict different helplessness and success outcomes as a function of differences in generalized expectancy, especially for a measure more specific to bodily self-control.

Carlson (1982) described a follow-up to the Carlson and Feld (1981) study that further evaluated the applications of the reactance concept. Expectations of self-control and perceived loss of control were manipulated with the same pretreatment subjects. Contrary to expectations, a group given success pretraining followed by failure pretraining did not show facilitated performance relative to control subjects. However, a group comparable to the failure pretreatment group in the Carlson and Feld study showed "some tendency" toward a facilitation effect, as did a group given actual but unsuccessful biofeedback training on a hand temperature task during pretreatment. Carlson (1982, p. 368) suggested that "the exposure to actual contingencies in the temperature task accompanied by failure heightened the credibility of the task and the perception of loss of self-control in these subjects."

The interaction of locus of control and expectancy manipulations was also examined by Russell, Dale, and Anderson (1982). In an initial session, selected internal and external locus of control subjects were instructed to relax the frontalis muscle aided by auditory proportional feedback. A brief baseline preceded the biofeedback treatment (see Table 3.3). There were no significant differences between I–E groups on any dependent measure during the initial session, although all groups decreased in muscle tension levels. The procedures for the second session were identical except that subjects were divided into positive and negative expectancy conditions. Positive expectancy was manipulated by instructions as follows: "Since you did well on the first day and because this is the second time and you are familiar with the set up and procedure, you should be able to do much better" (p. 529). The authors did not obtain success estimates, so it is difficult to know whether this instructional set conflicted with subjects' perceptions of success or failure on the task after the initial session. Instructions for the negative expectancy subjects were somewhat problematic: "Because you did very well on the first day, your muscle tension was very low. However, my baseline data is not set that low, so if it does not appear that you are getting any lower, don't worry about it. It might be because your muscle tension is already low." I leave it to the reader to decide whether these instructions would be likely to elicit the intended expectancies. Unfortunately, there is no evidence for a validity check on these manipulations.

Analysis of the second session results (which unfortunately included the baseline trial) led to the conclusion that externals with a positive expectancy had significantly higher levels of muscle tension relative to internals in the same condition. No differences in tension levels were reported as a function of I–E for the negative expectancy condition. The authors further suggested that increased anxiety and respiration rates (in anticipation of biofeedback trials) in external subjects support their interpretation that "biofeedback subjects identified as having an external locus of control seemed to be very disrupted by experimenters' comments of positive expectancies" (p. 531). The high initial baseline in the external subjects who received the positive expectancy instructions, relative to first session baseline, suggests an increase in general arousal (or at least arousal of the frontalis muscle) as a consequence of the manipulation that gradually habituated throughout the session. Paradoxically, if the baseline was assumed to be unaffected by the manipulation, then a change score analysis would suggest superior EMG relaxation on the part of the external subjects. Whatever interpretation one makes of these results, however, they do suggest that externals may be more influenced by expectancy manipulations, at least in the short term.

A study by R. H. Carlson, Bridges, and Williams (1983) is unique because these investigators examined the effects of I–E and perceived value of reinforcement on EMG biofeedback relaxation training. The Health Locus of Control Scale (Wallston, Wallston, Kaplan, & Maides, 1976) was used to assess locus of control expectancy and a value-ranking scale was used as an index of perceived value of reinforcement. Subjects who scored highly internal or external on the health I–E scale and who scored high or low on value attached to good health (relative to 9 other values) were given two sessions of frontalis EMG biofeedback training. Preliminary instructions "linked biofeedback with health benefits" (p. 113). The training consisted of 15 minutes of taped relaxation (autogenic) instructions and continuous feedback in the form of tones that decreased in frequency as the frontalis muscles "relaxed." Subjects were instructed to continue relaxing during a 5-minute "posttraining" period and the effects of training were assessed as changes in muscle activity, relative to a 5-minute pretraining baseline. Initial levels and changes in EMG activity during the actual training were not assessed. The same procedures were followed in a second session 2 weeks later.

The only significant finding was for the interaction between health locus of control and health value: Among subjects low in health value, internality was associated with the largest reductions in mean EMG, whereas among subjects high in health value, externals showed the largest reduction. This unexpected interaction and the failure to find main effects were explained by Carlson *et al.* (1983) on the basis of presumed higher generalized drive in internal, high health value subjects. Regardless of the post hoc theoretical speculations, the study suffers from several important methodological shortcomings, which preclude acceptance of the findings without independent replication. Nonetheless, the study further demonstrates the potential utility of a research strategy that goes beyond a search for simple generalized expectancy–physiological control relationships.

SELF-CONTROL AND OTHER PHYSIOLOGICAL MEASURES

Although most of the research has been on heart rate and electromyographic control, there have been a few reports on the relationship between I–E and regulation of EEG alpha, electrodermal activity, and, most recently, a single study on skin temperature. Several of these studies were published at the same time as Ray's work on cardiac control; however, there has been less interest in these measures in recent years.

Electroencephalograph (EEG) responses. Two 1974 studies examined the relationship between generalized expectancy for locus of control and the "operant conditioning" of EEG alpha (Goesling *et al.*, 1974), and alpha rhythm feedback (Johnson & Meyer, 1974). Goesling *et al.* predicted that internals would acquire more rapid control over occipital alpha rhythms than externals. Two groups of 15 subjects (gender unspecified) were defined by extreme scores on Rotter's I–E Scale (externals range = 13–21; internals range = 1–4). In a single session, baseline alpha activity was recorded for 8 minutes, followed by 40 minutes of EEG feedback training. Subjects were instructed to control the feedback beeps (activated by 8–13 Hz activity) by "mental processes" only, with eyes open. The measurements of alpha were recorded in 60-second intervals during both the baseline and conditioning periods. Although all subjects showed a significant increase in alpha activity relative to baseline, internal-oriented subjects spent significantly more time in alpha (and got there faster) than did externals. Thus although external locus of control subjects did learn to increase their alpha density, they did not do it "as quickly, as consistently, or as well" (p. 1343) as internals. Consistent with reports in the cardiac and EMG control literature, there were no between-group differences in self-reported strategies.

Johnson and Meyer (1974) published a brief report of a similar study in which they employed 24 female volunteers who expressed interest in participating in a biofeedback experiment. Differences included differentiation on the basis of the Nowicki–Strickland scale (means, Standard deviations, and selection procedure unspecified); control subjects who received pre- and postcontact only; and training consisted of three 40-minute sessions. In the base rate session subjects were given relaxation exercises and EMG feedback. Although no data are presented, it was reported that internals in the experimental condition ($N = 6$) were better able to use feedback to increase their alpha activity than were external subjects.

Jamieson and Dreger (1976) compared the responses to alpha feedback training in 10 internals ($M = 5.2$) and 10 externals ($M = 17.4$) selected from among 40 females who were administered Rotter's I–E Scale. Training involved four alternating sets of 5 minutes of auditory feedback and 2-minute rest periods (eyes closed throughout). Although externals showed a significant increase over trials in the difference between percentage of time in alpha during the feedback and rest periods, no difference was reported for internals. It was also reported that initial presentation of the feedback tone suppressed alpha in externals but not in internals. Interestingly, Jamieson and Dreger found that the resting baseline for the internals increased significantly over trials, whereas the baseline for the externals significantly decreased. This finding illustrates the importance of sampling baselines throughout biofeedback sessions, but it also demonstrates one of the pitfalls of a reliance on the running baseline in lieu of no-training control groups. Jamieson and Dreger (1976, p. 1) offered an explanation for the different baselines: "Internals easily gain autonomous control of alpha activity with training, while externals are impaired in their ability to autonomously produce alpha after it has been paired with the tone."

In a related vein, Tyson and Audette (1979) examined the variety of experiences associated with alpha enhancement. Participants were given eight continuous alpha feedback trials (8-minute trials, with 3-minute rest periods) and asked to complete a 40-scale semantic differential describing their experience. The eight principal components in the semantic differential were correlated with changes in alpha amplitude using canonical correlations, and two significant canonical variates were found. The influence of extraneous variables was estimated by manipulating perceived locus of control and the instructional set. Subjects were selected on the basis of total scores on the Reid and Ware (1974) I–E scale. The 10 extreme internals (less than 11 of 39) and 10 extreme externals (more than 25) were selected from a potential sample of 116 participants (gender unspecified). Within each group subjects were randomly subdivided into an instructional set ("alpha waves are usually experienced as quite pleasant giving one the feeling of comfortable relaxation," p. 67) and a naive group.

Consistent with previous studies, it was reported that internal individuals were more likely than externals to produce alpha activity. The focus was on the influence of I–E and instructions on the relationship between reported experience and alpha activity. (The interested reader is referred to the original article for a description of the statistical strategy and the complex results obtained.) Basically, the same scales that were influenced by locus of control were also influenced by instructions. The Weak and Slow scales were the strongest and most reliable indicators of the first variate (which represented the most frequent pattern) and Quiet and Hot the best indicators of the second variate. Experiences toward the Fast pole and some of the less Pleasurable feelings were attributed to external locus of control. The first canonical variate was generally consistent with other reports that instructed subjects do produce more alpha and report more typical experiences (e.g., Plotkin, 1976); participants given instructions tended to follow the most frequent patterns and the naive group the second canonical variate.

Brolund and Schallow (1976) conducted a single-session study demonstrating the hazard of inferring alpha control (or control of any physiological response, for that matter) from increases above initial baselines, as many studies have done, and at the same time failed to find any differences due to locus of control. These authors randomly assigned 80 undergraduates to one of four treatment conditions: A feedback group received an auditory stimulus that denoted the presence of alpha. A backup reinforcement group received feedback plus a choice of money or extra experimental credit contingent on increasing alpha 1.5 times baseline levels. A yoked control group received bogus feedback (taped feedback pattern of a baseline alpha matched feedback subject). Another control group received no feedback and was instructed that the study was about the effect of an auditory tone on a brain wave pattern. The subjects were instructed to rest for a 4-minute period prior to receiving instructions appropriate to each condition. The instructional period was succeeded by a 2-minute rest period. Following this subjects were given five 4-minute experimental periods and four 2-minute rest periods, during which the feedback system did not operate.

The backup reinforcement was clearly more effective in enhancing alpha than any other treatment condition. In fact, the conventional feedback group performed no better than the control group that received no feedback, although both significantly increased alpha over trials. The only group that failed to show a significant increase in alpha was the yoked control group. Performance in the yoked control group differed significantly over trials from the other controls. Self-reported strategies did not serve to differentiate the groups. Subjects were divided at the median (11) of their scores on the Rotter scale; however, adding I–E as another between-subject factor to the original design resulted in no significant effects and no interaction for locus of control. Furthermore, there were no differences between internals and externals on the questions about perceived control and strategies. Although subjects for the study were not preselected on the basis of locus of control scores, and the sample of internals and externals in each condition ($N = 10$) is relatively small, the study is methodologically quite sound. At the very least, the Broland and Schallow work suggests that the effects of other studies that have assessed control in a relaxation direction (e.g., alpha, EMG relaxation) may simply reflect adaptation to the experimental environment rather than acquisition, learning, or control.

Although these studies, with the exception of Brolund and Schallow (1976), are consistent with an expectation that internal-oriented persons are more effective alpha controllers and may describe the alpha experience differently relative to externals, it is necessary to conduct further research in this area. There are altogether too many problems with the particular studies and the alpha EEG control literature in general to make any definitive statement about I–E orientation and alpha performance. A replication of Broland and Schallow with highly selected internals and externals and multiple sessions would be valuable.

Electrodermal activity. Three studies have examined I–E in relation to some aspect of electrodermal activity. In a brief report, Wagner *et al.* (1974) tested their prediction that only scores on Levenson's Internal Scale (personal control) would be related to ability to control galvanic skin response within a single session. Participants included 30 students (number of each gender unspecified) who volunteered from a pool of 100 males and females who had previously completed the multidimensional I–E scale. The report does not describe a baseline and, more important, the criteria for determining an electrodermal response. Subjects were instructed to lower their GSR responses with visual feedback provided in the form of a display meter. There were five 2-minute trials interspersed with 1-minute rest intervals. The 10 most successful subjects were compared with 10 who were least successful on the task, and it was reported that the successful subjects scored more internally on the personal control scale. Although there were no differences for the Powerful Others and Chance scales, the authors concluded that only beliefs about self-control are relevant to voluntary control of autonomic function (but compare Logsdon et al., 1978).

In a recent follow-up to this work, Bourgeois, Levenson, and Wagner (1980) used essentially the same procedures but examined the effects of congruence and incongruence between locus of control and field dependence–independence on differential ability to decrease GSR responses. Past research has demonstrated that persons whose locus of control expectancies are congruent with their perceptual or cognitive styles (i.e., field-independent internals and field-dependent externals) perform better on cognitive tasks (Lefcourt & Telegdi, 1971) and are more accepting of themselves on a Q-sort measure of personality adjustment (Tobacyk, Broughton, & Vaught, 1975) than are incongruent subjects.

In the Bourgeois et al. study, 80 male and female undergraduates were divided into four groups based on median splits of scores on the Levenson Internal Scale and the Group Embedded Figure Test measure of perceptual differentiation (Witkin, Oltman, Raskin, & Karp, 1971). Then 15 subjects were randomly selected from each of the four groups (field-dependent and field-independent, internals and externals) for the GSR biofeedback study. It was reported that all subjects were able to learn to decrease GSR; however, congruent subjects decreased their GSRs significantly more than did incongruent subjects. This finding, if replicable, should prompt further research to determine the utility of the congruence–incongruence dimension for other physiological response systems, including heart rate and muscle activity. It would also be of interest to determine whether the different congruent groups employ different cognitive and/or somatic strategies to achieve the same ends (see Bourgeois et al., 1980).

Finally, Volow et al. (1979) explored the possibility of using biofeedback to arrest or facilitate spontaneous decline in tonic skin potential level, and obtained scores on the Rotter scale at the end of the study for the 10 male participants. For 3 days, subjects received 20 minutes of training in increasing skin potential level negativity, followed by training in decreasing negativity, with reverse order for half the subjects. Simultaneous analogue and binary (monetary reinforcement) feedback and a shaping procedure were employed. Training in the direction of skin potential level increases resulted in arrest of spontaneous decline (but not large-magnitude increases above presession baseline). Training in the direction of skin potential level decreases facilitated declines in skin potential level. The authors hypothesized that I–E scores might explain some of the variability in control. When locus of control scores were correlated with skin potential level changes for the third day, it was reported that scores in the internal range were correlated with better declines, but not significantly. However, the overall difference between decline and arrested declines (probably the best index of control, in light of the fact that directional control was highly correlated with the baselines) was uncorrelated with locus of control. Given the baseline problem in this study and the very small sample size, little significance can be attached to these findings.

As was the case for EEG alpha control, any conclusions about the relationship between locus of control and control of electrodermal activity, whether tonic or phasic, must remain extremely tentative.

Temperature control. Only one published study has examined I–E control in relation to attempted control of skin temperature (Stoffer *et al.*, 1979). An earlier paper by Fotopoulos and Binegar (1976) found no differences in the biofeedback control of skin temperature between groups of internals and externals. Stoffer *et al.* selected 24 internals (Rotter score less than 7) and 24 externals (greater than 13) from a group of 300 students who completed the locus of control scale 3 months prior to subject selection. Gender of the subjects was not specified. The two personality types were randomly assigned to one of three different treatment groups: contingent feedback (high-, medium-, or low-pitched tones corresponding to rising, unchanging, or falling temperatures); yoked sham feedback; or no feedback, resulting in six cells of eight subjects each. The only treatment difference among the three groups concerned the presence, absence, or source of temperature feedback signals the subjects received through headsets. A pretest included baseline recording and a cold pressor test. The temperature training phase included five 13-minute sessions during which subjects were instructed to raise finger temperature by mental means. Training was initiated when skin temperature stabilized or at the end of 15 minutes.

In a posttest session the subjects' ability to increase finger temperature without feedback was assessed and the cold pressor was readministered to test whether temperature training had any effect on physiological responses and pain perception during cold stress. Blood pressure and heart rate were also monitored. The results demonstrated voluntary control of peripheral temperature following the contingent feedback training, but not after yoked feedback training. However, the acquisition of voluntary control did not attenuate the stress response to thermal pain. Contrary to expectations, there was no indication that internals were superior to externals either during the training phase or during the no-feedback test phase.

SUMMARY AND EVALUATION

In his recent review, Carlson (1982, p. 370) concluded that "the accumulated literature relating bodily control to I–E control as assessed with a variety of tests at least points to the validity of the fundamental relationship" (also see Carroll, 1979; Williamson & Blanchard, 1979; Zimet, 1979). At least for EMG responses and heart rate, the systems that have received the most research attention, the evidence suggests that persons with a generalized expectancy for internal control, relative to external-oriented persons, are better able to reduce EMG activity and to increase heart rate. Some studies have demonstrated that when appropriately instructed, internals can produce the desired response without the assistance of biofeedback. However, it must also be concluded that the results are not always consistent from study to study, nor are they consistent with theoretical expectations from the literature on perceived control. The interpretation of data and comparisons across experiments, both within and between physiological systems, is particularly difficult. Inspection of Tables 3.2 and 3.3 indicates that the studies vary considerably on a number of points: measurement of locus of control, selection of subjects, gender of subjects, duration of the adaptation or baseline periods, control conditions, specifics of the interventions (including type of instructions and feedback parameters), length and number of training sessions, characteristics of the laboratory, and dependent measures.

Many of the studies reviewed suffer from important methodological weaknesses. In some of the studies that failed to obtain predicted effects, it is possible that with more careful subject selection and larger sample sizes effects could have been detected. A perturbing aspect of these studies is the method of assessing control of the relevant physiological response. This is a continuing source of confusion and discrepant results. For example, in the case of heart rate control, some investigators assess control relative to a pretraining baseline, whereas others take account of changes in tonic heart rate during the session. These different strategies lead to very different conclusions about the direction and magnitude of control achieved. Researchers in the area of EMG control have typically compared experimental groups to a no-treatment control condition; however these studies usually fail to control adequately for changes in baseline. A noncontingent control for biofeedback effects was rarely used in the reviewed studies.

Despite the methodological differences and problems, there appear to be important differences between internals and externals on the bodily control task. Some of the most impressive results have been obtained with measures that seem to be more directly relevant to self-control (e.g., Mirels's personal factor, the Nowicki–Strickland scale), and it is possible that a scale more specific to perceived physiological control will be even more predictive of differences. In this regard, it should be noted that self-control (i.e., response control in the absence of external feedback) deserves more attention. Research into the maintenance and generalization of the observed differences between internals and externals is imperative. The few studies that have employed helplessness manipulations, or manipulated expectancy by instructions, suggest that situational constraints may be important in influencing the relationship between generalized expectancies for control and bodily regulation.

Assuming that persons with an internal locus of control are generally better at the task of controlling specific aspects of their physiology, we are still left with this question: How do they do it? What behaviors do internals engage in to facilitate control of internal physiological responses? Carlson (1982) skirted this issue by stating that "specifying the mediators and their modus operandi is an entirely separate area for research" (p. 371). This issue is complex; however, it is also very important and deserves more creative and imaginative research effort. Some researchers have attempted to provide answers to this question, at least at the theoretical level, and further integration of concepts and hypotheses from the perceived control, biofeedback, and psychophysiological literature may provide some answers.

Let us take heart rate as a specific example (but realize that possible explanations for differences between internals and externals may not apply in precisely the same way to other physiological responses, such as EMG activity). Internals seem to be better able to speed heart rate; however, the evidence is less clear with respect to heart rate slowing. Consideration of methodological problems and recourse to psychophysiological principles to explain early conclusions that externals were better at slowing heart rate, in conjunction with recent findings, leads to the tentative conclusions that there is no difference between internals and externals where heart rate slowing is concerned. However, extrapolation from the EMG literature suggests that investigators may have provided insufficient training. Further, it is difficult to see how subjects who are well-habituated to the laboratory and who already have low resting heart rates could produce consistent large-magnitude decreases, given that "further reductions would press built-in physiological limits" (Schwartz, 1974, p. 463). Differential ability of internals and externals to slow heart rate should probably be assessed under conditions when heart rate is raised considerably above normal resting levels, as when induced by stressors. Although it has been suggested that different mechanisms underlie the two directions of heart rate control, there is no consensus on this issue (see Williamson & Blanchard, 1979).

Pleas for research on the psychophysiological mechanisms that may account for or enhance autonomic control have been virtually ignored by researchers of I–E and heart rate control. For example, several investigators have found that somatic activity successfully predicts differences in ability to decrease and increase heart rate with feedback (e.g., Levenson & Ditto, 1981) and that physiological-response patterning concomitant with the development of heart-rate control may be different earlier in training than it is later in training for both speeding and slowing conditions (Hatch & Gatchel, 1979). The possibility that these relationships may mediate I–E/heart rate control differences has not been explored systematically. Another simple, direct physiological explanation of the heart rate control effect was suggested by Blankstein and Egner (1977) based on a finding reported by Bell and Schwartz (1973): They found that internal subjects showed a wider range of bidirectional heart rate change on a variety of reactivity tasks in and out of the laboratory. Although this finding was not included in the published report (Bell & Schwartz, 1975), it should be followed up because it suggests that differences in cardiac control ability may be related to differences between internals and externals in the reactivity of the cardiovascular system.

Brener (1977) offered another explanation of the locus of control results. He speculated that I–E control might tap differences in visceral sensitivity, which he assumes to be an important mechanism of heart rate control. Although Whitehead, Dresden, Heiman, and Blackwell (1976, cited in Carroll, 1977) reported a significant correlation between locus of control and their index of cardiac discrimination ($r = +.74$), the direction of this correlation indicated that it was externals who showed superior cardiac perception. However, Brener's theory about the role of interoceptive stimuli has not received strong support (see Carroll, 1977).

Although Williamson and Blanchard (1979) concluded that studying cognitive mediators is not likely to increase understanding of individual differences in ability to control heart rate, they pointed out that the practice of asking subjects to report strategies at the end of a study may obscure potentially important differences. Given the important cognitive differences between internals and externals (e.g., Ducette & Wolk, 1973), more systematic assessments of the cognitive mediational strategies employed by internals and externals during the heart rate control task should be conducted. Favaro and Pye (1979) reported on the use of canonical correlation procedures to assess simultaneously the contributions of cognitive, physiological, and personality variables to performance on a heart rate control task. Motivational differences should also be explored. Even if it is assumed that both internals and externals want to succeed on tasks that allow the demonstration of personal ability and skill, such as the heart rate control task, externals have a relatively lower expectancy for achieving such valued goals, and this expectancy may be expressed in task-relevant behavior. Internals and externals may differ in their perceptions of ability to execute the desired response, either on instruction or with the assistance of biofeedback. Researchers should more systematically evaluate self-efficacy and outcome expectations and causal attributions (e.g., effort, task difficulty, ability, and luck) in the biofeedback situation. Although there is a clear need to integrate the concepts from various theories of perceived control with theoretical models of learned control (e.g., Brener, 1974; Lang, 1975; Schwartz, 1974), there is also a need to consider the social influence process in the biofeedback setting:

> Biofeedback training is not merely a form of manipulation of human physiology; it is a complex social–behavioral interaction in which not merely physiology but attitudes, expectations, motivations, attention, experience, alertness, and understandings are being directly and indirectly influenced independently of any contingencies between physiology and feedback [Plotkin, 1979, p. 1146].

Although the research on the relationship between I–E and physiological control has been useful from the perspective of theories of perceived control, it remains to be demonstrated that the differences have any relevance to the ability to control specific physiological responses in naturalistic settings (see Lynn & Friedman, 1979). Furthermore, researchers should consider investing in disentangling the relationship between I–E and alternative approaches to achieving relaxation or physiological control (see Cuthbert, Kristeller, Simons, Hodes, & Lang, 1981).

Progressive Deep Muscle Relaxation and Other Relaxation Procedures

A number of relaxation procedures, including progressive deep muscle relaxation (either alone or as a component of a treatment package such as Wolpe's systematic desensitization), transcendental meditation or Yoga and Zen, hypnosis, and autogenic training have enjoyed widespread clinical and popular use. In fact, since Jacobson's introduction of relaxation training in 1938, the use of this clinical approach to the treatment of anxiety and stress disorders has expanded to become a consistent component of the behavioral clinician's armamentarium of intervention techniques. Its ubiquitous use had led some to label relaxation training the "behavioral aspirin" (see Russo, Bird, & Masek, 1980). Maharishi Mahesh Yogi introduced transcendental meditation (TM) in 1958, and it is alleged that by 1974 nearly one million people had been instructed in the use of the technique, and more than 10,000 people were beginning the TM program each month (International Meditation Society, 1975).

There are, of course, many differences among the various relaxation procedures. For example, deep muscle relaxation typically involves tensing and releasing various muscle groups and discriminating differences. It is a much more active process than meditation, which usually involves a passive attitude and a mental device to prevent distracting thoughts. Even within the domain of progressive relaxation, there is extensive variability across a wide variety of procedural components (see King, 1980). Despite these differences, there is considerable evidence for the efficacy of these procedures with a broad range of symptoms and behavioral problems, although the actual mechanism responsible for improvement is not well-understood (e.g., Rachman, 1968).

Many researchers believe that these techniques have reliable psychophysiological consequences. For example, the psychophysiological correlates of meditation are reported to include a wide variety of changes that suggest decreases in arousal, including various EEG changes and decreases in heart rate, blood pressure, respiratory rate, muscle tension, skin conductance, oxygen consumption, carbon dioxide elimination, and arterial blood lactate (see West, 1980). Although some investigators have reported that decreases in arousal observed during meditation are not significantly different from decreases observed during other relaxing practices (Puente, 1981), other researchers talk of meditation producing a fourth major state of consciousness characterized as a unique wakeful hypometabolic physiological state (Wallace, Benson, & Wilson, 1971). Borkovec and Sides (1979) reviewed a number of critical procedural variables related to the physiological effects of progressive relaxation. They concluded that significant physiological reductions are more probable when multisession, subject-controlled procedures are employed, with populations for whom physiological arousal is a contributing factor.

Given the widespread interest in and extensive research on muscle relaxation, TM, and related procedures, it is surprising that very few investigations have used the locus of control construct as an independent variable or dependent measure. For example, in an extensive review of the progressive relaxation training literature published from 1970 to 1979, in 12 research journals, Hillenberg and Collins (1982) reported that only 1 of 80 studies employed Rotter's I–E Scale as a dependent measure.

It would be of interest to determine not only whether or not internals and externals respond differently to standard relaxation procedures, but also whether locus of control interacts with and mediates the effects of different types of relaxation treatments. The value of joint consideration of both client and treatment factors in maximizing therapeutic gain has received recognition by many researchers. Although explication of the interactive process awaits further investigation, Baker (1979) concluded on the basis of a review of a number of treatment studies that there is evidence for "an interactive effect of LOC differences and therapy variables upon treatment outcome" (p. 359). Consistent with the recent trends in the I–E and EMG and heart rate biofeedback research, Strickland's (1978) review of the literature on locus of control and psychological treatment led her to conclude that "congruence between locus of control expectancies and the structure of the therapeutic endeavor appears to lead to the most pervasive changes" (p. 1203).

One way of conceptualizing a match between type of relaxation intervention and the I–E dimension was suggested by Ollendick and Murphy (1977). These investigators argued that external-oriented subjects should be more responsive to relaxation-induction based on muscle tension and release, whereas internal-oriented persons should be most responsive to a cognitive form of relaxation. This distinction between somatic forms of relaxation (such as muscle tension and release) and more cognitive forms has been discussed at length by Davidson and Schwartz (1976). In their multiple-session study, Ollendick and Murphy compared selected groups of female internals and externals who received extended training in muscular relaxation, cognitive relaxation, or self-relaxation (control-for-time procedure). Although the sample sizes were relatively small ($N = 6$ per subgroup) and the effects were not very strong, the authors concluded that subjects matched with therapy type experienced greater decrements in heart rate and subjective anxiety than did subjects who were not matched.

A recent study by Pickett and Clum (1982) sought to examine this hypothesis further in a surgical situation—elective cholecystectomy (gall bladder) surgery. Although psychophysiological measures were not recorded, Pickett and Clum advanced two hypotheses about the effects of locus of control on postsurgery pain anxiety: (a) There would be an interaction between locus of control and therapist versus client control over a relaxation intervention, and (b) there would be an interaction between I–E and somatic versus cognitive treatment. In both cases it was hypothesized that congruent matches would yield lower postsurgery pain and anxiety than noncongruent matches. Subjects (16 males and 43 females) were divided on the basis of a median split of Rotter scale scores (Internals = 1–6; Externals ≥ 7) and divided into four groups consisting of three experimental groups (N = 16) and a no-treatment control group. The relaxation training condition was designed to be congruent with a generalized expectation for external control. Communication to the patient gave a sense of other- rather than self-control. Patients were then taught alternate tensing and relaxing of 19 muscle groups. In the relaxation information condition, designed to be congruent with internal control, patients were given a typed communication which emphasized that they could learn the muscle relaxation on their own (sense of self-control). An attention redirection condition consisted of an active cognitive imagery intervention designed to be congruent with internals' ability to use such techniques effectively. Multiple regression analyses were used to test for both treatment effects and I–E × treatment interactions.

The only treatment to reduce postsurgical anxiety successfully was the attention redirection procedure. Pickett and Clum suggested that relaxation training may be too complicated to learn in a single session (especially for subjects in a high-stress situation) and that the attention redirection procedure may be more consistent with typical approaches to dealing with stress (i.e., by attempting to divert attention). A second proposed explanation is that the more cognitive attention redirection approach was enhanced due to the samples' skew toward the internal end of the I–E dimension (highest I–E score = 14). This contention was buttressed by a significant interaction between locus of control and relaxation training versus attention redirection. This interaction indicated a linear relationship between I–E and anxiety within the attention redirection group and an inverted-U relationship between locus of control and anxiety in the relaxation training group (i.e., individuals in the I–E midrange had the highest anxiety scores). The same trend was found for analyses of pain intensity. Locus of control × directiveness of treatment interactions were not significant. It would be useful to pursue this line of research by extending the number of relaxation training sessions (Bernstein & Borkovec, 1973, recommend 10 sessions, although this recommendation has been followed in less than 6% of published studies; see Hillenberg & Collins, 1982), and recording physiological measures in order to determine whether I–E predicts changes in physiology that are related to other dependent measures of treatment outcome.

In a recent study, Theoret and Stoppard (1982) examined the effects of locus of control on two different methods of relaxation training—progressive muscular and autogenic methods of relaxation. They assumed that progressive muscle relaxation is the more structured and directive of the two (although, depending on how it is implemented, this may not be true). Sixty female students who had requested relaxation training were selected from a larger pool so that 30 were classified as internals and 30 as externals. In each I–E condition, 10 subjects were randomly assigned to progressive relaxation training, autogenic training, or an attention control. Subjects received three 30-minute sessions of relaxation training. Although heart rate was the only psychophysiological dependent measure, results indicated a significant interaction involving I–E and relaxation training method: Externals in the progressive relaxation condition manifested significantly greater pre–post reductions in heart rate than externals who received either autogenic training or the control condition. Internals showed changes in heart rate, but degree of change did not differ among training conditions. The authors concluded that progressive deep muscle relaxation is most appropriate for use with externally oriented clients.

Although I could not find a study relating locus of control to any of the forms of meditation and physiological processes, two 1979 studies did look at the effects on other dependent measures. Di Nardo and Raymond (1979) examined the relationship between I–E and deployment of attention during brief meditation. The task required subjects to focus their attention on an actual stimulus (candle flame) or an imagined stimulus (visualization of a candle flame) while recording intruding thoughts by pressing a button on a counter. Consistent with their hypothesis, Di Nardo and Raymond found that an internal locus of control (Rotter scale) was related to fewer intrusions than was an external locus. Goldman, Domitor, and Murray (1979) examined the effects of Zen meditation exercises (breath-counting technique) done in the laboratory under direct observation on measures of anxiety and perceptual functioning. The authors hypothesized that subjects with an internal locus of control would be better able than externals "to explore inner experiences and show the emotional and perceptual changes attributed to meditation exercises" (p. 552). However, internality–externality did not interact with treatment. This result must be placed in the context of the main findings: The measures of anxiety and perceptual functioning after brief (five sessions in 1 week) Zen meditation were not significantly different from control conditions.

In summary, although there are theoretical grounds to expect a relationship between generalized expectancies for control and relaxation and meditation, this is largely virgin territory. Although the untrodden research ground is extensive, there are a few indications that the area deserves careful study.

*Psychophysiological Interventions and Changes
in Generalized Perceptions of Control*

The viability of the role of psychological interventions in changing generalized perceptions of control was first proposed by Lefcourt (1966, p. 191). Recognition of this goal was based on his premise that "an internal locus of control may be one prerequisite for competent behavior, and an external-control orientation seems common to many people who do not function in a competent, 'healthy' manner." Since Lefcourt's theoretical statement, a number of studies have examined the effect of various treatment interventions and facets of therapy on locus of control (see reviews by Baker, 1979; Strickland, 1978). Surveys of the literature conclude that I–E has been systematically modified by several therapeutic and self-improvement approaches and in various subject populations.

The purpose of this section is to examine the impact of psychophysiologically oriented interventions on locus of control, as assessed by pre- and posttreatment and follow-up assessments. The relevant studies are summarized in Table 3.4. Inspection of this table indicates that a majority of the studies assessed the effects of EMG biofeedback— usually of the frontalis muscle—often in combination with muscle relaxation training and home practice. Although in some cases psychophysiological measures have been taken (usually frontal EMG), a majority of studies did not record physiological activity, and it cannot always be assumed that the intervention had significant physiological consequences. Nonetheless, these studies are included here because of a presumed relationship between the interventions and physiological functioning. In only a few cases have changes in EMG levels been correlated with shifts in locus of control.

An early study by Hjelle (1974) is at least suggestive of an impact of a psychophysiological self-control intervention on generalized expectancies for control. Although his findings are open to several interpretations, Hjelle reported that a group of regular meditators with about

TABLE 3.4
Changes in Generalized Locus of Control as a Function of Psychophysiological Interventions[a]

Study	Subjects and treatment	Treatment duration	I–E changes pre–post
Hjelle (1974)	Transcendental Meditation (SIMS) (15 regular meditators and 21 beginning meditators)	Regular meditators: M = 22.6 months Novice meditators: no experience	Regular meditators (TM) scored significantly more internal on Rotter scale than beginning meditators
Johnson & Meyer (1974)	EEG alpha biofeedback (plus some relaxation exercises) and no-treatment control (24 female volunteers)	3 40-min. periods over 2 weeks	No change for subjects able to control alpha (criterion unspecified) Trend for increased externality ($p < .10$) for subjects unable to control alpha
Cox et al. (1975)	EMG biofeedback, verbal relaxation (plus cue-control breathing and home relaxation) and placebo (27 adults with chronic tension headaches)	4 weeks 30-min. sessions	All groups experienced equally significant shifts toward internality (Nowicki–Strickland) at posttest and 4-month follow-up
Freedman & Papsdorf (1976)	Frontal EMG biofeedback, progressive relaxation, and placebo "relaxation" (13 onset insomniacs)	6 30-min. sessions (pre/post all-night laboratory sessions)	No significant I–E effects
Carlson (1977)	Frontal EMG biofeedback training and control group (48 undergraduates)	8 20-min. feedback sessions (2 per week)	External subjects shifted significantly in internal direction on Nowicki–Strickland scale (primarily in feedback condition) (I–E changes not correlated with changes in EMG levels)
Ollendick & Murphy (1977)	Muscular relaxation, cognitive relaxation, and control (36 undergraduate females)	5 45-min. weekly sessions	No significant I–E effects

TABLE 3.4 (*Continued*)

Study	Subjects and treatment	Treatment duration	I–E changes pre–post
Stern & Berrenberg (1977)	Frontal EMG biofeedback training, false feedback, and no feedback (33 undergraduate volunteers)	3 20-min. sessions	True biofeedback groups shifted toward internal personal control (Mirels's scale) (significant relationship between amount of EMG reduction and internal shift)
Carlson & Feld (1978)	Frontal EMG biofeedback training and control groups (subdivided into incentive and no-incentive groups) (56 male undergraduates)	6 20-min. feedback sessions (2 per week)	External subjects shifted significantly in internal direction on Nowicki–Strickland scale (primarily in incentive feedback condition) (I–E changes not correlated with changes in EMG levels)
Kappes & Michaud (1978)	Contingent versus noncontingent EMG feedback (12 moderately high test-anxious students)	5 20-min. sessions of noncontingent feedback plus 5 sessions of contingent feedback plus 5 sessions of contingent feedback (order reversed for second group over 2 weeks)	Trend toward a more internal locus of control (contingent–noncontingent group)
Holliday & Munz (1978)[b]	EMG biofeedback training plus daily home practice in muscle relaxation (7 psychosomatic and 6 nonpsychosomatic subjects)	3 1-hr. weekly feedback sessions (2 forearm, 6 frontalis)	Nonpsychosomatic group showed significant change toward internality (Rotter and modified Levenson scales) High correlation ($r = -.81$) between Rotter pretest score and % reduction in frontalis EMG for nonpsychosomatic group only

(*continued*)

TABLE 3.4 (*Continued*)

Study	Subjects and treatment	Treatment duration	I–E changes pre–post
Zaichkowsky & Kamen (1978)	Frontalis EMG biofeedback ($N = 14$), Transcendental Meditation ($N = 7$), and meditation (Benson technique) ($N = 14$), and control group ($N = 13$)	Biofeedback: 2 20-min. sessions per week for 12 weeks TM: as practiced Meditation: 2 20-min. sessions per day for 12 weeks.	Changes toward internal control only in biofeedback subjects (all experimental groups significantly reduced EMG activity)
Zuroff & Schwarz (1978)	Transcendental meditation (SIMS), muscle relaxation, and no-treatment control (30 male and 30 female student volunteers)	9 weeks (emphasis on home practice)	No change in I–E as a function of either treatment
Allen & Blanchard (1980)	Biofeedback-based stress management training, individual and group discussion, and waiting list control (22 male and 8 female middle-level managers, age 40–60 years)	6 55-min. weekly sessions	No change in I–E at the end of treatment and at 6-week follow-up
Hurley (1980)	Hypnosis, EMG biofeedback, and "trophotropic responses" Benson meditation), and no-treatment control (60 undergraduates)	3 60-min. weekly sessions plus home practice twice per day	No significant I–E effects (significant anxiety and ego strength changes in experimental groups)

2 years of experience with Transcendental Meditation were significantly more internal on Rotter's I–E Scale than was a group of novice meditators. However, Zaichkowsky and Kamen (1978) found no changes in I–E for a small group of TM practitioners and a group trained in Benson's meditation technique, despite the fact that significant reductions in EMG activity occurred over the 12 weeks of intervention. There was a trend toward changes in internality in a frontalis EMG biofeedback group. Zuroff and Schwartz (1978) also failed to find significant changes in I–E following TM and muscle relaxation training in a study that employed relatively large samples of both males and females.

3. PSYCHOPHYSIOLOGY AND PERCEIVED LOCUS OF CONTROL : 171

TABLE 3.4 (Continued)

Study	Subjects and treatment	Treatment duration	I–E changes pre–post
Linn & Hodge (1980)[a]	EMG biofeedback relaxation training groups (with or without contingent reinforcement), and no-treatment control (17 hyperactive children)	10 weekly sessions	EMG biofeedback groups became more internal
Reed & Saslow (1980)	Relaxation instructions, frontalis EMG biofeedback, and brief relaxation instructions (both groups received verbal reinforcement for progress), and no-treatment control (27 high test-anxious subjects)	8 20-min. sessions over 4 weeks	No significant I–E effects. Instructions only group changed in direction of increased internal control (p < .10) (significant test anxiety and general anxiety changes in experimental groups)
Achterberg, McGraw, & Lawlis (1981)	Study 1: Relaxation plus biofeedback temperature elevation or reduction (24 female rheumatoid arthritis patients) Study 2: Biofeedback (17 patients; "majority" from Study 1) and physiotherapy (8 patients	12 30-min. sessions over 6 weeks (Studies 1 and 2)	No significant effects on Levenson I–E and a health locus of control scale (Study 1); significant change on Powerful Others Scale (Study 2)

[a] Unless otherwise specified, I–E was measured using Rotter's I–E Scale, and assignment to groups was equal.
[b] Abstract.

Not surprisingly, the studies that have preselected subjects on the basis of I–E scores have found the most significant changes in locus of control as a function of treatment. These studies have typically examined the effects of EMG biofeedback either alone or in combination with home relaxation practice. Carlson routinely assesses locus of control before and after treatment, and in two frontal EMG biofeedback studies (Carlson, 1977; Carlson & Feld, 1978) he reported that external subjects shifted significantly in the direction of greater internality; however, these changes were not correlated with changes in EMG levels. Although Stern and Berrenberg (1977) did not report the differential effects of I–E (median split on unselected subjects) on treatment outcome, they did find that subjects who received true EMG biofeedback became more internal. The reader will recall that Carlson's laboratory employed the Adult Nowicki–Strickland Internal–External Control Scale, which is assumed to relate more closely to personal control. Stern and Berrenberg's significant finding was on Mirels's personal factor; treatment had no effect on items reflecting belief in political control and total (unfactored) Rotter scores. Stern and Berrenberg also reported a significant relationship between the amount of EMG reduction and the internal shift.

Cox et al. (1975) reported on the effects of EMG biofeedback, verbal relaxation, and a medication placebo treatment for a group of chronic tension headache sufferers. The active treatments also included cue-controlled breathing and home relaxation. All groups showed equally significant shifts toward internality on the Nowicki–Strickland scale at posttest and 4-month follow-up. Linn and Hodge (1980) also reported that hyperactive children became more internal after 10 EMG biofeedback sessions; however, Holliday and Munz (1978) reported that small samples of psychosomatic and nonpsychosomatic persons showed significant reductions in frontalis EMG following biofeedback and home practice, but only the nonpsychosomatic group showed a change toward internality. In the only biofeedback study to employ a modality other than EMG, Johnson and Meyer (1974) failed to find a relationship between success at alpha control and changes in I–E scores.

In summary, several of the studies presented in Table 3.4 suggest that personal locus of control can be modified by treatment approaches designed to promote relaxation, at least in the short run. However, the studies provide little in the way of information regarding the element(s) of the therapeutic process actually accounting for the changes. The available evidence suggests that I–E changes are related only remotely, if at all, to changes in physiological activity—specifically frontalis EMG—although this possibility has not been investigated systematically in most studies. Perhaps the instructional and procedural emphases on self-control and personal responsibility serve as strong situational expectancies for personal control which, over a period of time, influence generalized expectancies. Not all studies employed a no-treatment control, and some effects may be due to regression toward the mean. Several studies found no changes in locus of control despite the fact that the interventions included a relatively large number of sessions and produced significant effects on other dependent measures. Furthermore, most of the positive effect studies used college students as subjects, and only one study (Cox et al., 1975) employed a follow-up.

Clearly, more replications and extensions of this type of research, with appropriate control conditions, are needed in order to determine generalizability of findings to other populations. These studies should include assessments of psychophysiological measures and attempts to elucidate the processes mediating change in locus of control by dismantling strategies and assessments of the congruence between I–E expectancies and the structrure of the treatment intervention (see Strickland, 1978). Finally, most of this research has not controlled for the expectation of favorable outcome, a major consideration in all treatment studies (e.g., Murray & Jacobson, 1978).

Stress, Control, and Coping

How do individuals who differ in the generalized expectancy for control handle stressful situations? Do internals and externals differ physiologically when threatened? In an attempt to answer questions such as these, we can begin with the working hypothesis that externals are more vulnerable and less capable than internals of coping with stressful events in their environment (see Phares, 1976) and that this vulnerability is reflected at a physiological level. The previously cited research by Naditch (1974) on externality, life dissatisfaction, and hypertension and by Cromwell et al. (1977) on externality and undesirable physiological and biochemical indexes in recovering coronary patients, as well as the relatively extensive literature on the moderating influence of internality on life stress and illness (see Lefcourt's chapter on stress, present volume) all lead to an expectation of superior physiological adaptation in internals.

Although this hypothesis seems reasonable and appealing, we must also heed Strickland's (1979) warning that we cannot assume that autonomic functioning in relation to internality is always adaptive. The reader may be aware of the typical finding that cognitive, overt-motor, and physiological aspects of behavior are imperfectly coupled. Although as Phares (1976, p. 133) concluded, "the greater disposition to action of internals seems to equip them in a variety of ways for superior coping over the long term," this superior coping could be at considerable physiological cost. In his review of limited evidence on threat and stress reactions as a function of generalized control orientation, Phares seemed to adopt this position when he compared I–E to Byrne's (1964) repression-sensitization dimension and suggested that "repressors or internals may deny verbally what they fail to hide physiologically" (p. 132). Phares suggested that situation-specific findings would provide hints about the ways in which generalized I–E beliefs affect behavior.

In fact, most of the available literature on stress, coping, and physiological activity as a function of perceived control has examined the issue from a situation-specific perspective. Research that includes measures of dispositional differences has only rarely examined locus of control. The importance of control as a psychological factor in the modulation of physiological indicators of stress is evident from an extensive animal and human research literature. Averill (1973) and Lefcourt (1973) provided excellent reviews of many of the early studies on the relationship between controllability and stress in human beings. More recent reviews are presented by Miller (e.g., 1979), and Thompson (1981). Diverse methodologies have been used to examine this relationship. Aversive events have been manufactured in the laboratory (e.g., shock, noise, photos of accident victims) or used as they naturally occur (e.g., surgery, dental work, disease). Investigators have also focused on different parts of the process of receiving an aversive event: the anticipatory period, the impact period, the immediate postevent period, or the long-term postevent period. The types of reactions that have been assessed and the ways of measuring them have varied considerably but include self-report, behavioral, and physiological indicators.

Thompson's (1981) definition of control as "the belief that one has at one's disposal a response that can influence the aversiveness of an event" (p. 89) recognizes that control (a) does not need to be exercised and (b) does not need to be real to be effective. This definition has much in common with the I–E concept. Thompson presents a typology of control and reviews research and theory that relates four types of control (behavioral, cognitive, information, and retrospective) to reactions to aversive stimuli. As a unifying theme she proposed that reactions to potentially stressful events depend on their meaning to the individual. Although Thompson does not deal with dispositional differences in control beliefs, her review provides a useful framework for the discussion and evaluation of I–E in relation to stress. We focus on those complex designs that attend to the interaction of I–E expectancies and situational demands.

BEHAVIORAL CONTROL

The study that has had the most impact on reviewers' assessments of the differential physiological responsiveness of internals and externals was reported by Houston in 1972. It therefore deserves careful scrutiny. Houston investigated two factors asserted by Lazarus (1966) to influence a persons' perception of threat, and subsequent reactions, in a potentially stressful situation: the person's belief about capacity to counter or avoid threat *in that situation*, and the person's *general belief about control*.

Generalized perception of control was measured by Rotter's I–E Scale. The 66 male subjects were randomly assigned to three conditions and then subdivided, by median splits, into internals and externals. Under one experimental condition (avoidable shock), the subjects were led to believe that they could avoid an electric shock by not making mistakes on the Digits Backward subtest of the WAIS. This manipulation is an example of behavioral control in Thompson's typology—subjects had a behavioral response that could affect the aversive event. A second group of subjects (unavoidable shock) was told that there was no way of avoiding a shock, which would occur randomly while they performed the task. The design also included a nonstress condition. Heart rate was recorded during the last 30 seconds of a 5-minute rest period while subjects completed the Today form of the Affect Adjective Checklist (AACL). After an initial assessment of the subject's limit on the Digits Backward task, the differential instructions for the condition were given and the task followed. At the end of the experimental period, subjects completed the AACL again and heart rate was recorded for a further 30 seconds. These methodological details are important, for it is clear that Houston was evaluating the aversive event during the impact period; he did not assess the anticipatory period or postevent periods.

What did Houston find? Subjects who perceived that they had some control over shock (avoidable shock condition) reported less anxiety but tended to show a greater increase in heart rate than did the no-control group. However, the effect for heart rate was not significant, and, in fact, the threat of shock groups combined did not differ from the nonstress group. Nonetheless, Houston suggested that the subjects in the avoidable shock group showed greater physiological arousal because they "were making a substantial effort to achieve control over the situation" (p. 252). He further suggested that a component of this cardiac response was due to "apprehension about shock." Analyses of subjects' general and situational beliefs about control did not support a congruence–incongruence hypothesis for either anxiety or heart rate: Subjects in incongruent conditions did not evidence greater anxiety or heart rate increases. Further analyses tested the prediction from Lazarus' formulation that external subjects would be more anxious in both threat-of-shock conditions. Contrary to expectation, internal and external control subjects did not differ in reports of anxiety, but internal control subjects evidenced significantly greater heart rate increases than did externals. The means were not presented and there was no indication of the magnitude of these cardiac changes, although they could not have been great.

Houston's interpretation of these results is quite interesting, if somewhat acrobatic. He assumed that the heart rate difference (which, in the case of the manipulation of situational control, reflected effort) was due to threat-induced arousal in the internals who were also reluctant to report anxiety. Would it not be just as reasonable to assume that it is the externals who are the defensive ones (if either group must be) and that the increase in heart rate reflects effort on the task? Unfortunately, the performance data do not lend themselves to either interpretation because the congruence–incongruence hypothesis was supported by the analysis of Digits Backward performance.

This study illustrates, once again, the pitfalls of recording a single physiological measure. In her review, Miller (1979) suggested that the phasic skin conductance response is the purest measure of emotional arousal, whereas tonic skin conductance responses and tonic and phasic heart rate measures are more likely to be measuring focus of attention or general level of alertness. However, rather than subscribe to the classic "indicant fallacy," we should take into account the individual's transaction with the environment at the time of recording. The subjects were working on a cognitive task, and the increased heart rate observed in the internal subjects might well reflect greater task involvement (effort) or cognitive elaboration. Although the cardiac response may also include an emotional component, the response could be related just as well to somatic and respiratory coupling, given that subjects were not only verbalizing during the recording period but also checking adjectives on the AACL.

In addition to recording other measures of autonomic and somatic activity, it would be useful to gain a more complete picture of differences in physiological activity during different parts of the process of receiving the aversive event. As Thompson (1981) concluded, the effects of behavioral control on both physiological arousal and self-reported distress at impact are equivocal. However, the research literature is more clear-cut with respect to the anticipatory period: Knowing that one has a behavioral response available that can reduce the aversiveness of the event lessens anxiety and anticipatory physiological arousal. It would therefore be useful to replicate Houston's study with the inclusion of discrete anticipation and with postevent periods.

Molinari and Khanna (1980) also disagreed with Houston's interpretation of the data. They hypothesized that the reason for the discrepancy between changes in self-reported anxiety and heart rate for internal subjects was due not to the defensiveness of internal subjects but to the failure to consider the role of facilitating versus debilitating anxiety. Molinari and Khanna selected 30 male and 30 female subjects from a large sample of students who had completed the Levenson I–E Scale. They were chosen on the basis of whether their top standard scores occurred on either the Internal, Powerful Others, or Chance scales and respectively identified as internal, defensive external, or congruent external subjects. The design was complex: Each subject was assigned to two of the four treatment conditions (either avoidable shock-skill and nonstress chance, or nonstress-skill and unavoidable shock-chance) according to gender and locus of control. In addition to the possibility of carryover effects on the within-subjects treatments, shock avoidability–unavoidability was confounded with the skill (Digits Backward) and chance (an extra-sensory perception task) conditions. These confounds render the data uninterpretable. The only unconfounded comparison is between the unavoidable shock-skill condition and the nonstress-skill condition.

Inspection of the presented means suggests that internals reported less anxiety than both defensive and congruent external groups but that heart rate increased more in the internals relative to the other two groups; however, a separate analysis of these conditions was not reported. Apparently there were no significant differences in Digits Backward performance in the stress condition, although internal subjects did significantly better relative to defensive externals in the nonstress condition. Trait measures of facilitating and debilitating anxiety did not predict heart rate, anxiety, or performance behavior for any of the locus of control groups. Unfortunately, Molinari and Khanna did not acknowledge the methodological problems with their study. Even more unfortunate is their conclusion that the results question the comparability of Levenson's and Rotter's locus of control scales in identifying even internal subjects. Nonetheless, the trends in the data for the skill conditions are consistent with my previous interpretation of Houston's data and extrapolations from the situational expectancy literature on the effects of behavioral control at impact.

DeGood (1975) also investigated the interaction of behavioral control and I–E using an aversive shock-avoidance procedure. He preselected 24 male internal and 24 male external subjects. During the half-hour shock-avoidance task, half the subjects in each locus of control condition were permitted to escape the situation temporarily whenever they wished by requesting a rest period, whereas the remaining subjects had comparable rest periods imposed on them by the experimenter. The symbol-matching task was tailored to each subject's individual matching rate to guarantee that all subjects received approximately equivalent aversive stimulation ($M = 30$ shocks per session). In the available control condition subjects had the option of taking as many 1-minute time-outs from the task as they desired simply by saying "stop." In the no-control condition each subject was yoked to a subject from the behavioral control condition. The subjects averaged 3.5 time-outs per session. Systolic and diastolic blood pressure were manually recorded from a control room at 30-second intervals and converted to elevation scores by subtracting resting baselines (unspecified) from each score. Although there was a significant effect of the situational manipulation, indicating reliably less systolic arousal in subjects having control over time-outs, the I–E factor was not significant, nor did it interact with the manipulation of behavioral control. There were no main effects in analysis of the diastolic data; however, the blood pressure elevations were larger where personality was incongruous with experimental condition. DeGood pointed out the parallel between the patterning of cardiovascular changes during the experiment and the time course of changes often seen in the development of hypertension. He concluded that increase in peripheral resistance, reflected in diastolic pressure, was most responsive to the influence of locus of control.

Further research on the interaction of I–E with behavioral control–noncontrol over an aversive event was conducted by Lundberg and Frankenhaeuser (1978). This study is noteworthy because in addition to recording heart rate and self-reported discomfort, the investigators assessed catecholamine and cortisol excretion and self-reported effort as indexes of stress and arousal. It is also one of the few studies reviewed to employ an adequate baseline. They asked the question: Do subjects classified as internals and externals react differently when confronted with noise of controllable versus uncontrollable intensity? In the initial session, the 30 male students were exposed to a 10-minute test trial of 85 db white noise and then carried out a mental arithmetic task for 50 minutes during exposure to 50 db white noise. In a second session a day or two later, all subjects performed mental arithmetic for 50 minutes while exposed to white noise. Every other subject was offered a choice between noise intensities prior to each of five successive 10-minute periods, and the next subject, serving as his or her yoked partner, had to submit to the same noise (median noise intensities ranged from 76 to 84 db). Session 3 served to provide baseline values for physiological and subjective values.

Subjects completed the Swedish version of the I–E scale after completing the three sessions and were assigned to internal and external groups by median split. Although there was no difference in arithmetic performance in comparisons of the control versus no-control treatments, heart rate was consistently more elevated in subjects lacking control over noise intensity. Noradrenaline and cortisol excretion and effort and discomfort ratings were consistent with the heart rate effect, but the differences between groups were not significant. With respect to the effects of I–E, the authors concluded that the results were consistent with the congruence–incongruence hypothesis; however, there were no significant differences between groups on any variable. Although I consider the assessment of locus of control after the interventions to be a suspect procedure, this appears to be a methodologically sound study. Nonetheless, it illustrates the pitfalls of not reading beyond the abstract and discussion of research reports. What are clearly null results were elevated (along with heart rate) to significant findings consistent with theoretical expectations.

Although they have never examined the role of individual difference variables such as locus of control, findings by Obrist and his associates (see Obrist, 1981) are consistent with a hypothesis stating that characteristics that increase active coping efforts do evoke greater sympathetically mediated cardiovascular changes. I describe Obrist's notion of active versus passive coping and one recent study in some detail because from a psychophysiological perspective his approach can serve as a model for the kinds of research that could be done with locus of control groups.

Obrist's group has shown that phasic heart rate increases seen during a classical conditioning procedure involving unavoidable shocks may be parasympathetically mediated, while similar increases during a signaled reaction-time task involving shocks that could be avoided by good performance are largely sympathetic (beta-adrenergic in origin). They have further demonstrated that tonic increases in heart rate, systolic blood pressure, and indirect measures of cardiac performance (e.g., carotid dP/dt) were larger during an unsignaled shock-avoidance reaction-time task than during the cold pressor test or viewing an erotic film, events in which the subject is involved passively rather than actively. Obrist hypothesized that providing the subject with control over an aversive stimulus by making it contingent on task performance leads the subject to become more engaged in coping with the task actively, which thus results in an enhancement of sympathetic activity.

Light and Obrist (1980) examined the effects of opportunity for control over task outcomes on cardiovascular outcomes using the unsignaled shock-avoidance reaction-time task which their previous research has shown to evoke substantial beta-adrenergically mediated increases in heart rate, systolic blood pressure, and cardiac performance. The effects of control over receipt of shock were directly assessed by using a yoked control design to match avoidance and no-avoidance subjects in terms of the nature of the stressful task and also in terms of the number and time of receipt of shocks. They also manipulated prior experience with the shock and availability of performance feedback. Further, Light and Obrist assessed subjects' beliefs about whether the shock was avoidable and how involved the subject felt and how hard he or she was trying at different points in the task. Such perceptions have rarely been assessed in the I–E research reviewed. The main finding of interest here was that opportunity to avoid shock (active coping) was found to evoke greater cardiovascular changes (greater increases in heart rate and systolic blood pressure; greater decreases in pulse transit time) than being passively exposed to shocks, and these effects did not diminish over the 34 unsignaled trials. (These physiological changes were assessed during intervals that were collapsed across anticipation, impact, and postevent periods.) It should be noted that the magnitude of the heart rate changes was probably greater than that found by Houston (1972), averaging 9.7 beats per minute in the avoidance group and 5.6 beats per minute in the nonavoidance condition.

Although these results are in conflict with DeGood's (1975), the authors pointed out that control was easy to execute in the DeGood study, whereas in the Obrist and Light study exercising control was more difficult and the subject was uncertain in advance about how successful his or her control efforts would be. Thus Light and Obrist suggested that the changes in cardiovascular activity (enhanced sympathetic response) observed in their avoidance subjects "should be viewed as a consequence of both the availability of control over shock and the fact that exercising that control (coping) was uncertain and effortful" (p. 249). Data consistent with this interpretation have been reported from other laboratories (e.g., Manuck, Harvey, Lechleter, & Neal, 1978). These researchers further acknowledged that efforts to cope with the task by trying to react quickly, even in the absence of the incentive of avoiding shock, may be partly responsible for the cardiovascular changes observed in all subjects during the task (since all subjects, regardless of task condition, reported trying hard to react fast). Obrist and his colleagues have pointed to the parellels between these cardiovascular changes and changes reported in studies of borderline and mild hypertension. Light and Obrist (1980), for example, concluded that this and other demonstrations that specific types of stressful events, particularly those involving opportunities for control, evoke cardiodynamic changes similar to those early hypertensive states, provide renewed support for the position that stress may indeed play an important role in the etiologic process of some hypertensive disorders [p. 251].

It is important to assess differences between internal- and external-oriented persons in tasks similar to those employed by Obrist and his colleagues. Multiple physiological measures should be employed, especially measures sensitive to beta-adrenergic influences, before a hypothesis that effort at control has deleterious physiological consequences among internals is given credence.

INFORMATION CONTROL

Information may at times engender control and was included by Thompson in her fourfold typology. The information provided to subjects about an anticipated aversive event has taken the form of a warning signal, information about the sensations they will experience, information about the procedures they are about to undergo, or information about the causes of an event. Harrell (1979) hypothesized that anticipatory physiological reactions to a signaled stressful event would be related to locus of control. Presumably internals and externals should use the signal information differentially and also differ in coping strategies. Twenty unselected male students were assigned to locus of control groups by a median split of responses to Rotter's I–E Scale. Following a 5-minute initial rest phase, subjects were informed that a mild tone would be followed by a louder noise that "some people find unpleasant." The stress phase sequence consisted of five trials of a 60 db warning tone followed by a 105 db burst of white noise (stress tone). A variable interstimulus interval ($M = 21$ seconds) separated the warning and stress tones. Intertrial interval varied from 1 to 2.5 minutes. Skin conductance, respiration, and cardiac rate were measured continuously.

Although both second-by-second heart rate and skin conductance were affected by the stress manipulation, locus of control was not related to anticipatory physiological activity. Harrell pointed out that no explicit instructions were given to control physiological or psychological reactions to the stressful noise, and suggested that "instructions to control the reactivity to stress may enhance the predictive efficacy of the locus of control measure" (p. 668). These negative results are not surprising given the relatively small sample sizes and the fact that the effects of a warning signal on stress are not clear (see Thompson, 1981).

RETROSPECTIVE AND COGNITIVE CONTROL

The two remaining types of control described by Thompson—retrospective and cognitive control—are probably most relevant to locus of control. Unfortunately, studies of these types, in which generalized locus of control and physiological activity were both measured, are practically nonexistent. Retrospective control refers to beliefs about the causes of a past event. The issue here is not feelings of control while experiencing an event, but attributions about the cause of the event once it has happened. Wortman (1976) assumes that attributing responsibility to oneself is a way of asserting control and preserving one's sense of personal control. She further proposed (e.g., Bulman & Wortman, 1977) that attributions of control over a past aversive event lead to lessened long-term stress reactions to the event. Unfortunately, these hypotheses have not been related to physiological activity. However, the effects of believing that one has a cognitive strategy that can mitigate the aversiveness of an event have received a great deal of theoretical and empirical attention, including assessment of multiple physiological measures. For example, cognitive control in the anticipatory period has been found to reduce both the self-report of anxiety and physiological arousal (e.g., Holmes & Houston, 1974). Positive effects of cognitive control have been found at impact and during the short-term postevent period, although the available physiological evidence is not extensive.

Several studies have examined the relative effectiveness of different types of strategies (e.g., avoidant and nonavoidant). The evidence is mixed both between and within different response systems, including the physiological, and the strategies may have different effects during different parts of the process of coping with a traumatic event. However, the evidence is clear that not all strategies are equally effective. Avoidance, for example, seems to have positive effects during the initial part of the process of coping with a stressor; nonavoidant strategies are more useful later on. Another way to reconcile the mixed results of avoidant and nonavoidant strategies was suggested by Averill, O'Brien, and de Witt (1977). In their study, vigilant subjects experienced less stress than nonvigilant subjects when shock was avoidable. However, vigilant subjects experienced more stress when shock was unavoidable. Thus it may be that the usefulness of a particular strategy depends on the situation: If vigilance has no chance of paying off, it arouses a stress reaction; if it may potentially pay off, it is useful. I predict that under many circumstances an internal-oriented person would adopt a vigilant coping strategy (see Sanders et al., 1976).

Although not directly comparable to the Averill et al. paradigm, a brief report by Bennett, Webb, and Withey (1977) is relevant here. These investigators examined the effects of locus of control on attempts to maintain performance at a motor task during the stress of body vibration at acclerated levels typical of cross-country vehicle movement. Subjects had to perform a tracking task in which meter fluctuations were controlled by movements of a foot peddle. Although the sample included only 12 male subjects, they were assessed during 14 30-minute sessions. Internal subjects showed significantly smaller peformance decrements under all levels and types of vibration. Although subjective stress was not assessed, there were higher overall levels of heart rate for internal subjects (but no differences in oxygen uptake). The authors concluded that the better performance on the part of internals during vibration stress occurred at greater physiological cost. These results are subject to the same interpretations as were presented earlier for Houston's study; however, they are another indication that, at least under some stress conditions, internals may evidence greater physiological arousal than externals.

Despite the fact that some cognitive strategies are more effective than others, and that their relative effects may depend on situational parameters, Thompson concluded that cognitive strategies generally have beneficial effects. It would therefore be useful and important for future research to examine these strategies and their effects on performance and physiology in internals and externals during different periods of an aversive event. One possibility would be to manipulate coping strategies through instructions and other training procedures, as is typically done in the situational control and clinical treatment literature. However, these manipulations could swamp any effects due to I–E because general beliefs are expected to affect appraisal, coping, physiological processes, and emotional impact in more ambiguous situations (see Folkman, Schaefer, & Lazarus, 1979).

Rosenbaum (1980b) related scores on his Self-Control Schedule (Rosenbaum, 1980a) to ability to tolerate a cold pressor. In the first experiment, subjects instructed to think of a pleasant event while exposed to a cold stressor tolerated the pain longer than a control group. In a second study, one experimental group spent 5 minutes in self-planning of strategies to cope with the impending pain, and a second group was merely informed of the effectiveness of self-control methods in coping with pain. Subjects in both groups did not show longer tolerance than subjects in a control condition. The most important finding was that high self-control subjects (who are similar to internals) consistently tolerated the cold pressor longer than low self-control subjects (who are similar to externals) across the various treatment conditions.

Self-control was also related to perceived coping ability. Thought diversion appeared to be the most effective method of increasing pain endurance and it was used predominantly by high self-control subjects. Thus the self-control scale predicted both effective strategies and the occurrence of coping. Unfortunately, physiological measures were not taken.

In Anderson's (1977) field study of businessmen whose organizations had been disrupted by natural disaster, it was found that externals, relative to internals, used more emotion-directed coping and less problem-solving coping. Such differences in coping strategies could be assessed in more controlled laboratory situations in which psychophysiological measures are recorded. Folkman and Lazarus (1980) recently developed the Ways of Coping Checklist, which describes a broad range of behavioral and cognitive coping strategies an individual might use in a specific stressful episode. It includes items from the domains of defensive coping, information seeking, problem solving, palliation, inhibition of action, direct actions and magical thinking. Although it was originally scored in terms of problem-focused and emotion-focused scales, factor analyses have since identified seven coping scales. Appraisal of the situation (e.g., "must accept," "could change or do something about it") is also assessed. In future I–E research, situations could be structured such that a palliative strategy to regulate the stress and distress reaction would be considered generally to be most adaptive, or in which a problem-solving or instrumental approach would be adaptive. Coping could be assessed retrospectively and related to physiological activity. In addition to assessing coping, physiological, and performance outcomes (where appropriate), a more complete picture of possible differences between internals and externals in the different aversive situations could be obtained by assessing appraisals, attributions about causes and consequences of the events, and perceptions about the effectiveness of coping strategies.

Another useful strategy for assessing coping and emotional reactions during critical periods in relation to physiological activity is to use concurrent assessment techniques such as the "think-aloud" and "private speech" techniques described by Meichenbaum and Butler (1980) in their cognitive ethology approach. Briefly, the experimenter asks the subject to verbalize all the thoughts and feelings he or she has while doing a task. This strategy has been used successfully in my laboratory in conjunction with psychophysiological measurement to discriminate between different "incubation of threat" conditions (Toner & Blankstein, 1981) and between high and low test-anxious students (Toner, 1982). Concurrent assessment might permit assessment of simultaneously or sequentially employed coping processes in relation to physiological activity (see Folkman *et al.*, 1979).

Strickland (1979) expressed concern that the internal-oriented person will attempt to maintain control and continue to be vigilant when tasks are difficult or events are beyond personal control, and that these effects will take "a toll in personal functioning" (p. 227)—including maladaptive physiological functioning. She cites Wortman and Brehm's (1975) conclusion: "When an organism is confronted by outcomes that are truly uncontrollable, the most adaptive response may be to give up" (p. 331). I submit that the more adaptive responses would be to attempt to regulate the emotional response and physiological reactions, if excessive, engendered in the situation. For example, if a subject is instructed that he or she will receive a shock at the end of a waiting period and there is no instrumental response (short of fleeing the situation) to avoid the aversive stimulus, then it may be adaptive to focus on emotional coping, which could include control of physiological reactions, in order to master, tolerate, reduce, or minimize reactions to the aversive situation.

Locus of control and perceived efficacy are clearly relevant here. As Folkman *et al.* observed, "to disbelieve in one's own efficacy should generate passivity and disengagement, and at its extreme should be associated with a sense of helplessness and hopelessness, which are in turn linked to depression" (p. 286). This is not to say that there are not circumstances under which a mismatch of coping efforts and situational demands will occur for internals relative to externals. Folkman *et al.* (1979) speak in terms of "goodness of fit" between coping strategy and other agendas (goals, personal values, thinking styles, etc.) in the person's life. However, the available empirical evidence does not clearly support the idea that internals show a misfit of coping and physiological adaptation in uncontrollable situations. Nonetheless, it is possible that internals will make an effort after control over an aversive stimulus even though such control is not possible and that this tendency to exert control will have negative or adverse physiological consequences. Thus, at a theoretical level the goodness of fit among coping efforts, task demands and physiological and emotional consequences must be recognized. Janis and Mann have also given much attention to the conditions affecting "decision making" under stress and have written about "hypervigilance" which they regard as counterproductive. Effective control of a situation must be accomplished while "keeping the internal environment sufficiently close to homeostatic balance to maintain bodily health despite having to mobilize to cope instrumentally" (Folkman *et al.*, 1979, p. 292).

PHYSIOLOGICAL CONTROL

Perhaps we can add a further type of control to Thompson's ty-pology. Consistent with the recent interest in physiological self-regu-lation, we can explore the effects on stress of having a physiological response that can affect an aversive event. Although it might be argued that physiological control could be subsumed under cognitive or be-havioral control, Thompson did not include the available studies in her review. The rationale for a psychophysiological approach is, of course, to remove or reduce the physiological arousal that accompanies stress-ful situations. For example, a few studies have examined the effects of physical or psychological stress on heart rate control performance (e.g., Clemens & Shattock, 1979; Goldstein, Ross, & Brady, 1977; Sirota, Schwartz, & Shapiro, 1974, 1976; Victor, Mainardi, & Shapiro, 1978). Although there are methodological problems with most of these stud-ies, the general conclusion to be drawn is that subjects can regulate heart rate during both psychological and physiological stress. (The fact that significant decreases in heart rate are observed in these stress stud-ies may be related to the fact that an elevated heart rate is typically produced by the stress manipulation. Thus the biological constraints due to a low resting heart rate, which is very much a problem with studies of heart rate slowing under resting conditions, are no longer a factor. As stated previously, it is under these conditions that we should expect any differences to emerge between internals and externals in ability to slow heart rate.)

Breathing at a regulated lower rate may also be an effective and efficient physiological control technique. For example, Harris, Katkin, Lick, and Habberfield (1976) reported that subjects could reduce elec-trodermal responses to shock threat after only 10 minutes of training at reducing respiratory rate using a light-pacing stimulus. McCaul, Sol-omon, and Holmes (1979) reported that subjects exposed to slow-paced respiration showed less physiological arousal (finger pulse volume lev-els and skin conductance levels) to a shock threat than subjects who breathed at a normal rate and subjects in an attention-control condi-tion. Burish and Schwartz (1980) conducted an important study of EMG biofeedback in relation to stress. In the first phase, subjects received biofeedback training or were not trained, and half the subjects in each condition were threatened with electric shocks during the training pe-riods. Although the biofeedback training was effective in reducing fron-tal EMG levels and worry about the shock, it was not effective in reducing other measures of physiological arousal, or the perceived painfulness of the shock. Results of a second phase provided evidence that the effects would transfer to a stressful nontraining situation (frontal EMG and self-reported arousal). However, the specificity of the results led the authors to conclude that EMG biofeedback may be of limited usefulness as a general stress-coping procedure.

Nonetheless, a number of the aforementioned studies of physiological self-regulation under stress suggest that physiological control may also influence cognitive–emotional reactions to the task (e.g., McCaul et al., 1979). The effects on emotional reactions may, however, be mediated by cognitions about the association between physiological activity and affect. The notion that perceived physiological control may be a more important determinant of emotional experience than the occurrence of actual physiological change is supported by the effects of bogus physiological feedback on the appraisal of emotional experience (see Hirschman, Young, & Nelson, 1979).

In none of these studies were effects due to locus of control examined. In the previously cited study by Stoffer et al. (1979) on voluntary temperature control and cold stress tolerance, there were no differences between internals and externals either during temperature control, at rest, or during cold pressor. However, there was also no indication that previous temperature training influenced blood pressure, heart rate, subjective pain, or immersion time during the cold pressor test (no-feedback conditions) for the group as a whole. Although the psychophysiological response to thermal stress was generally similar between the two groups, heart rate tended to be higher during immersion in the internal group. In their study of perceived psychophysiological control, Glass and Levy (1982) found no evidence, on five of six measures, to support their prediction that self-control efficacy subjects would be more successful on a cold pressor task relative to self-control inefficacy subjects. Recall, however, that this study did not directly assess self-efficacy expectations. It is possible that subjects did not view the cold pressor task as an opprotunity to exert control.

Harrell (1980) tested the effects of locus of control and brief relaxation training in a signaled stress experiment. The methodology was similar to that employed by Harrell (1979), except that subjects received only three presentations of the stressful sequence in an initial phase. Subsequently, half of the subjects practiced progressive relaxation for 14 minutes while the remaining subjects were allowed to relax. During the final phase, subjects who had received progressive relaxation were instructed to use the technique to control stress reactions to the tones. Heart rate was assessed for the 8 seconds before and after the warning and stressful tones. Heart rate during training was not reported. The reduction in heart rate from the initial stressful phase to the final phase was greater for subjects who had received relaxation training, which, however, did not produce greater reduction in the ratings of the general aversiveness of the tones. Heart rate tended to be more rapid in internals ($r = .38$, $p < .05$). Although I–E was not related to the decrease in heart rate that occurred during stress after relaxation training, there was a tendency for the decrease in subjective ratings of aversiveness to be greater among internal subjects. Harrell concluded that "the coping strategies of individuals with internal locus of control may not facilitate the cultivation of reduced heart-rate reactions to stress through progressive relaxation even though subject ratings might suggest the technique is being utilized effectively" (p. 474). These findings are not unexpected given the relatively small sample size and brief training.

It would be valuable to determine the physiological coping skills of internal- and external-oriented persons during aversive situations as a function of autonomic and somatic control training. Further, since there seems to be some evidence that internals relative to externals can effectively control some aspects of physiological activity on instructions without feedback, it would be useful to determine whether internals could demonstrate physiological control under stress, such as in anticipation of an unavoidable aversive stimulus, when simply instructed to control their physiology.

LEARNED HELPLESSNESS AND TYPE A BEHAVIOR

Learned helplessness and Type A behavior appear to show a conceptual similarity to the locus of control construct. In a learned helplessness study, Hiroto (1974) reported that externals displayed greater performance deficits after exposure to aversive stimulation than did internals (although results showed no significant interaction between I–E and the nature of the pretreatment). Miller and Seligman (1975) did not report differences on this variable. However, given Wortman and Brehm's (1975) suggestion that initial expectations of control affect responses to uncontrollability, it might be expected that individuals who differ in locus of control would react differently to helplessness training. Pittman and Pittman (1979) hypothesized that internals would exhibit more pronounced reactance effects when given mild experiences with uncontrollability, but be affected more severely by helplessness training once they realize that they truly have no control (due to incongruence between expectations and the uncontrollable situation). These predictions were examined by exposing highly selected groups of internals and externals (gender unspecified) to one of several levels of helplessness training (noncontingent reinforcement on a series of concept formation problems). The internals exhibited greater performance deficits and reported greater depression under high helplessness than did externals. In the low helplessness condition, internals tended to perform better than control subjects, whereas externals tended to perform worse. Pittman and Pittman pointed to the need to determine the actual critical differences between internals and externals that account for their different responses to uncontrollability. They further suggested the utility of employing I–E scales or subscales specifically designed to tap expectations of control versus habitual reactions to uncontrollability.

Albert and Geller (1978) also investigated the relationship between locus of control and learned helplessness in two experiments. They found greater effects due to learned helplessness in externals.

It appears, then, that I–E is related to helplessness training but that the direction of the effect may be a function of the severity or duration of helplessness training. Assuming that replicable differences between internals and externals are found in the cognitive, motivational, and emotional deficits due to learned helplessness, it would be of interest to examine physiological differences. In fact, physiological assessment during pretraining may help to predict the direction of the effect. Several studies have investigated the emotional aspects of learned helplessness through physiological measures. Gatchel and Procter (1976) and Krantz, Glass, and Snyder (1974, Experiment 1) reported that subjects exposed to learned helplessness training conditions (inescapable noise) showed lower levels of electrodermal activity, presumed to relate to decreased task involvement and motivation. Gatchel, McKinney, and Koebernick (1977) used a similar paradigm to determine whether the physiological correlates of learned helplessness are similar to the response patterns found in mildly depressed college students. Although there was similarity in performance impairment, the findings indicated that learned helplessness was associated with less phasic skin conductance responding, whereas depression was associated with greater responding to uncontrollable aversive events. Given the reported relationship between depression and externality (see Lefcourt, 1976), it would be interesting to replicate the Gatchel et al. study with internals and externals as subjects and multiple physiological measures under high versus low helplessness training.

The Type A behavior pattern is an epidemiological construct described by Friedman and Rosenman (1974) as an independent risk factor for coronary heart disease. This status has now been firmly established (see Matthews, 1982). The major facets or core elements of the behavior pattern are extremes of aggressiveness, easily aroused hostility, a sense of time urgency, and competitive achievement striving. It is a set of overt behaviors that is elicited from susceptible individuals by appropriate environmental circumstances, such as challenge and stresses.

The most systematic and comprehensive effort to conceptualize Type A behavior comes from the work of Glass and his associates (e.g., Glass, 1977). Glass believes that the behavior pattern represents an attempt by Type A persons to assert and maintain control over uncontrollable events that are perceived as potentially harmful. When faced with a stressful event, they should struggle to control that event; however, if their control efforts meet with repeated failure, they give up responding and act helpless. Thus, Glass's uncontrollability approach suggests that Type A behaviors reflect a specific way of coping with stressful aspects of the environment (see Matthews, 1982, for a critique of the uncontrollability approach).

Strickland (1978, 1979) has drawn a parallel between the control aspect of Type A behavior described by Glass and locus of control: "Type A individuals . . . sound strikingly like internals" (1978, p. 1195). She states further (1979, p. 222) that "it is difficult to align the possible adaptive strategies of internals with tragic consequences of heart disease, which apparently affects overstriving, overcontrolling persons." It is "the puzzle of relating I–E to Type A behavior" (p. 227), in conjunction with the sparse evidence of heightened reactivity in internals under some stimulus conditions, which leads her to express concern that internals' attempts to maintain control takes a toll in personal functioning. In fact, while extreme, chronic internal control is undoubtedly maladaptive, the limited available evidence on the behavior of internals under stress—including physiological behavior—leads me to the conclusion that internals' behavior is generally more adaptive and positive than externals' (but see Gilbert and Mangelsdorff, 1979, for a position similar to Strickland's).

Although Glass (1977) reported a small but significant correlation between the Jenkins Activity Survey (a self-report measure of Pattern A) and the I–E scale ($r = -.17$, $p < .01$) suggesting that As may have higher expectations of environmental control than Bs (the opposite of Type A), more recent studies (e.g., Kennan & McBain, 1979; Nowack & Sassenrath, 1980) suggest that Type A behavior is related more to externality than to internality. Perhaps more important, an examination of the relatively extensive literature on the psychological nature of Type A behavior (Matthews, 1982) suggests few parallels with the comparable literature on internal-oriented persons (Lefcourt, 1976, 1982; Phares, 1976). Nonetheless, the reader who is interested in conducting psychophysiological investigations of internal–external locus of control and stress would be well-advised to examine the relevant Type A literature, especially with respect to the tasks and stressors used in the I–E research (shock, shock threat, cold pressor, cognitive tasks, etc.). Psychophysiological investigations of Type A behavior have employed intrapersonal and interpersonal competitive tasks (e.g., playing a TV computer handball game for a prize; stressful interviews, etc.), and differences emerge when stressors are personally relevant and challenging (see Matthews, 1982). Of course, the most valid stressors to relate to physiological differences between internals and externals are those that occur in the real-world environment (see Epstein, 1976).

SUMMARY AND EVALUATION

Although this chapter began with some dramatic examples of adverse physiological consequences (including death) presumed to be due to perceived or actual loss of control, there is very little evidence to support a hypothesis that persons whose generalized perception of control is either external or internal show superior or inferior physiological adaptation in the kinds of stressful situations encountered in the research laboratory. On balance, the limited available evidence leads me to conclude that my working hypothesis that internals show superior psychological and physiological adaptation in such stressful situations is still reasonable. Although some studies suggest that internals show greater reactivity in heart rate in situations that require active coping, there is little evidence that this response represents a significant physiological cost (although it may). Furthermore, I conclude that there is little evidence to support the incongruence hypothesis in stressful situations. However, in both cases much additional research should be done to corroborate these tentative conclusions. I have tried to point out some of the shortcomings of the available research and some directions for future research. Many of these suggestions are highly speculative; however, I hope that some of these ideas will stimulate productive research. From a psychophysiological perspective, future research in this area should take advantage of the building blocks of past research that has used multiple physiological measures, especially those that may be more sensitive to sympathetic influence. From the perspective of various cognitive theories of perceived control, workers should employ strategies and tools that will permit a better understanding of the appraisal processes and coping efforts, and the physiological consequences of these processes, of internals and externals in various situations of controllable and uncontrollable stress.

Conclusions

This review has concentrated on areas of interaction between the theoretical and empirical research on perceived control and psychophysiology. The primary focus has been on generalized expectancies for control as assessed by Rotter's Internal–External Locus of Control Scale and related measures.

The hope was expressed that a psychophysiological strategy would provide new insights into and greater understanding of the role of the I–E dimension in human experience. Although the list of the most striking contributions is probably short (I leave it for the reader to decide), there are some hints that a promising start has been made. Nonetheless, it seems prudent to conclude that the use of psychophysiological measures and principles has not yet provided deep insights into the processes that differentiate between internals and externals. Although some locus of control researchers will want to beware of psychophysiologists bearing gifts (the converse is also true!), it is very clear that many of the weaknesses of the reviewed studies relate to problems of conceptualizing and measuring locus of control.

A major methodological problem has to do with the selection of subjects and with the measurement of I–E expectancies. It was assumed that if physiological activity is related to perceived control, then study of persons at the extremes of the control continuum should maximize chances of observing relationships. Although some investigators used relatively strict selection procedures, many relied on a median split of the distribution of I–E scores for the experimental sample. The latter procedure probably taps a relatively narrow range of locus of control beliefs and probably contributes to appreciable suppression of I–E differences, especially in some of the more highly structured situations. This selection strategy, combined with failure to assess the reliability of I–E measurement (only one unpublished study assessed reliability *prior to* experimental manipulation), coupled with the extremely small sample sizes in some studies, probably precludes finding significant relationships or at least contributes to the disparate results. The concept of the defensive external appears to be an important one; however, with one or two exceptions, it has been virtually ignored by the research reviewed. Furthermore, only a single investigation examined the middle range of the I–E scale (Wong and Sproule's bilocals). Although this is not surprising given the past history of locus of control research, it is disconcerting to find that researchers are not following up on repeated recommendations to examine the moderates. This strategy may be particularly relevant in the area of stress and coping.

Although many studies used only males as subjects, a few used only females, and others used a mixed group of females and males or failed to specify the gender of the sample used. Since gender differences appear to be important in locus of control measurement and research (e.g., Nowicki, Duke, & Crouch, 1978; Strickland & Haley, 1980) and gender has been shown to be a significant variable in a number of psychophysiological studies, gender should be equated across groups and both males and females should be analyzed independently in future psychophysiological research on locus of control.

Rosenthal and Rosnow (1969) may have overstated the case when they wrote pessimistically about the existing science of human behavior as being largely a science of undergraduate psychology student volunteers. However, their criticisms ring true in the present case. Generalizability of findings should be assessed with other populations, such as older people. It is possible that locus of control will interact with age-related situational variables and biological changes (see Marsh & Thompson, 1977; Schulz, 1982).

Although research with the Rotter scale should be continued, we have seen that some of the more specific assessment scales or subscales are contributing to more precise prediction. Scales that are related more directly to self-control appear to be useful, although with few exceptions they have not received extensive use, and Rotter's I–E Scale is rarely compared with the newer scales for relative predictive power. It is interesting to note that almost all the research on heart rate control used Rotter's scale, and most of the research on EMG control used the Nowicki–Strickland scale. Development of a generalized expectancy scale specific to bodily control in stressful situations or physiological self-control is recommended.

Although many researchers attempted to assess the influence of different situations or types of tasks (usually as a test of the congruence–incongruence hypothesis), and some investigators have attempted to manipulate expectancies by instructions, subjects' expectancies are rarely assessed directly in different experimental conditions. Psychophysiological techniques and strategies can make significant contributions to the understanding of the I–E construct, but they are best used with cognitive and behavioral measures as part of a comprehensive assessment. Efficacy and outcome expectations, evaluations of task

importance, and appraisal and coping processes are obviously important and should be measured in many investigations. Although the mediating power of locus of control is assumed to reside in both its
cognitive and motivational qualities, "neither of which are sufficient
but both of which are necessary" (Ducette & Wolk, 1973, p. 426), in only
one of the reviewed studies was there an effort to evaluate reinforcement or goal value. As Phares (1976, p, 176) stated, "studying behavior
while assessing I–E status leaves out at least 70 per cent of the necessary predictive formula. This is analogous to swatting at tennis balls
with only 4 strings in the racquet." It is easy to be critical and suggest
that some of the players in the game are trying to win with faulty rac-
quets (or other damaged equipment)!

The relative shortage of really good work linking psychophysiological principles and measures to the locus of control construct is not
too surprising. The technical sophistication required and expense involved to collect, analyze, and interpret psychophysiological data may
stand as barriers to many locus of control researchers. We have witnessed many problems related to analysis and interpretation. Control
conditions were often inadequate, and baseline assessment and assessment of change in physiological activity has been especially problematic. Most investigators have failed to consider the possible
influence of initial levels (law of initial values) even though that failure
may contribute to discrepant results (see Kinsman & Staudenmayer,
1978).

Choice of method for quantifying responses also places limitations
on the interpretation of results (O'Gorman, 1977). Although it is generally agreed that monitoring one physiological system (e.g., skin conductance) is insufficient for assessing physiological reactivity, the vast
majority of studies of I–E and physiological processes have used only
one or two physiological variables. Thus drawing conclusions about
how several measures are interrelated (response patterning) is not yet
possible. Electrodermal and cardiovascular (heart rate and blood pressure) measures have been most commonly employed in the studies reviewed. EEG measures were employed only in the context of a
biofeedback task, and evoked cortical responses were not examined in
any reviewed study. Some studies are of relatively high quality; others
appear to reflect naivete about recent developments in psychophysiology.

Some progress is being made on several fronts, including assessment of resting levels, attention and cognitive processes, and regulation
of physiological activity, either as part of a biofeedback or physiological
self-control strategy or in relation to more traditional relaxation ap-

proaches. However, the research on stress and coping is disappointing in terms of both quality and quantity, especially in relation to its importance. Although previous reviewers have suggested that internals may cope with specific stresses at some physiological cost, the sparse data were interpreted as consistent with superior physiological adaptation in internals. However, the appropriate studies have not been conducted. A redirection of research investment is clearly called for. One glaring omission is in the area of susceptibility to social influence, attitudes, and interpersonal interactions. Despite the fact that locus of control is very much a social construct and that there is an extensive and recent literature on social psychophysiology (e.g., Cacioppo, 1982; Cacioppo & Petty, 1983; Schwartz & Shapiro, 1973; Shapiro & Schwartz, 1970), very little directly relevant research has been done. Leavitt and Donovan (1979) used heart rate to index the effects of attentional factors in developing mother–infant reciprocity. They reported that external women responded to continued eye contact encounters with heart rate acceleration. Clearly, psychophysiological investigations of internals and externals in more complex social psychological contexts merits study.

There is a clear need for more integration of research into Rotter's social learning theory and related theoretical frameworks of perceived control. By the same token, there needs to be more integration of psychophysiological principles and techniques. To quote reviewers from a different area, "a pious (if somewhat hackneyed) plea for interdisciplinary collaboration would seem to be in order" (Craik & Blankstein, 1975, p. 412).

This review is peppered with speculations, and in many cases I have probably demonstrated my own naivete. However, it is hoped that this chapter will provide some structure and directions for future research. Despite my sermonizing about the unfulfilled promise, it is important to continue this line of inquiry in order to improve our understanding of the fundamental psychophysiological differences between internals and externals.

References

Abramson, L. Y., Seligman, M. E. P., & Teasdale, J. D. Learned helplessness in humans: Critique and reformulation. *Journal of Abnormal Psychology*, 1978, *87*, 49–74.

Achterberg, J., McGraw, P., & Lawlis, G. F. Rheumatoid arthritis: A study of relaxation and temperature biofeedback training as an adjunctive therapy. *Biofeedback and Self-Regulation*, 1981, *6*, 207–223.

Albert, M., & Geller, E. S. Perceived control as a mediator of learned helplessness. *American Journal of Psychology*, 1978, *91*, 389–399.

Alexander, A. A. Psychophysiological concepts of psychopathology. In N. S. Greenfield & R. A. Sternbach (Eds.), *Handbook of psychophysiology*. New York: Holt, Rinehart & Winston, 1972.

Allen, J. K., & Blanchard, C. B. Biofeedback-based stress management training with a population of business managers. *Biofeedback and Self-Regulation*, 1980, 5, 427–438.

Anderson, C. R. Locus of control, coping behavior, and performance in a stress setting: A longitudinal study. *Journal of Applied Psychology*, 1977, 62, 446–451.

Andreassi, J. L. *Psychophysiology: Human behavior and physiological response*. New York: Oxford University Press, 1980.

Averill, J. Personal control over aversive stimuli and its relationship to stress. *Psychological Bulletin*, 1973, 80, 286–303.

Averill, J. R., O'Brien, L., & de Witt, G. The influence of response effectiveness on the preference for warning and on psychophysiological stress reactions. *Journal of Personality*, 1977, 45, 395–418.

Averill, J. R., & Opton, E. M., Jr. Psychophysiological assessment: Rationale and problems. In P. McReynolds (Ed.), *Advances in psychological assessment* (Vol. 1). Palo Alto, Ca.: Science & Behavior Books, 1968.

Baker, E. K. The relationship between locus of control and psychotherapy: A review of the literature. *Psychotherapy: Theory, Research & Practice*, 1979, 16, 351–362.

Bandura, A. Self-efficacy: Toward a unifying theory of behavioral change. *Psychological Review*, 1977, 84, 191–215.

Beatty, J. Task-evoked pupillary responses, processing load, and the structure of processing resources. *Psychological Bulletin*, 1982, 91, 276–292.

Bell, I. R., & Schwartz, G. E. *Individual factors in bidirectional voluntary control and reactivity in human heart rate*. Paper presented at the meeting of the Western Psychological Association, Anaheim, California, April 1973.

Bell, I. R., & Schwartz, G. E. Voluntary control and reactivity of human heart rate. *Psychophysiology*, 1975, 12, 339–348.

Bennett, M. D., Webb, R., & Withey, W. R. Personality, performance and physiological cost during vibration. *Journal of Physiology*, 1977, 270, 75P.

Berggren, T., Öhman, A., & Fredrikson, M. Locus of control and habituation of the electrodermal orienting response to nonsignal and signal stimuli. *Journal of Personality and Social Psychology*, 1977, 35, 708–716.

Bernstein, A. S. To what does the orienting response respond? *Psychophysiology*, 1969, 6, 338–351.

Bernstein, A. S. Electrodermal lability and the OR: Reply to O'Gorman and further exposition of the "significance hypothesis." *Australian Journal of Psychology*, 1973, 25, 147–154.

Bernstein, D. A., & Borkovec, T. D. *Progressive relaxation training: A manual for the helping professions*. Champaign, Il.: Research Press, 1973.

Bettelheim, B. *The informed heart*. New York: The Free Press, 1960.

Blankstein, K. R., & Egner, K. Relationship of the locus of control construct to the self-control of heart rate. *Journal of General Psychology*, 1977, 97, 291–306.

Blankstein, K. R., Zimmerman, J., & Egner, K. Within-subjects control designs and voluntary bidirectional control of cardiac rate: Methodological comparison between pre-experimental and pre-trial baselines. *Journal of General Psychology*, 1976, 95, 161–175.

Bohlin, G. Monotonous stimulation, sleep onset, and habituation of the orienting reaction. *Electroencephalography and Clinical Neurophysiology*, 1971, 31, 593–601.

Borkovec, T. D., & Sides, J. K. Critical procedural variables related to the physiological effects of progressive relaxation: A review. *Behaviour Research and Therapy*, 1979, 17, 119–125.

Bourgeois, A., Levenson, H., & Wagner, C. Success on a biofeedback task: Effects of congruence–incongruence between locus of control and psychological differentiation. *Journal of Personality Assessment*, 1980, *44*, 487–492.

Brener, J. Factors influencing the specificity of voluntary cardiovascular control. In L. V. DiCara (Ed.), *Limbic and autonomic nervous system research*. New York: Plenum, 1974.

Brener, J. Visceral perception. In J. Beatty & J. Legewie (Eds.), *Biofeedback and behavior*. New York: Plenum, 1977.

Brolund, J. W., & Schallow, J. R. The effects of reward on occipital alpha facilitation by biofeedback. *Psychophysiology*, 1976, *13*, 236–241.

Bulman, R. J., & Wortman, C. Attributions of blame and coping in the "real world": Severe accident victims react to their lot. *Journal of Personality and Social Psychology*, 1977, *35*, 351–363.

Burish, T. G., & Schwartz, D. P. EMG biofeedback training, transfer of training, and coping with stress. *Journal of Psychosomatic Research*, 1980, *24*, 85–96.

Byrne, D. Repression–sensitization as a dimension of personality. In B. A. Maher (Ed.), *Progress in experimental personality research* (Vol. 1). New York: Academic Press, 1964.

Cacioppo, J. T. Social psychophysiology: A classic perspective and contemporary approach. *Psychophysiology*, 1982, *19*, 241–251.

Cacioppo, J. T., & Petty, R. E. (Eds.), *Social psychophysiology: A sourcebook*. New York: Guilford, 1983.

Cannon, W. B. "Voodoo" death. *American Anthropologist*, 1942, *44*, 169–181.

Carlson, J. G. Locus of control and frontal electromyographic response training. *Biofeedback and Self-Regulation*, 1977, *2*, 259–271.

Carlson, J. G. Locus of control and frontal muscle action potential. In N. Birbaumer & H. Kimmel (Eds.), *Biofeedback and self-regulation*. Hillsdale, N.J.: Erlbaum, 1979.

Carlson, J. G. Some concepts of perceived control and their relationship to bodily self-control. *Biofeedback and Self-Regulation*, 1982, *7*, 341–375.

Carlson, J. G., & Feld, J. L. Role of incentives in the training of the frontal EMG relaxation response. *Journal of Behavioral Medicine*, 1978, *1*, 427–436.

Carlson, J. G., & Feld, J. L. Expectancies of reinforcement control in biofeedback and cognitive performance. *Biofeedback and Self-Regulation*, 1981, *6*, 79–91.

Carlson, R. H., Bridges, C. V., & Williams, P. S. Effects of Health Locus of Control and health value upon EMG biofeedback training. *Perceptual and Motor Skills*, 1982, *54*, 111–118.

Carroll, D. Cardiac perception and cardiac control. *Biofeedback and Self-Regulation*, 1977, *2*, 349–369.

Carroll, D. Voluntary heart rate control: The role of individual differences. *Biological Psychology*, 1979, *8*, 137–157.

Carroll, D., & Anastasiades, P. The behavioral significance of heart rate: The Laceys' hypothesis. *Biological Psychology*, 1978, *7*, 249–275.

Christie, M. J., & Todd, J. L. Experimenter–subject–situational interactions. In P. H. Venables & M. J. Christie (Eds.), *Research in psychophysiology*. London: Wiley, 1975.

Claridge, G. S. Psychophysiological techniques. In P. Mittler (Ed.), *The psychological assessment of mental and physical handicaps*. London: Methuen, 1970.

Clarke, A. M., Michie, P. T., Andreasen, A. G., Viney, L. L., & Rosenthal, R. Expectancy effects in a psychophysiological experiment. *Physiological Psychology*, 1976, *4*, 137–144.

Clemens, W. J., & Shattock, R. J. Voluntary heart rate control during static muscular effort. *Psychophysiology*, 1979, *16*, 327–332.

Cohen, J. Approximate power and sample size determination for common one-sample

198   :   KIRK R. BLANKSTEIN

and two-sample hypothesis tests. *Educational and Psychological Measurement*, 1970, *30*, 811–831.

Cox, D. J., Freundlich, A., & Meyer, R. G. Differential effectiveness of electromyograph feedback, verbal relaxation instructions, and medication placebo with tension headaches. *Journal of Consulting and Clinical Psychology*, 1975, *43*, 892–898.

Craik, F. I. M., & Blankstein, K. R. Psychophysiology and human memory. In P. H. Venables & M. J. Christie (Eds.), *Research in psychophysiology*. London: Wiley, 1975.

Cromwell, R. L., Butterfield, E. C., Brayfield, F. M., & Curry, J. L. *Acute myocardial infarction: Reaction and recovery*. St. Louis: Mosby, 1977.

Cuthbert, B., Kristeller, J., Simons, R., Hodes, R., & Lang, P. J. Strategies of arousal control: Biofeedback, meditation, and motivation. *Journal of Experimental Psychology: General*, 1981, *110*, 518–546.

Dale, A., Anderson, D., Klions, H., Tane, K., & Blankstein, K. Biofeedback and relaxation effects in electromyographic biofeedback training: A methodological note. *Perceptual and Motor Skills*, 1979, *48*, 848–850.

Dale, A., Anderson, D. E., DeGood, D., & Blankstein, K. *Physiological habituation as a function of anxiety, coronary proneness, field dependence and locus of control*. Presented at the Annual Meeting of the Canadian Psychological Association, Quebec City, 1979.

Davidson, R. J., & Schwartz, G. E. The psychobiology of relaxation and related states: A multi-process theory. In D. I. Mostofsky (Ed.), *Behavior control and modification of physiological activity*. Englewood Cliffs, N.J.: Prentice–Hall, 1976.

Davis, W. L., & Phares, E. J. Internal external control as a determinant of information seeking in a social influence situation. *Journal of Personality*, 1967, *35*, 547–561.

DeGood, D. E. Cognitive control factors in vascular stress responses. *Psychophysiology*, 1975, *12*, 399–401.

DeGood, D. E., & Valle, R. S. A state–trait analysis of alpha density and personality variables in a normal population. *Journal of Clinical Psychology*, 1975, *31*, 624–631.

Di Nardo, P. A., & Raymond, J. B. Locus of control and attention during meditation. *Journal of Consulting and Clinical Psychology*, 1979, *47*, 1136–1137.

Ducette, J., & Wolk, S. Cognitive and motivational correlates of generalized expectancies for control. *Journal of Personality and Social Psychology*, 1973, *26*, 420–426.

Duffy, E. The psychological significance of the concept of "arousal" or "activation." *Psychological Review*, 1957, *64*, 265–275.

Duffy, E. *Activation and behavior*. New York: Wiley, 1962.

Edelberg, R. Electrodermal recovery rate, goal-orientation, and aversion. *Psychophysiology*, 1972, *9*, 512–520.

Elliott, R. The significance of heart rate for behavior: A critique of Lacey's hypothesis. *Journal of Personality and Social Psychology*, 1972, *22*, 398–409.

Elliott, R. The motivational significance of heart rate. In P. A. Obrist, A. H. Black, J. Brener, & L. V. DiCara (Eds.), *Cardiovascular psychophysiology: Current issues in response mechanisms, biofeedback, and methodology*. Chicago: Aldine, 1974.

Epstein, L. H. Psychophysiological measurement in assessment. In H. Hersen & A. S. Bellack (Eds.), *Behavioral Assessment: A practical handbook*. Oxford: Pergamon, 1976.

Eysenck, H. J. *The biological basis of personality*. Springfield, Il.: Thomas, 1967.

Favaro, P., & Pye, D. *Individual differences in voluntary heart rate control: Physiological, personality and cognitive concomitants*. Paper presented at the meeting of the Society for Psychophysiological Research, Cincinnati, Ohio, October 1979.

Feldt, L. S. The use of extreme groups to test for a relationship. *Psychometrica*, 1961, *26*, 307–316.

Folkman, A., & Lazarus, R. S. An analysis of coping in a middle-aged community sample. *Journal of Health and Social Behavior*, 1980, *21*, 219–239.

Folkman, A., Schaefer, C., & Lazarus, R. S. Cognitive processes as mediators of stress and coping. In V. Hamilton & D. M. Warburton (Eds.), *Human stress and cognition: An information-processing approach*. London: Wiley, 1979.

Fotopoulos, S. Internal *vs.* external control: Increase of heart rate by thinking under feedback and no-feedback conditions (Doctoral dissertation, University of Kansas, 1970). *Dissertation Abstracts International*, 1971, *31A*, 3703–3704. (University Microfilms No. 70–25, 335) (a)

Fotopoulos, S. *Locus of control and the voluntary control of heart rate*. Paper presented at the Annual Meeting of the Biofeedback Research Society, New Orleans, Louisiana, 1970. (b)

Fotopoulos, S., & Binegar, G. A. Differences in baseline and volitional control of EEG (8–12 Hz and 13–20 Hz), EMG and skin temperature: Internal vs. external orientation. *Biofeedback and Self-Regulation*, 1976, *1*, 357. (Abstract)

Fotopoulos, S. S., Cook, M. R., & Larsen, L. S. *Skin temperature baseline and internal vs. external locus of control*. Paper presented at the Annual Meeting of the Society for Psychophysiological Research, Toronto, 1975.

Freedman, R., & Papsdorf, J. D. Biofeedback and progressive relaxation treatment of sleep-onset insomnia: A controlled, all-night investigation. *Biofeedback and Self-Regulation*, 1976, *1*, 253–271.

Friedman, E. P., Cleveland, S. E., & Baer, P. E. Heart rate control following myocardial infarction. *American Journal of Clinical Biofeedback*, 1980, *3*, 35–41.

Friedman, M., & Rosenman, R. *Type A behavior and your heart*. New York: Knopf, 1974.

Furedy, J. J. Operational, analogical and genuine definitions of psychophysiology. *International Journal of Psychophysiology*, 1983, *1*, (in press).

Furedy, J. J., & Arabian, J. M. A Pavlovian psychophysiological perspective on the OR: The facts of the matter. In H. D. Kimmel, E. H. Van Olst, & J. F. Orlebeke (Eds.). *The orienting reflex in humans*. Hillsdale, New Jersey: Erlbaum, 1979.

Furedy, J. J., & Riley, D. M. Classical and operant conditioning in the enhancement of biofeedback: Specifics and speculations. In L. White and B. Tursky (Eds.). *Clinical biofeedback: Efficacy and mechanisms*. New York: Guilford, 1982.

Gale, A., Coles, M., Kline, P., & Penfold, V. Extraversion–introversion, neuroticism and the EEG: Basal and response measures during habituation of the orienting response. *British Journal of Psychology*, 1971, *63*, 533–542.

Gale, A. The psychophysiology of individual differences: Studies of extraversion and the EEG. In D. Kline (Ed.) *New approaches in psychological measurement*. London: Wiley, 1973.

Gantt, W. H. Cardiovascular component of the conditional reflex to pain, food and other stimuli. *Physiological Reviews*, 1960, *40*, 266–291.

Gatchel, R. J. Change over training sessions of relationship between locus of control and voluntary heart rate control. *Perceptual and Motor Skills*, 1975, *40*, 424–426.(a)

Gatchel, R. J. Locus of control and voluntary heat-rate change. *Journal of Personality Assessment*, 1975, *39*, 634–638.(b)

Gatchel, R. J., McKinney, M. E., & Koebernick, L. F. Learned helplessness, depression, and physiological responding. *Psychophysiology*, 1977, *14*, 25–31.

Gatchel, R. J., & Proctor, J. D. Physiological correlates of learned helplessness in man. *Journal of Abnormal Psychology*, 1976, *85*, 27–34.

Gilbert, L. A., & Mangelsdorff, D. Influence of perceptions of personal control on reactions to stressful events. *Journal of Counseling Psychology*, 1979, *26*, 473–480.

Glass, C. R., & Levy, L. H. Perceived psychophysiological control: The effects of power versus powerlessness. *Cognitive Therapy and Research*, 1982, *6*, 91–103.

Glass, D. C. *Behavior pattern, stress, and coronary disease.* Hillsdale, N.J.: Erlbaum, 1977.

Goesling, W. J., May, C., Lavond, D., Barnes, T., & Carreira, C. Relationships between internal and external locus of control and the operant conditioning of alpha through biofeedback training. *Perceptual and Motor Skills*, 1974, *39*, 1339–1343.

Goldman, B. I., Domitor, P. J., & Murray, E. J. Effects of Zen meditation on anxiety reduction and perceptual functioning. *Journal of Consulting and Clinical Psychology*, 1979, *47*, 551–556.

Goldstein, D. S., Ross, R. S., & Brady, J. V. Biofeedback heart rate training during exercise. *Biofeedback and Self-Regulation*, 1977, *2*, 107–125.

Graham, F. K. Habituation and dishabituation of responses innervated by the autonomic nervous system. In H. V. S. Peeke & M. J. Herz (Eds.), *Habituation: Behavioral studies* (Vol. 1). New York: Academic Press, 1973.

Graham, F. K., & Clifton, R. K. Heart-rate change as a component of the orienting response. *Psychological Bulletin*, 1966, *65*, 305–320.

Groves, P. M., & Thompson, R. F. Habituation: A dual process theory. *Psychological Review*, 1970, *77*, 419–450.

Hahn, W. W. Attention and heart rate: A critical appraisal of the hypothesis of Lacey and Lacey. *Psychological Bulletin*, 1973, *79*, 59–70.

Harrell, J. P. Individual differences in anticipatory physiological responses to signalled stress: Role of locus of control and autonomic balance. *Perceptual and Motor Skills*, 1979, *48*, 663–669.

Harrell, J. P. Relationships among locus of control, heart rate, and ratings of stress. *Psychological Reports*, 1980, *46*(2), 472–474.

Hassett, J. *A primer of psychophysiology.* San Francisco: Freeman, 1978.

Harris, V. A., Katkin, E. S., Lick, J. R., & Habberfield, T. Paced respiration as a technique for the modification of autonomic response to stress. *Psychophysiology*, 1976, *13*, 386–391.

Hatch, J. P. Controlled group designs in biofeedback research: Ask, "What does the control group control for?" *Biofeedback and Self-Regulation*, 1982, *7*, 377–401.

Hatch, J. P., & Gatchel, R. J. Development of physiological response patterns concomitant with the learning of voluntary heart rate control. *Journal of Comparative and Physiological Psychology*, 1979, *93*, 306–313.

Heslegrave, R. J., & Furedy, J. J. Carotid dP/dt as a psychophysiological index of sympathetic myocardial effects: Some considerations. *Psychophysiology*, 1980, *17*, 482–494.

Heslegrave, R. J., & Furedy, J. J. Sensitivities of HR and T-wave amplitude for detecting cognitive and anticipatory stress. *Physiology & Behavior*, 1979, *22*, 17–23.

Hillenberg, J. B., & Collins, F. L. A procedural analysis and review of relaxation training research. *Behaviour Research and Therapy*, 1982, *20*, 251–260.

Hiroto, D. S. Learned helplessness and locus of control. *Journal of Experimental Psychology*, 1974, *102*, 187–193.

Hirschman, R., Young, D., & Nelson, C. Physiologically based techniques for stress reduction. In B. D. Ingersoll & W. R. McCutcheon (Eds.), *Clinical research in behavioral dentistry.* Morgantown: West Virginia University Foundation, 1979.

Hjelle, L. A. Transcendental meditation and psychological health. *Perceptual and Motor Skills*, 1974, *39*, 623–628.

Holliday, J. E., & Munz, D. C. EMG feedback training and changes in locus of control. *Biofeedback and Self-Regulation*, 1978, *3*, 223–224. (Abstract)

Holmes, D. S., & Houston, B. K. Effectiveness of situation redefinition and affective isolation in coping with stress. *Journal of Personality and Social Psychology*, 1974, *29*, 212–218.

Houston, B. K. Control over stress, locus of control, and response to stress. *Journal of Personality and Social Psychology*, 1972, *21*, 249–255.

Hurley, J. D. Differential effects of hypnosis, biofeedback training, and trophotropic responses on anxiety, ego strength, and locus of control. *Journal of Clinical Psychology*, 1980, *36*, 503–507.

Iacono, W. G., & Lykken, D. T. The effects of instructions on electrodermal habituation. *Psychophysiology*, 1983, *20*, 71–80.

International Meditation Society. *Fundamentals of progress.* Fairfield, Ia.: MIU Press, 1975.

Jacobson, E. *Progressive relaxation* (rev.ed.). Chicago: University of Chicago Press, 1938.

Jamieson, J., & Dreger, H. *Internal–external locus of control and response to alpha feedback training.* Paper presented at the Annual Meeting of the Canadian Psychological Association, Toronto, June 1976.

Janis, I., & Mann, L. *Decision making.* New York: Free Press, 1977.

Johnson, H. J., & May, J. R. Phasic heart rate changes in reaction time and time estimation. *Psychophysiology*, 1969, *6*, 351–357.

Johnson, R. K., & Meyer, R. G. The locus of control construct in EEG alpha rhythm feedback. *Journal of Consulting and Clinical Psychology*, 1974, *42*, 913.

Kallman, W. M., & Feuerstein, M. Psychophysiological procedures. In A. R. Ciminero, K. S. Calhoun, & H. E. Adams (Eds.), *Handbook of behavioral assessment.* New York: Wiley, 1977.

Kappes, B., & Michaud, J. Contingent vs. non-contingent EMG feedback and hand temperature in relation to anxiety and locus of control. *Biofeedback and Self-Regulation*, 1978, *3*, 51–59.

Katkin, E. Personal communication, October 13, 1982.

Keenan, A., & McBain, G. D. M. Effects of Type A behaviour, intolerance of ambiguity, and locus of control on the relationship between role stress and work-related outcomes. *Journal of Occupational Psychology*, 1979, *52*, 277–285.

Kilpatrick, D. G. Differential responsiveness of two electrodermal indices to psychological stress and performance of a complex cognitive task. *Psychophysiology*, 1972, *9*, 218–226.

King, N. J. The therapeutic utility of abbreviated progressive relaxation: A critical review with implications for clinical progress. In M. Hersen, R. M. Eisler, & P. M. Miller (Eds.), *Progress in behavior modification* (Vol. 10). New York: Academic Press, 1980.

Kinsman, R. A., & Staudenmayer, H. Baseline levels in muscle relaxation training. *Biofeedback and Self-Regulation*, 1978, *3*, 97–104.

Koriat, A., Averill, J. R., & Malmstrom, E. J. Individual differences in habituation: Some methodological and conceptual issues. *Journal of Research in Personality*, 1973, *7*, 88–101.

Krantz, D. S., Glass, D. C., & Snyder, M. L. Helplessness, stress level, and the coronary-prone behavior pattern. *Journal of Experimental Social Psychology*, 1974, *10*, 284–300.

Krupski, A., Raskin, D. C., & Bakan, P. Physiological and personality correlates of commission errors in an auditory vigilance task. *Psychophysiology*, 1971, *8*, 304–311.

Lacey, B. C., & Lacey, J. I. Studies of heart rate and other bodily processes in sensorimotor behavior. In P. A. Obrist, A. H. Black, J. Brener, & L. V. DiCara (Eds.), *Cardiovascular psychophysiology.* Chicago: Aldine, 1974.

Lacey, B. C., & Lacey, J. I. Two-way communication between the heart and the brain:

202 : KIRK R. BLANKSTEIN

Significance of time within the cardiac cycle. *American Psychologist*, 1978, *33*, 99–113.

Lacey, J. I. Psychophysiological approaches to the evaluation of psychotherapeutic process and outcome. In E. A. Rubinstein & M. B. Parloff (Eds.), *Research in psychotherapy* (Vol. 1). Washington, D.C.: American Psychological Association, 1959.

Lacey, J. I. Somatic response patterning and stress: Some revisions of activation theory. In M. H. Appley & R. Trumbull (Eds.), *Psychological stress: Issues in research*. New York: Appleton–Century–Crofts, 1967.

Lacey, J. I., Bateman, D. E., & Van Lehn, R. Autonomic response specificity: An experimental study. *Psychosomatic Medicine*, 1953, *15*, 8–21.

Lacey, J. I., Kagan, J., Lacey, B. C., & Moss, H. A. The visceral level: Situational determinants and behavioral correlates of autonomic response patterns. In P. H. Knapp (Ed.), *Expression of the emotions in man*. New York: International Universities Press, 1963.

Lacey, J. I., & Lacey, B. C. Some autonomic–central nervous system interrelationships. In P. Black (Ed.), *Psyiological correlates of emotion*. New York: Academic Press, 1970.

Lader, M. H., & Wing, L. *Physiological measures, sedative drugs, and morbid anxiety.* London: Oxford University Press, 1966.

Lang, P. J. The application of psychophysiological methods to the study of psychotherapy and behavior modification. In A. E. Bergin & S. L. Garfield (Eds.), *Handbook of psychotherapy and behavior change*. New York: Wiley, 1971.

Lang, P. J. Acquisition of heart rate control: Method, theory, and clinical implications. In D. C. Fowles (Ed.), *Clinical applications of psychophysiology*. New York: Columbia University Press, 1975.

Lang, P. J., Rice, D. C., & Sternbach, R. A. Psychophysiology of emotion. In N. S. Greenfield & R. A. Sternbach (Eds.), *Handbook of psychophysiology*. New York: Holt, Rhinehart & Winston, 1972.

Lang, P. J., Troyer, W. G., Twentyman, C. T., & Gatchel, R. J. Differential effects of heart rate modification training on college students, older males, and patients with ischemic heart disease. *Psychosomatic Medicine*, 1975, *37*, 429–446.

Lang, P. J., & Twentyman, C. T. Learning to control heart rate: Binary *vs.* analogue feedback. *Psychophysiology*, 1974, *11*, 616–629.

Lazarus, R. S. *Psychological stress and the coping process*. New York: McGraw–Hill, 1966.

Leavitt, L. A., & Donovon, W. L. Perceived infant temperament, locus of control, and maternal physiological response to infant gaze. *Journal of Research in Personality*, 1979, *13*, 267–278.

Lefcourt, H. M. Belief in personal control: Research and implications. *Journal of Individual Psychology*, 1966, *22*, 185–195.

Lefcourt, H. M. Recent developments in the study of locus of control. In B. A. Maher (Ed.), *Progress in experimental personality research* (Vol. 6). New York: Academic Press, 1972.

Lefcourt, H. M. The function of the illusions of control and freedom. *American Psychologist*, 1973, *28*, 417–425.

Lefcourt, H. M. *Locus of control: Current trends in theory and research*. Hillsdale, N.J.: Erlbaum, 1976.

Lefcourt, H. M. (Ed.). *Research with the locus of control construct* (Vol. 1). New York: Academic Press, 1981.

Lefcourt, H. M. *Locus of control: Current trends in theory and research* (2nd ed.). Hillsdale, N.J.: Erlbaum, 1982.

Lefcourt, H. M., Gronnerud, P., & McDonald, P. Cognitive activity and hypothesis formation during a double-entendre word association test as a function of locus of control and field dependence. *Canadian Journal of Behavioural Science*, 1973, *5*, 161–163.

Lefcourt, H. M., & Telegdi, M. Perceived locus of control and field dependence as predictors of cognitive activity. *Journal of Consulting and Clinical Psychology*, 1971, *37*, 53–56.

Lefcourt, H. M., & Wine, J. Internal versus external control of reinforcement and the deployment of attention in experimental situations. *Canadian Journal of Behavioural Science*, 1969, *1*, 167–181.

Levenson, H. Multidimensional locus of control in psychiatric patients. *Journal of Consulting and Clinical Psychology*, 1973, *41*, 397–404.

Levenson, R. W., & Ditto, W. B. Individual differences in ability to control heart rate: Personality, strategy, physiological, and other variables. *Psychophysiology*, 1981, *18*, 91–100.

Lichstein, K. L., Sallis, J. F., Hill, D., & Young, M. C. Psychophysiological adaptation: An investigation of multiple parameters. *Journal of Behavioral Assessment*, 1981, *3*, 111–121.

Light, K. C., & Obrist, P. A. Cardiovascular response to stress: Effects of opportunity to avoid, shock experience, and performance feedback. *Psychophysiology*, 1980, *17*, 243–252.

Lindsley, D. B. Psychological phenomena and the electroencephalogram. *EEG and Clinical Neurophysiology*, 1952, *4*, 443–456.

Linn, R. T., & Hodge, G. K. Use of EMG biofeedback training in increasing attention span and internalizing locus of control in hyperactive children. *Biofeedback and Self-Regulation*, 1980, *5*, 373. (Abstract)

Lobstein, T., Webb, B., & Edholm, O. Orienting responses and locus of control. *British Journal of Social and Clinical Psychology*, 1979, *18*, 13–19.

Logsdon, S. A., Bourgeois, A. E., & Levenson, H. Locus of control, learned helplessness, and control of heart rate using biofeedback. *Journal of Personality Assessment*, 1978, *42*, 538–544.

Lundberg, U., & Frankenhaeuser, M. Psychophysiological reactions to noise as modified by personal control over noise intensity. *Biological Psychology*, 1978, *6*, 51–59.

Lykken, D. T. Statistical significance in psychological research. *Psychological Bulletin*, 1968, *70*, 151–159.

Lynn, R. *Attention, arousal, and the orientation reaction.* Oxford: Pergamon, 1966.

Lynn, S., & Friedman, R. R. Transfer and evaluation in biofeedback treatment. In A. P. Goldstein & F. Kanfer (Eds.), *Maximizing treatment gains: Transfer enhancement in psychotherapy.* New York: Academic Press, 1979.

Mackworth, J. F. *Vigilance and habituation.* Baltimore: Penguin Books, 1969.

Mackworth, N. H. Vigilance. *The Advancement of Science*, 1957, *53*, 389–393.

Malmo, R. B. Activation: A neurophysiological dimension. *Psychological Review*, 1959, *66*, 367–386.

Maltzman, I., & Raskin, D. C. Effects of individual differences in the orienting reflex on conditioning and complex processes. *Journal of Experimental Research in Personality*, 1965, *1*, 1–16.

Mandler, G. Anxiety. In D. L. Sills (Ed.), *International encyclopedia of the social sciences.* New York: Macmillan, 1966.

Manuck, S. B., Harvey, A. E., Lechleiter, S. L., & Neal, K. S. Effects of active coping on blood pressure responses to threat of aversive stimulation. *Psychophysiology*, 1978, *15*, 544–549.

Marsh, G. R., & Thompson, L. W. Psychophysiology of aging. In J. E. Birren & K. W. Schaie (Eds.), *Handbook of the psychology of aging.* New York: Van Nostrand Reinhold Co., 1977.

Marshall–Goodell, B., Gormezano, I., Scandrett, J., & Cacioppo, J. T. The microcomputer in social–psychophysiological research: An Apple II/FIRST laboratory. *Sociological Methods & Research*, 1981, *9*, 502–512.

Matthews, K. A. Psychological perspectives on the Type A behavior pattern. *Psychological Bulletin*, 1982, *91*, 293–323.

Matus, I. Select personality variables and tension in two muscle groups. *Psychophysiology*, 1974, *11*, 91.

McCanne, T. R., & Lotsof, E. J. Locus of control and the autonomic response associated with a visual orienting task. *Physiological Psychology*, 1980, *8*, 137–140.

McCanne, T. R., & Sandman, C. A. Determinants of human operant heart rate conditioning: A systematic investigation of several methodological issues. *Journal of Comparative and Physiological Psychology*, 1975, *88*, 609–618.

McCaul, K. D., Solomon, S., & Holmes, D. S. Effects of paced respiration and expectations on physiological and psychological responses to threat. *Journal of Personality and Social Psychology*, 1979, *37*, 564–571.

McGhee, P. E., & Crandall, V. C. Beliefs in internal–external control of reinforcement and academic performance. *Child Development*, 1968, *39*, 91–102.

Meichenbaum, D., & Butler, L. Cognitive ethology: Assessing the streams of cognition and emotion. In K. R. Blankstein, P. Pliner, & J. Polivy (Eds.), *Advances in the study of communication and affect: Assessment and modification of emotional behavior* (Vol. 6). New York: Plenum, 1980.

Miller, I. W., & Norman, W. H. Learned helplessness in humans: A review and attribution-theory model. *Psychological Bulletin*, 1979, *86*, 93–118.

Miller, N. E. Biofeedback and visceral learning. *Annual Review of Psychology*, 1978, *29*, 373–404.

Miller, S. M. Controllability and human stress: Method, evidence and theory. *Behaviour Research and Therapy*, 1979, *17*, 287–304.

Miller, W. R., & Seligman, M. E. P. Depression and learned helplessness in man. *Journal of Abnormal Psychology*, 1975, *84*, 228–238.

Mirels, H. L. Dimensions of internal versus external control. *Journal of Consulting and Clinical Psychology*, 1970, *34*, 226–228.

Mischel, W. *Personality and assessment*, New York: Wiley, 1968.

Molinari, V., & Khanna, P. Locus of control and the denial of anxiety. *Psychological Reports*, 1980, *47*, 131–140.

Murray, E. J., & Jacobson, L. I. Cognition and learning in traditional and behavioral therapy. In S. L. Garfield & A. E. Bergin (Eds.), *Handbook of psychotherapy and behavior change* (2nd ed.). New York: Wiley, 1978.

Naditch, M. P. Locus of control, relative discontent, and hypertension. *Social Psychiatry*, 1974, *9*, 111–117.

Notarius, C. I., & Levenson, R. W. Expressive tendencies and physiological response to stress. *Journal of Personality and Social Psychology*, 1979, *37*, 1204–1210.

Nowack, K. M., & Sassenrath, J. M. Coronary-prone behavior, locus of control, and anxiety. *Psychological Reports*, 1980, *47*, 359–364.

Nowicki, S., & Duke, M. P. A locus of control scale for noncollege as well as college students. *Journal of Personality Assessment*, 1974, *38*, 136–137.

Nowicki, S., Duke, M. P., & Crouch, M. P. D. Sex differences in locus of control and performance under competitive and cooperative conditions. *Journal of Educational Psychology*, 1978, *70*, 482–486.

Nowicki, S., & Strickland, B. A locus of control scale for children. *Journal of Consulting and Clinical Psychology*, 1973, *40*, 148–154.

Obrist, P. A. The cardiovascular behavioral interaction—as it appears today. *Psychophysiology*, 1976, *13*, 95–107.

Obrist, P. A. *Cardiovascular psychophysiology: A perspective.* New York: Plenum, 1981.

O'Gorman, J. G. Individual differences in habituation of human physiological responses: A review of theory, method, and findings in the study of personality correlates in non-clinical populations. *Biological Psychology,* 1977, 257–318.

Öhman, A., & Bohlin, G. Magnitude and habituation of the orienting reaction as predictors of discriminative electrodermal conditioning. *Journal of Experimental Research in Personality,* 1973, 6, 293–299.

Ollendick, T. H., & Murphy, M. J. Differential effectiveness of muscular and cognitive relaxation as a function of locus of control. *Journal of Behavior Therapy and Experimental Psychiatry,* 1977, 8, 223–228.

Orne, M. T. Demand characteristics and the concept of quasi-controls. In R. Rosenthal & R. L. Rosnow (Eds.), *Artifact in behavioral research.* New York: Academic Press, 1969.

Peterson, C. *The sense of control over one's life: A review of recent literature.* Paper presented to the Social Science Research Council's meeting, New York City, October 1980.

Phares, E. J. Internal–external control and the recduction of reinforcement value after failure. *Journal of Consulting and Clinical Psychology,* 1971, 37, 386–390.

Phares, E. J. *Locus of control in personality.* Morristown, N.J.: General Learning Press, 1976.

Pickett, C., & Clum, G. A. Comparative treatment strategies and their interaction with locus of control in the reduction of post-surgical pain and anxiety. *Journal of Consulting and Clinical Psychology,* 1982, 50, 439–441.

Pittman, N. L., & Pittman, T. S. Effects of amount of helplessness training and internal–external locus of control on mood and performance. *Journal of Personality and Social Psychology,* 1979, 37, 39–47.

Plotkin, W. B. On the self-regulation of the occipital alpha rhythm: Control strategies, states of consciousness, and the role of physiological feedback. *Journal of Experimental Psychology,* 1976, 105, 66–99.

Plotkin, W. B. The alpha experience revisited: Biofeedback in the transformation of psychological state. *Psychological Bulletin,* 1979, 86, 1132–1148.

Porges, S. W. Peripheral and neurochemical parallels of psychopathology: A psychophysiological model relating autonomic imbalance to hyperactivity, psychopathy, and autism. In H. W. Reese (Ed.), *Advances in child developmental behavior* (Vol. 11). New York: Academic Press, 1976.

Pritchard, W. S. Psychophysiology of P300. *Psychological Bulletin,* 1981, 89, 506–540.

Puente, A. E. Psychophysiological investigations on transcendental meditation. *Biofeedback and Self-Regulation,* 1981, 6, 327–342.

Rachman, S. The role of muscular relaxation in desensitization therapy. *Behaviour Research and Therapy,* 1968, 6, 159–166.

Raskin, D. C. Semantic conditioning and generalization of autonomic responses. *Journal of Experimental Psychology,* 1969, 79, 69–76.

Raskin, D. C. Attention and arousal. In W. F. Prokasy & D. C. Raskin (Eds.), *Electrodermal activity in psychological research.* New York: Academic Press, 1973.

Raskin, D. C., Kotses, H., & Bever, J. Cephalic vasomotor and heart rate measures of orienting and defensive reflexes. *Psychophysiology,* 1969, 6, 149–159.

Ray, W. J. The relationship of locus of control, self-report measures, and feedback to the voluntary control of heart rate. *Psychophysiology,* 1974, 11, 527–534.

Ray, W. J., & Lamb, S. B. Locus of control and the voluntary control of heart rate. *Psychosomatic Medicine,* 1974, 36, 180–182.

Reed, M., & Saslow, C. A. The effects of relaxation instructions and EMG biofeedback on test anxiety, general anxiety, and locus of control. *Journal of Clinical Psychology*, 1980, *36*, 683–690.

Reid, D. W., & Ware, E. E. Multidimensionality of internal vs. external control: Addition of a third dimension and non-distinction of self versus others. *Canadian Journal of Behavioural Science*, 1974, *6*, 131–142.

Reinking, R. H. The influence of internal–external control and trait anxiety on acquisition of EMG control. *Biofeedback and Self-Regulation*, 1976, *1*, 350. (Abstract)

Richter, C. P. On the phenomenon of sudden death in animals and man. *Psychosomatic Medicine*, 1957, *19*, 191–198.

Roessler, R., & Engel, B. T. The current status of the concepts of physiological response specificity and activation. In Z. J. Lipowski, D. R. Lipsitt, & P. C. Whybrow (Eds.), *Psychosomatic medicine*, New York: Oxford University Press, 1977.

Rosenbaum, M. A schedule for assessing self-control behaviors: Preliminary findings. *Behavior Therapy*, 1980, *11*, 109–121. (a)

Rosenbaum, M. Individual differences in self-control behaviors and tolerance of painful stimulation. *Journal of Abnormal Psychology*, 1980, *89*, 581–590. (b)

Rosenthal, R., & Rosnow, R. L. (Eds.). *Artifact in behavioral research*. New York: Academic Press, 1969.

Rotter, J. B. Generalized expectancies for internal versus external control of reinforcement. *Psychological Monographs*, 1966, *80* (1, Whole No. 609).

Rotter, J. B. Some problems and misconceptions related to the construct of internal versus external control of reinforcement. *Journal of Consulting and Clinical Psychology*, 1975, *43*, 56–67.

Runcie, D., Graham, J. S., & Shelton, M. L. Locus of control and cardiac response to reaction time, mental arithmetic, and time-estimation tasks. *Perceptual and Motor Skills*, 1978, *46*, 1199–1208.

Russell, C. M., Dale, A., & Anderson, D. E. Locus of control and expectancy in electromyographic biofeedback. *Journal of Psychosomatic Research*, 1982, *26*, 527–532.

Russo, D. C., Bird, B. L., & Masek, B. J. Assessment issues in behavioral medicine. *Behavioral Assessment*, 1980, *2*, 1–18.

Sanders, M. G., Halcomb, C. G., Fray, J. M., & Owens, J. M. Internal–external locus of control and performance on a vigilance task. *Perceptual and Motor Skills*, 1976, *42*, 939–943.

Schneider, R. D., Sobol, M. P., Herrman, T. F., & Cousins, L. R. A re-examination of the relationship between locus of control and voluntary heart rate change. *Journal of General Psychology*, 1978, *99*, 49–60.

Schulz, R. Emotionality and aging. In K. R. Blankstein & J. Polivy (Eds.), *Advances in the study of communication and affect: Self-control and self-modification of emotional behavior* (Vol. 7). New York: Plenum, 1982.

Schwartz, G. E. Toward a theory of voluntary control of response patterns in the cardiovascular system. In P. A. Obrist, A. H. Black, J. Brener, & L. V. DiCara (Eds.), *Cardiovascular psychophysiology*. Chicago: Aldine, 1974.

Schwartz, G. E., & Shapiro, D. Social psychophysiology. In W. F. Prokasy & D. C. Raskin (Eds.), *Electrodermal activity in psychological research*. New York: Academic Press, 1973.

Seligman, M. E. P. *Helplessness: On depression, development, and death*. San Francisco: Freeman, 1975.

Shapiro, D., & Schwartz, G. E. Psychophysiological contributions to social psychology. *Annual Review of Psychology*, 1970, *21*, 87–112.

Siddle, D. A. Vigilance decrement and speed of habituation of the GSR component of the orienting response. *British Journal of Psychology*, 1972, *63*, 191–194.

Simkins, L. Biofeedback: Clinically valid or oversold? *The Psychological Record*, 1982, *32*, 3–7.

Sirota, A. D., Schwartz, G. E., & Shapiro, D. Voluntary control of human heart rate: Effect on reaction to aversive stimulation: *Journal of Abnormal Psychology*, 1974, *83*, 261–267.

Sirota, A. D., Schwartz, G. E., & Shapiro, D. Voluntary control of human heart rate: Effect on reaction to aversive stimulation: A replication and extension. *Journal of Abnormal Psychology*, 1976, *85*, 473–477.

Smith, R. P., Jr. Frontalis muscle tension and personality. *Psychophysiology*, 1973, *10*, 311–312.

Sokolov, E. N. The orienting reflex, its structure and mechanisms. In L. G. Veronin, A. N. Leontren, A. R. Luria, E. N. Sokolov, & O. S. Vinogradova (Eds.), *Orienting reflex and exploratory behavior*. Washington, D.C.: American Institute of Biological Sciences, 1965.

Sonstroem, R. J., & Walker, M. I. Relationship of attitudes and locus of control to exercise and physical fitness. *Perceptual and Motor Skills*, 1973, *36*, 1031–1034.

Stern, G. S., & Berrenberg, J. L. Biofeedback training in frontalis muscle relaxation and enhancement of belief in personal control. *Biofeedback and Self-Regulation*, 1977, *2*, 173–182.

Stern, J. A., & Janes, C. L. Personality and psychopathology. In W. F. Prokasy & D. C. Raskin (Eds.), *Electrodermal activity in psychological research*. New York: Academic Press, 1973.

Stern, J. A., & Plapp, J. M. Psychophysiology and clinical psychology. In C. D. Spielberger (Ed.), *Current topics in clinical and community psychology* (Vol. 1). New York: Academic Press, 1969.

Stern, R. M., Ray, W. J., & Davis, C. M. *Psychophysiological recording*. New York: Oxford University Press, 1980.

Sternbach, R. A. *Principles of psychophysiology*. New York: Academic Press, 1966.

Stoffer, G. R., Jensen, J. A., & Nesset, B. L. Effects of contingent versus yoked temperature control and cold stress tolerance. *Biofeedback and Self-Regulation*, 1979, *4*, 51–61.

Strickland, B. R. Internal–external expectancies and health-related behaviors. *Journal of Consulting and Clinical Psychology*, 1978, *46*, 1192–1211.

Strickland, B. R. Internal–external expectancies and cardiovascular functioning. In L. C. Perlmuter & R. A. Monty (Eds.), *Choice and perceived control*. Hillsdale, N.J.: Erlbaum, 1979.

Strickland, B. R., & Haley, W. Sex differences on the Rotter I–E scale. *Journal of Personality and Social Psychology*, 1980, *39*, 930–939.

Tarler–Benlolo, L. The role of relaxation in biofeedback training: A critical review of the literature. *Psychological Bulletin*, 1978, *85*, 727–755.

Theoret, R. L., & Stoppard, J. M. *Effects of relaxation training as a function of locus of control*. Paper presented at the Annual Meeting of the Canadian Psychological Association, Montreal, June 1982.

Thompson, S. C. Will it hurt less if I can control it? A complex answer to a simple question. *Psychological Bulletin*, 1981, *90*, 89–101.

Tobacy, K. J. J., Broughton, A., & Vaught, G. M. Effects of congruence–incongruence between locus of control and field dependence on personality functioning. *Journal of Consulting and Clinical Psychology*, 1975, *43*, 81–85.

Toner, B. *Self-report, psychophysiological and behavioral indices of test anxiety during anticipation and test periods*. Unpublished doctoral dissertation, University of Toronto, 1982.

Toner, B., & Blankstein, K. R. Heart rate increases and the pattern of self-verbalization in an "incubation of threat" situation. *Psychophysiology*, 1981, *18*, 164. (Abstract)

Tyson, P. D., & Audette, R. A multivariate approach to the relationship between alpha waves and experience during feedback. *Biofeedback and Self-Regulation*, 1979, *4*, 63–79.

Victor, R., Mainardi, J. A., & Shapiro, D. Effect of biofeedback and voluntary control procedures on heart rate and perception of pain during the cold pressor test. *Psychosomatic Medicine*, 1978, *40*, 216–225.

Vogt, A. T. Electromyograph responses and performance success estimates as a function of locus of control. *Perceptual and Motor Skills*, 1975, *41*, 977–978.

Volow, M. R., Erwin, C. W., & Cipolat, A. L. Biofeedback control of skin potential level. *Biofeedback and Self-Regulation*, 1979, *4*, 133–143.

Wagner, C., Bourgeois, A., Levenson, H., & Denton, J. Multidimensional locus of control and voluntary control of GSR. *Perceptual and Motor Skills*, 1974, *39*, 1142.

Wallace, R. K., Benson, H., & Wilson, A. A wakeful hypometabolic physiologic state. *American Journal of Physiology*, 1971, *221*, 795–799.

Wallston, B. S., Wallston, K. A., & Maides S. A. Development and validation of the Health Locus of Control (HLC) scale. *Journal of Consulting and Clinical Psychology*, 1976, *44*, 580–585.

Weiss, J. M. Effects of coping behavior in different warning signal conditions on stress pathology in rats. *Journal of Comparative and Physiological Psychology*, 1971, *77*, 1–13.

Weiss, J. M., Stone, E. A., & Harrell, N. Coping behavior and brain nonepinephrine in rats. *Journal of Comparative and Physiological Psychology*, 1970. *72*, 153–160.

Wenger, M. A., & Cullen, T. D. Studies of autonomic balance in children and adults. In N. S. Greenfield and R. A. Sternbach (Eds.), *Handbook of psychophysiology*. New York: Holt, Rinehart & Winston, 1972.

West, M. A. The psychosomatics of meditation. *Journal of Psychosomatic Research*, 1980, *24*, 265–273.

Williamson, D. A., & Blanchard, E. B. Heart rate and blood pressure biofeedback. I: A review of the recent experimental literature. *Biofeedback and Self-Regulation*, 1979, *4*, 1–34.

Witkin, H., Oltman, P., Raskin, E., & Karp, S. *Manual for the Embedded Figures Test*. Palo Alto, Ca.: Consulting Psychologists Press, 1971.

Wolk, S., & DuCette, J. Intentional performance and incidental learning as a function of personality and task dimension. *Journal of Personality and Social Psychology*, 1974, *29*, 90–101.

Wortman, C. B. Causal attributions and personal control. In J. H. Harvey, W. J. Ickes, & R. F. Kidd (Eds.), *New directions in attribution research* (Vol. 1). Hillsdale, N.J.: Erlbaum, 1976.

Wortman, C. B., & Brehm, J. W. Responses to uncontrollable outcomes: An integration of reactance theory and the learned helplessness model. In L. Berkowitz (Ed.), *Advances in experimental social psychology* (Vol. 8). New York: Academic Press, 1975.

Yates, A. J. *Biofeedback and the modification of behavior*. New York: Plenum Press, 1980.

Zaichkowsky, L. D., & Kamen, R. Biofeedback and meditation: Effects on muscle tension and locus of control. *Perceptual & Motor Skills*, 1978, *46*, 955–958.

Zimet, G. D. Locus of control and biofeedback: A review of the literature. *Perceptual and Motor Skills*, 1979, *49*, 871–877.

Zuroff, D. C., & Schwarz, J. C. Effects of transcendental meditation and muscle relaxation on trait anxiety, maladjustment, locus of control, and drug use. *Journal of Consulting and Clinical Psychology*, 1978, *46*, 264–271.

James A. Dyal

CROSS-CULTURAL RESEARCH WITH THE LOCUS OF CONTROL CONSTRUCT

Introduction

Since World War II the geopolitical structure of the world has been characterized by a proliferation of new nation-states. Parallel movements emphasizing tribal and ethnic identity have sought to enhance the relative power of national subcultures. In the United States the civil rights movement of the 1950s and 1960s focused the mainstream WASP culture on social and personal aspirations of American minorities who, contrary to expectation, had not disappeared into the melting pot. Responding to these sociocultural processes social psychologists directed their research energies toward a better understanding of socially relevant issues such as relative power, conflict resolution, resource allocation, and feelings of personal and social control. Similarly, American personality theorists focused on such culturally relevant constructs as need for achievement, anxiety, aspiration, expectation of success–failure, and locus of control. The key concept of American psychology—reinforcement—was extended and incorporated in the elaboration of a theory of social learning (Rotter, 1954) that contended that expectancies for reinforcement range from situation specific to quite generalized expectancies, which operate across a large number of situations. The early history of efforts to measure these generalized expectancies is thoroughly reviewed by Phares (1976).

Not surprisingly, these locus of control (LOC) instruments were almost immediately used for making comparisons among American

RESEARCH WITH THE LOCUS
OF CONTROL CONSTRUCT (Vol. 3.)
Extensions and Limitations

ethnic groups and more recently among national–cultural groups. As noted by Phares (1976), "such group differences are particularly important, not just because they may ultimately mediate group differences in certain kinds of behavior but also because of their implications with respect to the antecedents of I–E beliefs" (p. 45). Despite the fact that the research relevant to the cross-cultural application of the locus of control construct is now quite extensive, no complete review of the area has appeared, although passing reference to cultural variables is made in other treatments of LOC research (Lefcourt, 1976; Levenson, 1981; Phares, 1976) or in treatises on personality and culture (e.g., Draguns, 1979a, 1979b). As noted by Draguns (1979b), "the newer topic of 'locus of control' has neither been comprehensively reviewed nor has it currently yielded a coherent body of data" (p. 198).

It is the purpose of the present chapter to provide such a comprehensive review of the available literature. However, before the degree of coherence of the data is assayed, it seems desirable to consider some of the promises, problems, and perils of cross-cultural research on personality variables.

Why Do Cross-Cultural Research?
Promises, Promises

Even a cursory examination of the social–personality theories of twentieth-century psychology reveals an uncomfortably narrow data base in which the world view of Euro-American university students carries disproportionately large weight. It takes no great cultural awareness to suppose that White US university students might not be an entirely representative sample of humankind. As a consequence our psychological constructs and theories may be more ethnocentric than we like to admit. It is the task of cross-cultural psychologists continually to raise this concern. Indeed, our claim to any separate identity within psychology rests on our willingness to assert the importance of testing the generality of our psychological theories across cultural contexts. As noted by Garza and Lipton:

> One of the major shortcomings in the fields of personality and social psychology, particularly within the United States, has been a general failure of researchers to take ethnic or cultural variables into account. The result of this widespread myopia is that we are left with an essentially ethnocentric body of literature, a unicultural science often limited in its generalizability to a very specific population: white Anglo-Americans. It is timely to question how well our theories of personality and social psychology apply to nontraditional populations [1978, p. 743].

Although testing the cultural generality of Western psychology is indeed a legitimate and necessary undertaking, an exclusive focus on using "them" to test "our" knowledge generates overtones of intellectual imperialism. Furthermore, while acknowledging that a generality check is a necessary goal of cross-cultural psychology, Berry (1980) regards it as a "less exciting" first step of "limited importance."

There are two less ideocentric reasons for being interested in a cultural–comparative psychology. First, there is the excitement of discovery, description, and classification of cultural similarities and differences in psychological characteristics for their own sake. "The collecting of novel, exotic and exciting new data has always intrigued anthropologists: it has now captured the attention of cross-cultural psychologists as well" (Berry, 1980, p. 5). Though description and classification have always gained fewer scientific status points than explanation, it should be recalled that in most sciences it is an indispensable prerequisite for any robust theory building. Indeed, LeVine (1970, pp. 559–612) proposed that rather than focus on a search for theory-relevant cultural characteristics that may or may not be related to behavioral similarities and differences, we should first establish the reliability of our behavioral differences. As Segall noted:

This is a persuasive and valid argument. But, as LeVine himself properly notes, this "etiological approach" exposes some major weaknesses of cross-cultural research in its actuality—most especially the paucity of well-established differences! As LeVine (1970) has said with regard to cognitive performances of children in non-Western cultures, "We do not have comparable developmental data for children the world over or even for a diverse sample of societies, and much of the cross-cultural data we do have is of dubious quality because of questions concerning the validity and/ or comparability of the data collection procedures" (p. 22) [Segall, 1979, p. 103].

A second less theoretically oriented reason for an interest in cultural similarities and differences is the increasing demands for the *application* of psychological knowledge. "Only a cross-cultural psychology is capable of supplying the necessary basis for programmes in the service of diverse groups of people" (Berry, 1980, p. 6).

Although an increasing number of psychologists are accepting the challenge of including a culture-comparative thrust to their theoretical or applied research programs, they soon discover a simple truism: It is not easy validly to compare two things. This is particularly so when one of the entities is alien and may not structure the world in the same categories as the observer. As noted by Price-Williams (1975), "Our own categories of explanation and definition may not be appropriate when projected onto another cutlure" (p. 23).

Problems and Perils of Cross-Cultural Research

Perhaps the most difficult methodological problem confronting those who would use psychometric instruments to compare cultural groups is the problem of validity—or, more appropriately, the *problems* of validity. There are several interrelated problems here, but they all involve the challenge of demonstrating the *construct validity* (Berry, 1969; Cronbach & Meehl, 1955; Irvine & Carroll, 1980; Irwin, Klein, Engle, Yarbrough, & Nerlove, 1977) of the test in each of the cultures to be compared.

Construct validation is of necessity a spiraling process in which conceptual and metric equivalences are assumed and tested in iterative excursions between theory and data. Demonstration of the conceptual equivalence of a construct between two cultures, though based on the grand assumption of the psychic unity of mankind, becomes further refined and rigorous by repeatedly being subjected to empirical tests and theoretical revision which strengthens the nomological network of which the construct is a part. Cross-cultural tests of the construct permit the expansion of this theoretical network by including cultural variables. However, in order to provide a meaningful test of the utility of the construct in the new culture, it is necessary to show that both the *construct* and the *operations* for measuring it are as appropriate in the new culture as in the culture of origin. However, it should be recognized that there is no general concensus regarding the best tactics to demonstrate conceptual equivalence across cultures. Consequently, the question of the cultural relevance (conceptual equivalence) of the construct is usually finessed by elaborate "theoretical relevance display behavior" followed by carefully ignoring the issue. This so-called display and deny strategy is not logically defensible, but it may be practically necessary and it *is* expedient for data collection. Nonetheless, it seems appropriate to remain uneasy with a too-cavalier assumption of conceptual equivalence. As noted by Segall (1979), "the degree to which we are measuring the same thing in more than one culture, whether we are using the same or different test items, must always worry us. We must always assume the worst while hoping for the best" (p. 53).

Once the concept has been shown to be a part of the subjective culture of the target culture, it is necessary to operationalize it more formally. Two general approaches are available. One would seek to "start from scratch" and apply psychometric test construction principles to the creation of a truly indigenous (emic) instrument without reference to previous prototypical Euromerican instrumentation. The other approach would follow the transport, translate, and test (3-t) strategy which utilizes the Euromerican operationalizations of the construct with appropriate and accurate translation. The *de novo* construction of indigenous tests is seldom tried in practice, and certainly in the present case all cross-cultural research utilizing the locus of control construct has been of the transport and test variety.

This approach raises the second general problem with regard to validity; namely, the validity of the *operationalizing* of the construct. *Is the instrument that has been shown to have construct validity in our culture also valid in the target culture?* Two approaches may be taken to provide data relevant to this question. First, we may seek to demonstrate similarity of the internal structure of the test in the two cultural contexts. This tactic is accomplished by some variant of item comparison (Frederiksen, 1977; Irvine & Carroll, 1980) or factor comparison (Cattell, 1969, 1978; Irvine & Carroll, 1980). Second, we seek to show that similar relationships hold between our instrument and other psychological dimensions in the two cultures. We thus attempt to demonstrate convergent and discriminative validity in either concurrent or predictive contexts. In either case the inference that the two cultures exhibit similar or different patterns of internal or external relationships regrettably is often based on subjective "eyeball" comparison. Furthermore, if the judgment is that the relationships are different, we typically cannot know whether the difference is due to the fact that (a) the measuring instruments are not comparable; (b) the instruments are psychometrically comparable but the construct means different things in the two cultures; or (c) the instruments and the construct are equivalent but the processes (behind the construct) enter into different functional cognitive systems or are weighted differently in the two cultures. It is these latter two cases which reflect valid cross-cultural differences of interest to psychologists.

Having explored but not solved our methodological conundrum, we may now consider the available cross-cultural literature. We first review those studies that have been devoted to cross-cultural comparisons of differences in mean level of externality. We then consider the cross-cultural comparisons of internal structures, followed by the cross-cultural research relevant to the external correlates of the LOC construct. We conclude with some recommendations for future research.

Comparisons of Relative Levels of Externality

Unfortunately, a substantial portion of the research literature has been devoted to a simple comparison of two cultural groups in mean performance on some LOC instrument. The approach is undoubtedly the least interesting and informative of the possible cross-cultural ques-

214 : JAMES A. DYAL

tions unless it is posed in the context of a theoretical rationale and a priori cultural analysis, which dictates the selection of the two cultures. As we shall see, such a theoretical or cultural analysis is seldom attempted a priori, or in most cases even a posteriori.

Differences in LOC among Subcultural Ethnic Groups

It is perhaps not surprising that instruments measuring individual differences in LOC were applied almost immediately to the comparison of middle-class US Whites (typically referred to as WASPS) with representatives of underprivileged minority groups who presumably had less control over their reinforcement contingencies. The extensively discussed and controversial Coleman report (Coleman, Campbell, Hobson, McPartland, Mood, Weinfeld, & York, 1966) asked three locus of control questions in an extensive survey of minority group children in US high schools. Their sample included minorities of Mexican, Puerto Rican, Native American, Oriental, and African descent, along with a White majority comparison group. Each of the minority groups was found to be more external in its LOC than were Whites.

US BLACKS

The earliest comparison of Black–White differences in LOC was that of Battle and Rotter (1963), who contrasted the performance of children on the Bialer LOC questionnaire and a cartoon projective test. Both instuments indicated an interaction between race and SES such that lower-class Black children were the most external. Lefcourt and Ladwig (1966) evaluated a prison population of adults who were relatively homogeneous in SES and found Blacks to be more external than Whites. These results led Lefcourt (1966) to hypothesize that "groups whose social position is one of minimal power either by class or race tend to score higher in the external control direction."

For the most part, subsequent research involving Black–White comparisons has tended to support this generalization. At this point, 18 other studies using a variety of measuring instruments have tested for Black–White differences in LOC. From Table 4.1 it may be seen that 12 have found Blacks to be significantly more external, whereas 6 found no reliable differences. Though SES is undoubtedly confounded in some of the comparisons, for the most part this is not the case, and the data in which SES was controlled tend to support the hypothesis. Several metaanalyses were conducted on these data; all were in agreement that

TABLE 4.1
Studies that Have Compared US Blacks with Whites on Locus of Control

Reference	LOC Scale	p	z
Battle & Rotter (1963)	Bialer (1961)	.01	2.33
Lefcourt & Ladwig (1965)	I–E (Rotter, 1966)	.05	1.65
Coleman et al. (1966)	Coleman et al. (1966)	.05	1.65
Lefcourt & Ladwig (1966)	Dean Powerlessness (Dean, 1969)	.01	2.33
Katz (1967)	IAR (Crandall et al., 1965)	.50	0.00
Kiehlbauch (1968)	I–E	.50	0.00
Lessing (1969)	Lessing (1969)	.05	1.65
Owens (1969)	—	.05	1.65
Scott & Phelan (1969)	I–E	.05	1.65
Shaw & Uhl (1971)	Bialer	.05	1.65
Soloman et al. (1971)	IAR	.50	0.00
Milgram et al. (1970)	Bialer	.50	0.00
Hall (1971)	I–E	.50	0.00
Milgram (1971)	Bialer	.50	0.00
Pedhazur & Wheeler (1971)	Bialer	.05	1.65
Zytkoskee et al. (1971)	Bialer	.001	3.09
Strickland (1972)	Nowicki–Strickland (1973)	.001	3.09
Gruen et al. (1974)	Gruen et al. (1974)	.01	2.33
Garcia & Levenson (1975)	IPC (Levenson, 1974)	.05	1.65
Roueche & Mink (1976)	Nowicki–Strickland	.05	1.65
Giorgis (1978)	I–E	.05	1.65

the probability that US Blacks are more external than US Whites is extraordinarily high. For example, the conservative Edgington test (1972) resulted in $Zp = 5.05$; $p < .00000029$; the failsafe N would require 304 more experiments yielding null results before the combined probability failed to be significant.

HISPANIC AMERICANS

The data for Black Americans support the interpretation that real-life reinforcement structures may be reflected in LOC measures; however, the results for Hispanic Americans are mixed and implicate SES, age, and/or education as important moderators. Those studies with lower-class adult samples have found Hispanic Americans to be more externally controlled than Whites (see Table 4.2). Furthermore, Coleman et al. (1966) found both Puerto Rican American and Mexican American high school children to be significantly more external than the White majority. However, later research involving high school and college students casts this finding into doubt. The study of Hispanic Americans by Jesson, Graves, Hanson, and Jessor (1968) was prescient

TABLE 4.2
Studies that Have Compared US Hispanics with Whites on Locus of Control

Reference	LOC scale	p	z
Adults (Low SES)			
Jessor *et al.* (1968)	Jessor *et al.*	.05	1.65
Scott & Phelan (1969)	I–E	.05	1.65
Shearer & Moore (1978)	Levenson, IPC	.05	1.65
Public school children			
Coleman *et al.* (1966)	Coleman	.05	1.65
Jessor *et al.* (1968)	Jessor	.50	0.00
Scott & Phelan (1969)	I–E	.50	0.00
Pedhazur & Wheeler (1971)	Bialer	.05	1.65
Cole *et al.* (1978)	I–E	.50	0.00
Knight *et al.* (1978)	IAR	.50	0.00
Buriel (1981)	IAR	.50	0.00
College students			
Garza & Ames (1974)	I–E	.99	−2.33
Roueche & Mink (1976)	ANSIE	.01	2.33
Alvarez & Pader (1978)	I–E	.50	0.00
Buriel & Rivera (1980)	I–E	.50	0.00

of these later findings. They showed that in a triethnic community in Colorado, the Hispanic *adults* were more external than either the White or the Native American adults. However, no such differences were obtained among the high school students in the same community. Similarly, Scott and Phelan (1969) found that a group of chronically unemployed Mexican-American adults were more external than comparable White welfare recipients, but again no LOC differences were obtained among the adolescent children in the same community. Two other studies involving high school students and young adults failed to obtain differences between Mexican-American high school students (Cole, Rodriquez, & Cole, 1978) or Cuban-American college students (Alvarez & Pader, 1978) when compared with comparable Anglo-American students. Furthermore, Garza and Ames (1974) found that Mexican-American college students who were matched with Anglo-American students on socioeconomic status and gender scored significantly more *internal* on Rotter's I–E Scale. The greater internality of the Hispanics was especially notable on the Luck–Fate and the Respect dimensions. The authors contend that these findings "not only contradict the stereotype that Mexican Americans are fatalistic and controlled by external forces but they seem to suggest that their culture actually contributes to a great perception of internal control." In support of Garza and

Ames's results, three recent studies of Caucasian versus Hispanic differences in LOC have failed to obtain ethnic differences in high school children (Buriel & Rivera, 1980) or grade school children (Buriel, 1981; Knight, Kagan, Nelson & Gumbiner, 1978) when SES is controlled. On the other hand, an extensive study by Roueche and Mink (1976) found Mexican-American children to be more external than Whites on the Adult Nowicki–Strickland Internal–External Scale (ANSIE). However, the results with Levenson's IPC scales revealed that compared to Whites, Mexican Americans were more external on the Chance Scale and less internal on the Internality Scale; they were, however, less external on the Powerful Others Scale (see Table 4.7).

Of course, several alternative explanations could account for the conflicting results among the studies. Garza (1977) characterized much of the research as demonstrating a "blatant lack of theoretical and conceptual objectivity." The substance of this polemical assertion is that previous research has not taken sufficient care to match the groups in socioeconomic status, a variable that has been shown to influence perceived control (e.g., Franklin, 1963; Gruen & Ottinger, 1969). Inspection of the relevant research for possible SES confounds reveals the following: In studies in which there is either explicit matching or no reason to assume SES differences (Alvarez & Pader, 1978; Buriel, 1981; Buriel & Riveria, 1980; Cole et al., 1978; Garza & Ames, 1974; Knight et al., 1978), either no evidence or contrary evidence for Hispanic fatalism was obtained. Furthermore, in those studies that did obtain differences (Coleman et al., 1966; Roueche and Mink, 1976), SES confounds are clearly present. In two studies with college students (Alvarez & Pader, 1978; Garza & Ames, 1974) where SES was explicitly controlled, either no evidence or contrary evidence for Hispanic fatalism was obtained. Similarly, in the Cole et al. (1978) study, no ethnic differences on LOC were obtained, and it would appear that the Caucasian and Hispanic samples may have been reasonably equivalent in SES. On the other hand, although SES data are not reported, there seems little basis to assert that the adult felon samples of Shearer and Moore (1978) were confounded by SES differences; likewise, the greater externality of Hispanic adult welfare cases (Scott & Phelan, 1969) does not seem to be compromised by SES differences with the White comparison groups. Furthermore, there is little reason to believe that the hypothesis of "SES confounds of apparent ethnic differences" should be limited to Hispanics; and Garcia and Levenson (1975) showed that Black–White differences in perceived control persist when SES is controlled by covariance.

An alternative hypothesis focuses on the age variable. Meta-analyses of the data presented in Table 4.2 reveal that over all studies the effect is significant ($Zs = 2.21$, $p = .013$; $Zp = 1.75$, $p = .040$) indicating that Hispanics are more external than Caucasians. However, separate analyses for the adults, public school children, and college students confirm what is obvious from the table. The greater externality of Hispanics is significant for lower-class adults ($Zs = 2.86$, $p = .002$; $Zp = 2.70$, $p = .004$), of borderline significance for the school children ($p = .10$), and clearly nonsignificant for college students. Phares (1976) proposes that it is possible that "a rise in externality occurs as one leaves high school (when) there is the first encounter with the dominant culture and all its implications as regards job discrimination, prejudice etc." (p. 153). Again, although the hypothesis is plausible, there appears to be no cogent rationale for limiting its effect to Hispanics, and Garcia and Levenson's (1975) data showing greater minority group (Blacks) externality for students (even when SES differences are eliminated) becomes relevant. Furthermore, the "post-high-school–real-world effect" would not encompass the greater externality evidenced by the Puerto Rican elementary school children in the Pedhazur and Wheeler (1971) study. Parametric studies of age and LOC indicate that internality increases from youth through middle age and does not decrease in old age (Lao, 1974; Ryckman & Malikioski, 1975); however, these studies have been based on US Whites and it is not known if they apply to US minorities or other cultures.

A third alternative emphasizes *selection* factors in those studies that show no (or reversed) Hispanic–White differences. Specifically, it could be asserted that ethnic comparisons based on high school seniors or college students are biased in favor of finding no differences or reversed effects simply because the minority group subjects have been selected by educational–societal pressures in such a way that internals are overrepresented because the academically less successful (and more external) have dropped out along the way. Indeed, Garza and Ames seem to admit this bias when they say: "The fact the subjects were college students, however, limits generalization of the findings to the entire Mexican-American population" (p. 919). Additional support for this alternative comes from a cross-cultural comparison by Cole et al. (1978), who found college students in Mexico to be more *internal* that students in United States, Germany, or Ireland. They argue that being a minority student in Mexico is a more unique achievement and that an internal locus of control characterizes those who take a "counter normative step toward self improvement" (Cole & Cole, 1977). Cole et al. also provide data showing that Mexican college students are more internal than Mexican factory workers, whereas US students are more external than

US factory workers on some dimensions (Politics) but more internal on other dimensions (Respect and Leadership).

NATIVE AMERICANS

The Jessor *et al.* (1968) study found that Native Americans (Navajo) do not differ from White adults though both were more internal than the Hispanic group. Tyler and Holsinger (1975) compared Chippewa and White children in grades 4, 7, 9, and 11 on the Nowicki–Strickland (NOSIE) and the Rotter I–E scales. They found the Chippewa children to be more external than the Whites, with the ethnic difference being larger for females and younger children than for males and older children. They note that their grade 11 sample was probably biased by selective dropout of males and externals. It is also possible that there is an SES confound in this study, given that the Native Americans were primarily rural and the Whites were urban.

Echohawk and Parsons (1977) compared Native American children at boarding schools in Oklahoma with the White norms for the NOSIE and concluded that the "Indian students in this study are greater in externality than Nowicki–Strickland Ss but since control over socioeconomic levels was not established, this must be interpreted with caution." That caution is appropriate is indicated by the results of a study by Halpin, Halpin, and Whiddon (1981), who compared Flathead Native Americans who were junior and senior high school students with White students living in "close proximity under similar socioeconomic conditions" and attending the same schools. They utilized Crandall's Intellectual Achievement Responsibilities Questionnaire (IAR) and found no differences in total IAR score between the Native Americans and Whites. It is worth noting that these results are in fact rather consistent with those of Tyler and Holsinger, who found no differences for their grade 11 subjects and only for females in grades 7 and 9. Halpin *et al.*'s data also show the largest racial difference for junior high school females.[1]

ASIANS

Hsieh, Shybut and Lotsof (1969) compared Hong Kong Chinese adolescents (17 years old) with Chinese Americans and Anglo-Americans. They found the Chinese Americans to be significantly more external

---

[1] Since the Fs were not significant, Halpin *et al.* quite appropriately did not test for differences between these two means; however, a post hoc test of these differences reveals the difference to be highly significant for females.

than the Anglo-Americans and reliably *less* external than the Hong Kong Chinese. Similar results were obtained by Coleman et al. (1966), whose data show US Orientals tend to be somewhat more external than US Whites. They were, however consistantly less external than the other minority groups in the Coleman study. Christy (1977) found Chinese-American women to be more external than Hong Kong Chinese women.

Barling and Fincham (1978) compared South African children of Asian Indian descent with South African children of European descent on the CNSIE. They found that the overall performance of the two groups was the same, although some differences did emerge on specific factors; for example, the Indians were more internal on the helplessness and achievement factors. The authors suggest that the South African sociopolitical system results in Indian children learning from parental modeling that they must compete for a limited number of opportunities "through considerable personal effort and initiative." However, it should be noted that previous research has found no relationship between parental LOC and that of the children (Katkovsky, Crandall, & Good, 1967) and that the impact of modeling on LOC is unknown and needs further research (Phares, 1976). It may well be that the use of middle-class urban subjects in the Barling and Fincham study reflects SES as an important modifier of LOC both through selection (those who have been economically successful through personal efforts achieve or maintain middle-class status) and through modification of child-rearing practices to be more warm, protective, and nurturant of preadolescent children.

FRENCH CANADIANS

Kanungo and Bhatnagar (1978) assert that French Canadians perceive themselves as a minority group in Canada. They compared French-Canadian and Anglo-Canadian high school children in Montreal and found no differences between the two groups on overall externality on Rotter's I–E Scale. However, they did find that the Francophones placed considerably greater emphasis on interpersonal climate as opposed to task importance when choosing a work partner. These latter results suggest the interesting possibility that if Kanungo and Bhatnagar had examined affiliation and achievement control orientations separately (through Lefcourt's Multidimensional–Multiattributional Causality Scale [MMCS], differences between the two cultural groups would be obtained.

IMMIGRANTS–SOJOURNERS

To the extent that expectancies have some degree of veridicality to real-world reinforcement contingencies, it would be expected that new immigrants to a country would feel less control over what happens to them and test as more external than comparable groups who remained in their home culture or comparison groups of established (second-generation) minority group members in the host culture. Wolfgang (1973) compared ninth-grade Italian immigrant adolescents with comparable (gender and SES) adolescents in Italy and Canadian-born Italian-Canadians. As expected, he found the immigrant children to be more external than either of the comparison groups who did not differ from each other.

Chan (1981) administered Lefcourt's MMCS to Hong Kong Chinese student sojourners in Canada, Chinese students at the University of Hong Kong, and Anglo-Canadian students. She found the Hong Kong sojourners to feel more externally controlled than either of the comparison groups with regard to affiliation. However, in the area of achievement the foreign students were in the middle between the Hong Kong and the Canadian students; Hong Kong students were more external than the Canadian students. On the other hand, Kim (1977) found Canadian children to be more external than Korean-Canadian immigrants, and Mahler (1974) found no difference between US students in Japan and a US university sample. Likewise, Dyal and Bertrand (1982) found no difference (Rotter's I–E Scale) between Trinidadian student sojourners to Canada and a comparison group of Trinidadian students at the University of West Indies.

Dyal (1978) compared Anglo-Canadian children (grades 5 and 6) with Portuguese immigrant children on Crandall's IAR. There were no ethnic differences associated with responsibility for success, failure, or total internality. Dyal, Eckerman, Chan, Rai, and Lum (1979) compared IAR performance of Filippino children in Hawaii who came from the province of Ilocos with second-generation Ilocanos in Honolulu. They found no differences on the total score or responsibility for success but obtained a strong gender × country of birth interaction in the responsibility for failure scores. Females accepted more responsibility for failure than males, and immigrants were more internal for failure than were second-generation Ilocanos. Thus the nature of the interaction was that female immigrant children tended to attribute failure to themselves most often, whereas second-generation (US-born) males tended to self-attribute failure the least often. These results are consistent with

data reported by Dweck and Bush (1976) showing that female Caucasian children tend to self-attribute failure more than do males. Later in
this chapter it is shown that the self-attribution of failure may be correlated with mood disturbance and poor adjustment.

Although it may be the case that new immigrants are more likely
to be more external for success and internal for failure, the more stable
sociocultural differences that preceded immigration should also result
in group differences. Two studies conducted in Israel speak to this
point. Immigrants to Israel from the Soviet Union and the United States
were compared with native-born Israelis by Aviram and Milgram (1977).
They predicted that the children who had been socialized in the Soviet
Union would be more external than the other two groups. Their results
supported their hypothesis and were interpreted to indicate the importance of early socialization differences between Western countries
and the Soviet Union. The fact that the US immigrants did not differ
from the Israelis whereas the Soviets were much more external could
also reflect the presence of better coping or less stress for the US-born
children than for the Soviet-born children. Unfortunately, no stress and
coping measures were included in the study.

Bar-Tal et al. (1980) compared 2438 ninth-grade Israeli-Jewish students of Asian–African background with Israeli-Jewish children of
Euro-American background. On the basis of expected differences in
SES and child-rearing practices, it was predicted that the Asian–African children would be more external than the Euro-American-Israeli
children. The data supported this prediction, but it should be noted that
the racial–ethnic differences are completely confounded with obtained
differences in SES.

Nedd and Marsh (1979) found a fatalism–personal efficacy dimension to discriminate between New Zealand (Maoris and Polynesian Is-
lander) immigrants and European New Zealanders (native born and
immigrant), with Polynesians being more fatalistic and New Zealanders emphasizing personal efficacy.

As is typical of much research with the LOC construct, the data
on immigrants and minorities are not entirely consistent and sometimes contradictory. Nonetheless, the results are generally consistent
with the hypothesis that subjective expectancies of control of reinforcement tend to correspond to real-world control relationships. Second, it
is clear and obvious that if one is to make valid inferences regarding
the influence of one variable (e.g., ethnicity), other potentially confounding variables such as SES, age, gender, and education must be
controlled, preferably in such a way that their moderating effects on
each other can be evaluated.

Cross-Cultural Comparisons of Relative Externality

Although many cross-cultural studies of relative locus of control have compared several countries and cultures, we adopt the strategy of using the United States as the standard for comparison. The rationale for such an apparently ethnocentric tactic is twofold: First, the original normative data for all of the LOC instruments are from US samples; second, the vast majority of external validity studies that have explored and extended the meaning of the LOC construct have been based on US samples; and third, it is a discursive convenience. We also follow the heuristic of grouping the data by cultural areas; first considering Anglo-Celtic comparisons, followed by European, Asian, African, Latin American, and West Indies data.

ANGLO-CELTIC COMPARISONS

Because of the common historical roots and the strong cultural similarities among the Anglo-Celtic countries in the British Commonwealth, large differences in LOC would not be expected, and indeed none have been obtained. McGinnies, Nordholm, Ward, and Bhanthumnavin (1974) found no overall differences in I–E among students in the United States, Australia, and New Zealand. Similarly, Parsons and Schneider (1974) obtained no differences between Canadian and US students on the overall I–E score or on any of the subscale scores. Likewise Cole *et al.* (1978) report no differences between students in the United States and Ireland. Reid and Croucher (1980) recently validated the Crandall IAR questionnaire on 1000 British primary school children and obtained results that were highly similar to the earlier US data.

EUROPEAN COMPARISONS

The first cross-national comparisons of two Western cultures on relative LOC were reported by Parsons, Schneider, and Hansen in 1970. They compared Danish university students with US students. Their theoretical rationale for such a comparison was minimal; rather, they posed the general empirical question: "Is it possible that the high degree of social planning could lead to Danish Ss believing that they had less personal control over their behavior and hence score more external than United States Ss?" (p. 31). They found no differences in LOC level between US and Danish females, but Danish males were reliably more external than were US males. The male differences were regarded as small and aberrant, and the conclusion was drawn that the Danish and

US students were quite similar in their total I–E scores. However, in a companion paper based on the same samples, Schneider and Parsons (1970) reanalyzed the data in terms of five conceptual categories based on the manifest content of the I–E scale items. These categories were Luck–Fate; Respect; Politics; Academics, and Leadership–Success. They found the Danes to be reliably more external on the Leadership–Success category (Items 6, 11, 13, 16) and proposed that general cross-cultural similarities and differences would be revealed more adequately by the differentiation of these conceptual categories. Additional evidence for the greater externality of students from a Scandinavian welfare state was reported by McGinnies et al. (1974), who found Swedish college preparatory students to be the most external (overall I–E) of five countries (Sweden, Japan, Australia, United States, and New Zealand). Unfortunately, the generality of this finding may be questioned on the grounds of a substantially smaller N for the Swedish sample and the fact that they were somewhat younger and still living with their parents.

Three studies have reported comparisons of West German students with US students and found a weak tendency for the Germans to be more external. On the overall I–E scale, Maroldo and Flachmeir (1978) obtained a strong effect for German versus US females, whereas Cole et al. (1978) and Parsons and Schneider (1974) reported no differences on the overall I–E score. However, Cole et al. did find US students to be more external on Respect and Parsons and Schneider found the Germans to be more external on the Academic and Leadership–Success categories. They obtained quite parallel results for French, Italian, and Israeli students as well. Specifically, the pattern was that no overall I–E differences existed between the United States and France, Italy, or Israel; however, when the component scores were examined, the US students were more external on Respect but more internal on the Leadership–Success and Academic scales. Schmidt, Lamm, and Tromsdorf (1978) compared lower- and middle-class adult (and 35–45 years) Germans and, consonant with class differences obtained in the United States, found the lower-class Germans to be more external.

Rupp and Nowicki (1978) reported no difference between Hungarian and US adolescents on the children's version of the NOSIE. On the other hand, Malikiosi and Ryckman (1977) found Greeks to have a stronger belief that their lives were controlled by Powerful Others and Chance (Levenson IPC scale). No cultural difference was present on the internality dimension. The strong cultural differences on the Powerful Others and Chance dimensions may be understood as reflecting a veridical perception by the Greeks of their cultural constraints, in that the data were collected in 1973 shortly before the overthrow of the military dictatorship. Similarly, Jessor, Young, Young, and Tesi (1970) found two groups of Italian youths to be significantly more external than US youths.

We may summarize the results and implications of the application of LOC scales to compare nationalities within the Euro-Western tradition as follows:

1. When national comparisons are made using an overall LOC score, cultural differences are weak and may apply only in special subsamples differentiated by gender or SES.
2. Cultural differences that make ad hoc sense (sometimes) are more likely to be revealed by a finer–grained analysis of LOC components or factors.

ORIENTAL ASIANS

The first true cross-cultural comparison of LOC was reported by Hsieh *et al.* in 1969 and involved three groups of high school students (Hong Kong Chinese, US-born Chinese, and Caucasian Americans). The authors argued, following Hsu (1953), that US culture was individual-centered and placed a great deal of emphasis on self-reliance, achieved status, and power over other people and things, such that "life experiences appear to be largely a consequence of one's actions." Chinese culture, in contrast, is thought of as situation-centered, in that "luck, chance, and fate are taken for granted in life, which is considered to be full of ambiguity, complexity, and unpredictability (Hsu, 1953; 1963). Life situations may be viewed as being largely determined by circumstances outside his control" (p. 122). As a consequence, Hsieh *et al.* predicted that Hong Kong Chinese students would be more externally controlled on the I–E scale, whereas Chinese-Americans would be somewhere in between Chinese and US students in their perceived control. The results were precisely as hypothesized and were robust to adjustment for SES.

These results have been replicated and extended by Chan (1981) using a different LOC instrument (MMCS), a different comparison group (Anglo-Canadian) and different age level (college students). Lefcourt's MMCS scale permits full-scale I–E comparisons as well as subscale comparisons on achievement and affiliation domains. Overall I–E differences revealed the Hong Kong Chinese sample to be more external than the Canadian sample. Subscale analyses showed that this was due primarily to differences in the achievement domain, as there were no reliable differences on the affiliation scores.

Similarly, Lao (1978) found Taiwan Chinese (females) to be more external on the personal control (I) factor of the Levenson IPC scale. However, there was no difference in the degree to which they felt they were controlled by Chance (C), and the relationship was reversed in the case of Powerful Others (P) with US subjects avowing more external control than the Taiwanese. This latter outcome seems anomalous and may well be due to the fact that Lao's US sample, although quite large, is unusually external on the P scale. To demonstrate this fact, a weighted mean was computed from 12 independent samples of US Whites (N = 1256) reported by Levenson (1981). This value of 19.74 may be taken as the best available estimate of the population mean for US Whites on the P scale. Computation of the 1% confidence interval for this mean indicates the interval to be 17.70 to 21.78. Thus Lao's Chinese sample weighted mean (21.56) lies within the expected confidence interval, whereas the weighted mean of her comparison White sample (24.10) is significantly more external than the Levenson normative sample of US Whites. The appropriateness of Lao's comparison group is thus called into question.[2] A similar analysis applied to the Lao data for the Chance factor reveals that both the Taiwanese and the US sample are reliably more external than the US White norms, although they are not reliably different from each other.

Our conclusions from the Lao data are thus dependent on which comparison data are regarded as more appropriate: If Lao's South Carolina White group is utilized as the comparison, then the Chinese are more external on personal control (internality), more internal on control by powerful others (P), and equivalent on control by chance (C). However, if the normative data are utilized to provide the best estimate of the population of values for US Whites, then the Taiwanese are not different from the US norms on the Internal and Powerful Others scales but are significantly more *external* on the Chance scale. This latter result is consonant with theoretical expectations and the results of Hsieh *et al.* (1969) and Chan (1981).

The most consistent results in the cross-cultural literature on LOC have been obtained comparing Japanese with White Americans. Bond and Tornatzky (1973) administered Rotter's I–E Scale to university students in Japan and the United States and found the Japanese to be reliably more external. Mahler (1974) obtained confirming results using Levenson's IPC Scales; the Japanese were more external than the Americans on all three dimensions. Japanese students were included in the

[2]The same conclusion obtains if an even more liberal position is taken and the Lao data are included in the US White normative data in computing the weighted mean and confidence intervals, which become 19.02–22.64 at the 1% level.

extensive eight-country study by Parsons and Schneider (1974) and in the five-nation comparison of McGinnis *et al.* (1974). McGinnis *et al.* found Japanese (and Swedish) students to be more external than those from the United States, Australia, and New Zealand who did not differ from each other. Similarly, the Japanese were by far the most external of Parsons and Schneider's eight countries (Japan, United States, Canada, West Germany, Italy, France, Israel, and India). In addition to overall externality scores, Parsons and Schneider provided comparisons on their five conceptual dimensions. In comparison with the US sample, the Japanese were more external on Luck–Fate, Respect, and Academic subscales but were equivalent on the Politics and Leadership–Success subscales.

That Japanese externality is not limited to university students is demonstrated by Reitz and Groff (1974), who conducted a large-scale ($N = 1846$) comparison of nonsupervisory factory workers in the United States, Japan, Thailand, and Mexico. Like Parsons and Schneider, they found the Japanese workers to be more external on the Luck–Fate and Respect dimensions and to be equivalent on the Leadership–Success dimension. The only exception to exact replication of the Parsons and Schneider results was in the case of Politics, where Reitz and Groff found Japanese factory workers to be reliably more *internal* than Americans.[3] Compared to the US sample Thai workers were more external overall and particularly on the Respect and Leadership–Success subscales. In comparison with the Japanese, the Thai sample was even more external on Leadership–Success, Politics, and Luck–Fate. Analysis of the total score data revealed a significant culture × level of development interaction, such that the United States and Mexico were essentially the same, whereas the Oriental externality was more exaggerated in a developing country (Thailand) than in a developed country (Japan).

Chandler *et al.* (1981) administered Lefcourt's MMCS (Lefcourt, Von Baeyer, Ware, & Cox, 1979) in Japan, India, South Africa, the

---

[3]The political items (3, 12, 17, 22, and 29) include such internal alternatives as "one of the major reasons we have wars is because people don't take enough interest in politics"; "the average citizen can have an influence in government decisions"; and "by taking an active part in political and social affairs the people can control world events." It is tempting to speculate that the greater internality of the Japanese adults may be related to their political conservatism, as is true in the United States. However, no comparable data relating political ideology and LOC are available for Japan. Another plausible, though equally speculative, hypothesis suggests a guilt dynamic resulting from failure to prevent the military debacle of World War II and resulting affirmation of control over political excesses or wrongdoing. De Vos (1974) provided an illuminating analysis of the role of guilt in postwar Japan.

United States, and Yugoslavia. Their results clearly indicate the utility of a multiattributional instrument such as the MMCS. Consonant with previous research, they found the Japanese sample to be highly external in the attribution of their successes; however, they were the most internal of all the groups in attributing their failures. Their strongest attribution for failure was the lack of effort. In contrast, US subjects saw effort as the most salient cause of their successes. It is also notable that only the Japanese data failed to support a self-serving bias (Miller & Ross, 1975) such that successes are attributed more to personal responsibility than are failures.

The greater overall externality of the Japanese on the I–E scale has recently been replicated as part of a study of LOC and word association by Evans (1981). In contrast, Kim (1977) found Koreans to be more *internal* on total I–E and Respect than Canadians; there were no differences on other subscales. This latter finding, being dissonant with the rest of the Asian literature, requires replication before ad hoc exploration of the possible cultural basis for the Korean difference is attempted.

In sum, the data strongly support the generalization that Oriental Asians are more external in their locus of control than are North American Caucasians. The supporting data are strongest and most consistent for Japan and Thailand, somewhat less consistent for the Chinese but still generally supportive, and equivocal in the case of Koreans. Although greater externality of Oriental Asians is consistent with the previous characterization of Chinese culture by the cultural anthropologists (Hsu, 1953), a more precise unwrapping of the cultural "package" as it relates to perceived control awaits further analyses.

INDIA

Perhaps the cultural uniqueness of India was foreshadowed by its geotectonic history, which stipulates that the Indian subcontinent only recently (geologically speaking) joined the Asian land mass. This separateness from northern (Oriental) Asia has been reinforced by the uplifting of the barrier of the Himalayan massifs and has been exaggerated by continual migrations of diverse peoples from the Near East across the Indian plains. The consequent intermingling has resulted in a culture that is at one and the same time perhaps the most diverse and the most unique of all major developing nations. India is different and diverse. Its diversity must serve to caution overgeneralizations by overeager cross-cultural researchers who are attracted by its uniqueness.

That India resists generalizations is apparent in the inconsistencies of the available LOC literature.

Carment (1974) reported the first comparison of Indian and North American (Canadian) samples on LOC. In addition to the typical university student samples he also compared factory workers in the two countries. He found Indian students to be significantly more *internal* than Canadian students on the I–E full-scale score. Examination of subscales indicated that this full-scale effect was due to the greater internality of the Indians (students and workers) on Political Ideology and System Control factors (Gurin, Gurin, Lao, & Beattie, 1969). Carment comments that "this is somewhat surprising in view of the extensive nepotism, ingratiation and bribery found in India. . . . It may be that in India these techniques are viewed as involving effort, skill and ability, all internal characteristics." In contrast to the results on these sociopolitical factors, the Indian students were more *external* than the Canadians on the Personal Control factor. Carment interprets this difference to reflect the greater maternal indulgence and dependency–conformity training of the Indian family.

The greater overall internality of Indian students was also reported by Parsons and Schneider (1974). However, the pattern of differences on subscales is quite different from that obtained by Carment. Although Parsons and Schneider broke their results down according to their content-oriented conceptual categories rather than the factors utilized by Carment, it is nonetheless possible to make reasonable comparisons of the data because of item overlap. For example, Carment's Personal Control factor consisting of Items 9, 13, 15, 25, and 28 contains four Luck–Fate and one Leadership–Success item in the Parsons and Schneider category system. Whereas Carment found Indians to be more *external* than Canadians on personal control, the Parsons and Schneider sample found them to be more internal on Luck–Fate. The Gurin Systems Control factor used by Carment is exactly the same as Parsons and Schneider's Political category, and again different results were obtained. Carment found the Indians to be more internal, but Parsons and Schneider obtained no difference. Comparison between the two studies is less apt in the case of Control Ideology, given that this factor is quite heterogeneous with regard to content categories, with 10 of the 12 Control Ideology items being found in the Respect, Academic, and Leadership–Success content areas. Consistent with Carment's data, Parsons and Schneider found Indians to be more internal on Respect; however, they found no differences on Academic and Leadership–Success.

It should be noted that inferences about the relative standing of

Indians vis-à-vis North Americans depend on whether the comparison is made with Canadian or US subjects. That is, although Parsons and Schneider find no statistically significant difference between these two groups on any of the subscales, comparisons between India and the United States reveal a different pattern than that between India and Canada. These differences are summarized in Table 4.3, where it may be seen that only the inferences concerning Respect and Politics are the same independent of comparison group. Furthermore, when Carment's Canadian sample is compared to Parsons and Schneider's Canadian sample, only the inference regarding overall externality is consonant between the two studies.

In the Chandler et al. (1981) study the Indian sample was less internal overall on the achievement dimension of the MMCS than were US respondents. However, when attribution for success and failure were analyzed separately, Indians were found to be more internal for success and more external for failure than Japanese and US subjects.

Although this is not strictly comparable to cross-national comparisons, it will be remembered that when East Indians living in South Africa are compared with South African Whites on LOC, no differences were obtained on an overall LOC index (Barling & Fincham, 1978; Moodley-Rajab & Ramkissoon, 1979). However, Indian children were significantly more internal on Helplessness and Achievement factors but not on the Luck factor of the CNSIE (Barling and Fincham, 1978). These results are consistent with those of Chandler et al. (1981), who

TABLE 4.3

Direction of Effects in Studies by Parsons and Schneider (1974) and Carment (1974) Using US and Canadian Samples for Comparison with Asian Indians[a]

Dimension	Parsons & Schneider		Carment
	US	Canada	Canada
Overall	$=$I	$>$I	$>$I
Luck–Fate	$=$I	$>$I	$<$I
Respect	$>$I	$>$I	
Academic	$=$I	$=$I	$>$I
Leadership–Success	$<$I	$=$I	
Politics	$=$I	$=$I	$>$I

[a] $>$ means US–Canada is more external than India; $<$ means US–Canada is more internal than India; $=$ means no significant difference.

found that "subjects from all countries except India believed that luck contributed more to their success than their failure ($p < .01$). Indians, on the other hand, reported luck as contributing equally to success and failure" (p. 215).

The generally inconclusive nature of the data thus far available is perhaps not surprising when the internal heterogeneity of India is acknowledged. Apropos of this point, Khanna and Khanna (1979) recently reported comparisons of high school graduates in India. They conclude that contrary to earlier reports "the group was not more internal than previously reported for other cultures [however within the Indian culture] women were more external than men, Hindus were more external than non-Hindus, Ss who believed in Karma were more external than those who did not, and Ss of lower socioeconomic status were more external than Ss of higher status" (p. 207).

AFRICA

Available LOC research on indigenous Black African groups is limited to Nigeria and Rhodesia. Reimanis (1977) compared teachers' college students from the Biu area of northeastern Nigeria with community college students in New York. Overall the Nigerians were more external.[4] Comparison of the groups on specific item content revealed the Nigerians to be more external with regard to Destiny and Education items. However, there were no cultural differences on the Political items, with both groups feeling there is little one can do about war, corruption, and world events. In 1980 Reimanis and Posen added White Rhodesians (Zimbabweans) and Black Zimbabweans to the previously reported Nigerian–US comparisons. They proposed that both cultural and national (situation) factors would operate to influence overall control expectancy and that such molar variables would have differential influence depending on the I–E dimension that was being considered. Specifically, it was expected that *culturally* similar groups (Black Nigerians [BN] and Black Zimbabweans [BZ]; White Rhodesians [WR] and White Americans [WA]) would be similar to each other on Personal Control and that the Blacks would be more external than the Whites. The results supported both these expectations, with Personal Control externality scores ranging as follows: BN = BZ > WA = WR. However, because of political–situational uncertainty in Zimbabwe, it was expected that both Black and White Zimbabweans would be more ex-

---

[4]In the 1977 article the scale was scored in the internal direction, whereas in the 1980 study the more usual scoring in the direction of externality was utilized (Reimanis personal communication, 1981).

ternal on Systems Control than Black Nigerians or US Whites. The results are partially consistent with this hypothesis; the Black
Zimbabweans were significantly more external than the Black Nigerians and the US Whites. The authors also expected that Control Ideology
would be influenced by both cultural and situational factors in unknown ways and the specific ordering of groups could not be predicted.
The data indicated significant effects for cultural factors (BA > BN >
WA) and also for situational factors (BZ > WR).

Reimanis (1982) contributed a third study which permits comparison of Black African university undergraduates with US undergraduates. No cultural differences were reported on the overall I–E score,
and the data were not analyzed for differences on LOC factors.

Ryckman, Posen, and Kulberg (1978) compared US and Rhodesian
university students (a multiracial sample) on Collins's I–E Scale (Collins, 1974). They did not report cultural differences on Collins's factors,
but they did analyze for differences on each item, obtaining differences
on 11 of the 28 items. "In general, these differences indicated that the
Rhodesians had stronger feelings of self-determination than the Americans and that they also believed more strongly that governmental institutions were unresponsive to their needs" (p. 170). A later paper
presented a more complete comparison of the Rhodesian subgroups on
the Collins factors (Ryckman, Posen, & Kulberg, 1979). On the Authoritarian Control factor Black Africans were the most external followed
by Asians and then Europeans; US students were the most internal on
this factor. However, the Black Africans were the most internal of all
the groups on the Self-Determination for Success items. They also
tended to be more internal than the White Rhodesians on the Political
Responsiveness items, a difference that makes sense in terms of the
political climate in Rhodesia, now Zimbabwe. Ryckman et al. concluded that considerable caution must be exercised

> not only in drawing comparisons on I–E between cultures since the various com-
> ponents of locus of control may have different meanings between certain popula-
> tions, but also on I–E comparisons within a particular population. It is apparent that
> differences in perceptions of control are closely aligned to the experiences and na-
> ture of the environments confronting the individuals [1979, p. 171].

The importance of factor comparisons in addition to overall I–E
score in detecting cultural and subcultural differences is also indicated
by Giorgis (1978), who compared Black African students' responses with
those of US Black and US White students. She found no cultural differences on overall LOC. However, on the Personal Control items the
Black Africans were more external than the US Whites; US Blacks fell

between the two. There were no cultural differences on System Control, and the Africans were significantly more internal than the US Blacks on Control Ideology; US Blacks were more external than US Whites.

LATIN AMERICA

It is refreshing to find that in their comparison of industrially developed countries and developing countries in the East (Japan and Thailand) and the West (the United States and Mexico), Reitz and Groff (1974) tested specific hypotheses with respect to the conceptual dimensions (Parsons & Schneider, 1974) of the I–E scale. They hypothesized that workers from developing economies would be more external than those from developed economies on the Leadership–Success dimension. This hypothesis was strongly supported for both Eastern and Western countries. Mexican factory workers were more external than US factory workers and Thai workers were more external than Japanese. They also hypothesized that on the Respect dimension there would be no differences among Eastern countries or among Western countries but that the Eastern countries would be more external than the Western countries. The hypotheses were supported (J = T > US = M). On the Luck–Fate dimension they found, in opposition to their hypothesis, that workers from developing countries were significantly less external than those from developed countries. Specifically, their data contradicted the cultural stereotype that Mexicans are more fatalistic than US citizens. In fact, the Mexican workers were the most *internal* on Luck–Fate of the four countries.

That this counterstereotypic result is not unique to Mexican workers is supported by Cole et al. (1978), who found Mexican university students to be more internal than US university students on the Luck–Fate dimension. They were also more internal on the Respect and Academic dimensions and on the overall Rotter I–E score. Not surprisingly, their university student samples were reliably more internal than the factory workers in the Reitz and Groff study on all dimensions and overall.

That the failure to validate the fatalistic stereotype of Mexicans is not peculiar to the use of the Rotter I–E scale is indicated by Cole and Cole (1977), who utilized the Levenson IPC Scale. They found Mexican females who were business students to score more internal on the Powerful Others and Chance dimensions than a comparison group of US female business students; however, no such differences were found for male students. Similar differences were obtained by Wolfgang and Craig

(1971), who found middle-class Mexican students to be more internal (I–E scale) then Canadian students. Like the subcultural comparisons of Caucasians and Mexican Americans previously discussed, these cross-cultural data also call into question previously assumed cultural differences when the samples are confined to middle-class subjects.

Wolfgang and Weiss (1980) compared Jamaican and Trinidadian adolescents with Canadian White adolescents on Rotter's I–E Scale. They found the West Indian children to be more internal than the Canadians. However, they noted that the West Indian children may have been more highly selected for success in a highly competitive educational system based on a British model. Furthermore, there is a possible socioeconomic status difference, in that more of the West Indian children came from professional–white-collar families than did Canadian children. It is thus not clear whether Wolfgang and Weiss's results are due to cultural differences or selection and SES factors. Furthermore, Jones and Zoppel (1979) obtained no differences in I–E control among middle-class Jamaican high school students, middle-class US Blacks, and lower-class US Black.

Studies of Internal Structure

Structure of Rotter's I–E Scale for North American Whites

The first attempts at factor analyzing the Rotter's I–E Scale failed to yield coherent factors (Franklin, 1963; Rotter, 1966), and these results supported the original conceptualization of the scale as additive and unidimensional (Rotter, 1954). However, the issue of the dimensionality of the scale was forcibly raised by Gurin et al. (1969), who found a three-factor structure to best characterize the responses of US Black college students. These results required a reevaluation of the unidimensionality of the scale in its use with US Whites.

Independently of Gurin et al.'s research, Mirels (1970) reported a factor analysis of the I–E scale responses of introductory psychology students at Ohio State University. Mirels obtained two factors; one focused on the individual (personal control) the other on the citizen (political system control) as the target of control. MacDonald and Tseng (1971, reported in Lefcourt, 1976, p. 132) replicated Mirels's two-factor structure for males, but the female sample provided a third factor related to social respect, or likeability. Abrahamson, Schludermann, and

Schludermann (1973) replicated Mirels's two-factor structure but also obtained an indication of a third factor, which also could be interpreted as control over likeability. Bond and Tornatzky (1973), Joe and Jahn (1973), and Cherlin and Bourque (1974) reported success in replicating Mirels's two-factor solution. Reid and Ware (1973, 1974), while replicating the Mirels's two-factor solution, argue for a different interpretation of the factors than that proposed by Mirels. They label Factor 1 Fatalism and Factor 2 Social System Control, with the specification in both cases that the factor refers to the perceived *source* of control rather than the *target* of control à la Mirels. They show that half of the items loading high on the Fatalism factor referred to others as the target and half referred to control exercised by the respondent. A similar mix of self and other items was obtained on the Social System Control factor. Reid and Ware thus contended that the factors do not reflect self versus others as the target of control but luck–fate and social systems as the sources of control.

The results of factor analysis conducted on the responses of White North Americans to the unmodified Rotter I–E scale are thus reasonably consistent in finding two factors. However, it should be clear that this consistency in factor dimensions does not mean that the specific items that are salient on each factor are the same from one factor analysis to another. Indeed, the problem of comparison of the similarity of factor solutions across investigations is complicated and typically requires the technical ingenuity of specialized factor analysts. For example, Cattell (1969) provided an article that should be digested by all who attempt to make cross-cultural comparisons of factors. He noted,

> Surveying the inexplicit and much criticized current procedures for quantitative comparisons across cultures and between age groups, the present article proposes some methodological and conceptual improvements. They hinge on (a) first demonstrating conceptual identity, primarily by factor analysis, of the unique source trait dimensions on which comparison is to be made and (b) achieving common scale units and origins for the measurements [p. 258].

He went on to point out that when one has the same variables but different people in the samples to be compared—the typical cross-cultural comparison case—there are two general strategies: (a) comparison of factor patterns through such procedures as the use of congruence coefficients (Burt, 1941; Cattell, 1969; Cliff, 1966; Jöreskog, 1969; Sörbom, 1974) and (b) salient variable similarity indexes or calculation of configurative agreement. All of these methods entail highly technical problems in their calculation and in determining values of significance. None is "without defects from some assumption that one would prefer not to have to entertain" (Cattell, 1978, p. 265), and all require access to the original data. All of these constraints render them either inappropriate or of little utility in making post hoc comparisons of factor structure similarity across studies conducted by different researchers.

I have chosen to make use of a much simpler technique to obtain at least a first approximation (beyond eyeballing) of the similarity in item structure of factors between two studies. The technique simply attempts to answer the question "How successful was Researcher B in replicating the salient item loadings reported by Researcher A?" We thus prepare a four-cell table that reflects the hits and misses between the two studies. One such example is presented in Table 4.4. It may be seen that Cell a represents the number of salient variable agreements (hits) and Cell d the number of nonsalient variable agreements. Cells b and c represent the misses in which one study asserts that the item loads saliently on the factor but the other study fails to replicate this. The degree of salient variable overlap (factor content similarity) is reflected in the size of the ϕ coefficient computed on this four-cell table. The significance level of this factor content similarity (FCS) index is obtained from the corresponding chi-square statistic.

Application of this FCS index of item overlap to a comparison of replication attempts with Mirels's original two-factor solution provides the information represented in Table 4.5. In order to obtain a combined probability for the available analysis on White North American male university students, a meta-analysis was conducted for each factor. Application of both the Stouffer method (Mostellar & Bush, 1954) and the Edgington method (Edgington, 1972) resulted in highly consistent conclusions indicating that the combined probability for each factor was less than .0001. We may thus conclude that there is a highly significant item overlap in the factor structure between Mirels's factors and the factor structures obtained by later replication attempts.

In order to designate these consensus factors for White North Americans, it seems desirable to introduce factor names that will reconcile slight differences in factor interpretation (e.g., Mirels versus Reid

TABLE 4.4

Conceptual Representation of the Four-Cell Hit–Miss Table from which the ϕ Index of the Item Overlap (Factor Content Similarity—FCS) Is Computed

		Study B	
		+	−
Study A	+	a. Salient in both (hits)	b. Salient in A but not in B (misses)
	−	c. Salient in B but not in A (misses)	d. Nonsalient in both (hits)

TABLE 4.5

Factor Content Similarity Analysis Applied to Attempted Replications of Mirels's Factor Dimensions with North American White Male Samples

Study	Personal control L–F			Social system control		
	ϕ	χ	p	ϕ	χ^2	p
Bond & Tornatsky (1973)	.298	2.04	.16	.694	11.08	< .001
Joe & Jahn (1973)	.214	1.07	.30	.750	12.93	< .001
Reid & Ware (1974)	.411	3.89	.05	1.00	23.00	< .000
Cherlin & Bourque (1974)	.508	5.93	.015	.772	13.71	< .001
Escovar (1981)	.538	6.65	.01	6.84	10.74	< .005

and Ware). The first factor seems to refer to personal control over/by luck and fate and may most reasonably be designated as the Personal Control Luck–Fate factor (PCL–F).[5] The second factor refers to the degree to which the individual is perceived to have control over political and societal affairs. It is most reasonably designated, following Reid and Ware, as the Social System Control (SSC) factor.

Factor Structure of Other Instruments for North American Whites

Several different approaches to modification of Rotter's I–E Scale have been taken. As yet they have not generated a great deal of cross-cultural research but are strongly to be recommended for future cross-cultural applications. On the basis of attribution theory as it is applied to person perception, Collins (1974) argued that the Rotter scale should be conceptualized as reflecting two quite different dimensions: predictability–lawfulness versus chance, and situational versus dispositional attributions. Factor analysis of his revised instrument revealed four relatively orthogonal factors designated as reflecting a belief in (a) a difficult versus easy world, (b) a just versus unjust world, (c) a predictable versus unpredictable world, and (d) a politically responsive versus unresponsive world. Three replications of Collins's Likert-format procedure have been reported. Kaemmerer and Schwebel (1976) and Zuckerman and Gerbasi (1977) reported four-factor solutions that are "extremely similar to the four factors identified by Collins" (Zuckerman & Gerbasi, 1977, p. 162). Kleiber, Veldman, & Menaker (1973)

[5]The designation of Factor I as Fatalism (à la Reid & Ware) seems to carry a heavy load of philosophical excess meaning and could be misleading in the cross-cultural context.

failed to differentiate Collins's easy–difficult and predictable–unpredictable factors and thus reported a three-factor solution.

A special-purpose, multidimensional instrument also based on attribution theory as formulated by Weiner, Heckhausen, Meyer, and Cook (1972) was developed by Lefcourt and his colleagues (Lefcourt, 1981a; Lefcourt et al., 1979). The Multidimensional–Multiattributional Causality Scale (MMCS) consists of two 24-item scales measuring perceived control over academic achievement and over affiliation, goal areas of particular relevance to university students. Each of these goal areas comprises six items representing each of Weiner et al.'s (1972) four quadrants of attribution: internal stable (abilities and skills), internal unstable (effort and motivation), external stable (contexts), and external unstable (fortuitous events). Two cross-cultural applications of this instrument have been reported (Chan, 1981; Chandler et al., 1981; Dyal, Chan, & Bertrand, 1982).

Another approach to the development of a multidimensional LOC instrument was taken by Levenson (1972, 1981). Her scale was constructed to measure (a) the degree to which the individual believes he or she has personal control over his or her life (Internal Scale); (b) the degree to which the individual feels controlled by powerful others (Powerful Others Scale); and (c) the degree to which he or she feels controlled by chance or fate (Chance Scale). Each factor is represented by eight items in a 6-point Likert format. The factorial structure of the instruments was analyzed for undergraduates (Levenson, 1974) and psychiatric patients (Levenson, 1973). In each case the first three factors were perfectly isomorphic with the theoretical, a priori factors. An excellent review of the empirical research relevant to Levenson's IPC scale is available in Volume 1 of this series (Levenson, 1981). As noted by Levenson (1981), the IPC scale has also served as a model for the development of three health-related modifications of the scale. These are the Multidimensional Health Locus of Control Scale (MHLC) (Wallston & Wallston, 1978), the Health Attribution Test (Actenberg, reported in Levenson, 1981), and the Multidimensional Pain Locus of Control Scales (Levenson, 1981). It is to be expected that these special-purpose, multidimensional instruments will soon be employed in a cross-cultural comparative context.

Internal Structure for North American Minority Groups

The article by Gurin et al. (1969) opened up the issue of the equivalence of Rotter's I–E Scale for US Blacks by showing that Blacks differentiated between personal control and ideological control (self or other) items on the I–E. They argued on the basis of Rotter's factor analysis that such a differentiation did not hold for US Whites and that it was "a valid rather than artifactual difference between Negro and white populations" (p. 41).

Over a decade later it is still surprisingly unclear whether or not Gurin et al.'s argument is correct. In order to examine this question, several different approaches seem relevant. First, we may ask whether there has been successful replication of Gurin et al.'s factor structure with US Blacks. The answer seems to be that although no large-scale replication attempt has been reported, three studies have included Black subjects and are relevant to factor structure and reliability. Cherlin and Bourque (1974) tested a university sample and a community sample in California with the I–E scale. In both samples they obtained a two-factor structure comparable to that reported by Mirels. They commented,

This pattern also holds for a subsample of college students who identify themselves as belonging to minority groups. We found no personal versus ideological split in any analysis. The results are consistent with the findings of Mirels (1974) and inconsistent with the findings of Gurin et al. (1969) and Sanger and Alker (1972) [p. 573].[6]

Kinder and Reeder (1975) utilized four items from Gurin's Personal Control factor to examine the internal consistency of the items in a probability sample of 1000 persons from Los Angeles County. The results revealed striking ethnic differences in internal consistency of this four-item Personal Control factor. For Caucasians and Hispanics the Personal Control items showed an adequate degree of internal consistency, as indicated by both the intercorrelations and Cronbach's alpha. However, for the Black sample the item intercorrelations ranged from $+.15$ to $-.49$ and alpha $= .00$ (i.e., the scale was totally lacking in internal consistency for Blacks). These results were replicated in a second probability sample obtained a year later and thus raise serious questions regarding the equivalence of these Personal Control measures as applied to Black and Whites—a result that is, of course, consistent with Gurin et al.'s thesis.

Jones and Zoppel (1979) administered the I–E scale to middle- and

[6]The non-Caucasian minority group was composed of 32 Blacks, 17 Mexican-Americans, and 17 Asian-Americans. It will be recalled that Reid and Ware (1973, 1974) also obtained a two-factor structure similar to Mirels and no evidence for the Personal Control versus Control Ideology reported by Gurin et al. However, because Reid and Ware's subjects were White Canadians, the lack of a personal versus ideological split is in fact consistent with Gurin et al.'s expectation of Black–White differences in the meaning of the task.

lower-class high school samples of female US Blacks in the San Francisco Bay area. They obtained two factors for each of the groups but two *different* factors in each group. They contend that

> the discovery of factor solutions for Black populations that differ not only from those found on White samples, but from each other as well, raises serious questions about the equivalence of meaning of the I–E scale both cross-culturally and for populations dissimilar from that upon which it was constructed [p. 447].

The obvious and direct way of approaching the problem of whether the LOC scales are the same or different for Blacks and Whites is by conducting factor analyses of large parallel samples of Blacks and Whites and comparing the obtained factor structures. Unfortunately, such a definitive study has yet to be conducted, although a more modest study following this strategy has been reported (Roberts & Reid, 1978). However, the results of that study must be regarded as tentative because of the small samples involved (72 Whites and 89 Blacks who are low-income Head Start families in Jackson, Michigan). Nevertheless, Roberts and Reid found that the items in each of the three factors loaded differently for Blacks and for Whites.

> In most cases, the factor loadings for Blacks and Whites are *negatively* associated. For example, the item "Many times we might just as well decide what to do by flipping a coin" loaded on Factor 1 for both groups. However, for Whites, the loading was negative ($-.57$), while for Blacks the loading was positive (.65).

Clearly, these results represent either a serious challenge to instrument equivalence across ethnicities or an important confirmation of cross-cultural differences in the meaning of the construct. Roberts and Reid's data are deserving of more complete reporting than is now available; more important, they remind us that the definitive Black–White comparison of factor structures is long overdue.

Fortunately, a model research effort was made, directed at determining the cultural equivalence of Rotter's I–E Scale for Hispanics and Caucasians. Unfortunately, the results are not encouraging for those who would finesse the problem of cultural equivalance. Garza and Widlak (1977) separately factor analyzed the responses of 203 Caucasian and 244 Hispanic undergraduates to Rotter's I–E Scale. For both groups they obtained a five-factor structure that corresponded perfectly to the conceptually based dimensions proposed by Schnieder and Parsons (1970). These dimensions have been shown to differentiate cultural groups in several studies (Garza & Ames, 1974; Reitz & Groff, 1974; Schnieder & Parsons, 1970). Following Schnieder and Parsons (1970), the obtained factors were designated as Luck–Fate, Leadership–Success, Academics, Politics, and Respect. The cross-cultural comparability of factor structures was evaluated using Cliff's *coefficient of congruence* (Cattell, 1966; Cliff, 1966). Although this procedure yields an index of the similarity of two independently generated factors, it does not provide a test of the significance of the difference. Subjective evaluation is still necessary at this point. The results indicated that two of the factors (Luck–Fate and Leadership–Success) possessed an adequate degree of cross-cultural comparability, and a third factor (Politics) showed a modest degree of factor similarity. The similarity of the Academic and Respect factors was regarded as low.

Application of the ø-coefficient FCS index to the Garza and Widlak data requires first a decision regarding what factor loading value is to be regarded as salient or significant. This decision contains an uncomfortable degree of arbitrariness, as there are no generally accepted techniques for determining the standard error for factor loadings. As noted by Kerlinger (1967), some analysts advocate the use of the r value that is significant for the N used in the study; others refuse to accept any value below $\pm.25$ as the cutting score. As may be seen in Table 4.6, FCS analyses utilizing this latter cutting score permit the assertion of significant item overlap for all but the Leadership dimension. Although the Politics dimension shows significant similarity between the two ethnic groups regardless of the cutting score used, it is also clear that the inference of significant similarity is strongly influenced by the cutting score selected.

TABLE 4.6

ϕ Coefficient Index of Factor Content Similarity for the Garza and Widlak Comparison of Hispanics and Caucasians

Dimensions	Salience criterion[a]		
	$\pm.25$	$\pm.30$	$\pm.10$
Luck--Fate	.537**	.468*	.244
Leadership–Success	.388	.023	.586**
Academics	.724**	.228	.086
Politics	.844**	.586**	.411*
Respect	.583**	.797**	.220

[a] These salience criteria were selected for illustrative purposes based on the following consideration: $\pm.25$ is the cutting score used originally by Garza and Widlak; $\pm.30$ is a value most commonly used in the literature; and $\pm.10$ is the value of the significant (.05) r for the available N.

*$p < .05$.

**$p < .01$.

The most reasonable conclusions that may be drawn from the data on North American minorities seem to be the following:

1. The personal versus ideological distinction of Gurin *et al.* has still not be been tested adequately for US Blacks. However, consistent with their argument, the ideological factor does *not* seem to characterize the LOC factor structure for North American Whites for which Mirels's two-factor solution is more valid.[7]

2. Mirels's Personal Control Luck–Fate (PCL–F) factor is usually the largest factor for US Whites. This factor is similar for Hispanics and has high internal reliability for Caucasians and Hispanics; its reliability for Blacks is highly questionable.

3. The Social System Control factor, consisting of a core of four items (12, 17, 22, and 29), is highly replicable across analyses of White North Americans and Hispanics, but its equivalence in Black samples is questionable.

4. Garza and Widlak's (1977) conclusion is sufficiently apt and provocative to merit quotation in full:

> The findings of the present study underscore the intricate problems involved in assessing and comparing Chicanos and Anglos on a seemingly straightforward psychological dimension such as locus of control. The potential problems are much more complicated than most researchers are willing to admit. The use of Anglo personality tests or Anglo-derived experimental manipulations without determining their appropriateness for Chicano populations is highly irresponsible and lacking in scientific validity and sociocultural objectivity. The problem of cultural equivalence is extremely complex and entails more than merely controlling for the obvious factors such as readability and language usage. As clearly indicated by the data presented in the present study, even simple statements regarding beliefs in internal as opposed external control may evoke totally different meanings for Chicanos in comparison to Anglos. It is quite conceivable that a great deal of the research literature comparing Chicanos and Anglos may be based on equivocal measurements of a given psychological construct, casting serious doubt on the validity of the findings [p. 642].

Cross-Cultural Comparative Studies of Internal Structure

Three types of studies are relevant here. First to be considered are those in which factor analyses have been performed on LOC data obtained from non-US samples and parallel analyses on an American comparison group. Only three such studies have been reported (Bond & Tornatsky, 1973; Escovar, 1981; Lao, 1978).

[7]Following the completion of this review Trimble and Richardson (1982) published an extensive factor–cluster analysis of locus of control measures among Native Americans. Their results "substantiate previous findings of a separation of personal control . . . from ideological control."

Bond and Tornatzky (1973) performed parallel cluster analyses for Japanese and US university students on the I–E scale. Separate analyses were conducted for males and females. They obtained two factors for both the US and the Japanese samples which they interpret to "tap the dimensions of personal control and system modifiability in agreement with Mirels." They point out, however, that different content-specific items load on these clusters for different groups. Examination of the item with the highest loading on the personal control cluster for each group is revealing. For both US males and females that item is "many times I feel that I have little influence over the things that happen to me" (Item 25), whereas for Japanese males it is "Many of the unhappy things in people's lives are mostly due to bad luck" (Item 2). This latter item is not even significant for Japanese females, whose highest item loading is on "It is not always wise to plan too far ahead because many things turn out to be a matter of good or bad fortune anyhow" (Item 13). For Japanese males this item (13) is below the .40 item-cluster correlation Bond and Tornetsky regarded as significant. The authors note that "correlations with this generalized 'luck–fate' cluster yield revealing data on those situations which, for any given group, are regarded as part of the broad 'luck–fate' cluster" (p. 212).

Given that Bond and Tornatzky did not attempt to evaluate formally the cluster similarity, it is useful to apply our ø coefficient FCS Index to the cross-cultural comparisons. First, considering Factor 1 (Personal Control), the similarity between US and Japanese students was not quite significant for either males (ø = .324; p = .13) or females (ø = .358, p = .09). Similarly, the overlap between US males and US females did not approach significance, nor did the overlap between Japanese males and females. Thus the pattern of item overlap was not reliably similar for either cross-cultural or cross-gender comparisons, and this lack of significance was robust for cutting scores of .40, .30, and .15.

On the other hand, cross-cultural comparisons of similarity on Factor 2 (Political Control) reveal highly significant similarity (using Bond and Tornatzky's ±.40 cutting score) for Japanese–US males (ø = .844, p < .01) and Japanese–US females (ø = .511, p < .02).

In summary, the factor content similarity between Japanese and US samples is high for the Political Control factor, whereas the Personal Control factor reveals a strong tendency toward different item content in both cross-cultural and cross-gender comparisons. Again, it should be emphasized that these results may reflect either lack of psychometric equivalence for the Personal Control factor or real differences in perceived control across groups. However, the fact that Bond and Tornatzky's US White sample did not significantly overlap Mirels's US White sample for the personal control factor suggests that psychometric aberrations cannot be dismissed lightly.

The only other study to report factor analyses of I–E scale data based on parallel samples was conducted by Escovar (1981), who compared Latin American university students from Colombia and Venezuela with samples of Hispanics (Cuban Americans) and Whites (Caucasian Americans). He used both orthogonal and oblique rotations to simple structure and found that orthogonal solutions yielded meaningful factors only for the Hispanic group and in this case three factors emerged: General Control, Personal Control, and Political Control. For the Latin American group three oblique factors were defined as General Control, Academic Control, and Political Control. Two oblique factors emerged for the Caucasian group: General Control and Political Control.

Several important methodological advances are contained in the Escovar paper. First, the utilization of both orthogonal and oblique rotations presents a more accurate representation of similarities and differences that exist in the factor structures between groups. Second, the similarities and differences between cultural groups were evaluated more rigorously than the usual eyeball test. In his evaluation of the similarity of factors between groups, Escovar utilized two statistics. He observed that "the product-moment correlation coefficient (r) constitutes a good index for comparing factor loadings (Rummel, 1970). On the other hand, Cattell (1978) has suggested the salient variable similarity index(s) as a more adequate indicator of factor similarity" (p. 12).

Escovar's analyses are reproduced in Table 4.7, along with the ø-coefficient FCS analysis of significant item overlap I conducted. The

TABLE 4.7

Comparisons of Escovar's Factors Using the Product–Moment Correlation Coefficients (r), Cattell's Salient Variable Similarity Index (s), and the φ Coefficient FCS Index[a]

Control factors	r	p	s	p	θ	p
General control factors						
Anglo I and Latin I	.21	.337	.20	n.s.	.24	n.s.
Anglo I and Hispanic I	.36	.094	.48	.01	.08	n.s.
Latin I and Hispanic I	.13	.567	.35	.05	.02	n.s.
Political control factors						
Anglo II and Latin III	.75	.001	.56	.01	.69	.01
Anglo II and Hispanic III	.82	.001	.47	.01	.84	.01
Latin III and Hispanic III	.55	.01	.70	.001	.61	.01

[a]Salience = ±.30.

results are rather clear cut and show that there were no significant similarities among any of the three groups on the General Control factor. However, all three groups showed significant similarity in the Political Control factor.[8]

It is also reasonable to question the degree of overlap between Escovar's Caucasian data and those obtained by the referent US study by Mirels. The results of the FCS analysis of significant overlap is reassuring, yielding highly significant overlap for both the personal control factor (Escovar's General Control) and the Political Control factor (ϕ = .538, χ^2 = 6.65, p = .01; and ϕ = .684, χ^2 = 10.76, p < .005, respectively).

Lao (1978) performed parallel factor analyses on Taiwan Chinese and US Whites' responses on Levenson's IPC Scale. The Chinese factors accounted for about twice as much of the total variance as did the US factors. The first factor for the Chinese was Internality, accounting for 46.2% of the variance; among US respondents the first factor was Powerful Others (16.8%). As noted by Lao, these findings could suggest that general internality was a much more important factor for the Chinese.

Application of the FCS analysis to Lao's data indicates a significant similarity between US and Taiwanese subjects on the salient (.30) items for the Internality factor (ϕ = .80; p < .05). However, on the Powerful Others factor the similarity is not significant (ϕ = .466, p = .19), and in the case of the Chance factor the correlation approaches significance in the negative direction (ϕ = −.535, p = .14), reflecting the fact that five of the eight items were dissonant (misses) in their factor loadings. Because of the small number of items on each of the factors in the Levenson scale (N = 8), the size of the ϕ coefficient is unduly influenced by slight shifts in hit:miss ratios; therefore a contingency table was constructed reflecting performance on all three factors combined. The resulting correlation was only of borderline significance (ϕ = .30, p = .09). These analyses required tempering of Lao's conclusion that the "results indicate that the factor structures were quite similar" (p. 117). At the very least they suggest that although the Internality factor is highly similar between US and Taiwanese subjects, Chinese tend to structure the Chance factor quite differently.

Several researchers have conducted factor analyses on LOC data from other cultures but without parallel US samples. Their data must

[8]Dr. Chi-Chiu Harry Hui recently published an independent review of the cross-cultural research on LOC (Hui, 1982) and has made constructive comments on the present review. He notes that in a technical report Hui, Triandis, and Chang (1982) "found that the political items do not have similar meanings for the mainstream and Hispanic subjects."

then simply be compared to some referent US study. The most reasonable comparison is with Mirels's factors, as this is the comparison the authors themselves typically choose. However, in some instances a comparison with Reid and Ware's factor structure is also informative.

Five studies have performed factor analyses of Rotter's I–E Scale on non-North American samples. Viney (1974) tested male and female Australian adolescents (14–20) on the I–E scale and obtained two factors she regarded as comparable to those obtained in Mirels's US samples. Application of the FCS analysis to the Viney–Mirels comparison reveals significant overlap on the Personal Control factor for males (ø = .677; χ^2 = 5.31; p < .05). Likewise, on the Political Control factor, significant overlap was obtained for both males (ø − .444; χ^2 = 4.54; p < .05) and for females (ø = .723; χ^2 = 12.03; p < .005).

Tobacyk (1978) translated the I–E scale into Polish and factor analyzed the data from 199 female Polish university students. He obtained two factors that paralleled Mirels's General–Personal Control and Political Control factors. Tobacyk computed coefficients of congruence for the two and concluded that there was a "moderately high degree of quantitative factorial similarity." However, he cautioned that they are clearly not identical with the US factors containing more significant items. Application of the FCS analysis to Tobacyk's data reveals significant factor content overlap with Mirels's factors (ø = .505, χ^2 = 5.86, p < .02 and ø = .516, χ^2 = 6.12, p < .02, for Personal and Political Control factors, respectively). It thus seems reasonable to conclude along with Tobacyk that

the Political Control and Personal Control factors obtained in the Polish and American female university student samples show considerable thematic similarity. . . . It appears that Polish and American female university students may employ locus of control, as measured by Rotter's I–E Scale, similarly in understanding life events [p. 9].

On the other hand, three studies have partly or completely failed to replicate the Mirels factor structure in other cultures. In the Escovar study the factor structure obtained with the Hispanic and Latin American samples revealed no reliable overlap with Mirels on the Personal Control factor, although significant overlap was obtained on the Political Control factor. Furthermore, both the Hispanics and the Latin American data were best structured by three factors rather than two. In the case of the Latin Americans, an Academic Control factor was differentiated from General Control, whereas for the Hispanics General Control and Personal Control factors were differentiated.

Similar disparities in factor structure were reported by Nagelschmidt and Jakob (1977), who administered a Portuguese version of Rotter's I–E Scale to 170 Brazilian married women. The sample was heterogeneous with respect to SES. They obtained two factors, which they called General Externality and Fatalism. The authors note that the item content of these factors had minimal overlap with previous factor analyses by Cherlin and Bourque (1974), Collins (1974), Mirels (1970), and Gurin et al. (1969). Furthermore, computation of salient item overlap index (FCS) between Nagelschmidt and Jakob's Fatalism factor and the Fatalism factor reported by Reid and Ware (1973) reveals no significant overlap. Further testimony to the "differentness" of the Brazilian sample is obtained by comparison to Mirels's Personal Control factor, which also shows no reliable overlap with the Brazilian data. Again, such disparate results may be due to invalid instrumentation, to real cultural differences, or to lack of comparability of the comparison groups (i.e., confounding variables). Nagelschmidt and Jakob comment that "at least a part of the peculiarity of our results could be accounted for by the unusual nature of the sample investigated, being exclusively married women with a wide range of socioeconomic status, residing within an urban setting in a developing country" (p. 108). This comment may be accurate, but it does not carry us far in unwrapping the cultural package for a more specific inspection of the relevant variables.

Jones and Zoppel (1979) quote Nagelschmidt and Jakob sympathetically as concluding that "there is a general tendency for the factorial structure of the scale to differ as a function of the population under study, and that direct comparison of the I–E scale cross-culturally may, as a consequence, be misleading" (p. 439). Their research compared three groups of Blacks; Jamaican middle class, US middle class, and US lower class. Although two factors emerged for each group, the authors interpret the factors to be different for each group. The two factors are said to reflect Unpredictable World and Political Control for the Jamaicans; Personal Control and Success–Achievement for the middle-class US Blacks; and Fatalism and Personal Accomplishment for the lower-class US Blacks. Jones and Zoppel concluded that their "most striking finding . . . is the substantially different factor structure for the three populations; moreover, the present factor solutions generally fail to resemble those found by other researchers" (p. 447). However, it should be noted that Jones and Zoppel (1979) did not apply statistical tests to evaluate factor content similarity, and application of FCS analyses to their data reveals that certain caveats to this conclusion are in order.

First let us consider the similarity between the Jamaican factors and Mirels's factors. The Jamaican first factor (Unpredictable World) is revealed to have a highly significant overlap with Mirels's Personal Control factor ($\varnothing = +.477$; $\chi^2 = 5.23$, $p < .025$). The second Jamaican factor (Political Control) also shows borderline similarity to Mirels's Political Control factor ($\varnothing = +.324$; $\chi^2 = 2.41$; $p < .13$). It is clear that, contrary to their conclusion, Jones and Zoppel's Jamaican data constitutes at least a partial replication of Mirels's factor structure.

In the case of the two US Black groups, the picture is quite different. There was no significant overlap between the lower-class and the middle-class US Blacks, on the item content of either factor. Furthermore, the US Black factors were not significantly similar to either of Mirels's factors. In fact, the Fatalism factor for the lower-class US Black sample was *reliably different* from both Mirels's Personal Control factor and Reid and Ware's Fatalism factor ($\varnothing = -.423$; $\chi^2 = 4.115$, $p < .045$ in both cases). The appropriateness of Jones and Zoppel's factor label is thus open to question. One is reminded here that factor naming is a highly subjective creative task which should be approached in a circumspect manner. Indeed, as Cattell noted,

> Much trouble down the years in efforts to integrate factor studies has arisen from rather rashly giving premature interpretive labels, especially when derived from small studies. . . . Finally, it would hardly need to be said except for some blatant historical instances—that one should not cause confusion by failing to relate current research findings to previous research findings through employing a new term when a highly suitable behavioral term has already been given, unless a radical new interpretation can be proved. . . Provided that research maintains regard for these logical principles and social obligations, the game of factor interpretation can offer the theoretician an intellectual exercise at least as entertaining as a cross word puzzle, and as demanding as abstract philosophy [1978, pp. 232–233].

In sum, the Jones and Zoppel study replicates for middle-class Black Jamaicans the factor structure that typifies White North Americans on both Personal Control of Luck–Fate PCL–F and Social System Control (SSC). On the other hand, the factor structure for the US Blacks tends to be unlike that for the Jamaicans and unlike that for US Whites; furthermore, the magnitude of these differences tends to be greater for lower-class Blacks.

Niles (1981) administered the I–E scale to ninth-grade adolescents in Columbo, Sri Lanka. She obtained a two-factor structure whose item content she regarded as different from either of the two factors presented by Mirels. Application of the FCS index of item overlap confirms Niles's subjective impressions (Factor 1: $\varnothing = .04$; $p = .85$; Factor 2: $\varnothing = .00$; $p = .999$). Niles contends that her two factors reflect concerns with the sources of Control–Fate and Powerful Others (respectively) rather than the target of Control (self versus others) as in Mirels's analysis. It is recalled that Reid and Ware (1973) made a similar interpretation of their Canadian data. It is thus of interest to compare Niles's Fatalism factor with that of Reid and Ware. The FCS index of item overlap indicates substantially greater overlap than was present in the Niles–Mirels comparison (ø = .336; χ^2 = 2.60; p = .11).

Niles's interpretation of the two factors as Fatalism and Powerlessness, though based on an *informal* cultural analysis, seems worthy of quotation:

> The control of the individual by factors of chance and fate is a concept closely linked to beliefs such as the law of Karma (the law of cause and effect). The majority of the population in Sri Lanka profess the Buddhist or Hindu religions, and fatalism seems interwoven into their belief system. Apart from religion, however, in a poor country like Sri Lanka an appreciable proportion of the population is so controlled by external factors such as poverty that it is not surprising that a sense of powerlessness is created. Friere (1972) argues that the deprived (he describes them as the oppressed) nearly always express fatalistic attitudes toward their situation and this, he claims, generates a kind of docility and leads to their viewing their situation as the will of God (a kind of resignation), which can be interpreted in our religious tradition as accepting the inevitability of the laws of Karma.
>
> Therefore, in a developing society traditionally bound by ideas of the powerlessness of the individual against undefined cosmic forces, it is not surprising that the emphasis shifts from the typical western self–other differentiation to a consideration of the ways in which the individual is controlled and made powerless and ineffectual, not only by forces of chance or fate but also by powerful others. In a society experiencing rapid social change, where competition for scarce resources is maximized, society is sharply divided into the "haves" and the "have-nots." Forms of oppression of groups of people are common, and a feeling of being controlled by powerful others seems inevitable. In such a context of differentiation between forms of control rather than an objective control ideology seems the logical outcome. In this study, therefore, we may describe the first factor as "Fatalism," which acknowledges the importance of forces of chance and fate. The second factor describes "Powerlessness," in which the individual feels controlled by powerful others [p. 474].

Although the preceding cultural interpretation makes sense, it suffers from a strong post hoc element and lack of evidence of external validity. However, as will be noted later, Khanna and Khanna (1979) found in an Asian Indian sample that belief in the theory of Karma was significantly associated with greater total externality on the I–E scale. The relationship was particularly strong for the Control Ideology factor, 10 of 12 items of which were loaded on one or the other of Niles's two factors. In light of Niles's deemphasis of the importance of personal control with an attendant emphasis on fatalism and powerful others, it would clearly be useful for future studies of LOC in countries believing in Karma to include Levenson's IPC Scale in addition to Rotter's I–E Scale.

Cross-Cultural Studies of External Validity of Locus of Control

Two samples may differ not merely in their mean performance level on an LOC measure and on their internal structure; they may also differ in the relationship between LOC and other theoretically relevant variables—that is, in their convergent and discriminative validities. To the extent that the similar relationships are obtained between the LOC and other variables, we strengthen our belief that the measures are equivalent and that the variables *operate* similarly in the two cultures. That is, we have increased confidence in the similarity of the nomological networks in the two cultures. However, if substantial cultural differences are obtained between LOC and external variables, then we may question the equivalence of our tests and/or assert cultural differences.

It should be noted that the level of theory is rather rudimentary in the whole LOC domain. Furthermore, despite the hundreds of studies on the LOC construct, the degree of confidence we can have in any reported relationship may best be characterized as ranging from some to none. The state of our knowledge is no better revealed than by selected quotations from one of the most extensive summaries of the literature thus far available: the book-length treatment of the literature by Lefcourt (1976). Here we frequently encounter such characterizations as "the empirical data are not often without paradoxical inconsistencies or failures at replication," "interesting if mixed," "not always consistent or comprehensible," "far from complete," and "may be confounded." The search for a dependable set of standard data with which to compare our cross-cultural findings all too often proves to be an exercise in futility. Yet in order to examine the comparative validity of the LOC contruct, we must first ask ourselves what relationships LOC enters into *dependably* for North American White samples.

Personal Adjustment

One of the most reliable findings is that various indexes of inadequate functioning are more likely to characterize an externally oriented than an internally oriented person (Lefcourt, 1976). Among the indicators of dis-ease that have been related to LOC are debilitative anxiety, neuroticism, mood disturbance, and low self-esteem.

ANXIETY

Lefcourt cited three studies (Butterfield 1964; Ray & Katahn, 1968; Tolor & Reznikoff, 1967) that have reported modest but consistent relationships between measures of general or situation-specific debilitative anxiety and LOC for US White college students. Hersch and Scheibe (1967) obtained similar results relating anxiety (Minnesota Multiphasic Personality Inventory, Psychasthenia Scale [MMPI Pt scale]) to LOC, and Ware reported a significant relationship between the Taylor Manifest Anxiety and the I–E scale, which was not replicated by Efran (Rotter, 1966). Molanari (1979) found all three factors on Levenson's IPC Scale to be associated with anxiety, but Kleiber et al. (1973) found only their "system modifiability" factor to relate to anxiety (the more external, the more the anxiety).

The cross-ethnic and cross-cultural literature is generally supportive of a modest positive relationship between LOC and self-reported anxiety. Giorgis (1978) found a significant relationship between TMAS and overall score on Rotter's I–E Scale for US Black college students but not for Black student sojourners from Africa (nor for US Whites). Watson (1967) reported the expected positive relationship between debilitative anxiety measures and externality for Canadian university students; similar results were obtained by Feather (1967) for male Australian college students but not for females; In the Feather study, however, among mature adult part-time students the relationship was significant for females but not for males.

Chan (1981) related LOC as measured by Lefcourt's MMCS to measures of test anxiety (Speilberger, 1977), neurotic anxiety, and symptom formation (Langner, 1962). Subjects were Chinese students at the University of Hong Kong, Hong Kong Chinese student sojourners in Canada, and Canadian students. As expected, the overall tendency was for Achievement externality and Affiliation externality to be positively related to anxiety and symptom formation. However, the Achievement and Affiliation domains reveal quite interesting culture–situational similarities and differences. In the case of Affiliation externality, the same relationships characterize all three groups. Whether one is Chinese or Canadian or whether one attends university in Canada or in Hong Kong, externality for Affiliation is significantly related to neurotic anxiety and symptom formation but not to worrying about performance on tests. This pattern makes sense when one considers that feeling externally controlled in interpersonal relations leaves a late adolescent particularly vulnerable, for at least two reasons. First, interpersonal relations are highly valued at this stage of development and second, given that students often lose old friendship networks and create new ones, affiliation needs are cognitively salient.

The pattern of results for Achievement externality are even more striking because of the culture × situation interaction that is suggested. The data indicate that externality for Achievement is related to test anxiety (+.34), neurotic anxiety, and symptom formation (+.45) but only for the foreign student sojourners. These data are consistent with the common stereotype of the Hong Kong Chinese student who places great value on academic achievement because both family finances and "face" are invested in their academic success. Chan (1981) commented that for

> Chinese students who sojourn in the West . . . the primary goal is "to study", to "get a degree", "to obtain specialist training" and to equip themselves with better qualifications for Careers. . . . They usually expect to work harder than ever before, to learn more, to get better job opportunities and by doing so hopefully to improve family socio-economic status and to honour parents' wishes [p. 8].

NEUROTICISM

Morelli, Krotinger, and Moore (1979) hypothesized that externality would be related positively to neuroticism as measured by Eysenck's Personality Inventory. They found the Levenson Internality scale and the Chance scale to be significantly related to neuroticism for US White college students. It is noteworthy that the Powerful Others scale was not related reliably to neuroticism. Levenson (1981) argued that this may reflect "the possibility that some aspects of externality may not be indications of an unhealthy, maladjusted orientation." Specifically, a powerful others orientation may involve a more veridical perception of certain sociopolitical situations. This argument has been expressed most forcefully by the Gurins as it relates to US Blacks (Gurin et al., 1969) and to poverty groups (Gurin & Gurin, 1970). Although the theoretical argument is persuasive, unfortunately no data are available that directly test this relationship for low-SES US Blacks. The prediction would be that the relationship between neuroticism and externality on Powerful Others would be significant and positive for Blacks who were prone to self-blame on the Gurin scale but would be either nonsignificant or perhaps even negative for those who were high on both system blame (Gurin) and Powerful Others. Indeed, multiple regression analysis for the moderating effects of system versus individual blame on the relationship between Powerful Others externality and neuroticism for Black and White samples seem to be in order.

The only studies relating neuroticism and LOC in countries other than North America support a significant relationship for Australian Whites (Feather, 1967; Ray, 1980). Clearly, additional data on non-Anglo-Celtic samples would be desirable.

SELF-ESTEEM

A variety of measures of self-esteem has yielded consistently significant but small relationships to LOC orientation, such that greater internality is associated with greater self-esteem for US college students (Fish & Karabenick, 1972; Heaton & Duerfeldt, 1973; Hersch & Scheibe, 1967; Kleiber et al., 1973; Ryckman & Sherman, 1973). According to the argument advanced in the previous discussion of neuroticism, it could be predicted that the relationship between self-esteem and LOC might be reversed for Blacks in the United States. Hendrix (1980) tested 240 Black and White high school seniors in Louisiana using Rotter's I–E Scale and the Personal Control items from Gurin's factor analysis and a Self-Esteem scale. Consonant with our expectation, Hendrix found a highly significant and positive correlation between total externality on the I–E and Self-Esteem scales for Blacks. Unfortunately, interpretation of these results is rendered somewhat problematic by the fact that no significant relationship was obtained for the White sample. It should be noted that Hendrix's results are in conflict with those reported by Epstein and Komorita (1971), who found that high self-esteem Blacks were more internal than low to moderate self-esteem subjects. It is possible that the difference in these two studies reflects an increasingly veridical evaluation of external constraints (system blame) combined with an increased sense of personal–racial power during the 1970s.

MOOD DISTURBANCE

Reviewing research by Abramowitz (1969), Warehime and Woodson (1971), Goss and Morosko (1970), Burnes, Brown, and Keating (1971), Platt and Eisenman, (1968), and Powell and Vega (1972), Lefcourt (1976) concludes that "the evidence is sketchy. But what evidences do exist indicate that externals are more likely to admit to depressive feelings than internals" (p. 86). More recent evidence supports and extends this conclusion (Calhoun, Cheney, & Dawes, 1974; Lefcourt, Miller, Ware, & Sherk, 1981; Molanari, 1979).

Calhoun et al. (1974) replicated substantial correlations between general externality (I–E) and self-reported depression. In addition, they obtained suggestive gender differences in the relationship between mood and LOC and between mood and perceived causes of depression. Females showed a significant positive relationship between the degree of depressed mood and the tendency to hold themselves responsible for it. Recent work by Janoff-Bulman (1979) and Peterson, Schwartz, and Seligman (1981) has shown that the tendency toward *characterological* self-blame rather than self-blame for *behaviors* is correlated (but not causally related) with depression. This promising discovery about the attributional dynamics of depression can be extended profitably to the evaluation of SES, ethnicity, and gender in system versus self-blame as they are related to LOC. In addition, clarification of the role of LOC as it relates to symptom formation and self versus system blame would seem a useful direction for future research on acculturative stress of female refugees. Unfortunately, no relevant cross-cultural data concerning the relationship between LOC and mood disturbance or between LOC and the attribution of self-blame and symptom formation are currently available.

LOC and Sociopolitical Attitudes and Actions

ALIENATION

"Life is a spectator sport. The innocent bystander is not innocent, he is inevitable—an individual so detached that he cannot respond to the urgencies of his fellows. . . . Without a doubt, alienation is the state of the species" (Seeman, 1971, p. 83). Among the attitudes Seeman asserts as characteristics of alienation are individual powerlessness, cultural estrangement, meaninglessness, and social isolation. Seeman and his colleagues utilized an early version of the I–E scale to measure feelings of powerlessness and to relate that sociopolitical attitude to membership and participation in various organizational structures in the United States, France, and Sweden. They found in the US studies that members of work-based organizations had fewer feelings of powerlessness than did unorganized workers (Neal & Seeman, 1964). Comparable data on Mexican-American farm workers who that nonunion workers feel more powerless than do union workers (Hoffman, 1978).

Similar results were obtained in Sweden, where it was also shown that degree of involvement in the work organizations of manual workers was related negatively to feelings of powerlessness (Seeman, 1966). Seeman also found that feelings of powerlessness were related to lack of knowledge in control-relevant domains of information for both tuberculosis patients (Seeman & Evans, 1962) and reformatory inmates (Seeman, 1963). Again, the Swedish sample showed a similar relationship between power and control-relevant knowledge (Seeman, 1967). Congruent with these results, Gottesfield and Dozier (1966) reported that the amount of relevant information learned by participants in a community action training program was related inversely to their felt powerlessness and that their initiative on the job was related negatively to degree of externality. Additional support for the cross-cultural replicability of the general relationship between alienation and externality was obtained by Ray (1980) in a quota sample of adults in Sydney, Australia.

Jessor et al. (1970) measured, in addition to degree of powerlessness (I–E), the meaninglessness and social isolation components of alienation in Italian American and Italian samples in Rome and Palermo. The primary purpose of the study was to relate these attitude characteristics to drinking behavior. They found that external control (powerlessness) was related positively to frequency and quantity of drinking for the Italian Americans but not for the Italians. Unfortunately, no study has been reported that attempts to relate a measure of cultural estrangement to other aspects of alienation or dimensions of LOC. The application of Levenson's IPC Scale seems particularly useful in connection with home and host culture estrangement of immigrants.

IDEOLOGY AND SOCIOPOLITICAL ACTIONS

Early research on the relationship between LOC and social–political activism supported the uncomplicated view that those who most believed in the efficacy of their actions (internals) were also most likely to act in the support of social causes (Gore & Rotter, 1963; Strickland, 1965).

Forward and Williams's (1970) theoretical analysis of LOC and Black militancy opposed predictions of so-called blocked opportunity theory (militants will be more internal than nonmilitants) against alienation–powerlessness theory (militants will be more external). A serendipitous opportunity to test the theory was presented with the occurrence of the Detroit riot in 1967. Prior to the riot, Forward and Williams collected a great deal of educational and attitudinal measures on Black high school students in the riot area. These data included Rotter's I–E Scale as well as Gurin et al.'s extended I–E scale and Coleman's Personal Efficacy Scale (Coleman et al., 1966). Their measure of militancy was attitude toward the riot. Analysis of the Rotter scale on Personal Control and Control Ideology factors (Gurin et al., 1969) revealed that those with high personal control were uniformly positive in their attitude toward the riot, whereas those who were low in personal control tended to think the riot was bad. These differences in riot attitude were also related to the Control Ideology factor. These results support the blocked opportunity theory and are consistent with the data (Rotter, 1966; Strickland, 1965) indicating that activists are more internal.

The foregoing results are opposite to the alienation–powerlessness hypothesis, which was supported by data from Black neighborhoods in Los Angeles showing that those who were the most willing to engage in rioting were the most external on the I–E scale (Ransford, 1968). Similarly, Sank and Strickland (1973) found civil rights militants to be more external. Furthermore, Silvern and Nakamura (1971) questioned the generality of the positive relationship between internality and social action beyond the Black subjects whose cause was being served by the action. They argued on both theoretical and empirical grounds that the results do not generalize to left-wing White student activists whom they predicted to be more external (powerless) than demographically comparable nonactivists. However, they noted that the relationship between powerlessness and political action is complicated by that between LOC and political ideology. For example, Thomas (1970) found politically active liberals to be more external than right-wing activists. Similar results were obtained by Fink and Hjelle (1973), who found externals to exhibit more New Left ideology beliefs and internals to show greater political conservatism and endorsement of traditional US ideology. Likewise, a significant relationship between externality and the values inherent in the Protestant ethic has been reported by Mirels and Garrett (1971) and by MacDonald (1972).

In light of the demonstrated relationship between LOC and political ideology (for White North Americans), Silvern and Nakamura were cautious in evaluating their data from UCLA student activists. Their data may be summarized for males as follows: (a) Overall externality was related positively to overall level of political activity. (b) The relationship was strongest for political protest actions. (c) Consonant with the previous literature, externality was correlated positively with left-wing political views and countercultural attitudes. (d) It was primarily the personal control factor (Mirels) that accounted for the relationship with LOC; the political control factor was not related to either action or ideology. (e) These relationships held when controlled for religion, income, and education. (f) None of the relationships held for females in the sample. Silvern and Nakamura suggest that the results are not cause for rejecting the I–E scale as "simply a political attitude measure" (à la Thomas) but rather that the acceptance or rejection of traditional US cultural beliefs emphasizing personal responsibility accounts for the relationship between LOC and political ideology and action. A later study by Silvern (1975) showed that the relationship between LOC and political ideology that held for US Whites did not hold for Asian Americans and Hispanics. Indeed, unexpected *positive* relationships were found between political conservatism and externality for Asian Americans. This surprising result is based on a small sample and clearly needs replication.

Silvern's finding that externality was related positively to social action for Whites but not for minorities (Hispanics or Asian Americans) is supported by Lao (1970). She found that for US Blacks personal control was related to participation in civil rights activities, primarily through its interaction with individual versus system blame and belief in the modifiability of discrimination. Individual versus system blame was the strongest of the correlates of action intensity, with individual blamers preferring negotiation and system blamers preferring protest actions.

Zuckerman and Gerbasi (1977) correlated the Collins version of the I–E scale with a measure of political efficacy that has been shown to predict political participation (Campbell et al., 1954). They found the total score to be related *negatively* to political efficacy for males, females, and the combined sample—that is, the greater the externality, the lower the sense of political efficacy. This effect of total I–E was determined primarily by the Politically Responsive World factor.

Levenson and Miller (1976) reported several studies relating the IPC scale to activism. They also found that the relation between activism and perception of control by powerful others was moderated by political ideology. In the *liberal* males they found that as belief in the control of their lives by powerful others increased, so did their activism. The relationship was the opposite for *conservative* males, who decreased their activism as belief in powerful others increased. It was as though the liberals perceived the external control as being illegitimate and were rebelling against it, whereas the conservatives regarded the control by powerful others as legitimate. The acceptance of "law and order" (low risk) as opposed to "personal freedom" (high risk) has long been recognized as characterizing conservative versus liberal political ideology. Consonant with previous results, the conservatives tended to be more internal (I scale) and less oriented toward chance (C scale).

Levenson (1981) cited several studies (Huebner & Lipsey, 1979; Levenson, 1974; Trigg, Perlman, Perry, & Janisse, 1976) that examined LOC differences between activists and nonactivists regarding environmental issues. These studies reveal no clear pattern relating specific

LOC factors to activism in this area. In the Levenson (1974) study the Chance scale differentiated activists from nonactivists, whereas Trigg et al. found internality moderated by optimism to be critical; Huebner and Lipsey (1979) found that an apparent effect of the P scale in differentiating the groups disappeared when covaried for educational level. Taken together, the mixed nature of the results cautions against a too-easy generalization of results from one area of sociopolitical activism to another. Furthermore, they may suggest that situation-specific LOC scales (a la Heubner and Lipsey) will be more successful in predicting activism associated with specific issues or domains.

It may be true, Levenson noted, that "no area of research using the I–E construct has led to more confusing results with conflicting interpretations than that of social and political activism" (1981, p. 49); nonetheless, the relevance of this research area to cross-ethnic comparisons has both theoretical and practical implications, and persistence in clarifying the confusing literature is required.

MACHIAVELLIANISM (MACH)

Another social attitude that has been related to LOC is the tendency to advocate cynical manipulation of others to achieve personal or social ends (Machiavellianism). Small to moderate positive correlations have been obtained for several North American samples (Christie & Gies, 1970; Duffy, Shiflott & Downey, 1977; Levenson & Mahler, 1975; Miller & Minton, 1967; Solar & Breuhl, 1971).

Zuckerman and Gerbasi (1977) correlated the total score and each of the Collins factors with Mach V scores for male and female university students. Their results are consonant with those of Duffy et al. (1977) in showing that the Politically Responsive World factor related significantly for males and the combined sample but not for females alone. The total I–E score was significant for males only and was due almost entirely to the Politically Responsive World factor. The authors suggest that this factor probably reflects suspicion and anomie that may not be related to overall LOC. Maroldo and Flachmier (1978) obtained a modest relationship between total I–E and Mach with samples of German coeds and US students. Krampen and Nispel (1978) and Krampen (1979) found German alcoholics to be characterized by higher externality and higher Mach than nonalcoholics. Ray (1980) found the Luck–Fate cluster on the I–E to correlate .40 with Machiavellianism for a quota sample in Sydney, Australia. Nedd and Marsh (1979), in contrast, failed to obtain a significant relationship between a Fatalism–Personal

Efficacy scale and Machiavellianism for a combined sample of Polynesian and Anglo-New Zealanders.

It is apparent that further cross-cultural work relating LOC and Machiavellianism should utilize the multidimensional instruments that are available (Collins, 1974; Lefcourt et al., 1979; Levenson, 1972) in order to obtain a more precise characterization of the relationship. It would be expected, for example, that Lefcourt's MMCS Affiliation scale would be related more strongly to Mach V than the Achievement scale. Furthermore, there is a continuing need to relate cultural variables to theoretically relevant antecedents of both Machiavellianism and LOC in order to evaluate the sensitivity of the relationship to cultural characteristics.

LOC AND ACHIEVEMENT

Previous reviews of the LOC literature (Bar-Tal & Bar-Zohar, 1977; Gilmor, 1978; Lefcourt, 1976; Phares, 1976; Strickland, 1977) have documented the theoretical expectation that externality is related negatively to achievement behaviors for North American White children, "though not consistently and not without occasional paradox" (Lefcourt, 1976, p. 71). The predictive validity of Crandall's IAR measure for academic achievement and achievement-related behaviors has been well documented (Chance 1965; Crandall, Katkovsky, & Crandall, 1965; Crandall, Katkovsky & Preston, 1962; McGhee & Crandall, 1968). The use of other instruments to measure LOC has generally supported this relationship, indicating that the relationship is not instrument-specific (Gruen, Korte & Baum, 1974; Nowicki & Strickland, 1973). It should be noted, however, that the relationship between LOC and academic achievement is usually strongest for males; females show inconsistent and often insignificant effects depending on grade level and the specific instruments being related.

That children from Black, Hispanic, and Native American minority groups perform less well in school than their White counterparts is a consistent finding in the research literature. Many psychological variables have been proposed to account for this difference in academic achievement (e.g., intelligence, achievement motivation, cognitive style, test anxiety). The intuitively and theoretically strong connection between LOC and academic achievement suggested by the early data with White children mandated the determination of the LOC–achievement relationship among US minority group members. In their massive study, Coleman et al. (1966) showed perceived control to be the best single predictor of academic achievement for US Black high school students even when family background and school environment were controlled. Moreover, the LOC variable accounted for about three times as much achievement variance for Blacks as it did for Whites. A similar effect was reported by Crain and Weisman for Black and White adults (Crain and Weisman, 1972, cited in Glantz, 1977). Unfortunately, the effect of IQ was not controlled in many of the early studies (Entwisle & Greenberger, 1972; Gilmor, 1978). However, Lessing (1969) compared White and Black children in grades 8 and 11 on a shortened version of Strodbeck's personal control scale and did control for IQ differences. She found that personal control accounted for 12% of the variance of grade point average for grade 8 children, and that a significant effect remained (2%) after the affects of intelligence were removed. Personal Control accounted for less of the variance (5%) for grade 11 students, and this effect was not significant when covaried for IQ.

Lao (1970) conducted an extensive study of LOC and a variety of achievement measures with a large sample of Black college students in the southern United States. She found that Gurin's personal control factor "stands out as the most significant predictor" of academic confidence and academic aspirations. In a similar vein, Glantz (1977) hypothesized that Blacks who aspired to occupations which were traditionally closed to Blacks (e.g., nuclear physicist, airline pilot, architect) would be more internal than those who aspired to traditionally open occupations (such as physician, teacher, and clergyman). His results supported the hypothesis for US-born Blacks but not for West Indian Black immigrants to the United States. Compared to the US Blacks, the immigrant Blacks were characterized as greater risk takers, choosing traditionally closed occupations; a difference that as noted by Glantz could be related to selective factors in immigration.

Some of the inconsistencies in the predictive power of LOC for academic achievement variables may have been due to the fact that all of these early studies (with the exception of Lao) failed to differentiate the total I–E score into separate factors. It will be recalled that Hersch and Scheibe (1967) found externals to be more heterogeneous in their other personality characteristics and that these results, among others, influenced Levenson to differentiate between two types of external control (Chance and Powerful Others). Prociuk and Breen (1974) proposed that it might be particularly important to differentiate among types of externals when testing the LOC–achievement relationship. They correlated Levenson's IPC Scale with study habits and attitudes and academic performance. They found that Internality (I) was related positively to academic achievement and that primarily perceived control by Chance rather than by Powerful Others was negatively related to achievement. In light of the possibility that LOC is a more potent correlate of achievement for Blacks, and given that Blacks seem to score higher on Chance control than do Whites, it is unfortunate that no data speak to the possible differential relationship of Levenson's P and C scales for Blacks and Whites.

Given that LOC theory and achievement motivation theory emphasize similar variables as causes and consequences of these personality dispositions, it might be expected that LOC would be related significantly to achievement motivation. The available literature provides only modest support for this expectation, with low to moderate correlations between the two constructs using a variety of measures of achievement motivation for North American Whites (Mehrabian, 1968, 1969; Odell, 1959) and Blacks (Pedhazur & Wheeler, 1971). Jones and Zoppel (1979) obtained a comparable LOC–achievement motivation relationship for middle-class US Blacks but not for lower-class Blacks or Jamaican Blacks. Wolk and DuCette (1973) suggested that the modest and inconsistent relationship between achievement motivation and academic performance might be moderated by the LOC variable. They found that this was indeed the case; there were substantial correlations between achievement motivation and course grades (+.37) and SAT Verbal (+.41) and Quantitative (+.33) for *internal* subjects only. Externals showed no significant relationships, and the differences in correlation size between internals and externals was reliable for all achievement measures. Whether LOC serves as a moderator in the same way for minority groups is a research question that could have important applications.

The plausibility of ethnic differences in moderator effects is supported by an extensive cross-ethnic study conducted in Israel using a large (N = 2438) stratified sample of ninth-grade students. The ethnic comparison was between Jewish children of Asian-African descent and Jewish children of Euro-American descent. Bar-Tal *et al.* (1980) reported strong correlations between LOC and academic achievement, and between LOC and level of aspirations. These correlations were reduced but remained highly significant when the effects of SES were partialed out. The relationship between LOC and achievement was significantly higher for the Asian–African students than for the Euro-American students. Multiple regression analyses showed, after SES effects were removed, that LOC added 9.7% to the explained variance for the Asian-African group but only 3.7% for the Euro-American group. Similar ethnic group differences in the relationship of LOC and achievement were reported by Knight *et al.* (in press), who found IARQ scores to be a significant predictor of school achievement for Mexican-American children but not for Caucasian-American children.

Other studies have reported LOC–achievement relationships in Britain, India, Nigeria, and Hungary. Reid and Croucher (1980) administered Crandall's IAR Scale to more than 1000 British schoolchildren. As expected, they found I+ to be correlated with Vocabulary and Achievement in mathematics (.34 and .31) with I− having smaller but still reliable correlations (.17 and .19). When they used a mean split to separate their sample into internals and externals, they found consistently higher correlations for the internals (an apparent moderator effect à la Wolk and Ducette). Reid and Croucher reported (p. 257) that their results are quite consistent with the US data reported by Crandall and provide "further validation of the Crandall IAR scale in the setting of the British junior schools." However, they also assert that "the IAR scales appear to be relatively independent of intelligence"—an assertion that seems to be a tour de force independent of the data, given that the relationship between I+ and I− with Raven's IQ measure was of the same order of magnitude as the relationship between these LOC measures and achievement. For example, in the case of I+ the correlation with intelligence was .31; and comparable correlations with vocabulary and arithmetic achievement are .34 and .32, respectively. It is unfortunate that Reid and Croucher did not partial out the effects of intelligence on the LOC–achievement relationship.

Reimanis (1980) related the Gurin factors (Personal Control, Control Ideology, and Systems Control) related to past and expected academic achievement for Nigerian university students. Both the Personal Control and the Control Ideology factors were modestly but significantly related (rs range from −.19 to −.29) to past and projected academic achievement.

Working with a sample of East Indian university students, Aggarwal and Berry (1974) found a reversal of the theoretically expected LOC–achievement relationship, in that high externals obtained significantly higher academic marks than did internals. In contrast, Aggarwal and Gudwani (1978) utilized a Hindi version of Muckerjee's Sentence Completion Test (scored for achievement motivation) for ninth-grade classes in Rajpura (Punjab) and found that high internals were significantly higher on achievement motivation than low internals (externals). Likewise, Mishra (1980) found internals to have higher educational achievement scores in urban, rural, and tribal subcultures of Indian adolescents.

Further evidence of the generalizability of the US data have been reported by Faustman and Mathews (1980), who found that high achievers are significantly more internal than low achievers in a large sample of Sri Lankan children. Similarly, Rupp and Nowicki (1978) administered the NOSIE to 469 Hungarian children, ages 10–14 years. They found internals made significantly higher scores than externals on several measures of academic achievement (GPA, mathematics, and language).

What conclusions can be drawn regarding the empirical link between LOC and academic achievement? In the case of White North Americans, although the data are not free of inconsistencies, the general tenor of the results is consistent with theoretical expectation even when the effects of IQ and SES are partialed out. As noted by Lefcourt (1976),

> that a sense of control, measured by different devices, can add to the already high magnitude relationships between socioeconomic class, I.Q. and achievement behavior attests to the value of locus of control in formulas devised to predict academic behavior [p. 71].

With regard to other ethnic and cultural groups, it appears reasonable to entertain the hypothesis that the predictive power of LOC is greater for those groups whose environmental pressures make obtaining an education an exercise in persistence (e.g., US Blacks, Afro-Asian Israelis, Nigerians). It should be remembered, however, that although the empirical relationships with theoretically relevant variables may be stronger for disadvantaged groups, the discrepancies in factor structure between Blacks and Whites (e.g., Gurin et al., 1969; Jones & Zoppel, 1979) and the probable difference in reliability (Kinder & Reeder, 1975) raise serious questions regarding equivalence.

GENDER DIFFERENCES

It is commonly assumed that gender differences in LOC are minimal in the North American White standardization group. For example, Strickland and Haley (1980) noted that "no sex differences in I–E responding were assumed since overall patterns of means and standard deviations were generally the same for males and females" (p. 931). Unfortunately, this assumption, based on the lack of differences on the global total score measure of the I–E and a too-cavalier assertion of similarity of factor structures between males and females, now appears to be unfounded. A more analytic approach to a comparison of means and factor structure reveals many instances of six differences. Furthermore, gender differences in the pattern of relationships of LOC with other variables are commonplace. The following sections examine

TABLE 4.8

Mean LOC Scores on the ANSIE and Levenson's IPC Scale Broken Down by Ethnicity and Gender

	Black male (N = 118[a])	Black female (N = 112)	Caucasian male (N = 338)	Caucasian female (N = 196)	Hispanic male (N = 196)	Hispanic female (N = 227)
ANSIE[c]	12.55	14.10	9.73	10.27	12.33	12.02
I scale[b]	35.59	31.09	36.11	34.80	35.72	34.06
P scale[c]	22.07	18.47	20.33	20.19	19.99	18.28
C scale[c]	21.16	20.99	17.33	18.56	20.16	20.05

[a] Data from Roueche & Mink (1976). There are slight variations in the sample sizes in the various scales; the value given is the minimum sample size.

[b] Scored in the internal direction.

[c] Scored in the external direction.

cross-cultural differences between genders on the mean performance, item endorsement, factor structures, and external correlations.

In the most extensive study thus far available, Roueche and Mink (1976) compared over 1000 Black, White, and Hispanic community college students in Texas on the Adult Nowicki–Strickland Internal–External Control Scale (ANSIE) and Levenson's IPC Scale.[9] As the primary purpose of their study was to compare the impact of certain instructional and counseling procedures on various personality characteristics (including LOC and anxiety), the pretreatment racial and gender differences were of only incidental concern and were utilized as covariates. This is unfortunate from our perspective, but the pattern of the results is quite clear and application of post hoc t-tests (with alpha set at .01) confirms the eyeball impressions apparent in Table 4.8.

There were also reliable differences within each race, such that Black females and White females were more external than their male counterparts. For the Hispanics, however, the effect is in the other direction: Males were more external than females. It should be noted, however, that although this reversed effect is statistically reliable because of the large sample sizes, the absolute size of the effect is quite small. Furthermore, results for the Internal scale on the IPC, showing Hispanic males to be more internal than females, are dissonant with these ANSIE results. On the other hand, the Internal scale data for Blacks and Whites are consonant with the ANSIE data, with females

[9] Unfortunately these data are less accessible than would be desirable because they are published only in the NIMH Grant Final Report. I thank Dr. Hanna Levenson for making her copy of the report available to me.

being less internal (more external) than males. In the case of control by Powerful Others (P scale), Black and Hispanic males feel more controlled (more external) than do their female counterparts. The gender difference in P was not reliable for Caucasians. Overall, Blacks and Whites did not differ on the Powerful Others scale, but each was more external than the Hispanics. On the Chance scale the only reliable gender difference was for Caucasians, with females being more external.

The data collected in the Roueche and Mink study are probably the most extensive available using standard measures of LOC. It is thus particularly unfortunate that they are subject to the shortcoming of limited availability and incomplete analyses. The data could yield valuable information if subjected to a complete SES × sex × ethnicity analysis of variance in which the interactions that are apparent in the data could be properly evaluated. Despite these inadequacies, the data strongly suggest that reliable sex differences exist in LOC that vary with the ethnicity and SES of the subjects and the specific instrument being utilized to measure the construct.

Dyal (1978) compared Portuguese immigrant children to Anglo-Canadian children on several achievement-related variables, including IAR. On the IAR total score the main effect for gender was borderline ($F_{1, 187} = 3.12$, $p = .08$), but the triple interaction involving ethnicity × grade × sex was significant ($F_{1, 187} = 4.18$, $p = .043$). In each case the Portuguese females were more internal than the males. Two of the most extensive cross-cultural studies have also reported strong gender effects in overall externality. Parsons and Schneider (1974, p. 257) sampled eight different countries and found that "consistently higher external scores for the females is a general finding across countries." However, it should be emphasized that the effect was small and that t-tests of gender differences within countries were significant only for Israel. Furthermore, the significant overall gender effect was limited to the Luck–Fate dimension and the Leadership–Success dimension. Similar overall gender effects were reported by McGinnies et al. (1974) in their five-nation study; the gender effect was small, but women were consistently more external. In the national samples, the effect was strongest with the Australian and Swedish samples. The sex differences, though not statistically reliable, were in the direction of greater externality for females in Japan, New Zealand, and the United States.

Reliably greater externality (overall I–E) of females has been reported for American university students by Strickland and Haley (1980), and Feather (1967) found female Australian university students (ages 17–18 years) to be more external than their male peers. Zytkoskee,

Strickland, and Watson (1971) obtained no significant main effect for gender but did find a significant race × gender interaction for US Black and US White high school students. The effect was such that Blacks were more external, and the size of the Black–White difference was greater for females than for males. Furthermore, Mahler (1974) found Japanese women to be more external on the Powerful Others scale of the IPC. He also obtained a reliable country × gender interaction on the Chance scale, such that Japanese women were substantially more external than Japanese men, whereas US women were somewhat less external than US men.

Two studies have reported Asian Indian females to be more external than males. Aggarwal and Kumari (1975) administered the Hindi version of Rotter's I–E Scale to a sample of 228 high school students. Though they found a significant main effect for gender, the meaning of the effect was clarified by the significant gender sex × SES interaction. The sex difference increased as one moved from upper to middle to lower class. Khanna and Khanna (1979) reported an extensive study of two cohorts of high school graduates in which they examined the effects of age (20–30 versus 40–50 years), religion (Hindu versus non-Hindu), SES, and gender. On the total I–E score they found women to be more external than men. However, when they performed their analyses on the separate factors used by Carment in his earlier study of Asian Indians (i.e., Gurin's factors), they found women to be reliably *more internal* on Personal Control; there were no main effects for gender on Control Ideology or Systems Control, although the authors obtained a significant age × gender interaction on the latter factor.[10] The nature of the interaction was such that younger women were more internal than younger men, but there was no reliable gender difference for the older group.

It will be recalled that Parsons and Schneider (1974) included a sample from India in their eight-country study and that the gender difference obtained (total I–E) was very small and nonsignificant. Saraswathi and Sharma (1980) found an apparent interaction between social class and gender for Asian Indian adolescents, with girls of higher social class being more internal on success and failure on the IAR. Moodley-Rajab and Ramkissoon (1979) compared Black, White, and Asian Indian university students in South Africa and obtained a race × gender interaction indicating that the White females were significantly more external (total I–E) than the White males. The gender differences for the Indian and Black samples, though not significant, were in the opposite direction, with women being more internal than men. The authors speculate that the results for these two disadvantaged groups "may possibly be attributed to the fact that educational privileges, for cultural and social reasons, have been rare for females in both these groups and therefore females who did succeed in the system were atypical of their group with respect to their motivation and aspirations" (p. 147).

Indeed, these results are consistent with the hypothesis advanced by Cole and Cole (1977, p. 21), who proposed that "persons taking actions aimed at self-improvement, in cultural contexts where such action is counternormative should be more internal in locus of control when contrasted with persons for whom such actions are not counternormative." They analyzed for gender differences in LOC among Mexican university business students, economically disadvantaged students from Appalachia (United States), and economically advantaged US college students. They found, as predicted, that the Mexican women were more internal on the P and C scales than were Mexican men—that is, they more strongly rejected the influence of Powerful Others and Chance in controlling their lives. The gender differences on the Internal scale were in the appropriate direction but were not significant. Similarly, the economically disadvantaged US females significantly more often rejected control by Powerful Others and Chance than did the disadvantaged female students. In addition, among the economically advantaged students females were *less* internal on the I scale than were males. These results suggest that counternormative behavior may serve as a powerful moderator of gender effects in LOC, and future cross-cultural studies should take this variable into account.

As noted earlier, Chan (1981) compared Chinese students at the University of Hong Kong and Hong Kong Chinese student sojourners at a Canadian university with Anglo-Canadians using Lefcourt's MMCS Scale. She found the females of each group to be more external on the total I–E score and the Affiliation subscore. Both the gender main effect ($p = .12$) and the group × gender interaction ($p = .068$) were marginal in the case of the Achievement subscore; the nature of the interaction was that the sex differences were minimal for the Canadians, moderate for the University of Hong Kong Chinese, and largest for the Chinese student sojourners. Lao *et al.* (1977) also found Taiwan Chinese females to be more external on the Chance scale and less internal on the Internal scale of the IPC.

These studies tend to support the conclusion of the early multinational research of McGinnies *et al.* (1974) and of Parsons and Schneider (1974) that there was "convincing evidence for a greater degree of

268 : JAMES A. DYAL

belief in external control of one's destiny among women than among men" (McGinnies *et al.*, 1974, p. 454). In contrast, many other cross-cultural studies have failed to obtain a reliable gender difference. These include studies of Japanese (Bond & Tornatzky, 1973; Parsons & Schneider, 1974; Mahler 1974 [Internal scale], East-Indian and White South African children (Barling & Fincham, 1978), Nigerians (Reimanis, 1977, Reimanis & Posen, 1980), Mexican Americans (Buriel & Rivera, 1980; Cole *et al.*, 1978; Garza & Lipton, 1978), and Greeks (Malikiosi & Ryckman, 1977). Furthermore, a few studies have reported gender effects in the opposite direction, such that females are more internal: Israeli immigrants, (Aviram & Milgram, 1977), Filipino adolescents (Watkins, 1981), Australian mature students (Feather, 1967), Mexican-Americans (Buriel & Rivera, 1980 [on the Academic subscore]), US Black children (Crandall *et al.*, 1962; Gruen *et al.*, 1974), and Taiwan Chinese (Lao *et al.* 1977 [on the P scale of the IPC]). Lao's Chinese data are consistent with Levenson's (1972) original validating study for the IPC in which she found adult females to be significantly less external than adult males on the P scale. Levenson (1981) also reported that Freischlog obtained similar gender differences on the P scale for US high school and university samples. In neither the Chinese nor the US studies were gender differences found on the I or C scales.

In summary, it seems possible that there is an overall cross-cultural consistency for women to be somewhat more external; however, this fragile effect varies substantially (and capriciously) with the particular culture and sample characteristics. Indeed, the statistical reliability of this overall effect remains in doubt until a complete meta-analysis is applied to the available literature (see Strube, 1981, for an application of meta-analysis in cross-cultural comparisons). Furthermore, the assertion of gender differences based on comparisons of means is usually quite uninterpretable with regard to relevant cultural features. This problem has been observed frequently by cross-cultural methodologists (e.g., Campbell, 1961; Cole, Gay, Glick, & Sharp, 1971; Malpass, 1977), who usually advocate the examination of cultural differences in the *pattern* of relationships among several related variables. Following this recommendation in the present context, we now consider culturally related gender differences in the internal structures of LOC tests.

Chandler and Dugovics (1977) concluded that the factor structures between US male and female (Black and White) university students on a revised Adult Nowicki–Strickland I–E scale were highly similar even though their application of Tucker's (1951) exceptionally conservative coefficient of congruence failed to support the inference of significant similarity on three of the four factors. However, application of the ø coefficient FCS index for item overlap confirms the appropriateness of Chandler and Dugovics's inference as opposed to the Tucker analysis; there was highly significant overlap between males and females on each of the four factors (Personal Control, Helplessness, Luck, and Blame).

Hall, Joesting, and Woods (1977) obtained significant gender–race differences in the internal correlations between Levenson's IPC factors. Whereas the correlation between internality (I) and belief in control by powerful others (P) was zero for their combined samples, there were significant differences between the I–P correlations for Whites and Blacks ($r = -.15$ and $+.13$, respectively). Furthermore, this racial difference was due primarily to the difference in the correlation for females ($r = -.16$ for White females and $+.21$ for Black females).

Although Zuckerman and Gerbasi (1977) found no overall gender difference on the Collins I–E scale for US White college students, females were significantly more external on the Difficult World and Just World factors. Females, however, tended ($p < .10$) to be more internal on the Predictable World factor.

Four studies (Bond & Tornatzky, 1973; Joe & Jahn, 1973; Mirels, 1970; Strickland & Haley, 1980) have analyzed for gender differences in factor structure of Rotter's I–E Scale with samples of US White university students. Mirels (1970) concluded: "That the factors obtained from the male and female data were similar is evident in the fact that the six items which loaded highest on Factor I and four of the five items which loaded highest on Factor II were the same for both sexes" (p. 227). Application of our FCS analysis of item similarity provides an objective confirmation of Mirels's more subjective inference, in that the item overlaps between males and females was highly significant for both factors (Factor I: $\emptyset = .638$, $\chi^2 = 9.36$, $p < .01$; Factor II: $\emptyset = .871$, $\chi^2 = 17.44$, $p < .01$).

Joe and Jahn (1973) also reported two factors; the first (General Control) did not overlap significantly on Mirels's first factor (Personal Control), but the second (Political Control) overlapped perfectly with Mirels's factor. A comparison of the item overlap between males and females in Joe and Jahn's analysis reveals that there was no significant overlap on the first factor ($\emptyset = .124$; $\chi^2 = .35$; $p = .57$) but highly significant male–female overlap on the second factor ($\emptyset = .871$; $\chi^2 = 17.44$, $p < .01$). Results for Bond and Tornatzky's (1973) US comparison sample were consistent with those of Joe and Jahn: no significant overlap of the item content with Factor I (Personal Control) but significant overlap for Factor II (Social System Control). Strickland and Haley's (1980) factor analysis of the I–E scale obtained "a 'personal control' factor much like Mirels' Factor I. However, despite similar content of items, *no overlap in items across sex is apparent"* (p. 932) (italics added). Application of the ø index of item overlap to Strickland and Haley's data reveals a nonsignificant (but negative) overlap (ø = .21). In contrast, the overlap on the SSC factor is perfect (no misses) (ø = 1.00). In addition to these gender differences in factor structure within the PCF and SSC factors, Strickland and Haley obtained a third significant factor for males (Academic Control), which was not present for females.

The two non-US samples in which separate analyses were conducted for each gender obtained the same pattern: Japanese males and females (Bond & Tornatzky, 1973) did not overlap on composition of Factor I but showed significant overlap on Factor II (ø = .656; χ^2 = 9.90, p < .01). Likewise, in Viney's (1974) White Australian sample, the Personal Control–Fate factor (PCF) did not have significant gender overlap, but the Social System Control (SSC) factor did (ø = .549; χ^2 = 6.93, p < .01).

Meta-analyses (Strube, 1981) were applied to these data in order to estimate the combined probability of reliable factor content overlap between genders over all available samples. The results are consistent using both the more liberal Stouffer method (Zs) (Mosteller & Bush, 1954) and the more conservative Edgington method (Z$\bar{x}$p) (Edgington, 1972). In the case of the Social Systems Control factor, the results are highly significant (p < .0001) and uniform in indicating a high degree of item overlap between males and females. However, in the case of Factor I, Personal Control–Fate, the overlap between the genders is not significant when all six of the above samples (four US, one Australian, and one Japanese) are combined (Zs = .857 p = .14; Z$\bar{x}$p = .636, p = .26). Furthermore, when only the Caucasian samples are considered, the male–female factor pattern similarity is still borderline in significance (Zs = 1.535; p = .063; Z$\bar{x}$p = 1.216, p = .104). It would thus appear (from the minimal available data) that it is reasonable to expect only a modest gender similarity in the composition of the Personal Control–Fate factor for Anglo-Celtic cultures and substantial gender differences in the meaning of this factor for Japanese. It should be clear that this generalization must be tentative at this time, resting as it does primarily on the results of Mirels's data for Caucasians and Bond and Tornatsky's data for the Japanese. Clearly, additional factor analyses differentiating by gender in the two cultures are needed.

In conclusion, these analyses lead us to believe that the structure of the Personal Control–Fate factor is more susceptible to influence by the gender of the respondent than is the Social System Control factor. The PCF factor thus may be more likely to reflect cross-cultural gender differences in roles and/or opportunity structures (e.g., the Japanese data).

The differences in factor structure between Caucasian males and females suggests the possibility of meaningful sex differences in responding to specific items. Indeed, Strickland and Haley (1980) hypothesized that males would be more internal on Personal Control items than would females. They selected US college students matched on mean externality and analyzed the frequency of endorsement of each item by males and females. They found significant gender differences in 8 or the 23 items. However, contrary to their hypothesis, only 1 of these 8 items loaded on the Personal Control–Fate factor, and on this item (15)—contrary to prediction—more females selected the *internal* alternative (75% vs. 61%). Of the 8 items, 2 were SSC items (12 and 17), and more males than females selected the *external* alternative (72% vs. 58% and 69% vs. 52% respectively). Of the items 1 was an Academic item, and in this case males chose the internal alternative more often than did females (66% vs. 47%). The other 4 items did not load saliently on any of the factors. Strickland and Haley concluded the following:

> The finding that similarity of means, standard deviations, and factors does not necessarily demonstrate a lack of sex differences in frequency of item endorsement has important implications for the construction and validation of personality inventories. The results also suggest that the common practice of using factor analysis to explore group differences may be inappropriate. Factor analysis may be a valuable tool in identifying items that covary, but similar factor structures across groups do not necessarily imply that individuals within these groups are answering items in the same direction. The comparison of individual items leads to a finer-grained analysis and points to the fact that certain groups may achieve similar scores for different reasons [1980, p. 938].

Chandler and Dugovics (1977) also found significant sex differences on 5 of the 40 items in the ANSIE Scale and, using multiple regression, showed that a total of 10 items would be included as significant predictors of gender.

Unfortunately, only one cross-cultural study has analyzed for both sex differences and cultural differences in item endorsement frequency. Reimanis (1977) compared US and Nigerian students and, though finding no overall gender difference, did find specific items on which significant gender differences occurred. More US males than US females endorsed the internal alternative on Item 5 ("The idea that teachers are unfair to students is nonsense"). A similar but not significant gender difference was present for this item in Strickland and Haley's data. Likewise, both Reimanis and Strickland and Haley found more US women to endorse the item, "The average citizen can have an influence on world decisions." Reimanis also found that more Nigerian men than women endorsed Item 23: "There is a direct connection between how hard I study and the grades I get." Reimanis concluded that "locus of control data must take situational variables into consideration, and that analysis of individual items can contribute toward a better understanding of what the scale measures in different cultures" (p. 310).

From our examination of sex differences it seems clear that future LOC cross-cultural research should be designed to permit tests for a gender × culture interaction in frequency of item endorsement. However, the most important implication is that gender differences in LOC may interact with cultural variables in influencing the relationship of LOC with other significant psychological constructs and behaviors. Unfortunately, very few cross-cultural studies available are relevant to gender differences in external validity. One of the more interesting areas in which gender differences in external validity of LOC are implicated is the relationship to academic achievement. Although some studies have obtained significant LOC achievement correlations for females but not for males (DeCharms & Carpenter 1968; Massari & Rosenblum, 1972; Nowicki & Walker, 1974) and others have reported no gender differences (Nowicki & Segal, 1974; Prociuk & Breen, 1975), a more substantial number of studies have shown LOC scales to be better predictors of academic achievement for males than for females (Boor, 1973; Brown & Strickland, 1972; Crandall, et al., 1962; Duke & Nowicki, 1974; Nowicki & Roundtree, 1971; Nowicki & Strickland, 1973). Indeed, Nowicki (1973) found a reverse relationship between LOC and academic achievement for males and females—that is, internality predicted higher achievement for males, whereas externality correlated with high academic achievement for females. Similar results were obtained by Lee (1976, as reported by Levenson, 1981) using the IPC scale. Lee found that the more internal females (I scale) performed less well, whereas the more external (C scale) males performed less well. Furthermore, several studies have shown that the more females expect to be controlled by powerful others the *more* successful they are academically (Lee, 1976; Prociuk & Breen, 1975; and Zimmerman, Goldston, & Gadzella, 1977). As noted by Levenson, "it seems as though for females, some aspects of externality are facilitative" (1981, p. 46). However, it should be emphasized that the ethnic and cultural generalities of this finding are not clear. The Zimmerman et al. (1977) study found the effect to hold for White females but not for Black females; and Lao, Chuang, and Yang (1977) found the opposite relationship to hold for

Taiwanese females—the more internal they were on the Levenson I scale, the higher was their college entrance exam score ($r = +.25$, $p < .01$). The relationship was not significant for males, nor were the P and C scales related to entrance exams or GPA for either gender. There were also consistent gender differences between IPC variables and various academic–occupational aspiration indexes. The nature of the relationship was that externality on either Powerful Other or Chance scales was negatively related to academic–occupational aspiration and confidence for the females, whereas for males the relationships were typically lower and nonsignificant. Internality (I scale) was positively related to aspiration–confidence on each of the six indexes for both males and females.

It has been hypothesized that internals tend to prefer skilled tasks and externals prefer chance tasks; some support has been obtained for this effect with US White college students (Gold, 1966; Schneider, 1968). However, the effect often is small (Schneider, 1972) or gender-dependent (Schneider, 1968). Although these studies have made use of the total I–E scores as the LOC measure. Zuckerman and Gerbasi (1977) utilized Collins's four-factor I–E scale and found that although the total score yielded small but significant effects, it was primarily the correlation between skill preference and the Difficult World factor for females (but not for males) that accounted for the overall effect.

Ryckman, Stone, and Elam (1971) studied the effects of criticism on the degree of upset experienced under conditions of skill versus chance performance. They found, as expected, that internal females were more upset by criticisms in the skill condition, whereas external women were more upset by criticism under the chance condition. There was no such interaction between LOC and task requirements for the males. Ryckman, Rodda, and Stone (1971) repeated the experiment using a performance measure rather than reported disturbance to measure the disruptive effects of criticism. Again, there were gender × task and LOC × task interactions that were conditioned by a highly significant gender × LOC × task interaction. The nature of this interaction was such that the performance of internal males was disrupted more by criticism under skill than under chance conditions, whereas external males were disrupted more under chance than under skill conditions. There was no such interaction for females. The results, with regard to gender, are thus the opposite of those obtained in the Ryckman, *et al.* (1971) study, where the LOC × task interaction applied to women but not to men. The authors reconcile the two results "in terms of the kinds of role-linked behaviors that are appropriate or inappropriate for men and women in American culture." The specifics of their reconcilation, though plausible, need not concern us here; their conclusion, on the other hand, is most relevant:

> Both studies indicate clearly the importance of sex as a variable that influences performance of individuals with different locus of control orientations. It would appear that internal–external control orientation may have different implications for the behavior of women in our society than for men. The present study suggests the need for a systematic exploration of the differences in a variety of situations [p. 304].

Clearly the potential importance of cultural differences in the moderation of LOC effects by gender cannot be overlooked and deserves more serious experimental effort than it has thus far received.

It would not be surprising to find gender differences is LOC related to differences in socialization across both gender and culture. Rotter (1966) proposed that nurturance and consistency in child-rearing practices would be related positively to the development of internality. Supportive evidence came from a variety of early studies (Davis & Phares, 1967; Katkovsky, Crandall & Good, 1967; Shore, 1967) whose results are summarized by Lefcourt (1976) as "impressive in their relative consistency. Warmth, supportiveness and parental encouragement seem to be essential for the development of an internal locus of control" (p. 100). However, later research (e.g., Crandall, 1973) has shown that such nurturing is most critical in its influence in the early years and must be coupled with a later emphasis on independence training to yield the greatest likelihood of internality. Moreover, the timing of the greatest impact of independence training varies among males and females (Crandall, 1973) and in some instances is significant only for males (Chance, 1965). Similarily, Katkovsky et al. (1967) found the approval–criticism dimensions of parent training to be significantly related to the IAR total, I+ and I− for males but not for females, whereas Mac-Donald (1971) and Reimanis (1971) found a significant relationship between parental consistency and internality for males only. Likewise, Levenson (1973) obtained strong gender differences in the parental behavior that was associated with internality (I). For males, a helpful, teaching approach from the mother fostered internality, whereas for females internality was related negatively to the perceived protectiveness of the mother. This latter result is also consistent with Reimanis (1971), who found that perceived maternal rejection was related to internality for females.

Three studies have related family parenting antecedents to LOC for ethnic children. Solomon, Houlihan, Buss, and Parelius (1971) found that Black fathers who encouraged independent achievement had sons who were more internal. Halpin *et al.* (1980) studied the relationship between perceived parental behavior, LOC, and self-esteem for Native American and White children. Unfortunately, they did not report the relationship between LOC and self-esteem per se but only how each variable was related to parenting characteristics for the two culture groups. The results indicated that only 1 of the 12 parenting characteristics was significantly related to both LOC and self-esteem for both White and Native American children: "instrumental companionship." For the Native American children as the amount of physical punishment increased, internality (IAR) decreased. This variable was not related reliably to internality among the White children.

An extensive study by Buriel (1981) evaluated the relationships between LOC and parents' and teachers' socializing behaviors for Anglo-American and Mexican-American children. The LOC instrument was IAR, and socialization behavior was measured by the Cornell Parent Behavior Inventory (CPBI), which contains four global socialization dimensions: demanding, supportive, controlling, and punishing, each of which contains various subscales. The children (grades 4 and 5) rated their mother, father, and teacher. With regard to maternal behavior internal control for success (I+) was related positively to maternal demandingness and support for all children with no ethnicity or gender effects or interactions. In contrast, paternal demandingness interacted with ethnicity, such that it was related positively to internal control for success (I+) for Mexican-American but not Caucasian children. Buriel's interpretation of this effect is that

> the greater status and respect accorded fathers in Mexican-American families (Ramirez and Casteneda, 1974; Murello, 1974) may impart greater psychological importance to their demands for achievement and responsibility than in Anglo-American families. Consequently, Mexican-American children with demanding fathers may make a stronger effort to comply with their father's press for achievement and responsibility and thereby experience greater opportunities for learning internal control [p. 110].

Paternal *support* interacted, with gender being positively related to I+ for boys but not for girls. There were no gender × ethnicity interactions.

Teachers' demanding behavior was positively related to I+ with no gender × ethnicity interactions. Teacher demands were related positively to internal responsibility for failure (I−) for boys but negatively related to I− for girls. Two teacher characteristics also interacted with ethnicity. Teacher's controlling behavior was positively related to I+ for Mexican-Americans but not for Anglo-Americans;

similarly, teachers' supportive behavior was related positively to internal control for failure $(I-)$ for Mexican-American children but not for Anglo-American children. Buriel argued that these findings support the arguments of Ramirez and Castenada (1974) that Mexican-American children benefit more from teaching styles that are both structured (controlling) and supportive. He concluded that "the findings demonstrate the culturally relevant nature of the relationship between socialization practices and locus of control for Anglo- and Mexican-American children" (p. 111). Nonetheless, it should be emphasized that although there were abundant gender effects and ethnicity effects in these data, no gender $\times$ ethnicity effects were apparent, suggesting that socialization effects on the development of perceived control are not influenced differentially by these two variables. The generality of this assertion across cultural and ethnic groups requires further research that could be patterned profitably after Buriel's excellent study.

Four studies on US White college students have shown that the relationship between political involvement and LOC varies with gender. Silvern and Nakamura (1971) found that externality was related positively to overall involvement, to protest actions, and to left-wing and counterculture views, but only for males. Levenson (1974) found that male members of an antipollution group, who believed that chance controlled their lives, were less involved in environmental activities than those who scored low on the C scale. No such relationship existed for females. Zuckerman and Gerbasi (1977) found that Belief in a Difficult World was correlated significantly and negatively with political efficacy for males but not for females. Nowicki and Roundtree (1971) found that for females but not for males LOC predicted involvement in extracurricular activities; on the other hand, for males but not for females LOC predicted academic achievement. They commented that "these sex differences may, in part, be explained by the fact that our culture rewards males more than females for academic performance and females more than males for involvement in extracurricular activities" (p. 10). The last three studies suggest that when an activity is valued, internals will be more actively involved than externals; thus significant gender effects for LOC may be based on gender differences in values.

That the foregoing gender effects may not be limited to extracurricular involvement, or to US students, is revealed by a provocative study by Reitz and Jewell (1979). They determined the relationship between LOC and job involvement for male and female industrial workers in six countries (the United States, Turkey, Mexico, Yugoslavia, Thailand, and Japan). In every case the correlation was highly significant (the greater the internality, the greater the involvement) for males. However, for females only the Yugoslav sample resulted in a significant relationship.

Valecha (1972) evaluated a national probability sample of US Black and White males on an abbreviated I–E scale and several work-related variables, including three that indirectly reflect job involvement (number of hours worked per week, knowledge of work, and consistency of employment). In each case the White internals rated higher than the White externals. The Black internals worked significantly more hours than externals, but there were no differences on the other two variables.

Gender differences in the relationship of LOC and other personality–adjustment variables have been reported frequently. Platt *et al.* (1970) found that in the case of females, internals differed significantly from externals in 21 of 29 personality characteristics based on the MMPI; for males only one such variable yielded a difference related to LOC. In every case internals scored in the healthier direction than did externals. Calhoun *et al.* (1974) found no gender differences between LOC and relatively enduring symptoms of depression, but LOC predicted temporary mood depression significantly better for males than for females. In contrast, for females there was a strong relation between depressed mood and the attribution of this mood to causes within their personal control; that is, they tended to blame themselves for their depression more than did males. Ryckman and Sherman (1973), however, found no sex difference in the correlation between self-esteem and externality, whereas Warehime and Woodson (1971) found affect associated with feelings of self-confidence to be related to internality for men but not for women. Indeed, they found substantial gender differences in the relationship between LOC and several types of immediate affect. In general LOC was related to the affect associated with instrumental activities in the student role for men but to noninstrumental, general feelings (e.g., fullness, elation, tranquillity) for females.

The only non-US study relevant to gender differences in LOC–personality relationships was reported by Feather (1967) in a sample of Australian college students and adults. For females but not for males, LOC correlated significantly with social desirability, neuroticism and verbal ability, and test anxiety. For males but not females, the correlation was significant with debilitating anxiety.

It may be concluded that sex differences in mean performance of LOC scales and subscales, on frequency of item endorsement, on factor composition, and on correlation with external criteria are to be expected and should be accounted for in analyzing data. Furthermore, the cross-cultural, cross-ethnic comparisons should always provide an opportunity to test for gender × culture interactions. The paucity of available literature in this area is apparent.

LOC AND SES

We have already seen that SES is an important variable needing control when ethnic or cultural comparisons are to be made. Bartel (1968) found that middle-class children became more internal from grade 1 to grade 6, whereas the changes for lower-class children were not significant. The middle-class children were significantly more internal than the lower-class children by grade 4. Early research by Battle and Rotter (1963) found class and race to interact: Lower-class US Black children were more external than lower-class Whites, whereas middle-class Whites and middle-class Blacks did not differ from each other. SES main effects were also obtained by Franklin (1963), Strodbeck (1958), Gore and Rotter (1963), and Shaw and Uhl (1971). Jessor et al. (1968) found SES to be related significantly to LOC for their combined triethnic (White, Hispanic, and Native American) community sample but not for their high school sample. No ethnicity × SES interactions were reported. Similarly, Garcia and Levenson (1975) obtained significant SES effects for both Blacks and Whites on the Chance scale but no SES effects on the Internal or Powerful Others scales. Grebler, Moore, and Guzman (1970, reported in Buriel, 1981) found low-income Mexican-American adults to be more fatalistic than middle-income adults. Gruen and Ottinger (1969) obtained a significant SES effect for White children in the second grade but no SES effect for fourth- and sixth-grade children. A reversal of the usual effect was reported by Entwistle and Greenberger (1972), who found inner-city Black children in Baltimore to be more internal on both success and failure IAR scales than blue-collar Black chidlren.

In the previously discussed extensive study of community college students by Roueche and Mink (1976), significant ($p < .001$) and orderly SES (Income) effects (over gender and ethnicity combined) for the ANSIE and the Chance scale of the IPC were obtained. The income effect was not significant for the P scale, and although there were significant group differences on the I scale, the effect was not orderly. Unfortunately, Roueche and Mink did not evaluate the SES × ethnicity interaction. In the study of Portuguese immigrant children, Dyal (1978) obtained no SES effects or interactions with ethnicity or gender on the IAR.

Several cross-cultural studies have also been analyzed for SES effects. Bar-Tal et al. (1980) found SES to be correlated positively with internality for both his Asian-African sample (.23, $p < .001$) and his Euro-American–Israeli sample (.21, $p < .001$) Similarly small but significant correlations were found by Lao et al. (1977) for their Taiwanese sample. However, there was also the possibility of gender differences on the SES–LOC relationship. SES was indicated by an indigenously relevant index based on the number and type of appliances in the home. For males, SES was related significantly to I-scale internality (+.13; $p < .01$) but not for females. On the other hand, Powerful Others externality ws significantly related to SES for women but not for men (−.15, $p < .01$). Schmidt, et al. (1978) administered a test of future-time orientation to a sample of German lower- and middle-class workers; they also asked the subjects to indicate whether they believed the occurrence of hoped or feared events depended on themselves or on chance or fate. They found that middle-class in contrast to lower-class adults "envisioned the distant future more optimistically and believed more markedly that the realization of their hopes and fears depends on themselves" (p. 21). These SES differences were particularly strong with hopes–fears in the public as opposed to private domain.

Two studies with Asian Indian samples have analyzed for SES effects. Aggarwal and Kumari (1975) obtained a significant gender × SES interaction for secondary school children on the Hindi version of Rotter's I–E Scale. The nature of the interaction was such that the size of the gender difference (females more external than males) decreased with increasing social class. Khanna and Khanna (1979) also obtained significant SES effects for their Indian secondary school students but reported no interactions with the SES variable.

The message seems to be clear and simple: LOC is typically affected by real-world contingencies such that lower-class persons accurately perceive themselves to be more externally controlled than middle- or upper-class persons. This effect seems to be general across ethnicities and cultures (although the data base for this assertion is uncomfortably thin). Furthermore, since SES often interacts with other indicators of sociocultural disadvantage (e.g., sex, ethnicity), it is clearly necessary to control for SES effects—preferably by manipulating the variable rather than holding it constant—so that potentially important interactions may be evaluated.

FATALISM AND MODERNISM

An important sociological concept that has had considerable impact on both anthropological and social psychological cross-cultural investigations is that of individual modernism. The conceptualization of the construct has ranged from unidimensional (e.g., Inkeles and Smith's

[1974] "overall modernity") to situation- or value-specific factors that may be independent in their development and behavioral implications (Schnaiberg, 1970). An informative discussion of the major theoretical and methodological issues in the area may be found in Segall (1979) and the entire third issue of Volume 8 of the *Journal of Cross-Cultural Psychology* (1977). For present purposes it is sufficient to observe that one of the most pervasive features attributed to the individual modern outlook is the abandonment of passivity and fatalism and increased confidence in the efficacy of one's actions to achieve individual and group goals (Adinolfi & Klein, 1972; Doob, 1967; Kahl, 1968; Kiray, 1968; Inkeles & Smith, 1974). It would thus be expected that various indexes of perceived control would be related to a variety of examples of modern attitudes and behaviors.

One of the more ecoculturally relevant but politically sensitive issues that has received research attention is birth control and fertility. As noted by Crader and Belcher (1975), it has been a common sociological assertion that apathetic acceptance of circumstances tends to promote a high level of fertility (Lorimer, 1954, p. 248). However, the relevant data have not provided strong support for this fatalism–fertility relationship (Groat & Neal, 1967; Hill, Stycos & Bock, 1959). Crader and Belcher hypothesized that the general relationship between fatalism and fertility would be positive but small in their Puerto Rican Catholic families because of the cultural emphasis on having large families. As predicted, they found a borderline relationship between their measure of fatalism and number of live births. Fatalism strength increased as a function of age, and the fatalism–fertility relationship was strongest among nonsubsistence women who had completed their families. The authors postulated a fertility–fatalism reciprocity in which fatalism leads to greater fertility, which in turn leads to greater fatalism when there is a disparity between the number of children desired and the number born.

Blignault and Brown (1979) related contraceptive knowledge, attitudes, and practices to LOC in a sample of Australian women who were attending antenatal clinics. They found LOC to be significantly related to attitudes toward contraception but not to knowledge or practice. These results are consonant with those of Carment and Paluval (1973), who studied contraceptive attitudes and practices among male Indian Hindus and Sikhs. They found perceived control to be related significantly to attitudes toward vasectomy (externality was associated with negative attitudes). Although LOC was not related to whether or not the person had in fact had a vasectomy, there was an interesting relationship between LOC and attribution of the source of responsibility for having a vasectomy. The mean I–E total scores for those who said the decision resulted from (a) "personal decision alone" (b) "joint decision with wife" and (c) "wife made the decision" were 6.4, 7.9, and 11.0, respectively, suggesting "substantial support for the validity of the I–E scale" (Carment & Paluval, 1973, p. 116).

Individual modernity is also reflected by attitudes, values, and practices with respect to the adoption of "new techniques" versus "sticking with the tried and true ways of our fathers." The socioeconomic implications of willingness to adopt new practices are obvious in many areas and have been researched extensively with respect to farming practices in India by Pareek and Chattopadhyay (1966) and Chattopadhyay and Pareek (1964, 1967). Chattopadhyay and Pareek (1967) studied the adoption of new farming techniques as they related to five psychological variables (change proneness, level of aspiration, liberal–conservative value orientation, fatalism versus scientism, and authoritarianism). Fatalism was consistently the best predictor of adoption behavior, accounting for up to 36% of the variance in multiple regressions.

These studies encourage the belief that LOC is a potentially useful variable in prediction of attitudes and practices that may be part of the process of acculturation to an increasingly urbanized technological, scientized world. On both theoretical and pragmatic grounds it is essential to explore the psychological variables that moderate these acculturation processes (Dyal, 1979, 1980; Dyal & Dyal, 1981).

Conclusions and Directions for Future Research

Now that the literature on cross-cultural comparisons of locus of control has been reviewed comprehensively, what may be concluded? Regrettably, it is all too often the case that a pattern fails to emerge from the confusing patchwork of inconsistent and often unreliable fragments—cultural chards that resist reconstructive coherence. All too often we seem forced to agree with Draguns's (1979, p. 198) assertion that the research efforts have not yet yielded a coherent body of data.

It is certainly the case that we must content ourselves with less than the conclusive experiment. The nature of our quest requires that we stalk our quarry with correlational nets and quasi-experimental snares. Nonetheless, we have hunted in this domain with less than our best efforts—we have done less good research than we know how. We know that we cannot meaningfully compare differences in mean performance between only two groups on a single dimension. We know that we must compare *patterns* of responses both within our conceptually heterogeneous dependent variables and across subcultural units. We know that we must demonstrate—not just assume—that we have conceptually and psychometrically equivalent tests in the cultures to be compared. We know that cultural differences are often confounded by differences in SES, gender, education, and age, but we seldom design our research to eliminate or evaluate these influences. We know that the reliability of our instruments may vary with the culture and the sample, but we seldom test for their internal consistency. We know that the validity of our constructs–instruments must be demonstrated in each new cultural context by embedding them in theory-relevant nomological networks of convergent and discriminative relations. And we know that we should never use only a single instrument or a single method to measure our personality constructs. We must share the collective guilt of our scientific sins of omission–commission on all these counts.

Yet must we conclude that the efforts of the past two decades add up to nothing but an exotic seduction with no scientific redeeming value? Perhaps not. There *are* some points of relative clarity which may serve to illuminate and inform future efforts.

North American Minority Groups

The most consistent finding in the literature is that US Blacks tend to be more external than US Whites. This overall difference in externality can be interpreted as reflecting the ecological validity of the I–E scale in terms of different opportunity–reinforcement structures available to the two groups. Furthermore, it appears to be the case that US Blacks structure the content of Rotter's I–E Scale differently than do Whites, so that the overall differences reflect different structuring and weighting of component dimensions. Furthermore, the internal consistency of the responses of Blacks has been called into question and needs to be evaluated further.

Future LOC research on North American minority groups could profitably include large-scale developmental studies focusing on home and classroom socialization processes (à la Buriel, 1981). They should utilize several situation-sensitive LOC measures (e.g., IAR and CNSIE) and multidimensional socialization indexes (e.g., Cornell Parent Behavior Inventory [CPBI]). The analyses should be based on multiple regression techniques and should permit the evaluation of interactions among SES, gender, and ethnicity vis-à-vis these more molecular dimensions. In order to reduce and evaluate possible selection bias resulting from differential dropout from the school system, these studies should include samples from Grades 6, 8, and 12.

Cross-Cultural Comparisons

The most robust conclusion from the cross-cultural literature is the relatively greater externality of the Oriental Asian cultures, particularly Japan and Thailand. Future comparative research should be directed toward examining the cultural features that may be related to this externality. Again, of particular importance would be a large-scale study that focuses on the socialization antecedents using the design described earlier with regard to US minority groups. In addition, the external relationships to other personality characteristics that are particularly Japanese would help to embed the LOC construct in its psychocultural context. The observations of Caudill (1969) suggest that LOC-relevant Japanese personality features would include "a willingness to work hard and persevere toward long-range goals"; "an emphasis on self-effacement and a tendency to attribute responsibility to others rather than taking responsibility for one's own actions"; "an attitude of deference and politeness toward one's superiors"; and "a strong feeling of the ephemeral nature of things" (cited in Werner, 1979, p. 301). Futhermore, studies by Caudill and his associates (Caudill & Frost, 1973; Caudill & Schooler, 1973; Caudill & Weinstein, 1969) implicate the strong reinforcement of dependency-related behaviors as typical of Japanese mother–child interactions and a potentially strong antecedent for Japanese externality.

It should also be clear from our review that like Japan, India represents a special challenge and opportunity vis-à-vis future cross-cultural research on LOC. Although the obvious heterogeneity of India precludes any easy cross-cultural generalization (witness the conflicts in the literature with regard to the relative overall internality of Asian Indians), its cultural diversity also provides an unparalleled opportunity for analyses of subcultural factors that influence LOC. Future research should always involve subcultural comparisons (e.g., Khanna & Khanna, 1979) and include detailed specifications of demographic characteristics of the samples.

One feasible and reasonable beginning would be a collaborative effort among several Indian universities using student samples representing major language, geographical, sociocultural status and cast groups. The project should utilize several general and domain-specific measures of LOC, and factor structures should be determined and compared. Although it may not be possible to obtain reliable national norms, the closer we can approximate this goal, the more confidence we will have in subcultural and cross-cultural comparisons. Furthermore, a large-scale socialization antecedent study would be particularly inform-ative in India because the cultural heterogeneity would permit a broad range of potentially relevant socialization practices to be sampled. As noted by Krishnan (personal communication, 1982), research on family antecedents is notably lacking in the Indian setting.

Recent research on North American samples suggests that LOC can moderate the effects of stressful life events on mood states (Lef-court et al., 1981), depression, and anxiety (Johnson and Sarason, 1978) (see Chapter 7 by Lefcourt, in Volume 2). Although it does not seem unreasonable to suppose that cultural variables may influence the way in which LOC moderates life stresses, only two studies thus far re-ported have tested for such differential moderation effects (Dyal, 1982; Dyal et al., 1982). The Karma countries of the East provide a particularly promising contrast in which to search for cultural differences in the moderator effects of LOC. For example, if immersion in a Karma-ori-ented Zeitgeist fostered a "giving up" problem dissolution approach to anxiety-driven problem behaviors (Fogle & Dyal, 1983), then *externality* might in fact serve to reduce the stress of negative life events for Asians, whereas *internality* moderates life stresses for control-oriented cultures such as those of North America.

The Role of Theory and Experiment: Past and Future Promises

Consideration of where we have been and where we are going in cross-cultural LOC research would not be complete without ac-knowledging the critical role of theory and experiment. The failure of cross-cultural research to achieve its goal of testing the generality of Euro-American psychological principles is due in no small part to cross-cultural psychologists' failure to utilize extant theory and experiment to inform and advance the field. Mainstream Euro-American psychology is firmly grounded in theory-guided laboratory experimentation. Cross-cultural research, on the other hand, perhaps due both to practical con-siderations and temperamental bias, has been psychometrically ori-ented. Though it is true that the laboratory experiment has been used successfully in cross-cultural investigations of basic perceptual and cognitive processes, it is also the case that even these basic process areas remain relatively untouched and uninformed by the current con-ceptual–theoretical concerns of the field. The dearth of cross-cultural experimental tests (as contrasted to quasi-experimental tests) is even more apparent in the social or personality domain. The dominant social–personality theories are based on formal experiments, whereas cross-cultural research in the area is based on correlational psychometrics. An eloquent plea for recognition of the critical role of theory and experiment in cultural comparison has been made by Secrest (1977a, 1977b) and by Malpass (1977), leading, it is hoped, to an increasing number of theory-relevant experimental investigations. Furthermore, the dramatic movement toward multivariate causal modeling that has characterized personality research in the past few years augurs well for further convergence of the preferred methodologies of cross-cultural and mainstream personality research.

Several common LOC experimental paradigms seem to be prime candidates for replication in cross-cultural contexts because they test for effects that are likely to be influenced by cultural variables. Furthermore, at the practical level they require minimal high technological instrumentation and are thus more transportable. Two experimental paradigms that have already been shown to be culture-sensitive provide tests for the moderating effect of LOC on the impact of feedback and persuasibility. In her recent review of the LOC literature, Strickland (1977) summarized the North American research on conformity and resistance to social influences as follows:

> Generally, then, I–E appears to be clearly related to conforming and compliant behavior. Internals are more likely to maintain their own individual judgment in the face of contrasting evidence from external sources that call their perceptions and/or behaviors into question. Externals, on the other hand, succumb to pressure from others particularly when the outside source is seen as prestigious or an "expert" [p. 232].

Now consider an experiment by McGinnies and Ward (1974) showing that the influence of the credibility × LOC interaction on persuasibility depends on the country in which the experiment is conducted. McGinnies and Ward tested for the effects of source credibility and locus of control on persuasibility in Japan, the United States, New Zealand, Australia, and Sweden. The dependent variable was expressed attitude relevant to the subject matter of the persuasive communication. They obtained a significant credibility × I–E score × nationality interaction. The essentials of this interaction are presented in Figure 4.1.

It may be seen that for US subjects the previously reported results (e.g., Ritchie & Phares, 1969) are replicated: Internals show relatively little impact of source credibility, whereas externals are strongly influ-

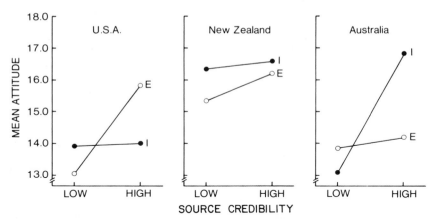

FIGURE 4.1 National differences in persuasibility (attitude ratings) as a function of source credibility and locus of control. (From McGinnies & Ward, 1974.) Closed circles refer to Internals; open circles refer to Externals.

enced. In contrast, New Zealand and Australian data reveal no inter-action effects and a *reversed* interaction, respectively. The Australian internals were strongly influenced by source credibility, whereas the externals showed relatively little influence. McGinnies and Ward concluded:

> The experimental findings support the theoretical predictions with regard to inter-action of Credibility and I–E Scores only for the American subjects. The failure to replicate Ritchie's and Phares's findings in three other countries and, indeed, the finding of an opposite pattern of interaction in the Australian group suggests that generalization of the findings from American subjects to other nationalities would be premature. Differences in "national character" may underlie the obtained effects, and this possibility remains to be explored [p. 370].

The McGinnies and Ward experiments are important in challeng-ing the cross-cultural generalizability of a well-established, theory-rel-evant, principle of American psychology. Yet such is the nature of cross-cultural psychology that no attempt has been made to replicate Mc-Ginnies and Ward's data in Australia or to test for alternative inter-pretations of the effect the authors provide. Clearly such a project is important, feasible, and long overdue.

Numerous studies have demonstrated that LOC serves to moderate the effects of various types of performance feedback (e.g., success–failure, praise–blame, praise–criticism). The state of the art with regard to feedback and its relation to attributions of causality and responsi-bility is well explicated by Strickland:

Several investigators have considered the degree to which I–E may be predictive of attribution of success and failure in task performance. Generally, internals are more likely to attribute success to their own abilities and externals attribute failure to luck or chance (Davis & Davis, 1973; Gilmour & Newton, 1974; Lefcourt, Hogg, Struthers, & Holmes, 1975; Sobel, 1974). . . . Basically, I–E beliefs do appear related to attributions about locus of causality and responsibility. Internals stress skill aspects of task performance and attribute success to their own behavior. Externals perceive chance as a determinant of outcome, particularly failure. . . . None of these findings is particularly surprising in that the I–E model developed originally from experimental manipulation of skill–chance situations and has always been tied theoretically to the perception of contingencies between behavior and outcome [Strickland, 1977, pp. 235–236].

At this point, it may not be particularly surprising that few cross-cultural tests have been made of the generality of the LOC–attribution of causality model. A notable exception is a study by Garza and Lipton (1978). The study was exploratory in the sense that no specific predictions regarding cultural differences were made. The design manipulated ethnicity (Caucasian or Mexican-American), performance feedback (praise versus criticism), LOC (internal versus external) and gender of subject. There were three types of dependent measures: (a) self-evaluation of performance, (b) evaluation of experience of being a subject, and (c) evaluation of the performance of the experimenter. Only this latter measure yielded interactions with ethnicity.

The results are presented in Figure 4.2, where it may be seen that there were no ethnic differences under the praise conditions but that Anglo externals strongly devalued the experimenter under criticism

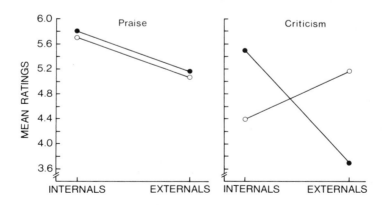

FIGURE 4.2 *Feedback* × *ethnicity* × *locus of control interaction for item: "How would you rate the overall performance of the experimenter?" (From Garza & Lipton, 1977.) Closed circles refer to Anglos and open circles refer to Mexican-Americans.*

conditions, whereas Mexican-American externals showed no such tendency. Indeed, the Mexican-American externals evaluated the experimenter even more positively than the internals. Garza and Lipton speculated that the attribution of positive characteristics to the experimenter by the Mexican-Americans under conditions of criticism may reflect defensive externality on the part of the Hispanics. *Defensive externality* (Prociuk & Breen, 1975; Rotter, 1966) refers to the idea that some externals may adopt a belief in external LOC as a defensive strategy against loss of self-esteem when environmental contingencies have reinforced a lack of trust in one's environment or belief in the lack of efficacy of one's actions.

More recent research efforts with defensive externality have attempted to differentiate "true" externals (i.e., those who truly believe in the importance of luck–fate in controlling their personal outcomes) and defensive externals (those who adopt the belief as a defensive stance). The general strategy has been to use an external criterion index of defensiveness and to split the LOC groups into high and low defensive. Three external criteria of defensiveness have been used: (a) the Interpersonal Trust Scale (Hochreich, 1974, 1975); (b) the Marlow–Crowne Social Desirability Scale (to reflect vulnerable self-esteem) (Evans, 1980), and (c) the degree to which the individual would take action to improve study techniques (Davis, 1970; Lloyd & Chang, 1979). Each of these studies revealed that the differentiation of defensive from congruent (true) externals was useful in predicting reactions to success–failure. The general tenor of the results was that defensive externals were more sensitive to the effects of failure–criticism than were congruent externals. Furthermore, the effect often was strongly influenced by the gender of the subjects (Hochreich, 1974, 1975; Evans, 1980). In addition to arguing for the importance of separating defensive from congruent externals, Evans (1980) contended that defensive and congruent internals should also be differentiated. He argued "that defensive behaviors such as blame projection may be characteristic of some identifiable group of internals when negative personal feedback is obtained" (p. 78).

The specific experimental procedures utilized by Evans are conceptually clean and clever, and his study deserves replication and extension to include cultural variables. It would not be unreasonable to infer, for example, that the defensive blame projection that is hypothesized to characterize defensive internals could account for the low ratings of the experimenter by Mexican-Americans in the Garza and Lipton study. Evans's results support his theoretical hypothesis by indicating that congruent externals accept the least responsibility for success, whereas congruent internals accept the most responsibility for failure. However, female congruent and defensive internals did not differ in their self-attribution of either success or failure. Thus the data support the usefulness of the defensive–congruent distinctions for externals of both genders: Defensive externals accept more personal responsibility for success than for failure and more responsibility for success than do congruent externals. However, the distinction between congruent and defensive internals seems to differentiate only in the case of males; defensive internals accept more personal responsibility for success than for failure. It should also be noted that defensive internal females blamed themselves for failure more than did defensive internal males, a result consistent with the findings of Douvan and Adelson (1966) and Calhoun et al. (1974). Recall that personal characterological self-blame has been implicated in depression for US women (Janoff-Bulman, 1979; Peterson et al. 1981). The cross-cultural generality of the defensive–congruent distinction and gender differences in characterological self-blame should intrigue and inform future research efforts.

An additional implication of the Evans data for future cross-cultural research would stress that the previously reported tendency of externals to attribute failure to luck (Epstein & Komorita, 1971; Strickland, 1977) may hold for defensive externals but not for congruent externals. The relevance of defensive externality to the adjustment of disadvantaged cultural groups is highlighted by Epstein and Komorita as follows:

> The implications of these results for the adaptability of the lower class Negro child may constitute a "double-edged" sword. Inability to assume personal responsibility for failure experiences may interfere with the use of negative environmental feedback for the purpose of modifying one's behavior in a more realistic, adaptive fashion. On the other hand, the defensive function served by this inability may enable the child to maintain some sense of personal integrity and self-esteem. Thus, the attribution of failure to external factors (e.g., luck, chance, or fate) may enable an aggrieved class of people to maintain a capacity for psychological resilience and survival for the short-term, but constitutes a self-defeating mechanism for long-term social adjustment [1977, p. 7]

In addition to the elicitation of attributions following experimental manipulation of success–failure, another tactic has been to elicit attributions to explain the behavior of protagonists presented through story or drama. A substantial number of such studies have tested for cross-cultural similarities and differences in attribution of responsibility—for example, comparing US subjects with Japanese (Shaw & Iwanwaki,

1972); Puerto Ricans (Shaw, 1968); Cubans and Puerto Ricans (Shaw, Briscoe, & Garcia-Esteve, 1968); and US Blacks and Whites (Shaw & Schneider, 1969); Mexican-Americans, Blacks, and Caucasians (Lipton and Garza, 1977); tribal and urban Asian Indian children (Dalal, Sharma, & Bisht, 1980). Attribution of causality, intent, or personal characteristics has also received considerable cross-cultural attention: Maori and Pakeha children (Nicholls, 1978); US and Pakistani subjects (Quereshi, 1978); Turkish and US adolescents (Lecompte and Lecompte, 1973); South Indian Hindus (Taylor and Jaggi, 1974); Iranian children and adolescents (Salili, Maehr, & Gillmore, 1976); Asian Indian university students (Singh, Gupta and Dalal, 1979); and Asian Indian and US native adults (Fry and Ghosh, 1980b). As noted by Alain (1980):

> Overall, the cross-cultural studies of locus of control, attribution of causality, and attribution of responsibility reveal strong cultural differences. However, there has been no effort to relate locus of control and attributional processes as has been done for the American culture [p. 14].

It is indeed unfortunate that this approach to attributional research has not yet been combined with manipulation of LOC in a cross-cultural context.

Other cross-cultural studies have tested for the effects of success and failure on attribution but have failed to manipulate the LOC variable. For example, Fry and Ghosh (1980a) compared Asian Indian-Canadian children with White Canadian children and obtained strong cultural differences in attribution of success and failure to effort, ability, luck, or evaluator accuracy. Recognizing the potential influence of LOC, Fry and Ghosh chose to match the subjects on a children's I–E scale. Their experiment could serve as a useful model for replications in which the LOC variable was manipulated and its possible interactions with culture and success–failure was evaluated.

It should be clear from the foregoing that a refined cognitive attributional analysis of more situation-specific aspects of LOC research has great explanatory and heuristic potential for advancing the practical application of LOC theory (see Gregory, 1981). The use of theory-guided experimentation may be expected to yield increased understanding of cultural variables operating to moderate the effects of LOC on the adjustment of such special populations as elderly people (Fry & Ghosh, 1980b; Rodin & Langner, 1977; Schulz & Hanusa, 1978), immigrants and foreign students (Dyal & Dyal, 1981; Dyal et al. 1982), problem drinking among various ethnic groups (Brod, 1975; Rohsenow

& O'Leary, 1978; Worrell & Tumilty, 1981), and learned helplessness among children of underachieving minority groups (Dweck & Goetz, 1978; Hiroto, 1974).

References

Abrahamson, D., Schludermann, S., & Schludermann, E. Replication of dimensions of locus of control. *Journal of Consulting and Clinical Psychology*, 1973, *37*, 320.

Abramowitz, S. I. Locus of control and self-reported depression among college students. *Psychological Reports*, 1969, *25*, 149–150.

Adinolfi, A., & Klein, R. The value orientations of Guatemalan subsistence farms: Measurement and implications. *Journal of Social Psychology*, 1972, *87*, 13–20.

Aggarwal, Y. P., & Berry, P. Internal–external control as a determinant of academic achievement. *Kurukshetra University Research Journal (Arts and Humanities)*, 1974, *7*, 27–31.

Aggarwal, Y. P., & Gudwani, S. Achievement maturation at high and low levels of perception of personal control. *Journal of the Institute of Educational Research*, 1978, *2*, 37–40.

Aggarwal, Y. P., & Kumari, M. A study of locus of control of boys and girls of various levels of socio-economic status. *Kurukshetra University Research Journal (Arts and Humanities)*, 1975, *9*, 26–32.

Alain, M. *Attribution of causality, I–E locus of control and cross-cultural research.* Unpublished paper, University of Waterloo, 1980.

Alvarez, C. M., & Pader, O. E. Locus of control among Anglo-Americans and Cuban-Americans. *Journal of Social Psychology*, 1978, *105*, 195–198.

Aviram, A., & Milgram, R. M. Dogmatism, locus of control, and creativity in children educated in the Soviet Union, the United States, and Israel. *Psychological Reports*, 1977, *40*, 27–34.

Barling, J., & Finchan, F. Locus of control beliefs in male and female Indian and White school children in South Africa. *Journal of Cross-Cultural Psychology*, 1978, *9*, 227–235.

Bar-Tal, D., & Bar-Zohar, Y. The relationship between perception of locus of control and academic achievement: Review and some educational implications. *Contemporary Education Psychology*, 1977, *2*, 181–199.

Bar-Tal, D., Kfir, D., Bar-Zohar, Y., & Chen, M. The relationship between locus of control and academic achievement, anxiety, and level of aspiration. *British Journal of Educational Psychology*. 1980, *50*, 53–60.

Bartel, N. R. *Locus of control and achievement in middle-class and lower-class children.* Unpublished doctoral dissertation, University of Indiana, 1968.

Battle, E., & Rotter, J. B. Children's feelings of personal control as related to social class and ethnic groups. *Journal of Personality*, 1963, *31*, 482–490.

Berry, J. W. On cross-cultural comparability. *International Journal of Psychology*, 1969, *4*, 119–128.

Berry, J. W. Introduction to methodology. In H. Triandis & J. W. Barry (Eds.), *Handbook of cross-cultural psychology: Methodology* (Vol. 2). Boston: Allyn & Bacon, 1980.

Bialer, I. Conceptualization of success and failures in mentally retarded and normal children. *Journal of Personality*, 1961, *29*, 303–320.

Blignault, I., & Brown, L. B. Locus of control and contraceptive knowledge, attitudes, and practice. *British Journal of Medical Psychology*, 1979, 52, 339–345.

Bond, M. H., & Tornatzky, L. G. Locus of control in students from Japan and the United States: Dimensions and levels of response. *Psychologia*, 1973, *16*, 209–213.

Boor, M. Dimensions of internal–external control and academic achievement. *Journal of Social Psychology*, 1973, *90*, 163–164.

Brod, T. M. Alcoholism as a mental health problem of Native Americans—A review of the literature. *Archives of General Psychiatry*, 1975, *32*, 1385–1391.

Brown, J. C., & Strickland, B. R. Belief in internal–external control of reinforcement and participation in college activities. *Journal of Consulting and Clinical Psychology*, 1972, 38, 148.

Buriel, R. The relation of Anglo- and Mexican-American children's locus of control beliefs to parents' and teachers' socialization practices. *Child Development*, 1981, 52, 104–113.

Buriel, R. & Rivera, L. The relationship of locus of control to family income and familism among Anglo- and Mexican-American high school children. *Journal of Social Psychology*, 1980, *111*, 27–34.

Burnes, K., Brown, W. A., & Keating, G. W. Dimensions of control: Correlations between MMPI and I–E scores. *Journal of Consulting and Clinical Psychology*, 1971, 36, 301.

Burt, C. L. *The factors of the mind: An introduction to factor-analysis in psychology.* New York: Macmillan, 1941.

Butterfield, E. C. Locus of control, test anxiety, reactions to frustration, and achievement attitudes. *Journal of Personality*, 1964, *32*, 298–311.

Calhoun, L. G., Cheney, T., & Dawes, A. S. Locus of control, self-reported depression, and perceived causes of depression. *Journal of Counseling and Clinical Psychology*, 1974, 42, 736.

Campbell, A., Gurin, G. & Miller, W. E. *The voter decides.* Evanston, IL: Row Peterson and Company, 1954.

Campbell, D. T. The mutual methodological relevance of anthropology and psychology. In F. L. K. Hsu (Ed.), *Psychological anthropology.* Homewood, IL: Dorsey, 1961.

Carment, D. W. Internal versus external control in India and Canada. *International Journal of Psychology*, 1974, 9, 45–50.

Carment, D. W., & Paluval, T. R. Correlates of birth control practices in India. *Journal of Cross-Cultural Psychology*, 1973, 4, 111–119.

Cattell, R. B. Comparing factor trait and state scores across ages and cultures. *Journal of Gerontology*, 1969, 24, 348–360.

Cattell, R. B. *The scientific use of factor analysis in behavioral and life sciences.* New York: Plenum, 1978.

Cattell, R. B. (Ed.) *Handbook of multivariate experimental psychology.* Chicago: Rand McNally, 1966.

Caudill, W. A. *The influence of social structure and culture on human behavior in modern Japan.* Honolulu: Social Science Research Institute, University of Hawaii (1969). (Mimeo)

Caudill, W. A., & Frost, L. A comparison of maternal care and infant behavior in Japanese-American, American, and Japanese families. In W. P. Lebre (Ed.), *Youth, socialization and mental health: Mental health research in Asia and the Pacific* (Vol. 3). Honolulu: University of Hawaii Press, 1973.

Caudill, W. A., & Schooler, C. Child behavior and child-rearing in Japan and the United States: An interior report. *Journal of Nervous and Mental Diseases*, 1973, *157*, 323–338.

Caudill, W. A., & Weinstein, H. Maternal care and infant behavior in Japan and America. *Psychiatry*, 1969, *32*, 12–43.

Chan, C. *A study of acculturative stress and internal–external control on Hong Kong foreign students at the University of Waterloo.* Unpublished honors thesis, University of Waterloo, September 1981.

Chance, J. E. *Internal control of reinforcements and the school learning process.* Paper presented at the meeting of the Society for Research in Child Development, Minneapolis, March 1965.

Chandler, T. A., & Dugovics, D. A. Sex differences in research on locus of control. *Psychological Reports*, 1977, *41*, 47–53.

Chandler, T. A., Sharma, D. D., Wolf, F. M., & Planchard, S. K. Multiattributional causality: A five cross-national samples study. *Journal of Cross-Cultural Psychology*, 1981, *12*, 207–221.

Chattopadhyay, S. N., & Pareek, U. Weighting practices in adoption studies. *Indian Journal of Applied Psychology*, 1964, *1*, 84–91.

Chattopadhyay, S. N., & Pareek, U. Prediction of multipractices of adoption behavior from some psychological variables. *Rural Sociology*, 1967, *32*, 324–333.

Cherlin, A., & Bourque, L. B. Dimensionality and reliability of Rotters I–E Scale. *Sociometry*, 1974, *37*, 565–582.

Christie, R., & Geis, F. L. *Studies in Machiavellianism.* New York: Academic Press, 1970.

Christy, L. C. Culture and control orientation: A study of internal–external locus of control in Chinese and American-Chinese women. *Dissertation Abstracts International*, 1977, *39*(2-A), 770.

Cliff, N. Orthogonal rotation to congruence. *Psychometrika*, 1966, *31*, 33–42.

Cole, D. L., & Cole, S. Counternormative behavior and locus of control. *Journal of Social Psychology*, 1977, *101*, 21–28.

Cole, D., Rodriguez, J., & Cole, S. A. Locus of control in Mexicans and Chicanos: The case of the missing fatalist. *Journal of Consulting and Clinical Psychology*, 1978, *46*, 1323–1329.

Cole, M., Gay, J., Glick, J. A., & Sharp, D. W. *The cultural context of learning.* London: Methuen, 1971.

Coleman, J. S., Campbell, E. O., Hobson, C. V., McPartland, J., Mood, A. M., Weinfeld, F. D., & York, R. L. *Equality of educational opportunity.* Washington DC: Government Printing Office, 1966.

Collins, B. Four components of the Rotter Internal–External Scale: Belief in a difficult world, a just world, a predictable world, and a politically responsive world. *Journal of Personality and Social Psychology*, 1974, *29*, 381–391.

Crader, K. W., & Belcher, J. C. Fatalism and fertility in rural Puerto Rico. *Rural Sociology*, 1975, *40*, 268–283.

Crandall, V. J. *Differences in parental antecedents of internal–external control in children and in young adulthood.* Paper presented at the American Psychological Association. Convention, Montreal, 1973.

Crandall, V. J., Katkovsky, W., & Preston, A. Motivational and ability determinants of children's intellectual achievement behavior. *Child Development*, 1962, *33*, 643–661.

Crandall, V. C., Katkovsky, W., & Crandall, V. J. Children's belief in their own control of reinforcements in intellectual academic achievement situations. *Child Development*, 1965, *36*, 91–109.

Cronbach, L. J., & Meehl, P. E. Construct validity in psychological tests. *Psychological Bulletin*, 1955, *53*, 281–302.

Dalal, A. K., Sharme, R., & Bisht, S. *Cultural differences in racial attribution: A comparison of ex-criminal tribal and urban children.* Paper presented at the Fifth International Congress of the International Association for Cross-Cultural Psychology, Bhubaneswar, Crissa, India, December 1980.

Davis, D. E. *Internal-external control and defensiveness.* Unpublished doctoral dissertation, Kansas State University, 1970.

Davis, W. L., & Davis, D. E. Internal–external control and attribution of responsibility for success and failure. *Journal of Personality*, 1972, *40*, 123–136.

Davis, W. L., & Phares, E. J. Internal–external control as a determinant of information-seeking in a social influence situation. *Journal of Personality*, 1967, *35*, 547–561.

deCharms, R., & Carpenter, V. Measuring motivation in culturally disadvantaged children. *Journal of Experimental Education*, 1968, *37*, 31–41.

DeVos, G. The relation of guilt toward parents to achievement and arranged marriage among the Japanese. In T. S. Lebra & W. P. Lebra (Eds.), *Japanese culture and behavior.* Honolulu: University of Hawaii Press, 1974.

Draguns, J. G. *Cultura y peronalidad* [Culture and personality]. In J. O. Whittaker (Ed.), *La psicologia social en el mundo de hoy* [Social psychology in the modern world]. Mexico City: Trillas, 1979, (a)

Draguns, J. G. Culture and personality. In A. J. Marsalla, R. Tharp, & T. J. Ciborowski (Eds.), *Perspectives on cross-cultural psychology.* New York: Academic Press, 1979. (b)

Doob, L. W. Scales for assaying psychological modernization in Africa. *Public Opinion Quarterly*, 1967, *31*, 414–421.

Douvan, R. & Adelson, J. *The adolescent experience.* New York: Wiley, 1966.

Duffy, P. J., Shiflott, S., & Downey, R. G. Locus of control: Dimensionality and predictability using Likert scales. *Journal of Applied Psychology*, 1977, *62*, 214–219.

Duke, M. P., & Nowicki, S. Locus of control and achievement: The confirmation of a theoretical expectation. *Journal of Psychology*, 1974, *87*, 263–267.

Dweck, C. S., & Bush, E. S. Sex differences in learned helplessness: II. Differential debilitation with peer and adult evaluators. *Developmental Psychology*, 1976, *12*, 147–156.

Dweck, C. S., & Goetz, I. E. Attributions and learned helplessness. In J. H. Harvey, W. Ickes, & R. F. Kidd (Eds.), *New directions in attribution research* (Vol. 2). Hillsdale, NJ: Erlbaum, 1978.

Dyal, J. A. *Locus of control and cognitive style in Portuguese-Canadian immigrant children and native born Canadian children.* Unpublished research, 1978.

Dyal, J. A. *A propaedeutic to a model of acculturation: Research implications from the stress and coping literature.* Paper presented at the First Asian Conference of the International Association for Cross-Cultural Psychology, University of Hong Kong, March 1979.

Dyal, J. A. *The psychosocial mediation of acculturative stress.* Paper presented at the Fifth International Congress of the International Association for Cross-Cultural Psychology, Bhubaneswar, Orissa, India, December 1980.

Dyal, J. A. Psychosocial mediation of acculturative stress. In R. Rath, H. S. Asthana, D. Sinha, & J. B. P. Sinha (Eds.), *Diversity and unity in cross-cultural psychology.* Lisse: Swets & Zeitlinger, 1982.

Dyal, J. A., & Bertrand, S. *Locus of control in Trinidadian university students and Trinidadian sojourners in Canada.* Unpublished research, 1982.

Dyal, J. A., Chan, C., & Bertrand, S. *Moderators of acculturative stress in student sojourners.* Paper presented at the meeting of the Canadian Psychological Association, Montreal, June 1982, and American Psychological Association Meetings, Washington, DC, August 1982.

Dyal, J. A., & Dyal, R. Y. Acculturation, stress, and coping: Some implications for research and education. *International Journal of Intercultural Relations*, 1981, 5, 301–328.

Dyal, J. A., Eckerman, A. K., Chan, G., Rai, N., & Lum, J. *Cognitive style and attributional variables differentiating immigrants and Hawaii-born Philipinos (Ilocanos)*. Paper presented at the First Asian Regional Conference of the International Association for Cross-Cultural Psychology, University of Hong Kong, March, 1979.

Echohawk, M., & Parsons, D. A. Leadership vs. behavioral problems and belief in personal control among American Indian Youth. *Journal of Social Psychology*, 1977, 102, 47–54.

Edgington, E. S. A normal curve method for combining probability values from independent experiments. *Journal of Psychology*, 1972, 82, 85–89.

Entwistle, D. R., & Greenberger, E. Questions about social class internality–externality and test anxiety. *Developmental Psychology*, 1972, 7, 218.

Epstein, R., & Komorita, S. S. Self-esteem, success–failure, and locus of control in Negro children. *Developmental Psychology*, 1971, 4, 2–8.

Escovar, L. A. *Dimensionality of the I–E scale: A cross-cultural comparison*. Unpublished paper, 1981.

Evans, H. M., Internal–external locus of control and word association: Research with Japanese and American students. *Journal of Cross-Cultural Psychology*, 1981, 12, 372–382.

Evans, R. G. Reactions to threat by defensive and congruent internals and externals: A self-esteem analysis. *Journal of Research in Personality*, 1980, 14, 76–90.

Faustman, W. O., & Mathews, W. M. Perception of personal control and academic achievement in Sri Lanka: Cross-cultural generality of American research. *Journal of Cross-cultural Psychology*, 1980, 11, 245–252.

Feather, N. T. Some personality correlates of external control. *Australian Journal of Psychology*, 1967, 19, 253–260.

Fink, H. C., & Hjelle, L. A. Internal–external control and ideology. *Psychological Reports*, 1973, 33, 967–974.

Fish, B., & Karabenick, S. A. Relationship between self-esteem and locus of control. *Psychological Reports*, 1972, 29, 784.

Fogle, D., & Dyal, J. A. Paradoxical giving up and the reduction of sleep performance anxiety in chronic insomniacs. *Journal of Psychotherapy: Theory, Research and Practice*, 1983, 20, 21–30.

Forward, J. R., & Williams, J. R. Internal–external control and Black militancy. *Journal of Social Issues*, 1970, 26, 75–92.

Franklin, R. D. Youth's expectancies about internal versus external control of reinforcement related to N variables. *Dissertation Abstracts International*, 1963, 24, 1684.

Fredriksen, N. How to tell if a test measures the same thing in different cultures. In Y. H. Poortinga (Ed.), *Basic problems in cross-cultural psychology*. Amsterdam: Scoets & Zeitlinger, 1977.

Freire, P. *Pedagogy of the oppressed*. New York: Viking, 1972.

Fry, P. S., & Ghosh, R. Attributions of success and failure: comparison of cultural differences between Asian and Caucasian children. *Journal of Cross-Cultural Psychology*, 1980, 11, 343–363. (a)

Fry, P. S., & Ghosh, R. Attributional differences in the life satisfactions of the elderly: A cross-cultural comparison of Asian and United States subjects. *International Journal of Psychology*, 1980, 15, 201–212 (b)

Garcia, C., & Levenson, H. Differences between Blacks' and Whites' expectation of control by chance and powerful others. *Psychological Reports*, 1975, 37, 563–566.

Garza, R. T. Personal control and fatalism in Chicanos and Anglos: Conceptual and methodological issues. In J. L. Martinez, Jr. (Ed.), *Chicano psychology*. New York: Academic Press, 1977.

Garza, R. T., & Ames, R. E. A comparison of Anglo- and Mexican-American college students on locus of control. *Journal of Consulting and Clinical Psychology*, 1974, 42, 919.

Garza, R. T., & Lipton, J. P. Culture, personality, and reactions to praise and criticism. *Journal of Personality*, 1978, 46, 743–761.

Garza, R. T., & Widlak, F. W. The validity of locus of control dimensions for Chicano populations. *Journal of Personality Assessment*, 1977, 41, 635–643.

Gilmor, T. Locus of control as a mediator of adaptive behaviour in children and adolescents. *Canadian Psychological Review*, 1978, 19, 1–26.

Gilmor, T., & Minton, H. L. Internal versus external attribution of task performance as a function of locus of control, initial confidence and success-failure outcome. *Journal of Personality*, 1974, 42, 159–174.

Giorgis, T. W. Locus of control and manifest anxiety in African, Afro-American, and Caucasian-American students. *Dissertation Abstracts International*, 1978, 39, 5–B, 2495.

Glantz, O. Locus of control and aspiration to traditionally open and traditionally closed occupations. *Journal of Negro Education*, 1977, 46, 278–290.

Gold, D. Preference for skill or chance tasks and I–E scores. *Psychological Reports*, 1966, 19, 1279–1281.

Gore, P. S., & Rotter, J. B. A personality correlate of social action. *Journal of Personality*, 1963, 31, 58–64.

Goss, A., & Morosko, T. E. Relation between a dimension of internal–external control and the MMPI with an alcoholic population. *Journal of Consulting and Clinical Psychology*, 1970, 34, 189–192.

Gottesfield, H., & Dozier, G. Changes in feelings of powerlessness in a community action program. *Psychological Reports*, 1966, 19, 978.

Grebler, L., Moore, J. W., & Guzman, R. C. *The Mexican-American people*. New York: Holt, Rinehart & Winston, 1970.

Gregory, W. L. Expectancies for controllabilities, performance attributions, and behavior. In H. M. Lefcourt (Ed.), *Research with the locus of control construct* (Vol. I). New York: Academic Press, 1981.

Groat, H. T. & Neal, A. G. Social psychological correlates of urban fertility. *American Sociological Review*, 1967, 32, 945–959.

Gruen, G. E., Korte, J. R., & Baum, J. F. Group measures of locus of control. *Developmental Psychology*, 1974, 10, 683–383.

Gruen, G. E., & Ottinger, D. R. Skill and chance orientations as determiners of problem-solving behavior in lower- and middle-class children. *Psychological Reports*, 1969, 24, 207–214.

Gurin, G., & Gurin, P. Expectancy theory and the study of poverty. *Journal of Social Issues*, 1970, 26, 83–104.

Gurin, P., Gurin, G., Lao, R. C., & Beattie, M. Internal–external control in the motivational dynamics of Negro youth. *Journal of Social Issues*, 1969, 25, 29–53.

Hall, E. R., Joesting, J., & Woods, M. L. Relationships among measures of locus of control for Black and White students. *Psychological Reports*, 1977, 40, 59–62.

Halpin, G., Halpin, G., & Whiddon, T. The relationship of perceived parental behaviors to locus of control and self-esteem among American Indian and White children. *Journal of Social Psychology*, 1980, 111, 189–195.

Heaton, R. C., & Duerfeld, P. H. The relationship between self-esteem, self-reinforcement, and the internal–external personality dimension. *Journal of Genetic Psychology*, 1973, *123*, 3–13.

Hendrix, B. L. The effects of locus of control on the self-esteem of Black and White youth. *Journal of Social Psychology*, 1980, *112*, 301–302.

Hersch, P. D., & Scheibe, K. E. On the reliability and validity of internal–external control as a personality dimension. *Journal of Consulting Psychology*, 1967, *31*, 609–613.

Hill, R. Stycos, J. M. & Back, K. W. *The family and population control*. Chapel Hill: University of North Carolina Press, 1959.

Hiroto, D. S. Locus of control and learned helplessness. *Journal of Experimental Psychology*, 1974, *102*, 187–193.

Hochreich, D. J. Defensive externality and attribution of responsibility. *Journal of Personality*, 1974, *42*, 543–557.

Hochreich, D. J. Defensive externality and blame projection following failure. *Journal of Personality and Social Psychology*, 1975, *32*, 540–546.

Hoffman, C. Empowerment movements and mental health: Locus of control and commitment to the United Farm Workers. *Journal of Community Psychology*, 1978, *6*, 216–221.

Hsieh, T. T., Shybut, J., & Lotsof, E. J. Internal versus external control and ethnic group membership. *Journal of Consulting and Clinical Psychology*, 1969, *33*, 122–124.

Hsu, F. L. K. *Americans and Chinese: Two ways of life*. New York: Akerlard-Schuman, 1953.

Huebner, R. B., & Lipsey, M. W. *The relationship of three measures of locus of control to environmental activism*. Unpublished manuscript, 1979. (Available from Psychology Department, Claremont Graduate School, Claremont, CA 91711)

Hui, C-C. H. Locus of control: A review of cross-cultural research. *International Journal of Intercultural Relations*, 1982, *6*, 301–323.

Hui, C-C. H., Triandis, H. C., & Chang, B-H. *Locus of control among mainstream and Hispanic Navy Recruits: A methodological and substantive study*. Technical Report No. CNR-9, Office of Naval Research, March, 1982.

Inkeles, A., & Smith, D. H. *Becoming modern*. Cambridge, MA: Harvard University Press, 1974.

Irvine, S. H., & Carroll, W. K. Testing and assessment across cultures: Issues of methodology and theory. In H. C. Triandis & J. W. Berry (Eds.), *Handbook of cross-cultural psychology*. Boston: Allyn & Bacon, 1980.

Irwin, M., Klein, R. E., Engle, P. L., Yarbrough, C., & Nerlove, S. B. The problem of establishing validity in cross-cultural measurements. In L. L. Adler (Ed.), Issues in cross-cultural research. *Annals of the New York Academy of Science, 285*, 1977.

Janoff-Bulman, R. Characterological versus behavioral self-blame: Inquiries into depression and rape. *Journal of Personality and Social Psychology*, 1979, *37*, 1798–1809.

Jessor, R., Graves, T. D., Hanson, R. C., & Jessor, S. L. *Society, personality, and deviant behavior*. New York: Holt, Rinehart & Winston, 1968.

Jessor, R., Young, H. B., Young, E. B., & Tesi, G. Perceived opportunity, alienation, and drinking behavior among Italian and American Youth. *Journal of Personality and Social Psychology*, 1970, *15*, 215–222.

Joe, V. C., & Jahn, J. C. Factor structure of the Rotter I–E scale. *Journal of Clinical Psychology*, 1973, *29*, 66–68.

Johnson, J. H., & Sarason, I. G. Life stress, depression, and anxiety: Internal–external control as a moderator variable. *Journal of Psychosomatic Research*, 1978, *22*, 205–208.

298 : JAMES A. DYAL

Jones, E. E., & Zoppel, C. L. Personality differences among Blacks in Jamaica and the United States. *Journal of Cross-Cultural Psychology*, 1979, 4, 435–456.

Jöreskog, K. G. A general approach to confirmatory maximum likelihood factor analysis. *Psychometrika*, 1969, 34, 183–202.

Kaemmerer, W. F., & Schwebel, A. I. Factors of the Rotter internal–external scale. *Psychological Reports*, 1976, 39, 107–114.

Kahl, J. *The measurement of modernism: A study of values in Brazil and Mexico*. Austin: University of Texas Press, 1968.

Kanungo, R. N., & Bhatnagar, J. K. Achievement orientation and occupational values: A comparative study of young French and English Canadians. *Canadian Journal of Behavioural Science*, 1978, 10, 202–213.

Katkovsky, W., Crandall, U. C., & Good, S. Parental antecedents of children's belief in internal–external control of reinforcement in intellectual achievement situations. *Child Development*, 1967, 38, 765–776.

Katz, I. The socialization of academic motivation in minority group children. In D. Levine (Ed.), *Nebraska symposium on motivation*. Lincoln, Nebraska: University of Nebraska Press, 1967, pp. 133–191.

Kerlinger, F. N. *Foundations of behavioral research*. New York: Holt, Rinehart & Winston, 1967.

Khanna, P., & Khanna, J. L. Locus of control in India: A cross-cultural perspective. *International Journal of Psychology*, 1979, 14, 207–214.

Kiehlbauch, J. B. Selected changes over time in internal–external control expectancies in a reformatory population. Unpublished doctoral dissertation. Kansas State University, 1968.

Kim, B. K. Attitudes, parental identification, and locus of control of Korean, new Korean-Canadian, and Canadian adolescents. *Dissertation Abstracts International*, 1977, 38, 5–A 3382.

Kinder, D. R., & Reeder, L. G. Ethnic differences in beliefs about control. *Sociometry*, 1975, 38, 241–272.

Kiray, M. B. Values, social stratification, and development. *Journal of Social Issues*, 1968, 24, 87–100.

Kleiber, D., Veldman, D. J., & Menaker, S. J. The multidimensionality of locus of control. *Journal of Clinical Psychology*, 1973, 29, 411–416.

Knight, G. P., Kagan, S., Nelson, W., & Gumbiner, J. Acculturation of second- and third-generation Mexican-American children: Field independence, locus of control, self-esteem, and school achievement. *Journal of Cross-Cultural Psychology*, 1978, 9, 87–97.

Knight, G. P., Nelson, W., Kagan, S., & Gumbiner, J. Cooperative–competitive school orientation and school achievement among Anglo-American and Mexican-American children. *Contemporary Educational Psychology*, in press.

Krampen, G. Generalized expectations of alcoholics: Locus of control, hopelessness, and Machiavellianism. *Journal of Counseling and Clinical Psychology*, 1979.

Krampen, G., & Nispel, L. Zur subjektiven Handlungsfreiheit von Alkoholikern. *Zeitschrift für Klinishe Psychologie*, 1978, 7, 295–303.

Langner, T. A twenty-two item screening score of psychiatric symptoms indicating impairment. *Journal of Health and Social Behavior*, 1962, 3, 269–276.

Lao, R. C. Internal–external control and competent and innovative behavior among Negro college students. *Journal of Personality and Social Psychology*, 1970, 14, 263–270.

Lao, R. C. *The developmental trend of the locus of control*. Paper presented at the meeting of the American Psychological Association, New Orleans, September 1974.

Lao, R. C. Levenson's IPC (Internal–External Control) Scale: A comparison of Chinese and American students. *Journal of Cross-Cultural Psychology*, 1978, 9, 113–122.

Lao, R. C., Chuang, C. J., & Yang, K. S. Locus of control and Chinese college students. *Journal of Cross-Cultural Psychology*, 1977, 8, 299–313.

Lecompte, W. F., & Lecompte, G. K. Generational attribution in Turkish and American youth. *Journal of Cross-Cultural Psychology*, 1973, 4, 175–191.

Lee, F. *A study of sex differences in locus of control, tennis, expectancy for success, and tennis achievement.* Unpublished doctoral dissertation, University of Oregon, 1976.

Lefcourt, H. M. Internal–external control of reinforcement: A review. *Psychological Bulletin*, 1966, 65, 206–220.

Lefcourt, H. M. The construction and development of the Multidimensional–Multiattributional Causality Scales. In H. M. Lefcourt (Ed.), *Research with the locus of control construct: Assessment methods* (Vol. I). New York: Academic Press, 1981. (a)

Lefcourt, H. M. *Research with the locus of control construct: Assessment methods* (Vol. 1). New York: Academic Press, 1981. (b)

Lefcourt, H. M. *Locus of Control.* Hillsdale, NJ: Erlbaum, 1976.

Lefcourt, H. M., Hogg, E., Struthers, S., & Holmes, C. Causal attributions as a function of locus of control, initial confidence, and performance outcomes. *Journal of Personality and Social Psychology*, 1975, 32, 391–397.

Lefcourt, H. M. & Ladwig, G. W. The American Negro: A problem in expectancies. *Journal of Personality and Social Psychology*, 1965, 1, 377–380.

Lefcourt, H. M., & Ladwig, G. W. Alienation in Negro and White reformatory inmates. *Journal of Social Psychology*, 1966, 68, 152–157.

Lefcourt, H. M., Miller, R. S., Ware, E. E. & Sherk, D. Locus of control as a modifier of the relationship between stressors and moods. *Journal of Personality and Social Psychology*, 1981. 41, 357–369.

Lefcourt, H. M., Von Baeyer, C. I., Ware, E. E., & Cox, D. J. The Multidimensional–Multiattributional Causality Scale: The development of a goal-specific locus of control scale. *Canadian Journal of Behavioural Science*, 1979, 11, 286–304.

Lessing, E. E. Racial differences in indices of ego functioning relevant to academic achievement. *Journal of Genetic Psychology*, 1969, 65, 153–167.

Levenson, H. Distinction within the concept of internal–external control: Development of a new scale. *Proceedings of the 80th Annual Convention of the American Psychological Association*, 1972, 7, 261–262.

Levenson, H. Multidimensional locus of control in psychiatric patients. *Journal of Consulting and Clinical Psychology*, 1973, 41, 397–404.

Levenson, H. Activism and powerful others: Distinction within the concept of internal–external control. *Journal of Personality Assessment*, 1974, 38, 377–383.

Levenson, H. Differentiating among internality, powerful others, and chance. In H. M. Lefcourt (Ed.), *Research with the locus of control construct: Assessment methods* (Vol. I). New York: Academic Press, 1981.

Levenson, H., & Mahler, I. Attitudes toward others and components of internal–external control. *Psychological Reports*, 1975, 36, 209–210.

Levenson, H., & Miller, J. Multidimensional locus of control in sociopolitical activists of conservative and liberal ideologies. *Journal of Personality and Social Psychology*, 1976, 33, 199–208.

LeVine, R. A. Cross-cultural study in child psychology. In P. H. Mussen (Ed.), *Carmichaels's manual of child psychology* (Vol. 2). New York: Wiley, 1970.

Lipton, J. P., & Garza, R. T. Responsibility attribution among Mexican-American, Black, and Anglo adolescents and adults. *Journal of Cross-cultural Psychology*, 1977, 8, 259–272.

Lorimer, F. B. (Ed.). *Culture and fertility.* Paris: UNESCO, 1954.

Lloyd, C., & Chang, A. F. The usefulness of distinguishing between a defensive and a nondefensive locus of control. *Journal of Research in Personality,* 1979, *13,* 316–325.

MacDonald, A. P. Internal–external locus of control: Parental antecedents. *Journal of Consulting and Clinical Psychology,* 1971, *37,* 141–147.

MacDonald, A. P. More on the Protestant ethic. *Journal of Consulting and Clinical Psychology,* 1972, *39,* 116–122.

MacDonald, A. P., & Tseng, M. S. *Dimensions of internal versus external control revisited.* Unpublished manuscript, University of West Virginia. 1971.

Mahler, I. A comparative study of locus of control. *Psychologia,* 1974, *17,* 135–139.

Malikiosi, M. X., & Ryckman, R. M. Differences in perceived control among men and women adults and university students in America and Greece. *Journal of Social Psychology,* 1977, *103,* 177–183.

Malpass, R. S. Theory and method in cross-cultural psychology. *American Psychologist,* 1977, *32,* 1069–1079.

Maroldo, G. K., & Flachmeir, L. C. Machiavellianism, external control, and cognitive style of American and West German coeds. *Psychological Reports,* 1978, *42,* 1315–1317.

Massari, D. J., & Rosenblum, D. C. Locus of control, interpersonal trust, and academic achievement. *Psychological Reports,* 1972, *31,* 355–360.

McGhee, P. E., & Crandall, U. C. Beliefs in internal–external control of reinforcements and academic performance. *Child Development,* 1968, *39,* 91–102.

McGinnies, E., Nordholm, L. A., Ward, C. D., & Bhanthumnavin, D. L. Sex and cultural differences in perceived locus of control among students in five countries. *Journal of Consulting and Clinical Psychology,* 1974, *42,* 451–455.

McGinnies, E., & Ward, C. D. Persuasibility as a function of source credibility and locus of control: Five cross-cultural experiments. *Journal of Personality,* 1974, *42,* 360–371.

Mehrabian, A. Male and female scales of the tendency to achieve. *Educational and Psychological Measurement,* 1968, *28,* 493–502.

Mehrabian, A. Measures of achieving tendency. *Educational and Psychological Measurement,* 1969, *29,* 445–451.

Milgram, N. A. Locus of control in Negro and White children at four age levels. *Psychological Reports,* 1971, *29,* 459–465.

Miller, A. G., & Minton, H. L. Machiavellianism, internal–external control, and the violation of experimental instructions. *Psychological Record,* 1967, *19,* 369–380.

Miller, D. T., & Ross, M. Self-serving biases in the attribution of causality: Fact or fiction? *Psychological Bulletin,* 1975, *82,* 213–225.

Mirels, H. L. Dimensions and internal versus external control. *Journal of Consulting and Clinical Psychology,* 1970, *34,* 220–228.

Mirels, H. L., & Garrett, J. B. The Protestant ethic as a personality variable. *Journal of Consulting and Clinical Psychology.* 1971, *36,* 40–44.

Mishra, C. *Differences in locus of control among children across SES and subcultures.* Paper presented at the Fifth International Congress of the International Association for Cross-Cultural Psychology, Bhubaneswar, Crissa, India, December 1980.

Molanari, V. *Locus of control.* Unpublished doctoral dissertation, Ohio State University, 1979.

Moodley-Rajab, D., & Ramkissoon, R. D. Internal–external control among South African students—A cross-cultural study. *South African Journal of Psychology,* 1979, *9,* 145–147.

Morelli, G., Krotinger, H., & Moore, S. Neurotism and Levenson's locus of control scale. *Psychological Reports,* 1979, *44,* 153–154.

Mostellar, F. M., & Bush, R. R. Selected quantitative techniques. In G. Lindzey (Ed.), Handbook of social psychology: Theory and method (Vol. 1). Reading, MA: Addison-Wesley, 1954.

Murillo, N. The Mexican-American family. In N. N. Wagner & M. J. Haug (Eds.), Chicanos Social and Psychological Perspectives. St. Louis: Mosby, 1971.

Nagelschmidt, A. M., & Jakob, R. Dimensionality of Rotter's I–E Scale in a society in the process of modernization. Journal of Cross-Cultural Psychology, 1977, 8, 101–112.

Neal, A. G., & Seeman, M. Organizations and powerlessness: A test of the mediation hypothesis. American Sociological Review, 1964, 29, 216–226.

Nedd, A. N. B., & Marsh, N. R. Social traditionalism and personality: An empirical investigation of the interrelationships between social values and personality attributes. International Journal of Psychology, 1979, 14, 73–82.

Nicholls, J. G. Development of causal attributions and evaluative responses to success and failure in Maori and Pakeha children. Developmental Psychology, 1978, 14, 687–688.

Niles, F. S. Dimensionality of Rotter's I–E Scale in Sri Lanka. Journal of Cross-Cultural Psychology, 1981, 12, 473–479.

Nowicki, S. Predicting academic achievement in females from locus of control orientation: Some problems and some solutions. Paper presented at the American Psychological Association Convention, Montreal, 1973.

Nowicki, S., & Roundtree, J. Correlates of locus of control in secondary school age students. Unpublished manuscript, Emory University, 1971.

Nowicki, S., & Segal, W. Perceived parental characteristics, locus of control orientation, and behavioral correlates of locus of control. Developmental Psychology, 1974, 10, 33–37.

Nowicki, S., & Strickland, B. R. A locus of control scale for children. Journal of Consulting and Clinical Psychology, 1973, 40, 148–155.

Nowicki, S., & Walker, C. The role of generalized and specific expectancies in determining academic achievement. Journal of Social Psychology, 1974, 94, 275–280.

Odell, M. Personality correlates of independence and conformity. Unpublished master's thesis, Ohio State University, 1959.

Owens, M. W. Disability–minority and social learning. Unpublished master's thesis, West Virginia University, 1969.

Pareek, U., & Chattopadhyay, S. N. Adoption quotient—A measure of multipractice adoption behavior. Journal of Applied Behavioral Science, 1966, 2, 95–108.

Parsons, O. A., & Schneider, J. M. Locus of control in university students from eastern and western societies. Journal of Consulting and Clinical Psychology, 1974, 42, 456–461.

Parsons, O. A., Schneider, J. M., & Hansen, A. S. Internal–external locus of control and maternal stereotypes in Denmark and the United States. Journal of Consulting and Clinical Psychology, 1970, 35, 30–37.

Pedhazur, L., & Wheeler, L. Locus of perceived control and need achievement. Perception and Motor Skills, 1971, 33, 1281–1282.

Peterson, C., Schwartz, S. M., & Seligman, M. E. P. Self-blame and depressive symptoms. Journal of Personality and Social Psychology, 1981, 41, 253–259.

Phares, E. J. Expectancy changes in skill and chance situations. Journal of Abnormal and Social Psychology, 1957, 54, 339–342.

Phares, E. J. Locus of control in personality. Morristown, N. J.: General Learning Fairway Press, 1976.

Platt, J. J., & Eisenman, R. Internal–external control of reinforcements, time perspective, adjustment, and anxiety. Journal of General Psychology, 1968, 79, 121–128.

Platt, J. J., Pomeranz, D., Eisenman, R., & Delisser, O. Importance of considering sex differences in relationships between locus of control and other personality variables. *Proceedings of the American Psychological Association*, 1970, 5, 463–464.

Powell, A., & Vega, M. Correlates of adult locus of control. *Psychological Reports*, 1972, 30, 455–460.

Price-Williams, D. R. *Explorations in cross-cultural psychology*. San Francisco: Chandler & Sharp, 1975.

Prociak, T. J., & Breen, L. J. Defensive externality and its relation to academic performance. *Journal of Personality and Social Psychology*, 1975, 31, 549–556.

Quereshi, M. Y. Attribution of personal characteristics in two cultures. *Social Behavior and Personality*, 1978, 6, 117–133.

Ramirez, N., & Castenada, A. *Cultural democracy, bicognitive development, and education*. New York: Academic Press, 1974.

Ransford, H. E. Isolation, powerlessness, and violence: A study of attitudes and participation in the Watts riot. *American Journal of Sociology*, 1968, 73, 581–591.

Ray, J. J. Belief in luch and locus of control. *Journal of Social Psychology*, 1980, 111, 299–300.

Ray, W. J., & Katahn, M. Relation of anxiety to locus of control. *Psychological Reports*, 1968, 23, 1196.

Reid, D., & Ware, E. E. Multidimensionality of internal–external control: Implications for past and future research. *Canadian Journal of Behavioral Science*, 1973, 5, 264–271.

Reid, D., & Ware, E. E. Multidimensionality of internal versus external control: Addition of a third dimension and nondistinction of self versus others. *Canadian Journal of Behavioural Science*, 1974, 6, 131–142.

Reid, I., & Croucher, A. The Crandall Intellectual Achievement Responsibilities Questionnaire: A British validation study. *Educational and Psychological Measurement*, 1980, 40, 255–258.

Reimanis, G. *Effects of experimental I–E modification techniques and environmental variables on IE*. Paper presented at the Annual Meeting of the American Psychological Association, Washington, DC, September 1971.

Reimanis, G. Locus of control in American and northeastern Nigerian students. *Journal of Social Psychology*, 1977, 103, 309–310.

Reimanis, G. *Anomie, locus of control, and educational variables in a cross-cultural perspective*. Paper presented at the Fifth International Congress of the International Association for Cross-Cultural Psychology, Bhubaneswar, Orissa, India, December 1980.

Reimanis, G. Relationship of locus of control and anomie to political interests among American and Nigerian students. *Journal of Social Psychology*, 1982.

Reimanis, G., & Posen, C. Locus of control and anomie in Western and African cultures. *Journal of Social Psychology*, 1980, 112, 181–189.

Reitz, H. J., & Groff, G. K. Economic development and belief in locus of control among factory workers in four countries. *Journal of Cross-Cultural Psychology*, 1974, 5, 344–355.

Reitz, H. J., & Jewell, L. N. Sex, locus of control, and job involvement: A six-country investigation. *Academy of Management Journal*, 1979, 22, 72–80.

Ritchie, E. & Phares, E. J. Attitude change as a function of internal–external control and communicator status. *Journal of Personality*, 1969, 37, 429–443.

Roberts, A. E., & Reid, P. N. Dimensionality of the Rotter I–E scale. *Journal of Social Psychology*, 1978, 106, 129–130.

Rodin, J., & Langer, E. J. Long-term effects of a control-relevant intervention with institutionalized aged. *Journal of Personality and Social Psychology*, 1977, 35, 897–902.

Rohsenow, D. J., & O'Leary, M. R. Locus of control research on alcoholic populations:
A review. I Development, scales and treatment. *International Journal of the Addic-
tions*, 1978, 13, 55–78.

Rotter, J. B. *Social learning and clinical psychology*. Englewood Cliffs, NJ: Prentice-Hall,
1954.

Rotter, J. B. Generalized expectancies for internal versus external control of reinforcement. *Psychological Monographs*, 1966, 80 (1, Whole NO. 609).

Roueche, J. E., & Mink, O. G. *Impact of instruction and counseling on high risk youth.*
Final Report, NIMH Grant R01MH22590, September 30, 1976. Dept of Educational
Administration, University of Texas, Austin, Texas.

Rummel, R. J. *Applied factor analysis.* Evanston, IL: Northwestern University Press, 1970.

Rupp, M., & Nowicki, S. Locus of control among Hungarian children. *Journal of Cross-
Cultural Psychology*, 1978, 9, 359–366.

Ryckman, R. M., & Malikioski, M. Relationship between locus of control and chronological age. *Psychological Reports*, 1975, 36, 655–658.

Ryckman, R. M., Posen, C. F., & Kulberg, G. F. Locus of control among American and
Rhodesian students. *Journal of Social Psychology*, 1978, 104, 165–173.

Ryckman, R. M., Posen, C. F., & Kalberg, G. E. *Multidimensional locus of control among
United States and Rhodesian university students.* Paper presented at the Interamer-
ican Congress of Psychology, Lima, Peru, 1979.

Ryckman, R. M., Rodda, W. C., & Stone, W. F. Performance time as a function of sex,
locus of control, and task requirements. *Journal of Social Psychology*, 1971, 85, 299–
305.

Ryckman, R. M., & Sherman, M. F. Relationship between self-esteem and internal–external control for men and women. *Psychological Reports*, 1973, 32, 1106.

Ryckman, R. M., Stone, W. F., & Elam, R. R. Emotional arousal as a function of perceived
locus of control and task requirements. *Journal of Social Psychology*, 1971, 83, 185–
191.

Salili, F., Maehr, M.L., & Gillmore, G. Achievement and morality: A cross-cultural analysis of causal attribution and evaluation. *Journal of Personality and Social Psychology*, 1976, 33, 327–337.

Sanger, S. P., & Alker, H. A. Dimensions of internal–external locus of control and the
women's liberation movement. *Journal of Social Issues*, 1972, 28, 115–129.

Sank, Z. R., & Strickland, B. R. Some attitudes and behavioral correlates of a belief in
militant or moderate social action. *Journal of Social Psychology*, 1973, 90, 337–338.

Saraswathi, T. S., & Sharma, P. *Personality characteristics and locus of control of competent children: Sex and social class comparisons.* Paper presented at the Fifth International Congress of the International Association for Cross-Cultural Psychology,
Bhubaneswar, Orissa. India, December 1980.

Schmidt, R. W., Lamm, H., & Tromsdorf, G. Social class and sex as determinants of future
orientation (time perspective) in adults. *European Journal of Social Psychology*, 1978,
8, 71–90.

Schnaiberg, A. Measuring modernism: Theoretical and empirical explanations. *American Journal of Sociology.* 1970, 61, 247–262.

Schneider, J. M. Skill versus chance acitivity preferences and locus of control. *Journal
of Consulting and Clinical Psychology*, 1968, 32, 333–337.

Schneider, J. M. Relationship between locus of control and activity preferences: Effects
of masculinity, activity, and skill. *Journal of Consulting and Clinical Psychology*, 1972,
38, 225–230.

Schneider, J. M., & Parsons, C. A. Categories on the locus of control scale and cross-cultural comparisons in Denmark and the United States. *Journal of Cross-Cultural Psychology*, 1970, *1*, 131–138.

Schulz, R., & Hanusa, B. H. Long-term effects of control and predictability-enhancing interventions: Findings and ethical issues. *Journal of Personality and Social Psychology*, 1978, *36*, 1194–1201.

Scott, J. D., & Phelan, J. G. Expectancies of unemployable males regarding source of control of reinforcement. *Psychological Reports*, 1969, *25*, 911–913.

Sechrest, L. On the need for experimentation in cross-cultural research. In L. L. Adler (Ed.), Issues in cross-cultural research. *Annals of the New York Academy of Sciences*, 1977, 285–305. (a)

Sechrest, L. On the dearth of theory in cross-cultural psychology: A return to basics? In Y. H. Poortinga (Ed.), *Basic problems in cross-cultural psychology*. Amsterdam: Sevets & Zeitlinger, 1977. (b)

Seeman, M. Alienation and social learning in a reformatory. *American Journal of Sociology*, 1963, *69*, 270–284.

Seeman, M. Alienation, membership, and political knowledge: A comparative study. *Public Opinion Quarterly*, 1966, *30*, 354–367.

Seeman, M. Powerlessness and knowledge: A comparative study of alienation and learning. *Sociometry*, 1967, *30*, 105–123.

Seeman, M. Alienation: A map of its principal territories: Individual powerlessness, cynicism, cultural estrangement, self-estrangement, and social isolation. *Psychology Today*, 1971, August, 83–84.

Seeman, M., & Evans, J. W. Alienation and social learning in a hospital setting. *American Sociological Review*, 1962, *27*, 772–782.

Segall, M. H. *Cross-cultural psychology: Human behavior in global perspective*. Monterey, CA: Brooks/Cole, 1979.

Shaw, M. E. Attribution of responsibility by adolescents in two cultures. *Adolescence*, 1968, *3*, 23–32.

Shaw, M. E., Briscoe, M. E., & Garcia-Esteve, J. A cross-cultural study of attribution of responsibility. *International Journal of Psychology*, 1968, *3*, 51–60.

Shaw, M. E., & Iwawaki, S. Attribution of responsibility by Japanese and Americans as a function of age. *Journal of Cross-Cultural Psychology*, 1972, *3*, 71–81.

Shaw, M. E., & Schneider, F. W. Negro–White differences in attribution of responsibility as a function of age. *Psychonomic Science*, 1969, *16*, 289–291.

Shaw, R. L., & Uhl, N. P. Control of reinforcement and academic achievement. *Journal of Educational Research*, 1971, *64*, 226–228.

Shearer, R. A., & Moore, J. B. *Personality dimensions of felonious probationers in Texas*. Paper presented at the Annual Meeting of the American Society of Criminology, Dallas, November 1978.

Shore, R. E. *Parental determinants of boys' internal–external control*. Unpublished doctoral dissertation, Syracuse University, 1967.

Silvern, I. E. The effect of traditional vs. counterculture attitudes on the relationship between the internal–external scale and political position. *Journal of Personality*, 1975, *43*, 58–73.

Silvern, I. E., & Nakamura, C. Y. Powerlessness, social–political action, and social–political views: Their interrelation among college students. *Journal of Social Issues*, 1971, *27*, 137–157.

Singh, R., Gupta, M., & Dalal, A. K. Cultural differences in attribution of performance: An integration–theoretical analysis. *Journal of Personality and Social Psychology*, 1979, *37*, 1342–1351.

Sobel, R. S. The effects of success, failure, and locus of control of postperformance attribution of causality. *Journal of General Psychology*, 1974, *91*, 29–34.

Solar, D., & Breuhl, D. Machiavellianism and locus of control: Two conceptions of interpersonal power. *Psychological Reports*, 1971, *29*, 1079–1082.

Soloman, D., Houlihan, R. D., Busse, T. V., & Parelius, R. J. Parent behavior and child academic achievement, achievement striving, and related personality characteristics. *Genetic Psychology Monographs*, 1971, *83*, 173–273.

Sörbom, D. A general method for studying differences in factor means and factor structure between groups. *British Journal of Mathematical and Statistical Psychology*, 1974, *27*, 229–239.

Spielberger, C. D. *Test Attitude Inventory.* Palo Alto, CA: Consulting Psychologists Press, 1977.

Strickland, B. R. The prediction of social action from a dimension of internal–external control. *Journal of Social Psychology*, 1965, *66*, 353–358.

Strickland, B. R. Delay of gratification as a function of the race of the experimenter. *Journal of Personality and Social Psychology*, 1972, *22*, 108–112.

Strickland, B. R. Internal–external control of reinforcement. In T. Blass (Ed.), *Personality variables in social behavior.* Hillsdale, NJ: Erlbaum, 1977.

Strickland, B. R., & Haley, W. E. Sex differences on the Rotter I–E scale. *Journal of Personality and Social Psychology*, 1980, *39*, 930–939.

Strodbeck, F. L. Family interaction values and achievement. In D. C. McClelland (Ed.), *Talent and society.* New York: Van Nostrand, 1958.

Strube, M. J. Meta-analysis and cross-cultural comparison. *Journal of Cross-Cultural Psychology*, 1981, *12*, 3–20.

Taylor, D. M., & Jaggi, V. Ethnocentrism and causal attributions in a south Indian context. *Journal of Cross-Cultural Psychology*, 1974, *5*, 162–171.

Thomas, L. E. The I–E scale, ideological bias, and political participation. *Journal of Personality*, 1970, *38*, 273–286.

Tobacyk, J. Factor structure of Rotter's scale in female Polish university students. *Journal of Social Psychology*, 1978, *106*, 3–10.

Tolor, A., & Reznikoff, M. Relations between insight, repression-sensitizations, internal–external control, and death anxiety. *Journal of Abnormal Psychology*, 1967, *72*, 426–430.

Trigg, L. J., Perlman, D., Perry, R. P., & Janisse, M. P. Antipollution behavior: A function of perceived outcomes and locus of control. *Environment & Behavior*, 1976, *8*, 307–313.

Trimble, J. E., & Richardson, S. Locus of control measures among American Indians: Cluster structure-analytic characteristics. *Journal of Cross-Cultural Psychology*, 1982, *13*, 228–238.

Tucker, L. A method for synthesis of factor analysis studies (Personnel Research Selection Report. No. 988, Contract DA–49–083, Department of the Army). Princeton, NJ: Educational Testing Service, 1951.

Tyler, J. D., & Holsinger, D. N. Locus of control differences between rural American Indian and White children. *Journal of Social Psychology*, 1975, *95*, 149–155.

Valecha, G. K. Construct validation of internal–external locus of reinforcement related to work-related variables. *Proceedings of the American Psychological Association*, 1972, *7*, 455.

Viney, L. L. Multidimensionality of perceived control: Two replications. *Journal of Consulting and Clinical Psychology*, 1974, *42*, 463–464.

Wallston, K. A., & Wallston, B. S. *Health-related locus of control scales.* Paper presented at the Annual Meeting of the American Psychological Association, Toronto, September 1978.

Warehime, R. G., & Woodson, S. Locus of control and immediate affect states. *Journal of Clinical Psychology*, 1971, *27*, 443–444.

Watkins, D. Sex role perception of Filipino adolescents. Unpublished paper, 1981.

Watson, D. Relationship between locus of control and anxiety. *Journal of Personality and Social Psychology*, 1967, *6*, 91–92.

Weiner, B., Heckhausen, H., Meyer, W. U., & Cook, R. E. Causal ascription and achievement motivation: A conceptual analysis of effort and reanalysis of locus of control. *Journal of Personality and Social Psychology*, 1972, *21*, 239–238.

Werner, E. E. *Cross-cultural child development*. Monterey, CA: Brooks/Cole, 1979.

Wolfgang, A. A cross-cultural comparison of locus of control, optimism toward the future and time horizon among Italian. Italo-Canadian and new Canadian Youth. *Proceedings of the 81st Annual Convention of the American Psychological Association*, 1973, *8*, 299–300.

Wolfgang, A., & Craig, S. C. *Beliefs of personal control, time perspective, and optimism of Mexican and Canadian students*. Paper presented at the Annual Meeting of the 13th Inter-American Congress of Psychology, Panama City, December 1971.

Wolfgang, A., & Weiss, D. A. A locus of control and social distance comparison of Canadian and West Indian born students. *International Journal of Intercultural Relations*, 1980, *4*, 295–305.

Wolk, S., & DuCette, J. The moderating effect of locus of control in relation to achievement-motivation variables. *Journal of Personality*, 1973, *41*, 59–70.

Worrell, L., & Tumilty, T. N. The measurement of locus of control among alcoholics. In H. M. Lefcourt (Ed.), *Research with the locus of control construct: Assessment methods*. (Vol. 1) New York, Academic Press, 1981.

Zimmerman, M. L., Goldston, J. T., & Gadzella, B. M. Prediction of academic performance for college students by sex and race. *Psychological Reports*, 1977, *41*, 1183–1186.

Zuckerman, M., & Gerbasi, K. C. Dimensions of the I–E scale and their relationship to other personality measures. *Educational and Psychological Measurement*, 1977, *37*, 159–175.

Zytkoskee, A., Strickland, B. R., & Watson, J. Delay of gratification and internal versus external control among adolescents of low socioeconomic status. *Developmental Psychology*, 1971, *4*, 93–98.

II

LIMITATIONS
IN LOCUS
OF CONTROL
RESEARCH

5

Paul T. P. Wong
Catherine F. Sproule

AN ATTRIBUTION ANALYSIS
OF THE LOCUS OF CONTROL
CONSTRUCT AND THE TRENT
ATTRIBUTION PROFILE*

The construct of locus of control is perhaps one of the most influential concepts in contemporary psychology. According to the February 1, 1982 issue of *Current Contents*, Rotter's 1966 monograph was cited over 2735 times. Research employing this construct continues to proliferate.

The popularity of locus of control research has also created some problems. One of the problems is that this construct has been interpreted differently by different investigators (Strickland, 1978) and has been subject to various misconceptions (Rotter, 1975). In this chapter we attempt to achieve three objectives. First, we examine the locus of control construct in light of current attribution research and attempt to clarify some of the misconceptions. Second, we provide the rationale and evidence for a two-dimensional hypothesis in comparison with the traditional bipolar, unidimensional conception of locus of control. Finally, we present additional validity data on the Trent Attribution Profile (TAP).

*The research reported here and the preparation of this chapter were supported by a grant from the Social Sciences and Humanities Research Council of Canada to the senior author. We also acknowledge the assistance of Jean Peel, Edward Peacock, Derek Watters, and Anna May Young in collecting and/or analyzing most of the data reported here. Portions of the data on the different meanings of internal and external control were collected by C. Gunthardt, B. O'Keefe, and B. Stripp as a class project.

An Attribution Analysis of Locus of Control

Collins (1974) noted that the orientation underlying locus of control research has much in common with the attribution approach. Lefcourt (1976, p. 28) also stated "It is not the simple registering of success and failure that is pertinent to the generalized expectancy of internal versus external control, but rather it is the interpretation of the causes of these experiences." Even lesser authorities can readily recognize that the construct of locus of control is somehow related to causal attributions. What we attempt to do here is examine closely the nature of this relation and clarify some of the conceptual difficulties.

Locus of Control versus Locus of Causality

One of the most common misconceptions is to equate locus of control with locus of causality. Ickes and Layden (1978, p. 128) argued that "there are a number of good reasons to believe that the variable of internal/external locus of causality . . . is not synonymous with the variable of internal/external locus of control. The theoretical and operational definitions of the two concepts differ in some important respects." Weiner (1979) proposed that locus of causality and of control should be treated as two separate causal dimensions, which have been defined by Wong and Weiner (1981, p. 655) as follows: "The *locus* dimension is concerned with the source of causality; that is, either the cause resides in you, in some other people, or in the situation. The *control* dimension is concerned with the extent of one's control or mastery over various causal factors."

However, the conceptual differences between these two dimensions often are not recognized. For example, Collins (1974) thought that locus of control research is concerned with the assignment of causality to the environment (external attribution) or to the action (internal attribution). Rotter seemed to equate internal causality with internal control, as is evident from his definition of locus of control:

When a reinforcement is perceived by the subject as following some action of his own but not being entirely contingent upon his action, then, in our culture, it is typically perceived as a result of luck, chance, fate, or under the control of powerful others, or as unpredictable because of the great complexity of the forces surrounding him. When the event is interpreted in this way by an individual, we have labeled this a belief in external control. If the person perceives that the event is contingent upon his own behavior or his own relatively permanent characteristics, we have termed this a belief in internal control [Rotter, 1966, p. 1].

Perhaps the best way to justify the distinction between the locus of causality and control dimensions is to demonstrate that these two dimensions may be orthogonal under certain conditions. In numerous cases the perception of internal causality is accompanied by a sense of uncontrollability or external control. When a negative outcome is attributed to stable personal characteristics, such as brain damage, chemical or physical handicap, or insufficient aptitude, one's sense of personal control is decreased rather than increased. Even internal and unstable causes, such as mood changes, fatigue, intrusion of unwanted thoughts, unsuppressible desires and impulses, and various kinds of obsessions, may also reduce one's sense of control.

Behavioral contingency figures prominently in Rotter's definition, which suggests that the perception of internal control is based on a perfect contingency between behavior and outcome. But is contingency both the necessary and sufficient condition for the perception of personal control? Does a slave experience control and freedom when his or her subsistence is contingent entirely on completion of an externally determined quota of hard labor? Similarly, does one feel in control in an authoritarian society when survival is contingent entirely on carrying out externally imposed rules? Clearly, the perception of internal control depends on a lot more than mere simple behavior–outcome contingency.

Following the same line of reasoning, external causality does not necessarily imply the absence of internal control. As proposed by Heider (1958) and recognized by jurisprudence, an individual may be held responsible for externally caused consequences when these outcomes are unintended, but foreseeable or avoidable. Thus, although an automobile accident was caused by a mishap, the driver is still held acountable if it is judged that the accident could have been prevented by better tire maintenance by the driver.

It should now become clear that an internally caused outcome may be under external control, and an externally caused outcome may be under internal control. Because locus of causality and locus of control are often orthogonal, they must be treated as separate dimensions. Locus of causality refers to the *assignment of causality* to various loci, such as persons, stimuli, or circumstances. Locus of control, on the other hand, is concerned with the *assignment of responsibility*. This distinction is important because the criteria for causal attribution and responsibility attribution are quite different. We have already shown that behavior–outcome contingency definitely promotes internal attribution but does not necessarily promote belief in internal control, which is also dependent on other considerations, such as freedom of choice, valence of the outcome, and the like. Further, Kelley's (1967, 1971) consistency criterion for causal attribution may not be applicable to responsibility attribution. When an effect is consistent across many individuals, we tend to attribute it to external sources such as situation or stimulus. However, this consistency criterion does not indicate whether the effect is controllable by the individual. An individual's reaction to a given stimulus may be consistent across a variety of situations, but this consistency need not imply responsibility on the part of the individual unless it is also assumed that the individual is able to avoid or seek this stimulus. Responsibility attribution seems to be a more complex judgmental process than causal attribution. The perception of control requires additional information concerning intention, choice, foreseeability, and predisposition; it also involves the allocation of credit and blame.

We propose a new definition of locus of control to make it more distinguishable from locus of causality. Locus of control is concerned with the assignment of responsibility, regardless of behavioral instrumentality. One perceives internal control when one assumes full responsibility for what has happened, even though it was externally caused. One perceives external control if the responsibility for an outcome rests entirely elsewhere, regardless of whether it is the direct consequence of one's own behavior. One perceives dual control when the responsibility for an outcome is shared by the individual as well as external sources. The full significance of this new definition of locus of control will become clearer as this chapter unfolds.

The Perception of Control

Another source of confusion surrounding the locus of control construct is the different ways in which the concept of control has been used. Mastery, responsibility, controllability, coping, efficacy, effectance, contingency, and competence are many of the terms that have been used to convey the idea of control. In this section we attempt to clarify what is meant by *control*.

CONTROLLABILITY OF CAUSE
VERSUS CONTROLLABILITY OF OUTCOME

According to Weiner (1979), control is treated as a causal dimension along with others, such as locus of causality and stability. Once a person has attributed an outcome to a certain cause, he or she will proceed to identify the dimensional properties of the cause: Is it internal? Is it controllable? Thus, in terms of Weiner's scheme, the control dimension has to do with perceived controllability–uncontrollability of cause rather than outcome.

It seems to be trivial to distinguish between cause and outcome with respect to controllability. However, this distinction becomes important when we realize that the controllability of a cause is not necessarily related positively to perceived controllability of an outcome. For example, ability, though typically considered an uncontrollable dispositional causal factor, actually enhances one's sense of control over an outcome. Carelessness, on the other hand, is generally considered a controllable cause, but it may decrease the likelihood of gaining control over one's environment. Generally, positively valued uncontrollable causes such as intelligence, ability, good looks, and charming personality increase one's sense of control over outcomes, whereas negatively valued uncontrollable causes such as incompetence and brain damage decrease one's sense of control. With respect to controllable causes, a similar generalization holds. Negatively valued controllable causes such as laziness or carelessness typically reduce the degree of personal control. Positively valued controllable causes such as effort, concentration, and strategy increase one's perceived control over outcomes.

In sum, whether a causal ascription is perceived as controllable or not has no direct bearing on perceived controllability of the outcome. Failure to distinguish between cause and outcome regarding perceived controllability may lead to the erroneous conclusion that an outcome is perceived as uncontrollable simply because the causal factor is uncontrollable. The present discussion concerns control as it relates to the perceived controllability of the outcome, not the controllability of the cause of the outcome.

THE PERSPECTIVE OF CONTROL

Within the framework of determinism, every event is controllable by someone or some force. Therefore it is not meaningful to talk about controllability (uncontrollability) of an outcome without specifying the perspective. For example, the difficulty level of an examination is uncontrollable from the student's perspective but controllable from the instructor's perspective.

To facilitate our discussion of locus of control, it is helpful to identify two important perspectives. First, we have the perspective of the *actor*—one who experiences as well as interprets an outcome. In this case, internal control means that the actor believes he or she has control over the event; external control means that he or she has no control. Second, we have the perspective of the *observer*—one who observes a target person involved in some kind of outcome. The observer interprets what has happened to the target person. The observer may pass judgments as to who is responsible for the outcome as an uninvolved observer. Internal control means that the observer *thinks* the target person is responsible for the outcome; external control means the observer attributes the responsibility to some other sources. Alternatively, the observer may choose to be more actively involved in the experience of the target person. The observer may put himself or herself into the shoes of the target person and try to understand how that person might have viewed the situation. It remains an empirical question whether the observer's tendency to project his or her locus of control beliefs onto the target person is in any way affected by the degree of involvement or empathy with the target person.

Whether from the eyes of an actor or an observer, responsibility attributions are always directed to the person who experiences the outcome under consideration. The experiencing person must be the focal point for attributional analysis. The locus of control construct would be meaningless without this focal point.

CONTROL AND COPING

Coping is a generic term that encompasses a wide range of responses, both behavioral and cognitive, that assist living organisms to adapt to stressful situations (Coelho, Hamburg, & Adams, 1974; Lazarus, Averill, & Opton, 1974; Mechanic, 1970).

There are different modes of coping. Lazarus (1966) differentiates between *problem-focused coping* and *emotional-focused coping.* The former consists of instrumental attempts to change the problematic situation; it may also be regarded to as behavioral control (Miller, 1979). The latter consists of ways of coping that make people feel better without actually changing the situation. It includes various intrapsychic defense mechanisms, such as rationalization and denial. These two models of coping are referred to as *internal* and *palliative control,* respectively.

Recently, Rothbaum, Weisz, and Snyder (1982) introduced the concept of secondary control. According to these authors, *primary control* involves the direct behavioral control to change the world to fit one's own needs, whereas *secondary control* refers to the process of changing oneself to fit into a world that cannot be changed. Passivity, withdrawal, and submission are given as examples of secondary control. Submission to powerful others may be considered as a case of vicarious control in which a powerless, helpless individual gains a sense of control by identifying himself or herself with the powerful controller.

Secondary control may involve the use of reality-based cognitive strategies, such as developing a more realistic and accommodating attitude. The use of such cognitive strategies has been referred to as *cognitive control* (Averill, 1973; Thompson, 1981).

Secondary control is of particular interest because it contains elements of both problem-focused and emotional-focused coping strategies. When a problem stems from one's own attitude, then this problem can be solved simply by changing one's attitude. For example, interpersonal conflict can often be resolved by changing one's attitude and behavior. When a person develops new interests, to make life more meaningful and satisfying, old problems may still exist, but no longer have the same negative impact. In this case, secondary control serves a palliative rather than instrumental function.

From our analyses, there are four broad categories of coping: internal control, external control, secondary control, and palliative control. Both internal and external control are problem-focused or instrumental modes of coping, but they differ in the kinds of coping resources employed. *Internal control* refers to dependence on internal resources, whereas *external control* refers to dependence on external resources. This distinction has important theoretical and practical implications. When a problem is appraised as uncontrollable by self, but controllable by some powerful others, then the appropriate coping strategy is external control. For those who are severely handicapped or chronically ill, external control will be more important than internal control in coping with various problems. In a recent study with an elderly sample, Wong and Reker (1982) found that Chinese elderly depended on external control more than their Caucasian counterparts, and that preference for external or internal control also depended on the nature of the problem encountered.

Secondary control and palliative control can be conceptualized as examples of self-control. *Palliative control* aims at controlling one's emotions through various defense mechanisms and cognitive means. *Secondary control* aims at changing one's attitudes and behaviors and indirectly changing the problem. The distinction between palliative and secondary control is not always clear. For example, learning to look at the brighter side of things not only makes one feel better, but also changes one's outlook and removes problems that stem from taking a negative view of everything. Similarly, trying to see the meaning and potential benefits of suffering eases the pain, but may also change one's basic attitude toward adversities in life. Perhaps no amount of debate could determine whether the foregoing illustrations are examples of palliative control or of secondary control, and the question of classification should be settled empirically.

There are, of course, ways of coping that are more clearly identifiable as examples of secondary control. These include *substitution, conversion,* and *personal growth.* In the case of *substitution,* one changes one's goals and priorities, so that the problem of failing to achieve certain goals is no longer stressful. According to Wong's stage model of coping with frustrative stress (Wong, in press), switching to alternative goals is treated as one of the preprogrammed coping mechanisms. *Conversion* involves a drastic change in one's belief systems, values, and lifestyle. Conversion, in some cases, can have such a profound influence on an individual that his or her relationships with others and with the world are altered in a fundamental way. These changes are likely to solve some old problems, but at the same time create new ones. *Personal growth* refers to attempts to broaden one's horizon, cultivate new interests, develop one's potentials, and form a more coherent and meaningful view toward life. Personal growth can be an effective way of coping, because it enables one to outgrow certain problems that arise from one's immaturity or personal weaknesses.

So far, we have equated different kinds of control with very different modes of coping. In other words, attempts to control the environment as well as oneself are coping processes. In this sense, control does not indicate whether these attempts are effective or successful. However, there is another use of control, which is perceived personal (internal) control or simply perceived control. With respect to both specific situations and life in general, one has a certain amount of perceived control. This perception depends on the process as well as the outcome of coping. Presumably one perceives greater control when one uses internal rather than external coping strategies and that success gives one a greater sense of personal control than of failure.

It is important that one differentiates between perceived control and control as a coping process. Secondary control is a coping process but it does not necessarily give one a sense of personal control. For example, when a person is stripped of all rights, freedoms, and dignities, and is forced to submit to every whim of a ruthless captor, the captive may attempt to cope with this stressful situation by means of submission, passivity, or even identification, but it is highly questionable whether the captive would relish his or her sense of control.

Rothbaum *et al.* (1982) seem to suggest that the evidence of personal (internal) control is the persistent way a particular coping strategy is used, be it submission or passivity. Following this logic, we must conclude that alcoholics are actually in control of their lives because they consistently resort to the bottle as an escape from stressful situations. Similarly, we must also conclude that chronic reactive depressives are in control because they persist in coping with life's problems by resignation, passivity, and withdrawal.

From our point of view, perceived control is primarily a phenomenological experience; therefore, it can only be ascertained by asking the individual. There is no evidence whatsoever that the frequency of employing a particular way of coping affects the perception of control. Systematic research is needed to determine how this perception is affected by different modes of coping, the frequency of employing different strategies, and the perceived efficacy of each coping strategy.

Finally, control also means objectively defined contingency between behavior and outcome. Perceived control is related to, but not completely determined by, objective contingencies. One may entertain an illusion of control even in uncontrollable situations (Lefcourt, 1973).

In sum, control has three distinct meanings: (1) coping, (2) subjective perceptions, and (3) objective contingency. Confusion inevitably occurs when these distinctions are not maintained. Only the first two meanings are relevant to the present treatise. Control is treated as a coping process, when the discusion is about *preferred* internal or external control, because it deals with the choice of coping strategies. Control is used as a subjective perception when we simply talk about internal or external control. In this case, *internal control* means perceived self-efficacy or personal responsibility, whereas *external control* means perceived external influences in bringing about certain outcomes.

What Does Rotter's I–E Scale Measure?

Research employing Rotter's I–E Scale has produced results that are consistent with the earlier definition of control. For example, it has been found that internals are more likely to take responsibility for their actions than are externals (Davis & Davis, 1972; Phares, Wilson, & Klyver, 1971). Further, internals not only perceive themselves as more capable of controlling reinforcements, but they also prefer personal control to a greater extent than do externals. In short, those who are classified as internals on Rotter's I–E Scale not only perceive but also desire more personal control than externals.

The interpretation of externals is less clear-cut. Rotter (1966, 1975) suggested two reasons for endorsing the external alternatives on the I–E scale. One reason is ego-defensiveness. By attributing negative outcomes to external forces beyond one's control, one is free from blame or responsibility. Defensive externals, according to Rotter (1975), might not differ from internals in terms of achievement motivation or striving for mastery. The reason for the weak correlations between the I–E scale and academic achievement in college could be due to the fact that many of the externals are only defensively external.

Another reason for endorsing external control beliefs is that the individual consistently holds the belief that he or she has little or no control over what is going on, regardless of success or failure. This type of individual, referred to as a congruent or passive external, usually lacks achievement motive and exhibits performance deficits. Several investigators have attempted to substantiate the distinction between defensive and congruent externality (e.g., Prociuk & Breen, 1975).

Given the established phenomenon of externality bias for negative outcomes (Zuckerman, 1979), there is little question that some individuals may endorse external control belief statements for that reason. It is also likely that some individuals see themselves as powerless pawns in a hostile and unresponsive world, and they tend to exaggerate the extent of external control. However, there is a third reason for favoring some of the external alternatives: realism.

REALISM VERSUS IDEALISM—A REINTERPRETATION
OF ROTTER'S I–E SCALE

Over the years we have administered Rotter's I–E Scale to our class on social cognition. Each year we have found highly motivated and competent students who would be classified as externals according to North American norms (Lefcourt, 1976). When we interviewed them, the reason cited most frequently for choosing several external alternatives was realism, reflected in comments like "That's reality"; "That is the way life is!"; "There will always be war, no matter how hard you try to promote peace"; "There will always be corruption or bad government, because the politicians usually promise one thing to get elected and then do something quite different once in office"; and "There will always be someone who does not like you for some strange reason." Who can argue against the truth of these statements? The students were serious in asserting the reality basis for their external choices. They supported their arguments with both personal experiences and historical facts and pointed out the naiveté of believing people can stamp out war and corruption by taking an interest in politics.

We cannot classify these students as either defensive externals or passive externals; they are realistic externals.

Recently we conducted a study to determine the reasons for favoring external (or internal) alternatives in Rotter's I–E Scale. We gave subjects the standard instructions. In addition, we stated that "an alternative may be judged more true, because it is more consistent with your experiences or *reality* as you have observed. An alternative may also be judged more true, because it is more consistent with your *ideals*, values, and wishes." Subjects were asked to indicate on a 7-point scale the extent to which their choice in each pair of statements was influenced by reality considerations and by their own ideals.

The results are generally in agreement with the hypothesis that external alternatives are chosen primarily because of reality considerations, whereas internal alternatives are chosen primarily because of ideals. Some of the findings are summarized in Table 5.1. It is quite clear that choices for some of the internal alternatives were motivated by students' ideals more than reality; the reverse was true for external choices.

These findings have important implications for both the interpretation of Rotter's I–E Scale and for the conceptualization of the locus of control construct. Our findings suggest that the choice of internal (external) alternatives is influenced by idealism versus realism considerations. Heider (1958, pp. 120–121) also pointed out that "attributions and cognitions are influenced by the more subjective forces of needs and wishes as well or by the more objective evidence presented in the raw material." Differences in locus of control beliefs, as measured by Rotter's I–E Scale, may reflect different amounts of influence by one's own desires for control. Viewed this way, Rotter's I–E Scale measures not merely one's interpretation of experiences but also one's ideals, wishes, and desires. In some individuals ideals may have a dominant influence to the point of systematically distorting all their interpretations of reality.

The foregoing discussion does not mean that the I–E scale measures idealism–realism, but it does mean that the interpretation of Rotter's internality (externality) score must be tempered by idealism–realism considerations. More specifically, we propose that those who have a very high internal score (perhaps the top quartile) may be characterized as individuals who have such a strong desire for control that they even entertain the illusion of control in situations where individuals have little or no control. They are the *idealistic–optimistic controllers* who are oversold on their own capability to control and underestimate the extent of external constraints. They tend to believe

TABLE 5.1
Mean Ratings on Reality and Ideal Scales for Internal and External Alternatives[a]

Question	Internal		External	
	Ideals	Reality	Ideals	Reality
Number 2	Wars are due to people's lack of interest in politics ($N = 9$)		There will always be war. ($N = 29$)	
$\overline{X}$	3.33	3.33	2.79	5.90
SD	2.18	2.06	2.09	1.37
	$t = 0.000$		$t = -5.700$**	
Number 6	People don't like you because you don't know how to get along. ($N = 14$)		There will always be people who don't like you. ($N = 24$)	
$\overline{X}$	4.79	5.00	3.04	5.79
SD	1.93	1.41	1.85	1.10
	$t = -0.586$		$t = -5.791$**	
Number 10	Average citizen can influence government ($N = 19$)		Average citizen can't influence those in power. ($N = 19$)	
$\overline{X}$	5.95	3.95	2.16	5.74
SD	1.31	1.43	1.30	1.41
	$t = 4.084$**		$t = -7.281$**	
Number 14	People can control world affairs. ($N = 15$)		World affairs are beyond our control. ($N = 23$)	
$\overline{X}$	5.47	3.47	3.17	5.48
SD	1.55	1.60	1.90	1.59
	$t = 2.81$*		$t = -4.277$**	
Number 18	We can wipe out political corruption. ($N = 10$)		Difficult to control what politicians do in office. ($N = 28$)	
$\overline{X}$	6.00	3.90	3.07	5.39
SD	1.89	1.20	1.65	1.47
	$t = 3.042$*		$t = -4.952$**	

[a] Questions presented here are taken from Rotter's I–E Scale but are shortened for this table. Number of subjects choosing each alternative is shown in parentheses.
* $p < .01$.
** $p < .001$.

that the world is easy, just, politically responsive, and subject to their influence.

At the other extreme, those who have a very low internal score (probably the last quartile) see themselves as helpless pawns even in situations where they actually have considerable control. In other words, their belief in external control is excessive and goes far beyond what is called for by realistic considerations. They are the *unrealistic, pessimistic controllees* who have relinquished all their control and become passive, unmotivated, and often depressed. The established negative effects of externality are most likely associated with unrealistic controllees.

Of special interest to us are those whose internal (external) score is in the middle range. They are moderately high in internality (externality). They may be referred to as realistic internals (externals) because they are realistic about the limitations of personal control and refuse to see the world through rose-colored glasses. They perceive the world as full of problems that are largely beyond their control—inflation, high interest rates, violence in the streets, war in different parts of the globe, unresponsive bureaucracy and corruption in high places etc., but these perceptions do not render them helpless and hopeless; on the contrary, they strive to achieve realistic goals in the context of external constraints. In fact, they could be just as motivated to achieve as are idealistic internals.

In light of the present distinction between realism and idealism, externality should no longer be viewed merely as reflecting ego-defensiveness or passivity. Realistic externality is not necessarily incompatible with belief in personal efficacy. A realistic person necessarily perceives a fair amount of external control in many of life's situations. Lange and Tiggemann (1981) suggested that "it may be that a substantial number of people believe in the efficacy of personal effort in individual achievement situations, but not in reference to control over political or world affairs" (p. 405). O'Brien and Kabanoff (1981, p. 197) also argued that the perception of having no control over political events, or grades obtained, may be "accurate perceptions of the environment and may not be necessarily associated with a sense of personal inadequacy in obtaining valued rewards in other settings."

There has been an increase in external control belief in both the U.S. (Rotter, 1975) and the Australian population (Gorman, Jones, & Holman, 1980; Lange & Tiggemann, 1980). One of the reasons for the shift, as suggested by Lange and Tiggemann (1980), is that people have gradually moved to a "more realistic viewpoint."

In this section we argued that the locus of control construct has to do with responsibility attribution, and that Rotter's I–E Scale measures both perceived control and desired control. We have also shown that the realism versus idealism issue must be taken into account in interpreting the I–E scale.

A Dual-Dimensional View of Locus of Control

The construct of internal versus external locus of control is typically treated as a bipolar dimension. According to this unidimensional view, internal and external control are pitched against each other such that an increase in external control *necessarily* means a decrease in internal control. We are so accustomed to this conception that we rarely pause to question its validity or generality. In this section we examine this unidimensional view critically and propose a dual-dimensional view of locus of control.

The issue addressed here is the dimensionality of the locus of control construct, not the dimensionality of Rotter's I–E Scale. However, we first attempt to show that there are two separate issues. Several studies (e.g., Collins, 1974; Gurin, Gurin, Lao, & Beattie, 1969; Mirels, 1970; Sanger & Alker, 1972; Zuckerman & Gerbasi, 1977) have shown that Rotter's I–E Scale was not unidimensional as claimed by Rotter (1966). For example, Collins (1974) found that the I–E scale actually contains four subscales: belief in an easy–difficult world, belief in a predictable world, belief in a just world, and belief in a politically responsive world. This finding was replicated by Zuckerman and Gerbasi (1977). Gurin et al. (1969) and Sanger and Alker (1972) identified two factors: personal control and control ideology. Mirels (1970) also identified two factors: general control and political control. Rotter (1975, p. 63) argued that "factor analyses do not reveal 'the true structure of the construct'; they only reveal the kinds of similarities perceived by a particular group of subjects for a particular selection of items." We agree with Rotter's argument, especially in view of the fact that the subscales are correlated with the total score, and the factors identified so far are all conceptually and functionally related to perceived and desired control over different domains. Thus, there is no reason to revise our thinking that the locus of control construct has to do with perceived and desired efficacy or responsibility and that the I–E scale has been successful in measuring this construct.

The issue we are concerned with here is whether the locus of control construct is best conceptualized as a bipolar dimension or a dual-dimensional space. According to the first conception, internal and external control are opposite poles on a single dimension, such that an increase in external control necessarily means a decrease in internal control. According to the second conception, internal and external control are two separate dimensions, and the locus of control can be located anywhere in this two-dimensional space. Thus, it is possible to be high in both internal and external control. The distinction between these two conceptions seems small, but it has profound theoretical and practical implications. In the next section we contrast these two views of locus of control and present some evidence in support of the dual-dimensional view.

A Unidimensional View versus
a Dual-Dimensional View of Control

A unidimensional view of control is a conflict model, because internal and external control are treated as competing or opposing tendencies. It never allows the possibility of the simultaneous presence of a high degree of internal control and a high degree of external control.

This conflict model reflects Western culture, which has long witnessed the see-saw battle between forces of determinism and free will. Aristotelian causal analyses, Calvin's determinism, and Skinner's utopia of behavioral control are parts of a long philosophical tradition that human beings are shaped by external forces they neither fully understand nor control.

On the other hand, there also has been no shortage of advocates for personal autonomy and free will. The current emphasis on personal control may be viewed as a revolt against deterministic behaviorism. We seem constantly to be caught between the cross-currents of external and internal control, swinging like a pendulum between these two opposing poles.

Western psychologists are so steeped in Western culture that even their conceptual analysis of control is imbued by the conflict model. The tendency is to characterize people as internals or externals (Lefcourt, 1976; Rotter, 1966), origins or pawns (deCharms, 1968). Instrumental behavior is seen either as behavior control exercised by external agents (Skinner, 1971) or mastery exercised by the individual (Seligman, 1975).

Those who embrace this unidimensional view tend to see themselves as either the controllers or the controllees. They either gloat in the position of control or groan in a subordinate position. To safeguard their sense of personal control, they consider the presence of any external control as a threat to their personal autonomy, resulting in psychological reactance (Brehm, 1966). The battle for control seems to dominate many of their relationships—management–worker, husband–wife, parents–children, and so on. They come from this battle either as winners or as losers.

The winners see themselves as controllers. They strive aggressively to expand their spheres of personal control. Their appetite for domination grows with each conquest. They have an inflated view of their efficacy and indulge in the illusion of control. They also tend to delude themselves by believing that the world is easy, predictable, just, and politically responsive. They find it intolerable to take orders from others and would experience great stress if they were reduced to a state of dependence, to be avoided at all costs. They are highly motivated to achieve, driven by the fear of dependence as well as the desire for control. They tend to be among the successful achievers of our society.

Losers in the battle for control tend to have a deflated view of themselves. They see themselves as helpless and powerless pawns. Some of them may even withdraw into their shells and feel depressed. They tend to relinquish all attempts to control because of their very bleak view that everything is beyond their control. They suffer from the illusion of incompetence and often grossly overestimate the extent of external control. Their desire for dependence is much stronger than their desire for autonomy. Passivity and withdrawal become their typical ways of coping.

Needless to say, not everyone who holds a unidimensional view can be classified as either a controller or a controllee. Many fall between these two extremes; however, because of their conflicting views, they are in the process of either struggling to reach the position of controller or sliding into the position of controllee. The dynamic at work is either fighting against external control or surrendering to it.

It should also be pointed out that individuals who hold a unidimensional view do not do so consistently in all situations. They recognize that some situations, such as growing crops, demand cooperation between internal control and external control. However, their typical view of the world is that internal control and external control are constantly at war with each other. They tend to vacillate between the illusion of control and the illusion of incompetence. Their drive to control and their despair at being a controllee often overshadow other motives and distort their perceptions of reality.

It is quite obvious that the world is neither a bowl of cherries nor a burning inferno; that an individual is neither an almighty controller nor a powerless controllee. Nevertheless, the unidimensional conflict view of control, and its tendency toward polarization, continues to dominate psychological thinking. Psychologists classify people according to the internal–external distinction, and most research findings are concerned with the difference between these two groups. So pervasive is this unidimensional view that its limitations are rarely noted and its adaptiveness is seldom questioned. We exalt the controller's belief in internal control and lament the controllee's external view, not realizing that both are products of the same unrealistic, unidimensional view of the world.

The dual-dimensional view detailed here represents a major departure from the traditional locus of control research. We believe that it is a more realistic conception of control, makes us aware of new locus of control orientations, and opens up new horizons for research.

To put it simply, locus of control is conceptualized as two-dimensional space, with internal and external control dimensions as the two coordinates. The locus of control for an event can be located anywhere in this two-dimensional space. One obvious advantage of this new conception is that it allows us to assess more realistically the degree of responsibility shared by the person and external sources. For example, the weather condition is an important external determinant of the success or failure of crops, but farmers also play an important role. Thus both internal and external control should be high. However, according to the unidimensional view, which considers internal and external control as inversely related, to believe in a high degree of internal control necessarily means to minimize the importance of external control, and vice versa.

Different from the conflict model of control, the accent of this dual-dimensional view is *shared responsibility,* or *dual control.* It does not look at control in terms of internal *versus* external control, but in terms of internal *and* external control. Individuals who believe in shared control are neither internals nor externals but *bilocals,* because they perceive and desire control from both the internal and external loci. They do not see themselves as either controllers or controllees, but as *co-operators* who interact with external constraints to achieve realistic goals. They are too realistic to try to control all aspects of their environment and yet too independent to relinquish all controls. Realistic bilocals do not attempt to play God or pretend to be superheroes. Yet at the same time, they do not "roll over and play dead." They attempt to *alter what can be changed but accept what cannot be changed.*

How do bilocals look at control? First, they are not threatened by external control. They do not fight against it, as do controllers, nor do they surrender to it, as would the controllees. Instead, they accept it as a fact of life and assume the responsibility of working productively within its constraints. External control is no longer viewed as something negative or degrading. Both the advantages and disadvantages of external control are recognized.

Second, personal autonomy is never defined in the dichotomous way: It is not a matter of being in complete control or in complete bondage. One cannot always will or do as one pleases, nor can one exist as a puppet. The idea of being the captain of one's own fate is dismissed as a controller's dream. The notion that people are helpless pawns in a hostile universe is also dismissed as a controllee's self-defeating excuse. Personal autonomy is always defined in the context of external constraints. One does not attempt to banish external control completely from one's life in order to maintain a sense of personal autonomy. Bilocals do not live to conquer and dominate; they attempt to live in harmony rather than in conflict with the ecosystem of which they are parts. Self and the external universe are seen in a kind of symbiotic relationship, and personal autonomy is developed not according to one's power to control but according to one's unique role, however limited, in achieving certain goals in the interconnected system. Self is seen as a unique part of a much larger world, interacting with various parts in different ways. One's relationship with the external world is not to be characterized simply in terms of domination–subordination. Other types of relationships, such as cooperation, dependence, trust, and sharing become as important as control. One's exercise of autonomy is always balanced by one's acceptance of certain forms of external control.

How to Identify Bilocals

We have just sketched a rather general picture of bilocals. Are there such individuals? Clearly, there must be those who have learned their limitations, perhaps through painful experience or the irreversible process of aging, but who at the same time recognize the responsibility of personal autonomy. Surely there must be those who are wise enough not to try to control everything and yet optimistic enough not to give up trying altogether. There must be the adaptive realists, who are neither overly ambitious nor hopelessly passive. They are likely to be found among the ordinary folks who do not need to receive psychiatric help because of burnout syndrome or depression. But how do we identify them?

Since the dual-dimensional view is new, no instruments have been developed to identify those who believe in shared control. Here are some clues that may give them away.

Given that bilocals are known for their realism, it is only logical that they will not score as high on Rotter's I–E Scale as do idealistic controllers, because of their endorsement of those external alternatives that are generally accepted as true reflections of reality. Furthermore, they will not be as low as the pessimistic controllees, because they do perceive self-efficacy in situations that are typically within the realm of individual control. In short, they are most likely to score in the moderate range of internality (externality) on the I–E scale. Unfortunately, these individuals are seldom singled out for investigation. They are typically divided, and labeled either internals or externals, on the basis of a median split of the I–E scores.

Bilocals also betray themselves by their attribution schema. It is predicted that both controllers and controllees tend to evoke simple causal schema to explain outcome. Controllers generally invoke a single sufficient internal causal schema for success, whereas controllees explain events usually in terms of a single sufficient external causal schema. Neither schema is a realistic portrayal of reality in most situations. Bilocals are more likely to evoke a multiple causal schema. This more complex schema permits bilocals to develop a variety of coping strategies. They are more flexible in coping than either controllers or controllees.

In terms of responsibility attributions, bilocals also differ from controllers and controllees. To boost their sense of efficacy, controllers tend to take more credit for success than others would grant them and blame others for unsolvable problems. Controllees, on the other hand, because of their exaggerated view of incompetence, tend to externalize success and blame their own inadequacy for failure. In contrast, bilocal cooperators are more likely to share credit—and blame—regardless of the outcome.

Another way to differentiate individuals who believe in shared control from those that hold a unidimensional conflict view of control is that the former tend to show a positive correlation between internal and external control, whereas the latter show a negative correlation. To put it differently, bilocals tend to believe in the covariation between individual effort and external influences for the outcome. Such covariation cannot be deduced from a unidimensional view that considers internal and external control as inversely related.

The most direct approach to identify bilocals is to obtain separate measurements of perceived internal control and external control for various situations and identify those who score high in both internal and external control. Controllers should be high in internal but low in external control; controllees should be the reverse.

The validity of any of these approaches can be established only through extensive research. We consider this an important new direction for locus of control research, because it fills a glaring gap that has long been overlooked due to preoccupation with the internal–external distinction, and because it will also provide a new model of adaptive coping, as will be discussed in the next section.

Locus of Control and Adjustment

Rotter (1966, 1975) always believed in a curvilinear relationship between locus of control and adjustment. He pointed out that "there must also be a limit on personal control. Many people may already feel that they have more control than is warranted by reality, and they may be subject in the future (or may have already been subjected) to strong trauma when they discover that they cannot control such things as automobile accidents, corporate failures, diseases, etc." (1975, p. 60).

From the present perspective, those who are in the middle range on the I–E scale should be most adaptive, not just because they are more realistic but because their bilocal view of control allows them to be more flexible and effective in coping with stressful situations.

The wisdom of Rotter's curvilinear view has not received much attention or empirical support. This is quite understandable, given that the importance of personal control has been so widely advocated and highly exalted that most, if not all, of the published studies were designed to demonstrate the various virtues that are supposedly associated with the internal locus of control orientation (Lefcourt, 1976, 1981). To our knowledge, no one has designed experiments explicitly and specifically to demonstrate some of the weaknesses and disadvantages of having a strong belief in internal control. Needless to say, since bilocals have never been recognized, their superiority in coping relative to the highly internal controllers remains to be tested.

Here we briefly describe areas where bilocals should be superior to controllers. We do not question the established findings that internals are superior to externals in various tasks; we simply propose that bilocals may be even better than highly internal controllers in many situations. Given that controllers attain satisfaction only when they have reduced those around them to the status of puppets, they tend to be aggressive, obtrusive, domineering, and will be perceived as such by others. Controllers often jostle and scheme for even more control and try to destroy everything or anyone that impedes their progress toward domination. In contrast, bilocals accept their own limitations and are cognizant of the rights and powers of others. These two rather different orientations toward control should lead to very different predictions in the area of interpersonal interactions.

First, bilocals should be better liked by coworkers than controllers. Wright (1969) defined friendship as voluntary interdependence. Because controllers are interested only in domination, they would have difficulty forming or maintaining close bonds with others on the basis of interdependence. Second, controllers would have difficulty tolerating subordination to people they do not perceive as legitimate authority figures. We hypothesize that controllers, relative to bilocals and controllees, are more likely to experience stress and anxiety when placed in a subservient role, especially when role assignment is perceived as illegitimate. In such situations, their desire for control being frustrated, they will not only experience stress but also show hostility toward those who give them orders. Generally, controllers resent following; they feel satisfied only when they are leading the way.

We can readily think of many tasks in which bilocals may outperform controllers. In general, bilocals should do better than controllers in any task where success is determined by both internal and external factors. For example, in tasks that involve coordinated effort and interdependence, controllers are expected to do poorer because of their tendency toward independence. Generally they are not good team players. It is predicted that they will be less cooperative and solicit help from team members less frequently. Therefore they have to complete the task without sufficient information and help, resulting in less than optimal performance. It is also predicted that they are less willing to provide help to others on the team to ensure that others do not outperform them.

So far we have described situations that involve either subordination or cooperation. However, even in some solitary types of tasks, controllers may be inferior to bilocals. We predict that controllers will be less motivated than bilocals in repetitive or unchallenging tasks that require thoroughness rather than a show of mental prowess. This prediction is based on the assumption that controllers are interested only in tasks that enhance their position or self-image as controllers.

Given their desire to control the uncontrollable and their tendency to overestimate their own efficacy, it is predicted that the controllers will have a greater illusion of control, exert more futile effort, and experience a greater amount of frustration than bilocals in noncontingent situations.

Finally, we hypothesize that bilocals are better problem solvers and adapters than controllers because of their greater flexibility and greater likelihood to use a variety of coping strategies, including dependence on external control. It is our hypothesis that a combination of external control and internal control is more effective in coping with a wide spectrum of stressful situations than sole reliance on either internal or external control.

We have briefly outlined a number of situations that may favor bilocals. In each of these situations, different experimental tasks may be devised to compare bilocals with controllers. This line of research

330 : PAUL T. P. WONG AND CATHERINE F. SPROULE

will determine the relative merits of these two kinds of control beliefs. To complete our analysis of locus of control and adaptation, we should also mention that a high degree of perceived and desired control may even be detrimental to one's health.

Although the beneficial effects of perceived control on health have been well-documented (Strickland, 1978), there is some evidence that a high degree of perceived and desired internal control may contribute to coronary heart disease. The linkage between the Type A behavior pattern and cardiac disorders has received a fair amount of support (Friedman & Rosenman, 1974; Matthews, 1982; Rosenman, 1978). This has been defined as "an action–emotion complex that can be observed in any person who is aggressively involved in a chronic, incessant struggle to achieve more and more in less and less time, and if required to do so, against the opposing efforts of other things or other persons" (Friedman & Rosenman, 1974, p. 67). This description can be readily applied to the controllers. In fact, the connection between the desire to control and the development of Type A behavior has been investigated systematically by Glass (1977), who suggested that this behavior pattern represents a strong tendency to cope with stress by means of behavioral control. Glass (1977) also hypothesized that Type A individuals are likely to become helpless if their attempt to control stressful aspects of the environment is met with repeated failure. The research by Glass and his associates suggests that controllers are high risks for heart disease and perhaps even reactive depression. At present, locus of control research has concentrated on college students and has not attempted to identify possible long-term negative consequences of excessive desire for control in these students later in life.

The present rather negative portrayal of high internals may come as a shock to those who firmly believe in the virtues of internal control. However, it should be emphasized that we are not disputing the importance of personal control, because there is overwhelming evidence that a sense of control is vital to the healthy functioning of the individual. What we do try to establish is, first, that an excessive degree of belief in internal control is less adaptive than a moderate degree, and second, that a dual-dimensional conception of control is more adaptive than a unidimensional conception.

The first point has been acknowledged either implicitly or explicitly by people working with the locus of control construct. However, it has never received empirical support because, as we have argued, most of the experiments were designed to show the superiority of internals over externals and to our knowledge no one has employed appropriate testing conditions to identify the weaknesses of very high internals relative to moderate internals.

If future research demonstrates some of the undesirable and unadaptive qualities attributed to highly internal controllers, we will have a more complete picture of internal control. More important, we will know whether there is a limit beyond which internal control might be harmful to the individual and to society. Our interest in this line of research is not motivated simply by scientific curiosity. We also believe that psychologists have the social obligation to learn and to inform the public whether excessive internal control may be harmful. Our present analysis should provide a balance to the widely promulgated idea that internal control is always beneficial.

The second point concerning dimensionality is related to the first point, because the unidimensional view of control tends to foster an unrealistic belief in internal or external control. Those who hold this view tend to see the world as a battlefield for control. They would say "I should strive for control at any cost. I must always be in control of all situations, because the alternative is degrading dependence." Alternatively, they will say "I am losing the fight for control. I am a loser." Therefore, their belief in internal (external) control tends to be either very high or very low. When they do hold a moderate view concerning locus of control in a particular situation, it is unstable and full of conflict because the internal and external forces are viewed as opposing tendencies along the same continuum.

The dual-dimensional view of control, on the other hand, tends to promote a more realistic and more moderate level of belief in internal (external) control. The adaptiveness of the dual-dimensional conception, as we have shown, goes far beyond a realistic assessment of locus of control. The dual-dimensional view also promotes a more cooperative relationship with others and a more flexible way of coping with stress. We believe that belief in shared control is more beneficial than belief in mere internal control in most stressful situations. This hypothesis can and should be subjected to a systematic empirical test, because it has important implications for psychotherapy as well as for the average individual attempting to cope with life's many problems.

Lefcourt (1972, p. 27) stated that "internal locus of control, with its assumed correlates of competence and the hope of success, is a common goal of psychotherapy." The current popularity of the self-efficacy approach to psychotherapy (Bandura, 1982) further illustrates our preoccupation with the value of internal control. In view of our prior arguments concerning the adaptiveness of the two-dimensional view, we propose that belief in shared control is a more worthwhile therapeutic goal than belief in internal control. Wortman and Brehm (1975) pointed out the danger of emphasizing personal control when the individual is facing an uncontrollable problem, echoing the concern voiced by Rotter (1975). Strickland (1978) also warned against the assumption that beliefs in internal control are always beneficial. The present dual-dimensional view, of course, circumvents the problem of exclusive and undue emphasis on personal control. Given that most of life's situations are subject to internal and external influences, belief in shared control is clearly more realistic.

One clear advantage of belief in shared control is that dependence on external control, when needed, does not absolve one of personal responsibility. Silvestri (1979) showed that God-dependent individuals are also internally oriented as measured by Rotter's I–E Scale. These individuals may even have a heightened sense of self-efficacy when it is linked to God-dependence. Belief in shared control actually opens up unlimited external resources to supplement one's own limited resources. Belief in shared control views dependence as a supplement rather than a substitute of personal control.

Our arguments in favor of shared control must be based on empirical findings, and we present some of these findings in the next section. However, we also need to recognize the cultural bias against shared control.

Western culture highly values independence or personal control in the socialization process (e.g., Berkowitz & Daniels, 1963; Merton, 1968; Mussen, 1970), and dependence is typically cast in a rather negative light (e.g., Coleman, 1976; Kagan & Moss, 1960). Given this cultural bias, it is not difficult to see why Western psychologists have been advocating internal control rather than shared control.

From a different cultural perspective, dependence takes on a more positive connotation. In introducing Dr. Takeo Doi's work, Douglas (1978) wrote that "so complete is the sustained dependence of the child upon the mother that it results in a lifelong search for belonging, a primary identification as a member of a group rather than an independent person" (p. 154). In his book *The Anatomy of Dependence*, Doi (1973) argued that the suppression of this longing for dependence and belonging in the West may have serious consequences, such as a sense of alienation and loneliness. The spreading of various cult groups in North America may reflect many individuals' attempts to fulfill the longing for dependence in a society that suppresses it.

The differences in Western and Eastern cultures are reflected not only in different emphases in psychology but also in different approaches to management. Ouchi (1981) observed some interesting differences between West and East. The United States model of management stresses personal autonomy—individual decision-making and personal responsibility. The incentive system, which is tied to individual performance, fosters competition rather than cooperation. Individuals are motivated primarily to climb the corporate ladder without any sense of loyalty to the company. Ouchi observed that graduates of graduate schools of business tend to change employers if they are not promoted rapidly.

> In a company, with rapid advancement and turnover, people learn to operate without depending on or consulting others. . . . In order to accomplish anything, each must stick to those things which they can do alone. In such a situation, broad influence over decisions and events is impossible, frustrating a manager. Some move on to yet another hopeful setting. The story, of course, does not have a happy ending [Ouchi, 1981, p. 50].

In contrast, trust, cooperativeness, accommodation, and the maintenance of harmony are the important ingredients in the Japanese approach (DeBettingnier, 1971, pp. 75–93; Drucker, 1971; Pascale, 1978; Ouchi, 1981). Japanese businesses emphasize collective decision-making and shared responsibility. "Productivity is a problem that can be worked out through coordinating individual efforts in a productive manner and of giving employees the incentives to do so by taking a cooperative, long-range view" (Ouchi, 1981, p. 5). Because industrial life is typically far too complex for any individual, the Japanese emphasis on interdependence and shared control is more adaptive. In terms of productivity, the Japanese approach to management is superior to the United States approach.

In sum, we believe that belief in shared control is more adaptive than belief in internal control, not just for the individual but also for society. A great deal of research has demonstrated the merits of internal control, but perhaps it is now time to consider when personal control hurts rather than helps and when shared control is more beneficial than personal control. We believe a proper blend of internal and external control should result in better adjustment than the exclusive emphasis on either independence or dependence. The present emphasis on shared control may be considered a fusion of West and East.

Empirical Evidence for the Dual-Dimensional View of Control

Some evidence for the dual-dimensional view can be gleaned from prior research. For example, findings on political activism and locus of control can be understood best in terms of two separate dimensions of perceived control. Levenson and Miller (1976) found a positive correlation between political activism and belief in external control by powerful others. This finding is inconsistent with a unidimensional view, which predicts negative correlation. Reid (1975) argued that those who believe that social–political powers determine one's outcomes but also believe that individuals can somehow change the system are most likely to engage in social political activism. According to a unidimensional view, a strong belief in external control by powerful others necessarily leads to a sense of powerlessness and passivity; similarly, as strong belief in self-efficacy leads to the belief that the world is easy and politically responsive.

In the case of political activism, external control hinders rather than supports internal control. The conflict between these two sources of control seems to suggest a unidimensional view. However, it should be reiterated that according to a unidimensional view, a high degree of external control necessarily means a low degree of internal control. The simultaneous presence of strong external and internal control is consistent with a dual-dimensional conception of control.

Levenson (1974) also found that length of incarceration increased inmates' belief in control by powerful others but had no effect on belief in internal control. This finding indicates that increasing recognition of external control does not reduce prisoners' belief in internal control. Such findings are possible only when internality and externality exist as separate dimensions rather than opposite poles of the same continuum.

Given that Levenson (1973, 1974) used separate scales for belief in internal control, belief in powerful others, and belief in chance, it is not surprising that most of the evidence in support of the dual-dimensional view comes from studies based on Levenson's Multidimensional–Multiattributional Control Scale. However, even for Rotter's I–E Scale, when the format is changed from forced-choice to separate rating scales for internal and external alternatives, the findings are consistent with a dual-dimensional view. For example, Collins (1974) failed to find consistent and significant negative correlations between internal and external ratings as demanded by a unidimensional view. He also reported that the factor structure of Rotter's internal items differs from that of external items.

Evidence for a two-dimensional concept of locus of control has been obtained in the achievement context as well. In one experiment (Wong, 1982), subjects were told to obtain as many points as possible by choosing the correct route in a finger maze that contained many possible routes leading to a goalbox, which was equipped with a small light bulb and a counter. Both the light onset and counter increment could be activated simultaneously by the experimenter. Under the success condition, reinforcement in the form of light onset and counter increment was delivered independently of the subject's behavior and according to a predetermined variable time schedule. Under the failure condition, reinforcement was never delivered, regardless of which routes were chosen by the subject. Various attribution measures were obtained before and after the test. Two of the measures relevant to our present discussion were the following: (a) To what extent do you think that the points you got were related to or dependent on the route you chose? (b) To what extent do you think that your total points were due to the operation of chance factors or luck? The first question was designed to measure the subjects' contingency judgment or illusion of control in a noncontingent situation. Wong (1982) found that females, as compared to males, had greater illusion of control as well as greater luck attribution. The paradox is how females could simultaneously perceive a higher degree of internal and external control than males.

The same paradox emerged in a study by Kettlewell (1981). She used the Trent Attribution Profile to measure different attributions of women who had different levels of career achievement. She found that women who perceived themselves as successful were simultaneously more internal and more external than women who perceived themselves as less successful. She also found that successful women's higher external attribution scores were due primarily to their greater dependence on luck. This finding reminds us of the time-worn sports saying: "Ya' gotta' be lucky to be good, and good to be lucky."

One way to resolve this paradox is to conceptualize internal and external dimensions as two separate dimensions. Thus internal and external attributions may be related positively. It is likely that females perceive more external constraints in a male-dominated world; they may also feel that in order to succeed they not only have to try harder but need more lucky breaks.

We recently conducted some experiments that bear more directly on the issue of dual-dimensionality (Wong & Sproule, 1982). We briefly report portions of the findings that are relevant to our present discussion.

We have argued that Rotter's I–E Scale reflects both perceived and desired control. In the first study, we obtained measures of perceived and desired control for persons with both internal and external control orientations. One popular notion related to the unidimensional view of control is that more individuals prefer internal control and detest external control. However, according to the dual-dimensional view, external control may be more desirable than internal control under highly complex and negative circumstances. Thus the purpose of the first study was to demonstrate that people not only perceive but actually desire external control under these circumstances. Complexity and valence were manipulated as the independent variables. The three levels of complexity were peace–war, employment–unemployment, and completion–incompletion of a school assignment. For each level of complexity there was a positive and a negative outcome, for a total of six different outcomes.

Subjects were 58 students from Trent University; males and females were equally represented. They were asked to complete a questionnaire to indicate on five-point scales the extent to which they perceived or believed certain outcomes are controlled by internal (or external) causes. Similarly, they were asked to indicate the extent to which they desired or wished certain outcomes to be controlled by internal (or external) causes. Thus subjects were requested to rate four separate scales (perceived internal, perceived external, desired internal, and desired external) for each of the six outcomes. These 24 rating scales were presented in random order. Subjects were instructed that both internal and/or external causes may contribute to an outcome and were given some examples of internal causes (e.g., ability, effort) and external causes (e.g., other people, circumstances, luck). The predictions were that both perceived and desired internal control would decrease with complexity, whereas perceived and desired external control would increase with complexity. It was also predicted that perceived and desired internal control would be higher but perceived and desired external control would be lower for positive than for negative outcomes.

Results are shown in Figure 5.1. It is clear that all predictions were supported. For all four scales (perceived internal, perceived external, desired internal, desired external), the main effect of complexity was significant: $F(2, 112) = 272.47, 87.72, 123.40,$ and 47.01, respectively, all $ps < .001$; the main effect of outcome was also significant: $F(1, 56) = 36.68, 7.18, 118.14,$ and 31.97, respectively, all $ps < .001$. The outcome $\times$ complexity interaction was significant for perceived internal and desired external: $F(2, 112) = 13.74$ and 10.23, respectively, both $ps < .001$, because for these two scales the outcome effect did not occur under the high level of complexity. Another interesting finding was a significant gender main effect for desired internal control: $F(1, 56) = 4.93, p < .05$, in that females desired greater internal control than did males (3.37 vs. 3.07).

We have demonstrated that people actually desire a high degree of external control for complex events, such as peace and war. Even for the moderate level of complexity, people desire a fair amount of external control. These findings are contrary to the unidimensional conflict view of control and the implicit assumptions of control psychologists

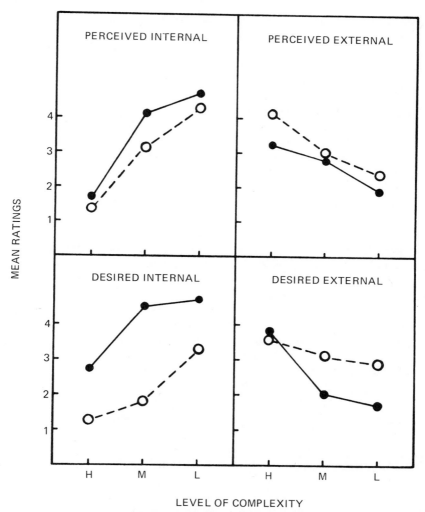

FIGURE 5.1. *Perceived and desired internal (or external) control ratings as a function of complexity, (solid line = positive, broken line = negative).*

(see Rothbaum et al., 1982) that people desire only internal control. However, these findings are consistent with the dual-dimensional view that except for highly internal controllers, most people actually desire external control or prefer shared control for situations that are too complex for their own resources. The validity of the present findings becomes obvious when one considers the ever-increasing governmental control in the affairs of citizens. Despite frequent campaign rhetoric against big governments, politicians have not been successful in reducing the size of government bureaucracy. Many citizens actually want government to do more for them, especially in the areas of employment–unemployment and peace–war.

In the second study, we intended to replicate and extend Study 1 by asking subjects to indicate, according to their perception or judgment, how many internal (or external) causes might be responsible for each of the six outcomes described in Study 1. They were allowed to use any number of causes ranging from 0 to 100 and told that some outcomes were more complex and involved more causal factors than others. This new dependent variable—the number of causes—would allow us to verify the level of complexity for different outcomes.

For Study 2 we also included a locus of control variable. All subjects completed Rotter's I–E Scale. The order of administering the scale and our responsibility attribution questionnaire was counterbalanced for the subjects. The I–E test was scored in the internal direction, and the 66 subjects were then divided into Internals and Externals on the basis of a median split. It was predicted that Internals would assume more responsibility than Externals.

The results of Study 2, as shown in Figure 5.2, clearly replicated Study 1, in that subjects perceived fewer internal causes and more external causes for more complex situations: $F(2, 128) = 21.49$ and 75.18, respectively, $ps < .001$. When internal and external judgments were combined, the mean numbers of causes for the three levels of complexity in a descending order were 47.76, 43.49, and 40.09, respectively, $F(2, 128) = 7.71$, $p < .001$, thus providing direct support for our assumption that the three types of situations represent three different levels of complexity.

The main effect of I–E was significant in perceived external causes: $F(1, 64) = 4.11$, $p < .05$, demonstrating that Internals perceived fewer external causes than did Externals. For perceived internal causes, the I–E × complexity interaction was significant: $F(2, 128) = 3.76$, $p < .05$, in that Internals perceived more internal causes than did Externals only under moderate and low levels of complexity. It may be concluded that except for highly complex events such as peace and war, Internals do assume more responsibility for the outcome than do Externals, thus providing some evidence for the validity of the present measure of responsibility attribution.

Past research on situational variables and locus of control beliefs has focused on skill versus chance manipulations. The present studies have shown that both complexity level and valence are important determinants of perceived and desired control. These two studies repre-

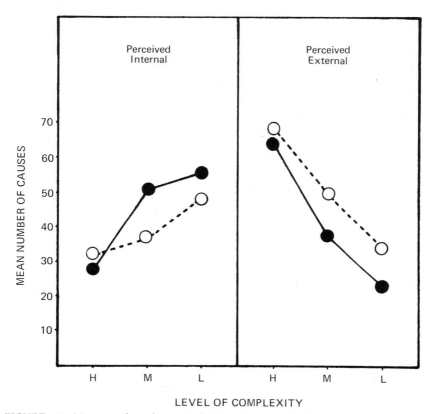

FIGURE 5.2. *Mean number of perceived internal (external) causes as a function of complexity and Rotter's Locus of Control Scale (solid line = internal; broken line = external).*

sent the first step toward mapping out conditions under which shared control or external control is more beneficial and desirable than internal control. This new direction of research clearly stems from the dual-dimensional view of control.

One of the important implications from the two-dimensional view is that as people become older, they are more likely to adopt a two-dimensional view of control and believe in shared control. Evidence for belief in shared control is the simultaneous presence of relatively high internal and external control. A recent study by Wong and Reker (1982) measured perceived and desired internal (or external) control in five different life situations (health, personal safety, financial situations, social contact with relatives and friends, and living conditions) for four different age groups (10–29, 30–49, 50–69, and 70–89 years).

Subjects were asked to indicate on five-point scales the extent to which they perceived and desired internal (or external) control for each of the five domains. Thus there were 20 questions, which were arranged in random order. Results are shown in Figure 5.3.

For the present purposes, we comment only briefly on relevant aspects of the results. As predicted, internal and external control (both perceived and desired) tend to converge for the oldest group. A main effect for age was significant in nearly all of the measures. Past research has shown that internal belief as measured by Rotter's I–E tends to peak around 50 years of age (e.g., O'Brien & Kabanoff, 1981). The results of our present study are comparable to past findings. Figure 5.3 shows that the group aged 30–49 years tends to stress the highest level of internal control in most of the life situations. A similar picture emerged when these subjects completed Rotter's I–E Scale (higher scores indicating internality). The mean internality scores for the age groups 10–29, 30–49, 50–69, and 70–89 years were 13.16, 16.30, 16.03,

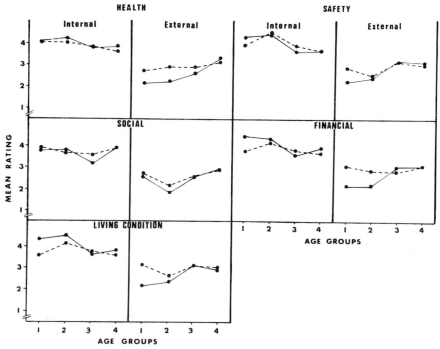

FIGURE 5.3. Perceived and desired internal (external) control ratings as a function of different age groups in different life situations (solid line = desired; broken line = perceived; 1 = 10–29; 2 = 30–49; 3 = 50–69; 4 = 70–89 years.

and 15.40, respectively, $F(3, 112) = 4.70$, $p < .01$. It is only reasonable that the middle age group shows the highest degree of internal control, because they are indeed financially more independent and more capable of looking after their own affairs than either the younger or the older groups. It is also realistic that the oldest group not only perceived but also desired more external control than did the younger groups because of the increasing limitations (often physical and financial) that come with advanced age. For the oldest group, perceived and desired internal control was still very high. Thus both internal and external control were fairly high, showing some evidence of belief in shared control for this age group.

The correlation data of this study were also supportive of the dual-dimensional view. The Pearson product-moment coefficients for perceived internal and external control and for desired internal and external control are shown in Table 5.2. The pattern of correlations is instructive. For Groups 1 and 2, most of the correlations are in the negative direction, reflecting a tendency toward a unidimensional view of control; for Groups 3 and 4, most of the correlations are low but positive, consistent with a dual-dimensional view of control.

The present findings of belief in shared control by the elderly support our earlier arguments that the goal of psychotherapy should not be exclusively the promotion of internal locus of control. It is hypothesized that belief in shared control is more adaptive than belief in internal control for the elderly. This hypothesis warrants close attention from those who are interested in the well-being of the elderly.

The Dual-Dimensional View of Control and Social Learning Theory

We have presented attributional analyses as well as empirical findings that argue for a dual-dimensional view of locus of control. In this section we attempt to show that the present conception of locus of control is consistent with a social learning theory formulation. The generalized expectancy of dual control simply refers to the generalized belief that the reinforcement occurs typically as a function of personal control and external control. External control may come from a variety of sources, such as powerful others, circumstances, God, fate, and luck. Overall, external control may be viewed as either positive or negative. Positive external control supports and cooperates with personal control, increasing the expectancy of success. Negative external control hinders or limits personal control, decreasing the expectancy of success.

According to the traditional unidimensional view of locus of con-

TABLE 5.2
Pearson Product–Moment Correlation Coefficients between Internal and External Control for Four Different Age Groups (N = 30)

Life situation	Correlations between perceived internal and external control				Correlations between desired internal and external control			
	Group 1 (10–29)	Group 2 (30–49)	Group 3 (50–69)	Group 4 (70–89)	Group 1 (10–29)	Group 2 (30–49)	Group 3 (50–69)	Group 4 (70–89)
Health	−.520*	.048	.077	.118	−.6970*	−.248	.285	.201
Safety	−.236	−.264	−.044	.062	−.100	.230	.332	.052
Social	−.271	−.272	.118	.068	−.422*	−.307	.470*	.110
Home	−.218	−.092	.265	−.046	−.294	−.314	.133	.098
Financial	−.393*	−.011	−.300	−.215	−.197	−.377*	−.235	.090

*p < .05.

trol, expectancy of external control need not be treated as a separate variable because it is simply the inverse of expectancy of internal control. However, according to the dual-dimensional view, expectancy of external control must be treated as a separate variable. Given the same generalized expectancy of internal control, a generalized expectancy of positive external control increases the expectancy of success, whereas a generalized expectancy of negative external control decreases it.

It should be mentioned that our present analysis of dual control is consistent with Heider's (1958) view of social causality, which assumes some additive function of internal and external causes. The external causes can either facilitate or hinder the internal causes.

One advantage of including generalized expectancy of positive or negative external control in the expectancy × value formulation is to enable us to make a more precise prediction of expectancy of success in different situations. Another advantage is that it provides a more complete picture of individual differences in locus of control beliefs, as shown in Table 5.3.

Controllers maximize belief in internal control. Controllees, on the other hand, exaggerate the external control and believe the presence of such a high degree of external control renders internal control ineffectual and unnecessary. Both controllers and controllees tend to have a unidimensional view of control. Their generalized expectancies of both internal and external control are unrealistic and excessive.

It is important to bear in mind that we are talking about generalized expectancies. Even controllers may perceive a low degree of internal control in certain situations, such as peace and war. However, generally controllers tend to have a high opinion about their ability to control their environment.

Bilocals, as the term implies, believe in the importance of both internal and external control. To them, these two types of control are not

TABLE 5.3
Schematic Classification of Different Profiles of Generalized Locus of Control Beliefs

Classification	Internal control	Positive external control	Negative external control
Controllers	Very high	Very low	Very low
Controllees	Very low	Very high	Very high
Realistic bilocals	High	High	High
Optimistic bilocals	High	High	Low
Pessimistic bilocals	High	Low	High

necessarily inversely related as demanded by the unidimensional view. They do not unrealistically exaggerate the influence of either internal or external control as do controllers and controllees. They have a fairly high generalized expectancy of control because the exercise of a fair amount of personal autonomy is a common experience in a democratic society, and it is essential for the normal functioning of an individual. It is our contention that the majority of people, especially among the elderly, embrace a dual-dimensional view of control.

Bilocals can be further differentiated on the basis of their outlook concerning external control. Realistic bilocals recognize the simultaneous presence of both beneficial and hostile kinds of external control. They also recognize the importance and the extent of these two kinds of external control. They see the threats and hindrance that come from without, but they also know that they can depend on the support of external resources. In situations where positive external control outweighs negative external control, their expectancy of success could be even higher than the highly internal controllers.

Optimistic bilocals are those individuals who tend to see the world as benevolent and think that Fate always smiles on them. Like controllers, they have an unrealistic expectancy of success; but different from internals, they do not see the presence of external control as a threat to their personal autonomy—in fact, they see powerful others and providence as their friends. Their unrealistic expectancy of success is based not on an unrealistic assessment of their own capability, as is true of controllers, but on an overly optimistic view of external support. Optimistic bilocals are also different from controllees, in that they do not cast themselves at the mercy of external forces; they would do their part and at the same time expect external sources to provide what is needed to ensure success.

Finally, pessimistic bilocals believe the odds are stacked against them and that external control is hostile, but they still believe that with determination they could achieve some success. They see the world as an obstacle course, and they clench their teeth to run the race. Some of the political activists described earlier seem to be pessimistic bilocals because they see a repressive sociopolitical system, and yet they attempt to promote some social change. There are, of course, also idealistic political activists who are more like controllers because they entertain the naive view that the world is easy and politically responsive, and that they can change the world simply by marching and shouting slogans.

One may question whether external aid should be conceptualized as external control. From a unidimensional view, dependence on anything external—be it reward or help—reduces one's autonomy (deCharms, 1968). Thus controllers should find it aversive to be in conditions of dependence. This prediction is consistent with the model of threat to self-esteem of recipient reactions to aid (Fisher, Nadler, & Whitcher-Alagna, 1982) and has some indirect support from the finding that individuals with a high need for achievement or high self-esteem are more likely to find external aid threatening (Nadler, Altman, & Fisher, 1979; Nadler, Fisher, & Streufert, 1976; Tessler & Schwartz, 1972).

Given that controllers view external aid as an undesirable external control that threatens personal autonomy, they would be more reluctant to receive it. When aid is necessary, controllers demand it as an entitlement rather than ask for it as a favor. External aid is viewed as a form of external control by controllees because it reminds them of their own helpless condition and their being pawns in the hands of powerful others.

From the perspective of dual control, external aid is a form of external control because it is one of the factors that determine the final outcome. External aid does not threaten or reduce a sense of autonomy for bilocals; external aid is treated as a necessity for successful coping.

It should be pointed out that dependence on external aid sometimes involves relinquishing certain rights or freedoms. For example, the helper may dictate the terms that must be fulfilled if the individual is to receive help. In this case, external aid is clearly a means of manipulating and controlling other individuals, regardless of whether one holds a unidimensional or a dual-dimensional view. When external aid is blatantly restrictive and oppressive, it is likely to be viewed as a negative rather than a positive kind of external control.

Finally, even external control that restricts an individual's freedom may be viewed favorably if it actually helps the individual to achieve certain desirable goals. Rules and regulations, reward and punishment, and even the constant presence of authority figures may be favorably viewed as external aids if external control actually helps the individual to gain better control over his or her own life and to achieve cherished goals. For example, externally imposed restrictions may help prevent an individual from indulging in habits, such as drug-taking, that will eventually destroy him or her, and enable that person to pursue more worthwhile goals.

In sum, the dual-dimensional view permits a more thorough analysis of external control within the framework of social learning theory so that external control may be viewed as either facilitative or inhibitive with respect to one's expectancy of success. This analysis is quite different from the traditional view of internal versus external locus of control, which considers them opposites. Further research is needed to determine the conditions under which people are more likely to perceive external control as beneficial help rather than harmful restriction. More research is also needed to investigate the individual differences in accordance with the different profiles of locus of control beliefs outlined in Table 5.6.

The Trent Attribution Profile

Rationale for the TAP

The TAP was developed in the fall of 1976 in response to the limitations inherent in Rotter's I–E Scale and the more recent findings from attribution research. Earlier we alluded to some of the limitations. One limitation is the forced-choice format. Many of our subjects—especially the elderly—expressed real difficulty in choosing an alternative in several pairs of statements, claiming "Both statements are equally true." The forced-choice format does not permit subjects to demonstrate their belief in shared control.

Another limitation of Rotter's I–E Scale is that some of the statements are not clearly related to attributions. For example, the statement "There will always be war, no matter how hard people try to prevent them" is simply a generalization based on human history and the daily news about wars in various parts of the globe. It is a projection into the future rather than a causal explanation of past or present events. Similarly, the statement "I have often found that what is going to happen will happen" is a reflection of reality rather than an attribution concerning causality or responsibility.

It seemed that the best way to assess locus of control beliefs was to measure people's causal beliefs directly. At the time of the study, locus of causality and locus of control had not been clearly differentiated in the literature and the difference between causal attribution and responsibility attributions had not yet been spelled out.

The TAP was based on Weiner's earlier model of causal attributions (e.g., Weiner, Frieze, Kukla, Reed, Rest, & Rosenbaum, 1971). According to this model, the two prominent causal dimensions are locus of control (internal versus external) and stability (stable versus unstable). The major causal factors in the achievement domain are ability, effort, task difficulty, and luck, which could be classified according to the two-dimension scheme. For example, ability is internal and stable, but effort is internal and unstable.

At the time the TAP was conceived, the hedonic bias was already well-established. This bias refers to the phenomenon that success tends to be attributed to internal causes, whereas failure is more often ascribed to external causes (e.g., Ross, 1977). There was also some evidence that perceived causes of failure are better predictors of persistence, expectancies, and actual future performance than perceived causes for success (Dweck & Goetz, 1978; Ickes & Layden, 1978, p. 120–156). Therefore we had separate attribution measures for success and failure in the TAP.

Another important and well-documented attribution bias is the effect of self versus other perspectives on the attribution of causality. First demonstrated by Jones and Nisbett (1971), attributions for one's own behavior tend to be more situational (external), whereas attributions for other people tend to be more dispositional (internal). It seemed desirable to differentiate between self-attributions and attributions about others in the TAP.

Our plan at the time was to provide a profile about an individual's causal belief under four conditions: self-success, self-failure, other-success, other-failure. Under each condition we had three items related to three different life domains: academic, social, and financial. Thus the TAP consists of twelve test items. They were selected from a large pool of items generated by us and our students. The criterion for selection was that these items be representative of success and failure experiences in these three domains of life in a Western society.

To put it differently, in each of the three common life domains, the two different outcomes (success and failure) are factorially combined with two different perspectives (self and others), yielding twelve different items. Each item is followed by four possible explanations based on Weiner's four causal ascriptions. For example, the item on academic failure for others is presented this way: "When people fail school, it is because of (a) lack of academic skills, (b) bad breaks, (c) lack of effort, and (d) harsh judgments by the teacher." Respondents were asked to rate the relative importance of each of these four explanations for each of the 12 test items. (See Appendix A for the complete scale.)

Validity and Normative Data

Some of the initial validity and reliability data of the TAP have already been published (Wong, Watters, & Sproule, 1978). We now present some additional validity and normative data.

STUDY 1: ROTTER'S I–E SCALE AND THE TAP

We demonstrated earlier that internals and externals differed significantly in some attribution measures on the TAP (Wong et al, 1978). In the present study we gave the TAP to 48 subjects (24 males and 24 females) chosen from the first and last quartile of subjects who had completed the I–E scale. We have argued that the highly internal controllers would be high in competence-related internal attributions (i.e., ability and effort) but low in external attributions, whereas the highly external controllees would be just the reverse. We were able to obtain significant differences in the predicted direction between internals and externals in all four attribution measures, as shown in Table 5.4. Significant I–E $\times$ domain interactions were obtained only for Internality and Luck measures. For Internality scores, controllers are higher than controllees in all three life domains, although the magnitude of the difference is dependent on the situation. For the Luck measure, the reverse is true; again, the magnitude of difference is dependent on the domain. Overall, our findings indicate that attributional differences between controllers and controllees are generalizable to at least three life domains, although for some attribution measures the magnitude of these differences may be dependent on the situation.

It should be noted that ability and effort correspond to Heider's "Can" and "Try," both considered essential in achieving personal goals. Given that these two causal ascriptions are related to self-efficacy and competence, a high Internality measure in the TAP (based on the summation of ratings in these two causes), reflects not only high internal causality but also a high degree of perceived control. (We argued earlier that high internal causality, in some other cases, may reflect a low level of perceived control.)

STUDY 2: ACHIEVEMENT MOTIVATION AND THE TAP

There is considerable evidence that differences in achievement motivation are related to attribution differences (Weiner, 1979; Weiner

TABLE 5.4

Mean Attribution Ratings on the TAP by Controllers and Controllees as Defined by Rotter's I–E Scale

	Ability	Effort	Task	Luck	Internality	Externality
Controllers	4.13	4.39	2.61	2.02	8.52	4.63
Controllees	3.69	3.76	2.98	2.65	7.45	5.63
$F(1, 44)$	13.8	34.20	8.93	18.56	39.56	17.23
p	$< .001$	$< .001$	$< .01$	$< .001$	$< .001$	$< .001$

& Kukla, 1970). For example, Weiner and Kukla (1970, Exp. V) reported that individuals high in resultant achievement motivation as measured by Mehrabian's Achieving Tendency Scale (1969) are more likely to take personal responsibility for success than individuals low in achievement motivation.

In the present study we administered Mehrabian's Scale and the TAP to 105 subjects and chose 32 with the highest achievement score (16 males and 11 females) and 32 subjects with the lowest achievement score (16 males and 16 females). These 64 subjects came from a variety of backgrounds: Some were housewives, some were office workers, but the majority were university students. Their average age was 25.7 years, ranging from 16 to 48 years.

The prediction was only partially supported, in that high achievement individuals were significantly less external than low achievement individuals (4.74 vs. 5.44), $F(1, 60) = 11.66$, $p < .001$; the difference in Internality score was in the right direction (7.94 vs. 7.66) but not significant. Overall, the TAP seems to be sensitive to differences in achievement motivation. The results might be more clear-cut if a more homogeneous sample were used.

STUDY 3: NORMATIVE DATA FOR TWO AGE GROUPS

The 120 subjects in this study represented a broad cross-section of the population. Half of the subjects were between 16 and 25 years of age, with a mean age of 20.02 (young adults); the other half were between 26 and 50 years, with a mean age of 33.42 (middle age). Males and females were equally represented in each age group. Most of the young adults were students, whereas most of the middle-aged subjects were working people. We chose these two particular age groups because our prior research (Sproule, Watters, & Wong, 1976) showed that most of the differences in attribution on the TAP were obtained between these two age groups.

Significant age differences were obtained in most of the attribution measures, as shown in Table 5.5. Age × outcome interaction was sig-

TABLE 5.5
Mean Attributions between Young Adults (N = 60) and Middle-Aged Subjects (N = 60)

	Ability	Effort	Task	Luck	Internality	Externality
Young	3.68	3.71	2.76	2.51	7.12	5.27
Middle	3.91	3.96	2.43	2.56	7.87	4.99
$F(1, 116)$	4.43	4.54	12.05	< 1	5.19	2.22
p	$< .05$	$< .05$	$< .001$	N.S.	$< .05$	N.S.

nificant for effort: $F(1, 116) = 7.92$, $p < .001$, and task attribution: $F(1, 116) = 3.96$, $p < .05$. For the effort attribution, the two age groups did not differ for success, but the middle-aged group attached greater importance to insufficient effort for failure than did young adults. Similarly, the two age groups did not differ for success in task attribution, but the young adults were more likely to blame the task for failure. In other words, the middle-aged group assumed greater personal responsibility for failure than did the young adults.

The present findings of age differences are consistent with the literature, which shows that the middle-aged group is more internal than younger groups (Bradley & Webb, 1976; O'Brien & Kabanoff, 1981; Staats, 1974). Thus the TAP is capable of detecting age differences in perceived personal control.

Attribution Biases

SELF–OTHER DIFFERENCES

Given that the TAP provides attributional measures, it should demonstrate the actor–observer bias reported by prior research (i.e., Jones & Nisbett, 1971). It is predicted that subjects would make a stronger dispositional attribution (i.e., ability) for others but stronger situational attribution (i.e., task) for self. This prediction was supported in all three studies reported here. These differences are shown in Table 5.6.

SUCCESS–FAILURE DIFFERENCES

The TAP is also sensitive to the well-documented success–failure bias in attribution. Table 5.7 clearly shows that in all three studies success produced greater internal attribution, whereas failure produced

TABLE 5.6
Mean Ability and Task Attributions for Self (Actor) and Others (Observer) Perspectives

	Ability attribution		Task attribution	
	Self	Other	Self	Other
Study 1	3.56	4.26	3.17	2.42
	$(F[1, 44] = 103.01)^*$		$(F = 78.59)^*$	
Study 2	3.52	4.08	3.08	2.41
	$(F[1, 60] = 86.08)^*$		$(F = 89.38)^*$	
Study 3	3.50	4.04	2.75	2.48
	$(F[1, 116] = 155.71)^*$		$(F = 17.64)^*$	

$^*p < .001.$

TABLE 5.7
Mean Attributions under Success (S) and Failure (F) Conditions

	Ability		Effort		Task		Luck		Internality		Externality	
	S	F	S	F	S	F	S	F	S	F	S	F
Study 1	3.98	3.84	4.27	3.88	2.47	3.12	2.50	2.17	9.25	7.72	4.97	5.29
$(F[1, 44] = 3.57)$			$(F = 15.58)$***		$(F = 42.58)$***		$(F = 17.14)$***		$(F = 17.41)$***		$(F = 4.48)$*	
Study 2	3.95	3.65	4.14	3.82	2.36	3.13	2.60	2.09	8.09	7.47	4.96	5.22
$(F[1, 60] = 14.70)$***			$(F = 26.68)$***		$(F = 93.54)$***		$(F = 60.78)$***		$(F = 41.92)$***		$(F = 6.29)$*	
Study 3	3.86	3.70	4.06	3.64	2.52	2.74	2.57	2.56	7.92	7.34	5.09	5.30
$(F[1, 116] = 9.93)$**			$(F = 61.51)$***		$(F = 11.69)$***		$(F < 1)$		$(F = 72.97)$***		$(F = 11.73)$***	

*$p < .05$.
**$p < .01$.
***$p < .001$.

greater external attribution. With respect to specific attribution elements, ability and effort attributions are higher after success than after failure, but task attribution is higher after failure than after success. Luck attribution seems to be the opposite of task attribution. Because of the conventional usage of the word "luck," it is often considered an internal rather than external attribution (i.e., being a lucky person). In fact, there is some empirical evidence (Fischhoff, 1976) that luck may be perceived as a dispositional.

In sum, the demonstration of both self–other and success–failure differences in attribution lends further substance to the construct validity of the TAP. However, it remains to be seen whether variables such as ego involvement and empathy that affect the magnitude of these attributional biases would have similar effects on TAP measures.

A Preliminary Evaluation of the TAP

At the time of this writing, the TAP is being used by different investigators for a variety of purposes, ranging from the study of cultural differences to research on alcoholism. Because most of these studies are still under way, it is not known how predictive the TAP is in various situations. However, we can discuss some of the positive and negative features of the TAP on the basis of our own experience with this instrument.

On the positive side, the TAP seems to be a reliable and valid instrument to tap an individual's general attributional style; the test items are based on three common life domains, the test–retest reliability coefficient is quite high (See Wong et al., 1976), and the attribution profile is sensitive to differences in locus of control orientations as measured by Rotter's I–E Scale. It could be used to portray the general attribution schema of different populations, such as depressives or schizophrenics.

Another advantage of the TAP is that it provides information not only on attribution elements and attribution dimensions but also on the magnitude of hedonic and self–other biases. A simple way to plot the attribution profile is to list the values of the four attribution elements separately for the success and failure conditions. It is obvious that the profile is more informative than a single internality or externality score.

A third advantage is that the TAP permits the assessment of relative interdependence between internal and external causes. For individuals who believe in shared control, internal and external causes tend to covary. For example, success may be attributed to ability and effort but at the same time to lucky breaks and the task being easy. We have not yet explained the patterns of correlations between different attribution elements or between internal or external scores. The test scores of the TAP could be readily subjected to a variety of multivariate analyses to reveal the structure of an individual's attribution schema.

Furthermore, results from the TAP could be related to findings and theories in the attribution domain, because the TAP explicitly measures an individual's attribution about various events. The interpretation of the TAP, then, benefits from advances in attribution research in general.

On the negative side, the TAP could be criticized for offering a limited set of causal explanations. However, the inclusion of additional causal factors could be justified only when it increases the predictive power of the TAP.

Another weakness is that locus of causality and locus of control were not recognized as two separate dimensions at the time the TAP was developed. In fact, these two dimensions are confounded in the TAP because, as we showed earlier, high internal causality based on ability and effort also means a high degree of personal control, whereas high externality based on task difficulty and bad luck means a low degree of perceived control. As long as one recognizes this confounding, one should not have difficulty in interpreting the TAP results.

The TAP may also be faulted for having a limited sample for each life domain. This is a valid criticism. To increase the number of test items in each domain would likely increase the generalizability of the profile. Some interested investigators may consider such an undertaking.

Finally, the meaning of the five-point scale of attribution rating in the TAP seems ambiguous to the subject because of its bipolar nature. In future uses of the TAP, perhaps the meaning of the scale should be redefined in a unipolar fashion, ranging from not at all important to extremely important. Because this proposed change increases the range of perceived importance of causes, it might increase the magnitudes of individual differences in the attribution profile.

Conclusions

The traditional construct of internal versus external control treats the two loci as opposites of a continuum; therefore, internal and external control are held to be inversely related. We have discussed several implications of this unidimensional view of control and argued that this view tends to promote perceived conflict between autonomy and dependence and fosters an unrealistic view of the extent of internal (or external) control.

In contrast, the new conception of locus of control treats internal and external control as two independent dimensions; therefore, different kinds of relationships may exist between these two dimensions, including positive as well as zero correlations. We presented both the rationale and evidence in support of this dual-dimensional view. We stated the reasons why this new conception of control minimizes the perceived autonomy–dependence conflict and promotes belief in shared control. It seems valid to conclude that the dual-dimensional view is more realistic and more consistent with attribution research than is the unidimensional view.

Several new directions of research have emerged from the present dual-dimensional formulation. One important area requires mapping out the conditions under which shared control is more beneficial than internal control. Another challenging direction of locus of control research is to identify bilocals—those who hold a generalized expectancy of dual control—and determine whether bilocals are more adaptive than unidimensional controllers.

There is now a loud chorus lauding the beneficial effects of internal control and the voice seems to come from all quarters. The occasional suggestion that excessive personal control may be harmful has been either ignored or dismissed as being a sour note. We propose that the pendulum toward internal control has already swung too far, and that now is the time to return to the more realistic position of shared control.

Since the early 1960s, "control" psychologists have been busy demonstrating the importance of internal control. Their main practical concern is how to enhance a person's belief in self-efficacy or internal control. In contrast, the psychology of shared control emphasizes both personal responsibility and reliance on external resources. It is our contention that perceived personal control must be tempered by a realistic assessment of one's limitations and supplemented by available external resources. "Shared control" psychologists are concerned with finding the optimal mix between internal and external control to maximize efficiency, harmony, and the well-being of the individual as well as of the group. To achieve such an optimal balance would contribute a great deal to the health of the individual and to the moral climate of the society.

Our study of why people chose a particular alternative in Rotter's I–E scale reveals realism versus idealism as an important factor. More specifically, for several items on the I–E scale, choice of the external alternative seems motivated by realistic more than idealistic considerations; the reverse seems to be true for choice of the internal alternatives. This finding demands that in interpreting the I–E score we recognize the realistic externals.

Our attributional analysis of the locus of control construct has led not only to a two-dimensional view of control, a reinterpretation of Rotter's I–E scale, but also the development of the TAP. We have provided additional validity data that recommend the TAP as a useful instrument to measure locus of control and general attributional style.

Appendix A: The Trent Attribution Profile

Instructions: For each of the following statements, please rate the importance of each of the five reasons according to your judgment. Please circle the appropriate number.

Note that: 5 means very important
4 means somewhat important
3 means undecided
2 means somewhat unimportant
1 means not at all important

For example, consider the following item:

One's height is the result of: Nutrition 1 2 3 4 5
Exercise 1 2 3 4 5
Parents' height 1 2 3 4 5
Climate 1 2 3 4 5

Thus, if you believe that parents' height is very important you would circle number 5; if you believe that exercise is somewhat important you would circle number 4; and so on.

---

1. Most scientific inventions are the result of:

   a. chance happenings 1 2 3 4 5
   b. the inventor's intelligence 1 2 3 4 5
   c. easy, routine scientific work 1 2 3 4 5
   d. much time and effort by the inventor 1 2 3 4 5

2. My good marks in school were due to:

   a. easy marking by the teacher 1 2 3 4 5
   b. hard work on my part 1 2 3 4 5
   c. good luck 1 2 3 4 5
   d. my academic skills 1 2 3 4 5

3. When a person is popular, it is because:

   a. of lucky breaks 1 2 3 4 5
   b. he or she tries hard 1 2 3 4 5
   c. of their social skills 1 2 3 4 5
   d. it's easy to be popular 1 2 3 4 5

4. When I did not do well in a class in school, it was because:

   a. I didn't try hard enough 1 2 3 4 5
   b. the teacher was very demanding 1 2 3 4 5
   c. of my lack of skills in that subject-area 1 2 3 4 5
   d. of unlucky breaks 1 2 3 4 5

5. If my financial situation were to get worse, it would probably be due to:

   a. difficult circumstances 1 2 3 4 5
   b. my poor judgment 1 2 3 4 5
   c. unlucky breaks.......................... 1 2 3 4 5
   d. my lack of effort 1 2 3 4 5

6. When people fail school, it is because of:

   a. lack of academic skills................ 1 2 3 4 5
   b. bad breaks 1 2 3 4 5
   c. lack of effort......................... 1 2 3 4 5
   d. harsh judgments by the teacher 1 2 3 4 5

7. Most wealthy people are rich because:

   a. of their skill at making money......... 1 2 3 4 5
   b. they worked very hard 1 2 3 4 5
   c. of lucky breaks....................... 1 2 3 4 5
   d. it's easy to make money 1 2 3 4 5

8. When I have a good time at a party, it is because:

   a. it was a good party 1 2 3 4 5
   b. I'm a good mixer 1 2 3 4 5
   c. it was a lucky day 1 2 3 4 5
   d. I make an effort to have fun 1 2 3 4 5

9. My future financial successes will be because:

   a. of hard work on my part............... 1 2 3 4 5
   b. of lucky breaks....................... 1 2 3 4 5
   c. of my skill to make money 1 2 3 4 5
   d. it's not hard to make money 1 2 3 4 5

10. When people dislike me, it is usually because:

   a. I don't try hard enough to be friendly 1 2 3 4 5
   b. luck isn't on my side 1 2 3 4 5
   c. it's hard to be liked by everyone..... 1 2 3 4 5
   d. I lack the social skills 1 2 3 4 5

11. Most poor people have little because:

   a. of bad breaks 1 2 3 4 5
   b. it's difficult to get ahead in the world..... 1 2 3 4 5
   c. they don't work hard enough 1 2 3 4 5
   d. of lack of financial skills 1 2 3 4 5

12. The fact that some people are not well-liked is because:

   a. they don't know how to get along with others 1 2 3 4 5
   b. it's hard to be popular 1 2 3 4 5
   c. they don't try to be friendly 1 2 3 4 5
   d. they have had bad breaks.............. 1 2 3 4 5

References

Averill, J. R. Personal control over aversive stimuli and its relationship to stress. *Psychological Bulletin*, 1973, *80*, 286–303.

Bandura, A. Self-efficacy mechanism in human agency. *American Psychologist*, 1982, *37*, 122–147.

Berkowitz, L., & Daniels, L. R. Responsibility and dependency. *Journal of Abnormal and Social Psychology*, 1963, *66*, 429–436.

Berkowitz, L., & Daniels, L. R. Affecting the salience of the social responsibility norm: Effects of past help on the response to dependency relationships. *Journal of Abnormal and Social Psychology*, 1964, *68*, 275–281.

Bradley, R. H., & Webb, R. Age-related differences in locus of control orientations in three behavior domains. *Human Development*, 1976, *19*, 49–55.

Brehm, J. W. *A theory of psychological reactance.* New York: Academic Press, 1966.

Coelho, G., Hamburg, D., & Adams, J. (Eds.). *Coping and adaptation.* New York: Basic Books, 1974.

Coleman, J. C. *Abnormal psychology and modern life* (5th ed.). Glenview, Il.: Scott, Foresman, 1976.

Collins, B. E. Four separate components of the Rotter I–E Scale: Belief in a just world, a predictable world, a difficult world, and a politically responsive world. *Journal of Personality and Social Psychology*, 1974, *29*, 381–389.

Davis, W. L., & Davis, D. E. Internal–external control and attribution of responsibility for success and failure. *Journal of Personality*, 1972, *40*, 123–136.

DeBettignier, H. C. Japanese organizational behavior: A psychocultural approach. In D. Graser (Ed.), *Management research: A cross-cultural perspective.* San Francisco: Jossey-Bass, 1971.

deCharms, R. *Personal causation: The internal affective determinants of behavior.* New York: Academic Press, 1968.

Doi, T. [*The anatomy of dependence*] (John Bester, translator). Tokyo: San Francisco: Kodansha International, 1973.

Douglas, J. H. Pioneering a non-Western psychology. *Science News*, 1978, *113*, 154–158.

Drucker, P. What can we learn from Japanese management? *Harvard Business Review*, 1971, *49*, 110–122.

Dweck, C. S., & Goetz, T. E. Attributions and learned helplessness. In J. H. Harvey, W. J. Ickes, & R. F. Kidd (Eds.), *New directions in attribution research* (Vol. 2). Hillsdale, N.J.: Erlbaum, 1978.

Fischhoff, B. Attribution theory and judgment under uncertainty. In J. W. Harvey, W. J. Ickes, & R. F. Kidd (Eds.), *New directions in attribution research* (Vol. 1). Toronto: Wiley, 1976.

Fisher, J. D., Nadler, A., & Whitcher-Alagna, S. Recipient reactions to aid. *Psychological Bulletin*, 1982, *91*(1), 27–54.

Friedman, M., & Rosenman, R. *Type A behavior and your heart.* New York: Knopf, 1974.

Glass, D. C. *Behavior patterns, stress, and coronary disease.* Hillsdale, N.J.: Erlbaum, 1977.

Gorman, P., Jones, L., & Holman, J. Generalizing American locus of control norms to Australian populations: A warning. *Australian Psychologist*, 1980, *15*, 125–127.

Gurin, P., Gurin, G., Lao, R. C., & Beattie, M. Internal–external control in the motivational dynamics of Negro youth. *Journal of Social Issues*, 1969, *25*, 29–53.

Heider, F. *The psychology of interpersonal relations.* New York: Wiley, 1958.

Ickes, W., & Layden, M. A. Attributional styles. In J. H. Harvey, W. J. Ickes, & R. F. Kidd (Eds.), *New directions in attribution research* (Vol. 2). Hillsdale, N.J.: Erlbaum, 1978.

358 : PAUL T. P. WONG AND CATHERINE F. SPROULE

Jones, E. E., & Nisbett, R. E. The actor and the observer: Divergent perceptions of the causes of behavior. In E. E. Jones, D. E. Kanouse, H. H. Kelley, R. E. Nisbett, S. Valins, & B. Weiner (Eds.), *Attribution: Perceiving the causes of behavior.* Morristown, N.J.: General Learning Press, 1971.

Kagan, J., & Moss, H. The stability of passive and dependent behavior from childhood through adulthood. *Child Development,* 1960, *31,* 577–591.

Kelley, H. H. Attribution theory in social psychology. In D. Levin (Ed.), *Nebraska symposium on motivation.* Lincoln: University of Nebraska Press, 1967.

Kelley, H. H. *Attribution in social interaction.* Morristown, N.J.: General Learning Press, 1971.

Kettlewell, G. *Attributional patterns of high achieving career women.* Unpublished honours thesis, Trent University, Peterborough, Ontario, 1981.

Lange, R., & Tiggemann, M. Changes within the Australian population to more external control beliefs. *Australian Psychologist,* 1980, *15,* 495–497.

Lange, R. V., & Tiggemann, M. Dimensionality and reliability of the Rotter Internal–External Locus of Control Scale. *Journal of Personality Assessment,* 1981, *45*(4), 398–406.

Lazarus, R. S. *Psychological stress and the coping process.* New York: McGraw-Hill, 1966.

Lazarus, R. S., Averill, J. R., & Opton, E. M., Jr. The psychology of coping: Issues of research and assessment. In G. V. Coelho, D. A. Hamburg, & E. J. Adams (Eds.), *Coping and adaptation.* New York: Basic Books, 1974.

Lefcourt, H. M. Recent developments in the study of locus of control. In B. A. Maher (Ed.), *Progress in experimental personality research* (Vol. 6). New York: Academic Press, 1972.

Lefcourt, H. M. The function of illusion of control and freedom. *American Psychologist,* 1973, *28,* 417–425.

Lefcourt, H. M. *Locus of control: Current trends in theory and research.* Hillsdale, N.J.: Lawrence Erlbaum, 1976.

Lefcourt, H. M. (Ed.). *Research with the locus of control construct: Assessment methods* (Vol. 1). New York: Academic Press, 1981.

Levenson, H. Multidimensional locus of control in psychiatric patients. *Jurnal of Consulting and Clinical Psychology,* 1973, *41,* 397–404.

Levenson, H. *Multidimensional locus of control in prison inmates.* Paper presented at the annual American Psychological Association Conference, September 2, 1974.

Levenson, H., & Miller, J. Multidimensional locus of control in sociopolitical activists of conservative and liberal ideologies. *Journal of Personality and Social Psychology,* 1976, *33,* 199–208.

Matthews, K. A. Psychological perspectives on the Type A behavior pattern. *Psychological Bulletin,* 1982, *91*(2), 293–323.

Mechanic, D. Some problems in developing a social psychology of adaptation to stress. In J. McGrath (Ed.), *Social and psychological factors in stress.* New York: Holt, Rinehart & Winston, 1970.

Mehrabian, A. Measures of achieving tendency. *Educational and Psychological Measurement,* 1969, *29,* 445–451.

Merton, R. K. Contributions to the theory of reference group behavior. In R. K. Merton (Ed.), *Social theory and social structure.* New York: Free Press, 1968.

Miller, S. M. Controllability and human stress: Method, evidence and theory. *Behavior Research and Therapy,* 1979, *17,* 287–307.

Mirels, H. L. Dimensions of internal versus external control. *Journal of Consulting and Clinical Psychology,* 1970, *34,* 226–228.

Mussen, P. (Ed.). *Carmichael's manual of child psychology* (3rd Ed., Vol. 2). New York: Wiley, 1970.

Nadler, A., Altman, A., & Fisher, J. D. Helping is not enough: Recipients' reactions to aid as a function of positive and negative self-regard. *Journal of Personality*, 1979, *47*, 615–628.

Nadler, A., Fisher, J. D., & Streufert, S. When helping hurts: The effects of donor–recipient similarity and recipient self-esteem on reactions to aid. *Journal of Personality*, 1976, *44*, 392–409.

O'Brien, G. E., & Kabanoff, B. Australian norms and factor analysis of Rotter's Internal–External Control Scale. *Australian Psychologist*, 1981, *16*(2), 184–202.

Ouchi, W. G. *Theory Z.* Reading, Mass.: Addison-Wesley, 1981.

Pascale, R. T. Zen and the art of management. *Harvard Business Review*, 1978, *78*, 153–162.

Phares, E. J., Wilson, K. G., & Klyver, N. W. Internal–external control and the attribution of blame under neutral and distractive conditions. *Journal of Personality and Social Psychology*, 1971, *18*, 285–288.

Prociuk, T. J., & Breen, L. J. Defensive externality and its relation to academic performance. *Journal of Personality and Social Psychology*, 1975, *31*, 549–556.

Reid, D. W. Locus of control as an important concept for an interactionist approach to behaviour with particular application to psychological stress. *York University, Department of Psychology Reports*, 1975, No. 10, 1–19.

Rosenman, R. H. The interview method of assessment of the coronary- prone behavior pattern. In T. M. Dembroski, S. M. Weiss, J. L. Shields, S. G. Haynes, & M. Feinleib (Eds.), *Coronary-prone behavior.* New York: Springer-Verlag, 1978.

Ross, L. The intuitive psychologist and his shortcomings: Distortions in the attribution process. In L. Berkowitz (Ed.), *Advances in experimental social psychology* (Vol. 10). New York: Academic Press, 1977.

Rothbaum, F., Weisz, J. R., & Snyder, S. S. Changing the world and changing the self: A two-process model of perceived control. *Journal of Personality and Social Psychology*, 1982, *42*(1), 5–37.

Rotter, J. B. Generalized expectancies for internal versus external control of reinforcement. *Psychological Monographs*, 1966, *80* (1, Whole No. 609).

Rotter, J. B. Some problems and misconceptions related to the construct of internal versus external control of reinforcement. *Journal of Consulting and Clinical Psychology*, 1975, *43*(1), 56–67.

Sanger, S. A., & Alker, H. A. Dimensions of internal–external locus of control and the women's liberation movement. *Journal of Social Issues*, 1972, *28*, 115–129.

Seligman, M. E. P. *Helplessness: On depression, development, and death.* San Francisco: Freeman, 1975.

Silvestri, P. J. Locus of control and God-dependence. *Psychological Reports*, 1979, *45*, 89–90.

Skinner, B. F. Beyond freedom and dignity. New York: Knopf, 1971.

Sproule, C. F., Watters, D. A., & Wong, P. T. P. *Attribution biases: Self vs others, success vs failure.* Paper presented at the Psychonomic Society Annual Meeting, St. Louis, 1976.

Staats, S. Internal versus external locus of control for three age groups. *International Journal of Aging and Human Development*, 1974, *5*(1), 7–10.

Strickland, B. R. Internal–external expectancies and health-related behaviors. *Journal of Consulting and Clinical Psychology*, 1978, *46*(6), 1192–1211.

Tessler, R. C., & Schwartz, S. H. Help-seeking, self-esteem, and achievement motivation:

An attributional analysis. *Journal of Personality and Social psychology*, 1972, *21*, 318–326.

Thompson, S. C. Will it hurt less if I can control it? A complex answer to a simple question. *Psychological Bulletin*, 1981, *90*, 89–101.

Weiner, B. A theory of motivation for some classroom experiences. *Journal of Educational Psychology*, 1979, *71*, 3–25.

Weiner, B., Frieze, I., Kukla, A., Reed, L., Rest, S., & Rosenbaum, R. M. Perceiving the causes of success and failure. In E. E. Jones, D. E. Kanouse, H. H. Kelley, R. E. Nisbett, S. Valins, & B. Weiner (Eds.), *Attribution: Perceiving the causes of behavior.* Morristown, N.J.: General Learning Press, 1971.

Weiner, B., & Kukla, A. An attributional analysis of achievement motivation. *Journal of Personality and Social Psychology*, 1970, *15*, 1–20.

Wong, P. T. P. Coping with frustrative stress: A stage model. *The Behavioral and Brain Sciences*, in press.

Wong, P. T. P. Sex differences in performance and contingency judgment. *Sex Roles*, 1982, *8*, 381–388.

Wong, P. T. P. & Reker, G. T. Do old people perceive and desire more external control? Unpublished manuscript, Trent University, 1982.

Wong, P. T. P., & Reker. G. T.Coping and well-being in Chinese and Caucasian elderly. Paper presented at the Canadian Association on Gerontology Annual Meeting, Winnipeg, 1982.

Wong, P. T. P., & Sproule, C. F. When do people desire external control? Unpublished manuscript, Trent University, 1982.

Wong, P. T. P., Watters, D. A., & Sproule, C. F. Initial validity and reliability of the Trent Attribution Profile (TAP) as a measure of attribution schema and locus of control. *Educational and Psychological Measurement*, 1978, *38*, 1129–1134.

Wong, P. T. P., & Weiner, B. When people ask "why" questions, and the heuristics of attributional search. *Journal of Personality and Social Psychology*, 1981, *40*, (4), 650–663.

Wortman, C. B., & Brehm, J. W. Responses to uncontrollable outcomes: An integration of reactance theory and the learned helplessness model. In L. Berkowitz (Ed.), *Advances in experimental social psychology* (Vol. 8). New York: Academic Press, 1975.

Wright, P. H. A model and a technique for studies of friendship. *Journal of Experimental Social Psychology*, 1969, *5*, 295–309.

Zuckerman, M. Attribution of success and failure re-visited, or: The motivational bias is alive and well in attribution theory. *Journal of Personality*, 1979, *47*, 245–287.

Zuckerman, M., & Gerbasi, K. E. Dimensions of the I–E scale and their relationship to other personality measures. *Educational and Psychological Measurement*, 1977, *37*, 159–175.

6

David W. Reid

PARTICIPATORY CONTROL AND THE CHRONIC-ILLNESS ADJUSTMENT PROCESS*

Introduction

The ideas expressed in this chapter derive from two conclusions regarding current research on the impact of chronic illness and disabilities. The first conclusion is that rigorous systematic studies of the long-term psychosocial ramifications of living with chronic illness are woefully lacking. The second conclusion is that research in which the locus of control variable accounts for variations in psychological adjustment is generally inadequate. Current formulations have discussed both the conditions contributing to external control and the immediate effects of being externally controlled, but they neither explain the long-term effects of being externally controlled nor clarify the process of adjustment to being externally controlled. Except for the work of Miller (1980), current locus of control formulations do not generally examine the ramifications of living in a state of external control except to suggest that a profound sense of helplessness, hopelessness, depression, self-denigration, or alienation is likely to develop. The implication is that to be externally controlled is bad or at least less than an optimal state. Perhaps, however, being externally controlled is not always so bad (for similar concerns, see Rodin, Rennert, & Solomon, 1980; Wortman & Dintzer, 1978; Schulz & Hanusa, 1980; Miller 1980).

*The preparation of this chapter was supported by a Social Sciences and Humanities Research Council of Canada Grant 492–79–0080–R1 & R2 (Strategic Grants Division).

RESEARCH WITH THE LOCUS
OF CONTROL CONSTRUCT (Vol. 3.)
Extensions and Limitations

The purpose of this chapter is to share some theoretical notions concerning adjustment to chronic disease and disability. Although it deals with adjustment to chronic physical illness, the ideas are general enough to be applied in an equally exploratory way to other situations where an individual must live with considerably increased external control of his or her life. Consequently, other literatures concerned with psychological stress, reactions to acute forms of illness, adjustment to treatments such as surgery and hemodialysis, and adjustment to cardiovascular diseases have also been examined. From these reviews I have derived some exploratory ideas, which require refinement but may provide us with some promising directions to further our understanding of adjustment processes.

Before pursuing this discussion some clarifications are necessary to avoid confusion. Chronic diseases referred to here are those which (a) by definition cannot be cured, (b) significantly influence one's everyday life, and (c) necessitate the assistance of or treatment by others. Furthermore, it is acknowledged that adjustment to some diseases, such as certain forms of cancer, may be different in many ways from adjustment to other ailments, such as myocardial infarction. However, this chapter focuses on more global adjustment processes that are likely to share commonality with all chronic diseases. Finally, personal control is used in a broad sense, notwithstanding the fact that other authors are becoming progressively more precise in distinguishing controllability from predictability and in specifying many additional facets of control, such as behavioral control, cognitive control, organization, prediction, choice (Averill, 1973), self-control (Reid & Ware, 1974), countercontrol (Mahoney, 1974), reactance (Wortman & Brehm, 1975), and retrospective control (Thompson, 1981). Though useful in some respects, such refinements are often easier to differentiate conceptually than empirically (e.g., Burger & Thompson, 1981).

The Reality of Living with Chronic Disease and Health Care Dependency

The research Ziegler and I (see Reid & Ziegler, 1981b, for a review) reported on psychological adjustment among the elderly has consistently demonstrated that those who have more internal scores on our Desired Control measure are relatively better adjusted. The findings were obtained from samples of both noninstitutionalized and institutionalized elderly. From an examination of the mean scores it was also found that the institutionalized elderly generally reported more external beliefs than did the noninstitutionalized elderly (Reid & Ziegler, 1980). Such mean differences are understandable given that the institutionalized commonly suffer from chronic disease or disabilities and such poor physical health is correlated with lower Desired Control scores (Reid & Ziegler, 1981b). More recently we found that the Desired Control scores of a sample of 124 senior citizens (initial mean age = 77 years) declined significantly (became more external) over a 5-year period (1976–1981). This decline may have reflected changes in physical health because persons in this sample with poor physical health generally reported lower Desired Control, and also because those persons deceased at the time of follow-up had obtained lower Desired Control scores 5 years earlier than had those who were still alive. Despite these mean score changes, the initial Desired Control scores still correlated with Life Satisfaction ($r = .43$) 5 years later. In summary, our data show that Desired Control scores decreased substantially, that these changes may well have reflected changes in health status, and yet even within the distribution of these scores those who were relatively more internal were better adjusted. In other words, everyone became more external in his or her beliefs and yet many were still relatively adjusted. Such a finding is consistent with those of Schulz and Hanusa (1980), who suggested that it is not the absolute level of control that is important but rather one's sense of control in light of one's reference group.

Becoming more external in one's beliefs seems to be a likely result of having a chronic disease or disability, which, in turn, leads to reduced ambulation, energy levels, and the like. Furthermore, living under the care of others (e.g., hospital staff) leads to excessive dependencies (Barton, & Baltes, & Orzech, 1980) and conformity to necessary routines, among other things, that might well undermine one's sense of control. Indeed, simply trying to gain or retain a high degree of personal control may lead to considerable frustration and stress. It even seems that the more adjustive strategy would be to become more external, to surrender one's control. Yet our correlational data do not suggest this.

The substance of this issue became more clear as a result of our more recent research (Sangster, Blackwell, Quek, Reid, & Ziegler, 1981) studying the adjustment to chronic disease and disability among elderly patients. In our initial study patients with diseases or disabilities participated in individual in-depth clinical interviews conducted by specially trained doctoral students. These interviews typically spanned two and sometimes three sessions. The resulting data (based on answers to

10 leading questions) were content analyzed carefully and extensively and the findings have been reported elsewhere (Sangster, et al., 1981). Subsequently, a second study was undertaken which involved three-person groups of patients meeting biweekly for 6 weeks of social skills training. The latter dealt not only with the social skill behaviors of the patients but also with their cognitions (expectations, reservations, and understandings) regarding their interactions with other patients and staff. A third pilot study was then completed in which four patients who were adjusting to disease or disability and institutionalized living were followed on a weekly basis over several months to monitor and facilitate their adjustment.

From these three studies we have become familiar with certain viewpoints common to the elderly that are relevant to the issue of whether adjustment is facilitated by increased control when circumstances militate against such control. First, we found that patients were generally reticent about their desire to gain more personal control and feared that the pursuit of control could result in a reduction of the care they currently received; or else that it was impossible to gain more control because they were either too old or too ill. These view-points suggest both a wish to retain the status quo with regard to control by others and resignation to this condition borne of inevitability. Supporting this view was the often stated belief that it was the staff's responsibility and right to take care of the patients. In short, our data indicated considerable externality in beliefs among the patients, and these beliefs seemed realistic and were often quite well-articulated. A second point we discovered was that the patients' ways of adjusting were complex and that any manifestation of personal control was different qualitatively from what one might otherwise expect. For example, a common theme for many patients was that they adjusted simply by living from day to day. Although such statements might be interpreted as symptomatic of passivity bordering on apathy, it can be also seen as a way of optimizing predictability. The patients found that at best they could anticipate and prepare only for events occurring within a short period of time. Given that the future and long-term events are so affected by the vicissitudes of health, changes in staffing, and other factors, they are less predictable and less subject to control. Consequently, patients focus more directly on their day-to-day existence.

Our data also led us to suspect that there was a conflict being shared by both patients and staff. An extended care setting is simultaneously a hospital and a patient's home. Hospital care is legally and historically under the control of hospital staff. But in our culture one's home and associated daily activities are assumed to be more private and self-directed. In many cases the staff may have expectations that they will care for the patient's physical comfort but that, within their capabilities, the patient needs to participate, to be active, and to be responsible for those aspects of his or her hospital life which do not directly pertain to physical care. But such distinctions easily become blurred for both staff and patients, and the resulting differential expectations may be conflicting. Staff who attend to physical health may try to care for other aspects of the patient's life, thus frustrating patients' needs to be able to choose and control the activities and conditions of their home. Alternately, patients who desire that their physical health needs be met by expert staff may function in ways that suggest they expect all aspects of their lives to be cared for. In either case the result is a milieu that encourages passive dependence on the part of the patient, which may be countertherapeutic in a psychological sense. Corroborating this view is an observational study by Barton *et al.* (1980) which demonstrated that dependency behaviors on the part of elderly patients are reinforced by staff, whereas independent behaviors are not.

It appears from our data, as well as considerations of anecdotal observations, that the reality of living with chronic disease and its accompanying health care dependency helps to foster the development of externality in one's attitudes. Indeed, becoming more external seems to be an adjustive strategy reflecting actual reductions of instrumental involvement in one's world.

There is other evidence in the literature that persons living with a chronic disease or disability (with regard to their personal control beliefs) become more external. Furthermore, in two of these studies there are indications that being external can be independent of or associated with decreases in anxiety and increases in the sense of well-being. Lewis, Gottesman, and Gutstein (1979), for example, used a Solomon four-group quasi-experimental design to follow the comparative course of experience among persons undergoing surgery for cancer and persons receiving surgery for other ailments. Comparisons were made between data collected the evening before surgery and then 2, 5, 8, and 12 weeks later. The cancer group was found to be more anxious on both state and trait anxiety measures, more depressed, and more external in their beliefs, with differences increasing over the test period. At 12 weeks there were signs that the state of crisis was abating, with a lessening of anxiety (state and trait) and depression. However, externality and diminished self-esteem remained. Wilson, Muzekari, Schneps, and Wilson (1974), in a study that involved counselling for home hemodialysis patients, reported a substantial shift over 15 months to greater externality on Rotter's I–E Scale and, at the same time, an increased sense of well-being as measured by the California Personality Inventory. Poll and Kaplan De-Nour (1980) concluded on the basis of I–E scores from their own study, and those of four others, that dialysis patients exhibit external control. However, in their study I–E scores did not correlate with time on hemodialysis, suggesting that the length of time in treatment does not alter beliefs. Moreover, the mean Rotter I–E scores in the studies they cited ranged from 8.00 to 9.55, and their own mean scores were 10.95. These means (12.18), as well as those in the Wilson et al. (1974) study (12.18) cited earlier, are not extreme and lie well within the Rotter scale norms obtained for university students.

Rotter's I–E Scale was used in a questionnaire study of the psychosocial aspects of mastectomy for 41 women (Jamieson, Wellisch, & Pasnau, 1978). Although mean scores were not provided, better overall postmastectomy emotional adjustment was associated with more external I–E beliefs, lower neuroticism scores (Eysenck Personality Inventory), longer marriages, and having more social support from significant others, including hospital staff and surgeons.

Assuming that the reality of living with chronic disease or disability and health care dependency leads to considerably more externality, the question that arises concerns the price of the adjustment to such conditions. Is it enough to accept the fact that the largest parts of one's existence are out of one's control and to feel instrumental within only the narrow limits that are still responsive to one's efforts? And if one is able to make such reconstructions of one's disabilities vis-à-vis one's reference group and/or physical conditions (Fisk, 1980), how might this be done? To try to answer these questions we need to look at what is known about the relationship between control and adjustment.

Relationship of Control to Adjustment: Application of Current Knowledge

A large and growing literature supports the view that the more people believe they are losing personal control over events that are of importance to them, the more detrimental and negative are the effects; conversely, having personal control is seen as preferable and as leading to positive effects. However, these relationships between personal control and adjustment are complex, and increased control has not always been found to lead to positive effects (e.g., Rodin, Rennart, & Solomon, 1980; Solomon, Holmes, & McCaul, 1980); nor, on the other hand, has the loss of control always been found to lead to detrimental effects (e.g.,

Roth & Bootzin, 1974). Given these anomalies and the resulting search for explanations of them, we hope to develop better understanding of the function of control phenomena in psychosocial well-being.

The current wisdom is that the relationship of control to adjustment depends on the meaning and/or the situational context (Averill, 1973; Silver & Wortman 1980; Solomon, et al., 1980; Thompson, 1981; Wortman & Dintzer, 1978). Now we have to understand what is meant by the meaning and/or the situational parameters mediating the control–adjustment relationship. However, it is first useful to identify a theoretical distinction in the literature, which is necessary to avoid further confusion in studies of control–adjustment relationships. Across studies (and among authors) there appears to be a difference in perspective whereby from one point of view control is seen as a means to an end whereas from another point of view having control is considered the preferred end in and of itself (Miller, 1980; Rodin et al., 1980). The latter is more consistent with writings implying a need for control (deCharms, 1968; Kelley, 1971; White, 1959) that assume that being in control is an integral part of psychological adjustment per se rather than as a potential means or tool for facilitating adjustment.

Control as a Means to an End

The perspective that control is a means to adjustment makes it easier to predict when control would be less preferable than lack of control. Put simply, whenever being in control is likely to lead to pain, embarrassment, or feelings of inferiority, external control will be the preferred condition. Consistent with this viewpoint is Miller's (1980) minimax hypothesis, which states that persons behave so as to minimize the maximum of likely aversive conditions. If one feels more able and more stable relative to other persons (external source), then one will prefer having control and anxiety will be less than it would be if the other person were to be given control. Alternately, if one feels that the other person is more capable and/or stable than oneself, then there would be a greater likelihood of minimizing danger of aversiveness if one depended on that other person. In this case one should prefer turning control over to the more stable other person. This eminently reasonable hypothesis fits with typical learning theory assumptions (i.e., increase positive reinforcement—minimize punishment) and follows a traditional, rational-cognitive model whereby subjects are expected to weigh the costs versus the benefits of retaining control. The most problematic aspect of this hypothesis for our interests is that it predicts preference or choice but not adjustment. To use Miller's example, one might choose to let one's doctor administer a hypodermic needle because he or she is more skilled, but one can still be highly anxious, unsettled, or discontent with such a circumstance. Furthermore, this hypothesis either fails to consider the intrinsic worth of being in control or else assumes that under excessive or particularly aversive conditions the instrinsic worth of control is overridden by the desire to minimize aversive experience. For acute, highly threatening situations, Miller is likely correct. But being externally controlled under the conditions she has discussed does not necessarily mean that one is or feels well adjusted.

Rodin et al. (1980) reported that under certain circumstances having more control can lead to a loss of self-esteem. Across a series of three studies these authors demonstrated that when greater control (choice, responsibility) is given to a person who is engaged in a task in which self-monitoring is salient (e.g., completing an important self-report or personality scale or conducting a real-life interview with minimal preparation while under potential psychological surveillance), self-esteem ratings decrease. It is notable, however, that these subjects apparently were receiving no feedback on tasks with which they had little familiarity. Thus it is likely that self-doubt was maximized by these procedures. In short, when one chooses to take control or responsibility and yet receives no pertinent feedback, one's self-monitoring and doubt concerning performance are likely to increase. These laboratory demonstrations were highly contrived, but they serve to support the point that taking control can put one's self- esteem at risk. However, in these studies being externally controlled was not manipulated, and the moot point remains whether one's self-esteem is more diminished when one is in control than when one's behavior is controlled by others. Obviously, it depends on the circumstances. In a similar study Solomon et al. (1980) found that having behavioral control leads to increased physiological arousal and self-reported anxiety only when the exercise of control is difficult; a condition likely operating in the Rodin et al. (1980) study.

Similar to this line of reasoning—that control is important only as a means—are the findings by Matthews, Scheier, Brunson, and Carducci (1980) which demonstrated that the reporting of fewer physical symptoms under conditions of unpredictability was eliminated when subjects in the predictability condition were instructed to attend to aversive stimuli. These results were interpreted as supporting the hypothesis that unpredictable events exert a deleterious influence because they cause more attention to be directed to the aversive stimuli. Although this hypothesis is compelling, the data demonstrate only that the *addition* of instruction to attend to aversive stimuli leads to increased reporting of physical symptoms among those in a predictability condition; but this does not prove that attention per se is the mediating distinction between predictability and unpredictability with resulting differences in performance. Furthermore, had the authors been able to include an additional experimental condition demonstrating the reduction of symptom reporting following reduced attention in an unpredictable condition, their hypothesis would have been better served.

Thompson (1981) suggests that a unifying theme in understanding the control–adjustment relationship involves the extent to which either gaining or losing control alters the meaning of events to the person. One dimension of meaning she describes is that of endurable–unendurable. This dimension, similar to Miller's minimax hypothesis, suggests that the critical distinction is the extent to which a person sees either surrendering or retaining control as making an outcome more endurable. From this point of view it may be predicted that one may even willingly accept aversive conditions under an external control situation provided one believes this choice would lead to more positive outcomes. An example would be a person's submitting himself or herself to the rule of a brutal leader instead of choosing to retain his or her own independence, if he or she believes the former would lead to greater rewards than would the latter.

The assumption that control is a means to an end is also central to social learning theory, proposed by Rotter (1954, 1966; Rotter et al., 1972). According to this theory, control refers to the persons' expectancy that the outcome is contingent on the person's actions. The greater the expected contingency between acts and outcomes, by definition, the more control the person anticipates having. However, the likelihood of a person acting in given ways is determined not only by perceived control but also by the value of the outcomes. No matter how much the person has control, the likelihood of particular actions is diminished if the outcome is not valued. Although the theory does not necessarily predict either when having control may be detrimental or when not having control might be beneficial, the theory does place considerable emphasis on combining situational parameters and learning history in predicting behavior. It seems reasonable from social learning theory that one could learn either to give up control or to accept noncontingency if it would ensure a desired outcome. But once again this would occur only if the external agent of control was predictably rewarding. In essence, controllability would be given up if predictability of the desired outcome increased.

From the preceding discussion, it appears that we can better understand the personal control to adjustment relationship if (a) we find that the situational meaning of control to a person is as a means to a desirable end and not an end in itself, and (b) assume that the end results are more important than the means. This theoretical perspective allows one to understand why a person may at times prefer not to have control. Indeed, the logic can even be extended to the notion that people will give up personal control if doing so ensures greater control in the future.

Control as an End or a Need

The assumption that having control is a desired goal in and of itself is implicit in the writings of many authors. In a classic article White (1959) reviewed existing theories of motivation and concluded that they were inadequate to account for such phenomena as play or exploration. He proposed the concept of *effectance motivation* based on a neurogenic, innate need to manipulate the environment. This need is a basic and prevailing one, but it can be overridden by other primary needs such as hunger and thirst when they are aroused. But when these primary needs are satisfied, the effectance motive continues to be a basis for our behavior. Related concepts are those of *personal causation* (deCharms, 1968) and Bandura's (1977) *self-efficacy*. Lefcourt (1976) contends that persons are generally better off when they have personal control. Langer's (1975) studies demonstrating the ways persons will misconstrue chance events so as to give themselves a sense of control suggests that persons intrinsically want to perceive control over events. Kelly (1967, 1971), one of the seminal contributors to attribution theory, based his theory on the assumption that persons tend to perceive their worlds in ways that optimize their control over events. Wortman (1976), Rodin *et al.* (1980), and Averill (1973) provided reviews of studies and/or theoretical positions that posit a need or preference for control.

In Volume I of this series Reid and Ziegler (1981, Chapter 4) proposed a cognitive social learning basis for control beliefs. They suggested that there is a natural bias for persons to see their worlds in terms of cause–effect relationships and that these causes in turn are differentiated as dimensions of personal control versus control by external sources. This bias toward making interpretations in terms of internal versus external sources is indigenous to our reactions to the world, for it has always been an important element in the adaptation process one makes to one's world. Put in these terms, wishing to see the world in orderly, causal, internal–external ways is not only a need, it is a natural way of thinking. When our experiences are not readily interpretable in terms of causation or the internal–external sources, we become uncomfortable and seek to restore an order or understanding of a cause–effect relationship along an internal–external pattern. However, given order, we prefer to see ourselves as the causal or instrumental agents because this permits us to be more adaptive.

The assumption that having control is a desired end in and of itself leads one to assume that being externally controlled is undesirable. Furthermore, being externally controlled would be contrary to one's natural tendencies and frustrating to one's needs. As such, being externally controlled would lead to poor psychological well-being. Given such assumptions, we are led to wonder why some persons may desire to be externally controlled and how persons can continue to live in a state where being externally controlled is a salient reality. Any answer that simply suggests that a person in such a state somehow manages to retain a sense of control (illusory or not) merely begs the question (cf. Lefcourt, 1976). How does one either regain, retain, or achieve a sense of control, particularly when doing so can be very distressful and contrary to the physical and/or social reality in which the person exists?

Multidimensional Compensation Model

One answer to the foregoing questions can be found in a compensation model whereby the person finds some alternate way to gain a sense of control. This is possible only if persons can make reasonably clear distinctions between where they do not have control and where they do have control. Thus a person dying from cancer whose treatments have been repeatedly unsuccessful and whose disease is out of control may find some reduction in anxiety either through helping others or undertaking instrumental actions in areas other than those concerned with the treatment of his or her own disease. This regaining of a form of control may contribute to a reduction of anxiety and the effects of trauma for the person.

When considering the feasibility of such a distinction we noted that among the 35 expectancy items in our Desired Control Measure only 2 were concerned with the control of one's health. Perhaps psychological well-being among our elderly samples would not have correlated with internality on health care items. This finding, along with the absence of relationships between health control beliefs and other personal control beliefs, supports the distinction noted earlier. Indeed, perhaps being more external on Health Control and more internal on Desired Control are associated with better adjustment. Supporting this multidimensional distinction is the Wallston and Wallston (1981) finding that their original Health Locus of Control Scale had only low positive correlations (20s and 30s) with Rotter's scale across four studies.

This multidimensional compensation model was tested in a recent study in which 50 hospitalized elderly patients receiving extended care for chronic disease and disabilities were interviewed at length. In addition, they completed the short form of the Desired Control measure (excluding the one item referring to health), a 16-item I–E Health Control scale (most items derived from the Wallston and Wallston multidimensional Health Locus of Control Scale), an expanded version of Bradburn and Caplowitz's (1965) mood measure, and a 9-item rating of patient adjustment by nursing staff. The contents of a 9-item rating were derived from an investigation by Bulman and Wortman (1977) and refer to such patient behaviors as accepting the reality of one's disease, showing interest in improving one's physical condition, and taking full advantage of services available. Greater Desired Control was not reliably correlated with either internality in Health Control ($r = -.21$, $p < .07$) or patient adjustment ratings by staff ($r = -.003$), but it did correlate with more positive affect ($r = .52$, $p < .001$) and less negative affect ($r = -.30$, $p < .01$). Greater personal Health Control, on the other hand, correlated with better patient adjustment ($r = .23$, $p < .05$) but with neither positive ($r = -.03$) nor negative affect ($r = -.02$). Positive patient adjustment correlated marginally with more positive affect ($r = .22$, $p < .06$) and with less negative affect ($r = -.25$, $p < .04$). The pattern of these data is consistent with a multidimensional model of I–E control and adjustment, but the relationship is possibly even more intricate than originally envisioned. Not only is the correlation between Desired Control and Health Control low, but each one correlates with a different aspect of psychological adjustment. Desired Control beliefs are pertinent to a more general measure of well-being, but not to one's actions as a patient. Health Locus of Control is more specific to how one performs the role of a patient. The psychological adjustment of chronic care patients also appears to be multidimensional (see Silver & Wortman, 1980, for a similar conclusion).

Relationships of Control to Adjustment: Reconsiderations and a Hypothesis

The current formulations concerning how persons adjust to living with greater externality seem incomplete for explaining adjustment to chronic disease and disability. Application of Miller's minimax hypothesis predicts that those with chronic diseases would gladly surrender control to health care staff if the staff were considered more competent than the patients. But health care staff as individuals—and as part of large, impersonal health care systems—can make mistakes and are not necessarily thorough or consistent in the care they provide. Thus surrendering control can engender a state of threat unless the patient comes to have complete faith in the health care staff. But such blind faith is unlikely, particularly over time, when opportunities to experience the inadequacies of external care become plentiful. But assuming control of oneself is not a likely choice after a probable history of frustration in trying to cope on one's own. Usually it is the case that the person has struggled to attain or retain as much personal control as possible, but the failures in doing so and the greater relief and reduced frustration when in the care of others make external control desirable. On this point Miller is probably right. Thus the loss of external control may be as threatening as the loss of personal control.

Such a situation portends a dilemma for the chronically ill or disabled person, one that could be of existential proportions. Only when the dilemma is accentuated by extreme threat to the person's existence is it likely that blind faith may develop in the integrity and competence of either the staff or, indeed, one's own potency in gaining relief.

Cousins's (1979) chronicle of his personal experiences with a terminal disease is a case in point. He described how he heroically defeated his disease, a struggle that included his self-administration of large dosages of vitamin C and spending long periods listening to humorous recording and movies with the hope that the resulting humor and mirth would have biochemical influences useful for eradicating his disease. It is interesting to note the admiration and gratefulness Cousins has for his personal physician, who was apparently a steadfast source of assurance and encouragement to Cousins in his monumental struggle. A person experiencing such a dilemma is a prime candidate for conversion to belief in a supernatural power, such as a benovolent and just God. But blind faith may be much less likely with chronic disease, where acute phases are less frequent and the dilemma develops more gradually. Nevertheless, adjustment to chronic disease and disability is an adjustment to a way of life, and it is likely that this adjustment involves coming to terms with how much control one has and does not have over one's life. It is not uncommon for those who have suffered a permanent disability or chronic disease to report a subsequent growth experience, one they may value for the lessons (e.g., reevaluation of one's values), liberation, and wisdom gained (Bulman & Wortman, 1977; Herzlich, 1973; Lipowski, 1970; Mechanic, 1977).

In summary, formulations such as the minimax hypothesis, which are rooted in the assumption that control is a means to an end, predict the direction of choice vis-à-vis surrendering or retaining control. But in and of themselves these formulations do not explain adjustment. Choosing to have one's health and well-being controlled by others may produce anxiety, leaving the person discontent and in a rather unhappy situation. The irony is that in many cases persons do not see themselves as having any choice in surrendering control to other persons.

To understand the relationship of control to adjustment we need to consider more carefully our use of the locus of control construct. For example, many articles in the locus of control literature portray a rather simplistic bivariate internal or external distinction. Most writers appreciate internality or externality as a dimension; nevertheless, there is a common tendency to talk about subjects being either internal or external. But if our current wisdom is that the relationship of personal control to adjustment depends on the meaning of control in the situation, I think we also need to pay much more attention to what is meant by either internal or external control vis-à-vis psychological adjustment. The following is such a reconsideration.

What Is Internal versus External Control?

First, it must be kept in mind that there is no such thing as internality without externality. To see ourselves as internal or external is clearly a relative rather than an absolute statement. Rotter (1966) warned that extremes of internality or externality are likely maladaptive and this is eminently reasonable, for to see oneself as entirely internal is to say there are not external sources of control. But if internal is relative to external and vice versa, what does this tell us and why might it be important? The answer may lie within a cognitive social learning theory of I–E and causal experiences.

Reid and Ziegler (1981), in the first volume of this series, postulated that one's sense of internality–externality is rooted in one's basic experience of causation. Internality–externality differentiations are part of the general process of distinguishing oneself from other objects in the world and as such it is a necessary part of adaptation to one's world. This I–E distinction, along with the sense of causation, comes from the child's earliest self-perceptions as being different from his or her world. This is the root process of developing a personal identity. This viewpoint obviously shares commonality with Piaget's theory, which emphasized an ongoing adaptation process of assimilation and accommodation. One is constantly maintaining a balance between assimilating experiences provided by one's environment and accommodating oneself to the environment. In a similar fashion one's sense or understanding of causation is constantly in terms of a balance between internal and external forces. Thus to the extent to which we see our outcomes as not within our control, we automatically search for external agents as explanations for the cause of the outcome.

This balance between one's sense of internality and externality is critical, for without this balance our sense of causation(s) is unresolved, and this state is highly unsettling and anxiety-arousing. Our awareness of external forces helps us to explain the occurrence of events we cannot influence. Conversely, when our understanding of external sources does not explain certain events adequately, it helps us to be able to attribute the results to our own doing or responsibility. Generally we all go about our lives adapting day by day with no particular problem, given that the causes of events are adequately accounted for by the internal–external sources we are aware of; and with this understanding we can act accordingly. Furthermore, events are not usually seen as due entirely to either internal or external sources, but rather to some combination of both. It is when our sense of internal versus external control does not account for events adequately that adaptation to our world becomes difficult. There are times—thankfully quite rare—when people experience an asynchronism in their understanding of causation along an internality–externality continuum. These are almost always times of crisis, such as when one is suddenly paralyzed for life, or when one learns that one is terminally ill with cancer or will lose a child to a rare disease. These asynchronisms are events that demand an understanding of their cause; but the events do not fit the usual determining balances between internal and external as we have known them. Thus when a tragic event occurs, we demand to know why. We are driven to find an explanation, a cause. Emotionally and intellectually we are impelled to search for meaning of the events. Of course, these particular examples are of crisis proportions because they hurt very deeply, not just because we do not understand them. Even when we understand them they are exceedingly distressful. But our adjustment to them hinges on our coming to terms with their causation or (depending on the situation) lack of reasonable causal explanations. Thus the Bulman and Wortman (1977) interviews with victims of spinal cord injury, Shanfield's (1980) interviews with survivors of cancer, and Markson's (1971) interviews with sufferers of rheumatoid arthritis found that *all* interviewees had searched for reasons for their victimization. Take, for example, a person who finds that he is terminally ill. His search for meaning may range from feelings of being punished for unknown wrongdoings to being called by the Lord, feeling that he hadn't lived properly (e.g., poor nutrition and smoking), or anger against mankind. Such examples abound in articles concerned with ways in which people cope with death and dying. The death of an elderly loved grandparent is not as likely to distress people as much as the death of an equally loved child. Perhaps the reason is that despite the hurt caused in both cases, the public's sense of cause for the death of a senior citizen is better balanced with minimal asynchronism among the attributed internal–external causes. Thus, the death of the child is seen as more unjust.

An important point is that some major events, such as having a chronic illness, becoming very old, and/or approaching death, are not necessarily crises that generate a great deal of questioning (e.g., Why me?) when the person has had time to attribute personally acceptable reasons for the events. But these reasons are going to lie along a continuum of internal and external causes. Knowing where causes lie and being able to accept them makes it easier for most people to adjust. Only when one has come to an understanding of how much control one has is one able to respond in ways that are likely to be beneficial or potentially rewarding to one's interests. In short, being internal is relative to one's perception of externality.

This reconsideration of internal–external beliefs as building on one's ongoing attempts to maintain an understanding of the causation of experienced events fits very closely with the current emphases on person–environment dialectics (Riegel, 1977; Windley & Scheidt, 1980) and person–environment congruence that inheres in the interactional models of psychology (Kahana, 1975; Lawton, 1977; Magnusson & Endler, 1977; Murray, 1938). The emphasis in these models is that there is an inseparability between humans and their environment and a reciprocal causation between such sources, and that people function best when a point of equilibration between those sources can be approximated. Thus optimal adjustment occurs when the competence of the person in meeting his or her needs is complemented by an environmental press that does not overly challenge or oppress the person's abilities to respond. In this context locus of control is very much an interactionist concept (Reid, 1977).

From this reconsideration of the theoretical meaning of control and its relationship to adjustment it is easier to see how persons can perceive themselves as becoming more externally controlled at the same time that they continue to strive for control. This striving in turn contributes to a sense of well-being. Thus, we can explain our earlier findings that over 5 years the mean Desired Control scores of a sample of elderly persons became more external, and yet those who continued to perceive themselves as relatively internal were more satisfied with their lives. In essence, reflecting the reality of becoming older and more frail, the balance of external to internal sources seen as influencing their outcomes had shifted in an external direction; but those retaining a relatively more internal orientation were nevertheless more satisfied and content.

The theoretical explanations for why persons in most cases tend both to prefer and to respond more positively to being in control are readily available from other sources (e.g., Lefcourt, 1973, 1976, 1981; Phares, 1976). However, an added emphasis here is that unless persons respond in reaction to or in opposition to their sense (perception) of events being externally controlled, they will not know how much input they have toward influencing events happening to them. *Thus, being able to react is important for validating or corroborating one's sense of control.* If this is so, then persons will rarely be content to be completely externally controlled. Rather, they will respond in ways so as to ensure that they have input and/or instrumental involvement. Those persons who are better able to react effectively to external forces are better able to adjust.

Thus, Miller's minimax hypothesis may be seen as incomplete. Although her hypothesis predicts when a person may choose to have an external source of control over events, it does not explain that the person will at the same time wish to continue an involvement and/or also maintain a relative sense of control over the events. The question remains how one retains a relative sense of control over events that one also sees as strongly determined by sources external to oneself. The answer may lie in a process called *participatory control.*

Participatory Control

The concept of participatory control is predicated on an argument that humans do not remain in a state of total helplessness (no personal control) for an extended period. Those extreme stresses, depressions, and so on that are associated with the loss of personal control are typically transitory. Similarly, most chronically ill or disabled patients, even in the later stages of their life, do not remain in a state of abject helplessness for very long. In one way or another, people manage to regain an acceptable sense of control and do so despite their realistic loss of considerable control.

There are two components of participatory control. First, chronically ill patients must come to the resolution whereby they concede and accept the fact that there are others who are better able than themselves to take care of their physical health. Thus, as they become more involved in participatory control they also become more external (but not extremely external) in their beliefs, and more willing to have others take control of outcomes important to them. These more external beliefs reflect an attitude of cooperation.

Second, because such a surrender of control is threatening, the patient must operate so as to minimize this threat. To do this, it helps for the patient to feel that he or she has input into the decisions of medical staff. For example, the patient would like the staff to have all available data necessary to make the best decisions. Furthermore, the patient, though clearly surrendering control to the caregivers, wants to know about the decisions being made so that he or she might be assured that his or her case is being examined and considered properly. Being kept informed provides the illusion of monitoring one's treatment and supports beliefs in the integrity of the caregivers. The underlying psychological dynamics of this surrender of control is that the patient, unable to control his or her physical condition directly, attempts to gain control over his or her condition through the abilities and efforts of others. One ramification is a developing sense of membership in a team dedicated, it is hoped, to the best care of the patient's conditions. Thus compliance and cooperation should be greater when participatory control is operating. The caregivers and the patient are working together, but with the staff viewed as being more expert and in control. In essence the chronically ill patient *participates* in a system in which he or she is ultimately externally controlled.

The style with which participatory control is maintained varies from patient to patient and setting to setting. However, there are some basic features necessary to assist the development of participatory control. First, patients require the ability to express their needs and fears, and also to communicate either their encouragement or displeasure to the staff in an effective way. Such abilities will operate more effectively if there are existing social norms which encourage such behaviors on the part of patients. Thus patients should be encouraged to be involved in their care as much as is reasonable. In short, there should be arrangements whereby all issues are discussed openly, regular consultations made with patients, reinforcement offered for their giving information and suggestions, and encouragement provided to take the initiative in everyday activities other than their health care.

The provision of participatory control makes it possible for the chronically ill to adjust more easily to the reality of being dependent on the care of others. At the same time, it can reduce the anxiety and stress attendent on having sole responsibility for oneself and thus lead to greater adjustment, contentment, well-being, and life satisfaction. In fact—and almost by definition—participatory control should lead to better health care, for it should facilitate a better information exchange and the kind of cooperation that is necessary for effective treatment. An added feature of participatory control is that it reduces total reliance on the caregivers. Thus if mistakes occur, patients should be less likely to become angry with the staff, provided that the staff were consistent in their consultations with the patients. Alternatively, patients who see their participatory control as high will be very upset with any health care practice that is adopted without due consideration of the expectations patients had of being consulted or advised.

Review of Supporting Literature

Acceptance is a poorly researched concept with regard to adjustment to disease and/or stress. One implication of locus of control research is that to reduce stress one should gain more control, even if it is illusory (e.g., Lefcourt, 1973; Glass & Singer, 1972). However, as we noted earlier, another way stress may be reduced in many situations is to cease trying to regain control and to accept the apparent circumstances. Similarly, adjustment to a chronic disease may be made easier if the person can first come to accept the permanence of the disease and its influence on everyday life. One needs to accept not only the disease but also the sequelae and the cause of the disease. Acceptance of the cause is akin to being able to forgive. Indeed, a number of writers have found inconsistent findings with regard to whether or not blaming oneself or others for one's circumstances leads to better adjustment

(Janis & Rodin, 1979; Silver & Wortman, 1980). Yet these studies may have missed the point that blame per se may not be as important as whether or not the target of the blame is forgiven.

Barker (1955) appears to be one of the first to suggest that the acceptance of one's loss is a step toward adjustment to being disabled without self-devaluation. In a questionnaire survey of adjustment to multiple sclerosis by 174 persons, Matson and Brooks (1977) found that from a list of 13 coping strategies, accepting the disease was the fourth most popular coping strategy. These authors speculated that acceptance is a significant part of the process of adjustment. Keegan, Ash, and Greenough (1976), in a study of the psychological and social implications of blindness, found that among a random sample of 114 legally blind persons the most significant variable affecting a variety of adjustment measures was whether or not the person had given up the false hope (acceptors) of regaining his or her vision. The acceptors scored lower on dependence and depression, reported more adequate coping, were more likely to be employed, and were more likely to be involved in rehabilitation programs.

Similarly, Weisman and Worden (1976) interviewed and tested 120 consecutive patient admissions, who had received a diagnosis of cancer, with the Minnesota Multiphasic Personality Inventory, the Thematic Apperception Test, and the Profile of Mood States at four different times in the first 100 days after diagnosis. Although the interviewer's assessment of the patient's "vulnerability" (adjustment) may not have been independent (blind) of the psychometric scores, some interesting findings were obtained. For example, one of the five factors characteristic of good adjustment was acceptance of one's condition together with finding something favorable about it. Kipinowski (1981) reported that the content analysis of interviews designed to assess the psychological coping of 42 hemophilia patients revealed that of the 25 identifiable coping strategies, the most common was acceptance of the condition. Acceptance in this case referred to both accepting one's own limitations as well as accepting the situation. This acceptance strategy was correlated with greater compliance with treatment and fewer psychosomatic reactions. In summary, these studies of three different chronic diseases and one disability all found that acceptance is a particularly important factor influencing adjustments.

The participatory control concept places considerable emphasis on a *mutually beneficial relationship* between the patient and the treatment staff, such that (a) the staff gives particular attention to the patient, which encourages his or her feelings of being involved; and (b) the patient becomes instrumental in assisting or promoting the care given to him or her by the treatment staff.

A number of studies and anecdotal, professional opinion publications support the importance of this reciprocal relationship. In the Weisman and Worden (1976) study cited earlier, those cancer patients who were low in mood disturbance, better adjusted, and lower in vulnerability were characterized as being able to seek direction from authority and comply with it and to face the facts of their illness and take firm action rather than resort to suppression and a fatalistic submission to the inevitable. Weisman and Sobel (1979) also found from their 5-year study (Project Omega) of coping with cancer that so-called good copers were resourceful in shifting back and forth from one strategy (independence–self-reliance) to another (rely on resources available). Furthermore, these good copers would insist on more information and good treatment whenever they felt neglected.

In a study examining individual differences in promptness at returning to employment and a full life following reconstructive vascular surgery, Boyd, Yeager, and McMillan (1973) identified a characteristic theme among those who adjusted more quickly. From in-depth interviews it was found that these better-adjusted persons had a more active reciprocal communication with their surgeon whereby "a basic trust and acceptance of authority of the surgeon rather than acquiescence to omnipotence of the parental substitute" was fostered (p. 38). These studies were correlational, however, and it is possible that those factors related to participatory control were preexisting personality variables rather than reactions to the situation.

Using a quasi-experimental design, Klein, Kliner, Zipes, Troyer, and Wallace (1963) followed two successive groups of patients who were transferred from an intensive care unit during rehabilitation from cardiac arrest. The first group consisted of seven patients whose transfer from the intensive care unit to the general medical ward were abrupt and unpredictable. Five of these patients showed negative adjustment, such as cardiovascular reactions and increases in catecholamine secretions indicative of high stress. The next seven patients received advanced warning of the transfer, had one medical doctor and a nurse who were actively involved in following through treatment, and after transfer to the general ward were visited by a nurse to provide assistance in adjustment (e.g., by giving information regarding rehabilitation). In this latter group none of the adverse reactions noted in the first group was found. Notwithstanding the nonrandomized, nonequivalent groups and small sample size, these findings are consistent with the notion that an active reciprocal relationship is conducive to less stressful rehabilitation.

Krantz and Schulz (1980) summarized a study by Cromwell, Butterfield, Brayfield, and Curry (1977) in which care of acute myocardial infarction patients was manipulated in a 2 (information) × 2 (participation) × 2 (diversion) factorial design. High information involved a combination of a recording, literature, and informative comments from physicians regarding the causes, treatment, and physiology of myocardial infarctions. The high participation condition had subjects active in their own treatment, recording their own EKG tracings, and doing isometric and foot-pedaling exercises. It is notable, however, that they were to give the EKG recordings to the physician for his or her examination and the exercises were to be performed under the close surveillance of hospital staff. Patients in the high diversion treatment had greater access to television, newspapers, magazines, and visitor privileges. They also had nurses coming to visit and talk informally whenever the staff chose to do so. Each of these treatment conditions reflects distinct aspects of participatory control whereby the patient was given detailed information about his or her condition (together with the attention of the expert physician), was encouraged and supervised in taking an active role in his or her care, as well as receiving the special attention of nursing visits where he or she would have a greater opportunity to discuss care received.

The rationale behind the participatory control concept predicts that all three high conditions (a three-way interaction) together optimize participatory control and lead to the greatest adjustment. Cromwell et al. (1977) found that the two 2-way interactions—of high information with high participation, and high information with high diversion—led to earlier release from intensive care (2–3 days) and from the hospital (7–8 days). More careful scrutiny also found a trend whereby intermediate levels as opposed to low or high levels of participation and diversion together were associated with short hospital stays. Although this is a somewhat more speculative interpretation, one wonders whether the extremes (low and high levels of participation) might not be more disruptive of the relationships between patients and their nurses and physicians. In other words, to be too self-treating or too attentive to television and book-reading may be less optimal for realizing a cooperative relationship with the staff. A final note of caution in the interpretation of these data is necessary. The differential discharge rates may reflect the fact that the health status of those patients in the low information, low participation and low diversion conditions were not as well-known to the staff, who were therefore more hesitant in discharging them.

Part of the reciprocal relationship aspect of participatory control is the emphasis on the role of staff in giving explanations, encouragements, and guidance for adjustment to illness (Mechanic, 1977; Stewart & Rossien, 1978). Shanfield (1980) interviewed 20 persons who had apparently survived cancer for 1–20 years. All had continued to live with a sense of precariousness and vulnerability to the disease. He noted that important to the psychological well-being of these persons was a high level of loyalty to and trust in their physicians, and this developed when the physicians were "able to accept, clarify, and deal with the anxiety of their patients on a sustained basis" (p. 133). Similarly, in a review of articles pertinent to psychosocial adjustment to breast cancer, Lewis and Bloom (1978) cited several studies suggesting that the early (pre-surgical) involvement of physicians in giving guidance with regard to stress and the pursuit of functional, physical, and cosmetic rehabilitation was important in facilitating adjustment to treatment of the disease. Finally, Jamieson et al. (1978) found that greater social support from hospital staff and surgeons was associated with better overall postmastectomy adjustment.

Another promising aspect of the participatory control concept is that it explains how a person's I–E beliefs can become more external as an adjustive strategy when external sources of control are clearly important. Alternatively, the concept explains how being more internal, when the environment allows such control, would be more adjustive. Such reasoning fits with a congruence hypothesis whereby preexisting beliefs concerning one's degree of internality versus externality may play a role regarding ease of adjustment to one's environment. Those who already have a relatively more external sense of control should find it easier to adjust to an environment that does not permit a high degree of personal control. Conversely, adjustment to an environment that provides opportunity for personal control should be easier for a person with a relatively strong sense of personal control. Strickland (1979), in reviewing studies of locus of control and cardiovascular functioning, noted that the most successful treatment of health-related problems (e.g., smoking cessation treatment, weight loss programs, rehabilitation from cardiovascular arrest) occurred when the individual's I–E beliefs were congruent with the treatment methods; those methods promoting self-treatment worked best for internals, whereas those promoting care controlled by health professionals worked better for those with more external beliefs.

Turner, Tobin, and Lieberman (1972), in a prospective study examining institutional adaptation among the aged, found that those survivors who adapted best in three different nursing homes revealed one distinguishing personality trait cluster, which was derived from a personality assessment questionnaire. This cluster reflected vigorousness, an active style of seeking interaction, intrusiveness when it was necessary, and insistence on responsibility from others regarding one's needs. These authors pointed out that such a style was congruent with the atmosphere of these homes that rewarded active engagement and a combative stance and tolerated complaints and individuality as long as these remained within institutional limitations.

In completing this selective review it is important to point out that the concept of participatory control may not be entirely new. Krantz and Schulz (1980) briefly cited a book by Taylor and Levin (1976) that examines theory and research on the psychological aspects of breast cancer. In this book the authors refer to "informed participation," which presumably refers to some middle position between self-care and care by staff. Similarly, Viederman (1978), in a discussion on the need for control in patients confronted with hemodialysis, talked about a "therapeutic alliance" between the patient and the health care treatment. This alliance includes internalization of the initially external constraints, which involves incorporation of treatment procedures as if they were the patient's own. It seems that those who already have preexisting "character constellations involving a strong sense of control" (p. 455) should be better able to develop such an alliance.

The catalyst for my own ideas came when I had lengthy conversations with a former Jesuit at a time when I was trying to come to grips with my research findings and clinical experience with elderly persons. As a social scientist, I have been impressed with the prevalence of faith and the strength of placebo effects. When my Jesuit friend informed me that a person's relationship with God was not a passive one, but rather required frequent checking of one's understanding of God's will, praying, confessing one's fears and wishes, and so on, my curiosity about the psychological dynamics of such relationships was aroused. It had always seemed paradoxical that a person in the same sentence could say that God determined his or her life and that at the same time he or she gained personal strength, among other things, from God. Such statements are not easily explained by current locus of control formulations. However, one wonders if there is a similar psychological function occurring when the newly converted Christian says that he or she has regained his or her personal strength through God's counsel and when the victim of cancer or the survivor of a deceased loved one regains his or her personal strength through the counsel and guidance of significant others. In each case there is personal participation with an external source of strength and direction to help one adapt to one's existence and conditions. Perhaps this is a basic function of so-called social support groups, particularly at times of increased anxiety, crisis, or confusion.

Summary

The purpose of this chapter was to point out current limitations of locus of control concepts in explaining how persons can adjust to a reality where one has lost control and where health care needs necessitate reliance on others. Hitherto most psychological research had emphasized the value of personal control for alleviating the effects of stress and contributing to one's well-being.

Discussion of the limitations of the locus of control concept led us to consider two directions for further development. One suggested that persons living in circumstances where external controls are dominant learn to compensate by differentiating those areas where they have control from those where they do not, and gaining a sense of control through the former. The second direction involved the concept of participatory control, which was derived from a reconsideration of internal–external control as a cognitive, social learning concept rooted in one's sense of causality (Reid & Ziegler, 1981b). Participatory control refers to a twofold process whereby people first learn to accept the reality of their disease or disability and their reliance on others and, second, learn to become instrumental in their lives through participating with others in controlling events of importance to them. Participatory control helps to explain how a person adjusts to chronic disease and disability, and it may also help to explain part of the process of adjustment to sudden, life-threatening, or crisis situations.

Acknowledgment

I would like to thank Annette Young for her assistance and Sandra Sangster, Bess Blackwell, and Jonathan Quek for their collaboration in the research reported herein.

References

Averill, J. R. Personal control over aversive stimuli and its relationship to stress. *Psychological Bulletin*, 1973, *80*, 286–303.

Bandura, A. Self-efficacy: Toward a unifying theory of behavioral change. *Psychological Review*, 1977, *84*, 191–215.

Barker, R. G. Adjustment of physical handicap and illness: A survey of the social psychology of physique and disability. *Social Science Research Council Bulletin* No. 55, 1955, 1–5.

Barton, E. M., Baltes, M. M., & Orzech, M. J. Etiology of dependence in older nursing home residents during morning care: The role of staff behavior. *Journal of Personality and Social Psychology*, 1980, *38*(3), 423–431.

Boyd, I., Yeager, M., & McMillan, M. Personality styles in the postoperative course. *Psychosomatic Medicine*, 1973, *35*(1), 131–134.

Bradburn, N., & Caplowitz, D. (Eds.). *Report on happiness*. Chicago: Aldine, 1965.

Bulman, R. J., & Wortman, C. B. Attribution of blame and coping in the "real world": Severe accident victims react to their lot. *Journal of Personality and Social Psychology*, 1977, *35*, 351–363.

Burger, J. M., & Arkin, R. M. Prediction, control, and learned helplessness. *Journal of Personality and Social Psychology*, 1980, *38*(3), 482–491.

Cousins, N. *Anatomy of an illness as perceived by the patient*. New York: Norton, 1979.

Cromwell, R. L., Butterfield, E. C., Brayfield, F. M., & Curry, J. J. *Acute myocardial infarction: Reaction and recovery*. St. Louis: Mosby, 1977.

deCharms, R. *Personal causation*. New York: Academic Press, 1968.

Fisk, P. C. The effects of loss of meaning on the mental and physical well-being of the aged. *Dissertation Abstracts International*, 1980, 3925B. (University Microfilms No. 40–8B)

Glass, D. C., & Singer, J. E. *Urban stress*. New York: Academic Press, 1972.

Herzlich, C. *Health and illness*. New York: Academic Press, 1973.

Jamieson, K. R., Wellisch, D. K., & Pasnau, R. O. Psychosocial aspects of mastectomy: I. The woman's perspective. *American Journal of Psychiatry*, 1978, *135*(4), 432–436.

Janis, I. L., & Rodin, J. Attribution, control and decision making: Social psychology and health care. In G. Stone, F. Cohen, & N. A. Adler (Eds.), *Health psychology*. San Francisco: Jossey-Bass, 1979.

Kahana, E. A congruence model of person–environment interaction. In P. G. Windley, T. O. Byerts, & F. G. Ernst (Eds.), *Theory development in environment and aging*. Manhatten, KA: Gerontological Society, 1975.

Keegan, D. L., Ash, D. D. G, & Greenough, T. Blindness, some psychological and social implications. *Canadian Psychiatric Association Journal*, 1976, *21*, 333–340.

Kelley, H. H. Attribution theory in social psychology. In D. Levine (Ed.), *Nebraska Symposium on Motivation* (Vol. 15). Lincoln: University of Nebraska Press, 1967.

Kelley, H. H. Attribution theory in social interaction. In E. E. Jones *et al.* (Eds.), *Attribution: Perceiving the causes of behavior*. Morristown, NJ: General Learning Press, 1971.

Kipnowski, A. *Psychological coping with physical illness*. Paper presented at the Annual Meeting of the Society for the Study of Behavioural Development, Toronto, August 16–24, 1981.

Klein, R. F., Kliner, V. A., Zipes, D. P., Troyer, W. G., & Wallace, A. G. Transfer from a coronary care unit. *Archives of Internal Medicine*, 1968, *122*, 104–108.

Krantz, D. S., & Schulz, R. A model of life crisis, control, and health outcomes: Cardiac rehabilitation and relocation of the elderly. In A. Baum & J. E. Singer (Eds.), *Advances in environmental psychology: Applications of personal control* (Vol. 2). Hillsdale, NJ: Erlbaum, 1980.

Langer, E. J. The illusion of control . *Journal of Personality and Social Psychology*, 1975, *32*, 311–328.

Langer, E. J., Janis, I. L., & Wolfer, J. A. Reduction of psychological stress in surgical patients. *Journal of Experimental Social Psychology*, 1975, *11*, 155–165.

Lawton, M. P. The impact of the environment on aging and behavior. In J. Birren & K. W. Schaie (Eds.), *Handbook on the psychology of aging*. New York: Van Nostrand Reinhold, 1977.

Lefcourt, H. M. The function of the illusions of control and freedom. *American Psychologist*, 1973, *28*, 417–425.

Lefcourt, H. M. *Locus of control: Current trends in theory and research*. Hillsdale, N.J.: Erlbaum, 1976.

Lefcourt, H. M. *Research with the locus of control construct* (Vol. 1): *Assessment methods*. New York: Academic Press, 1981.

Lewis, F. M., & Bloom, J. R. Psychosocial adjustment of breast cancer: A review of selected literature. *International Journal of Psychiatric Medicine*, 1978, *9*(1), 1–17.

Lewis, M. S., Gottesman, D., & Gutstein, S. The course and duration of crisis. *Journal of Consulting and Clinical Psychology*, 1979, *47*(1), 128–134.

Lipowski, Z. J. Physical illness: The individual and coping processes. *Psychiatry in Medicine*, 1970, *1*(2), 91–102.

Magnusson, D., & Endler, N. S. *Personality at the crossroads: Current issues in interactional psychology*. Hillsdale, NJ: Erlbaum, 1977.

Mahoney, M. J. *Cognition and behavior modification*. Cambridge, MA: Ballinger, 1974.

Markson, E. W. Patient semeiology of a chronic disease (rheumatoid arthritis). *Social Science and Medicine*, 1971, *5*, 159–167.

Matson, R. R., & Brooks, N. A. Adjusting to multiple sclerosis: An exploratory study. *Social Science and Medicine*, 1977, *11*, 245–250.

Matthews, K. A., Scheier, M. F., Brunson, B. I., & Carducci, B. Attention, unpredictability, and reports of physical symptoms: Eliminating the benefits of predictability. *Journal of Personality and Social Psychology*, 1980, *38*(3), 525–537.

Mechanic, D. Illness behavior, social adaptation, and the management of illness. *Journal of Nervous and Mental Disease*, 1977, *165*(2, Serial No. 1137), 79–87.

Miller, S. M. Why having control reduces stress: If I can stop the roller coaster, I don't want to get off. In J. Garber & E. P. Seligman (Eds.), *Human helplessness: Theory and applications*. New York: Academic Press, 1980.

Murray, H. A. *Explorations in personality*. New York: Oxford University Press, 1938.

Phares, J. E. *Locus of control in personality*. Morristown, NJ: General Learning Press, 1976.

Poll, I. B., & Kaplan De-Nour, A. Locus of control and adjustment to chronic hemodialysis. *Psychological Medicine*, 1980, *10*, 153–157.

Reid, D. W. Locus of control as an important concept for an interactionist approach to behavior. In D. Magnusson & N. S. Endler (Eds.), *Personality at the crossroads: Current issues in interactional psychology*. Hillsdale, NJ: Erlbaum, 1977.

Reid, D. W., & Ware, E. E. Multidimensionality of internal versus external control: Addition of a third dimension and nondistinction of self versus others. *Canadian Journal of Behavioural Science*, 1974, *6*, 131–142.

Reid, D. W., & Ziegler, M. Validity and stability of a new desired control measure pertaining to psychological adjustment of the elderly. *Journal of Gerontology*, 1980, *35*(3), 395–402.

388   :   DAVID W. REID

Reid, D. W., & Ziegler, M. *Longitudinal studies of desired control and adjustment among the elderly.* Paper presented at the joint meeting of the Gerontological Society of America and the Canadian Association of Gerontology, Toronto, Canada, November 8–12, 1981.(a)

Reid, D. W., & Ziegler, M. The desired control measure and adjustment among the elderly. In H. M. Lefcourt (Ed.), *Research with the locus of control construct: Assessment methods* (Vol. 1). New York: Academic Press, 1981.(b)

Riegel, K. F. History of psychological gerontology. In J. E. Birren & K. W. Schaie (Eds.), *Handbook of the psychology of aging.* New York: Van Nostrand Reinhold, 1977.

Rodin, J., Rennert, K., & Solomon, S. K. Intrinsic motivation for control: Fact or fiction. In A. Baum & J. E. Singer (Eds.), *Advances in environmental psychology (Vol. 2): Applications of personal control.* Hillsdale, NJ: Erlbaum, 1980.

Roth, S., & Bootzin, R. R. Effects of experimentally induced expectancies of external control: An investigation of learned helplessness. *Journal of Personality and Social Psychology,* 1974, *29,* 253–264.

Rotter, J. B. *Social learning and clinical psychology.* Englewood Cliffs, N.J.: Prentice-Hall, 1954.

Rotter, J. B. Generalized expectancies for internal versus external control of reinforcements. *Psychological Monographs,* 1966, *80* (1, Whole No. 609).

Rotter, J. B., Chance, J. E., & Phares, E. J. *Applications of a social learning theory of personality.* New York: Holt, Rinehart & Winston, 1972.

Sangster, S. L., Blackwell, J. E., Quek, J., Reid, D. W., & Ziegler, M. *Adjustment in the chronically disabled elderly.* Paper presented at the joint meeting of the Gerontological Society of America and the Canadian Association on Gerontology, Toronto, Canada, November 8–12, 1981.

Schulz, R., & Hanusa, B. H. Experimental social gerontology: A social psychological perspective. *Journal of Social Issues,* 1980, *36,*(1), 30–46.

Shanfield, S. B. On surviving cancer: Psychological considerations. *Comprehensive Psychiatry,* 1980, *21,*(2), 128–134.

Silver, R. L., & Wortman, C. B. Coping with undesirable life events. In J. Garber & M. E. P. Seligman (Eds.), *Human helplessness: Theory and applications.* New York: Academic Press, 1980.

Solomon, S., Holmes, D. S., & McCaul, K. D. Behavioral control over aversive events: Does control that requires effort reduce anxiety and physiological arousal? *Journal of Personality and Social Psychology,* 1980, *39*(4), 729–736.

Stewart, T. D., & Rossien, A. B. Psychological considerations in the adjustment to spinal cord injury. *Rehabilitation Literature,* 1978, *39*(3), 75–80.

Strickland, B. R. Internal–external expectancies and cardiovascular functioning. In L. C. Permuter & R. A. Monty (Eds.), *Choice and perceived control.* Hillsdale, NJ: Erlbaum, 1979.

Taylor, S. E., & Levin, S. *Psychological aspects of breast cancer: Theory and research.* San Francisco: West Coast Cancer Foundation, 1976.

Thompson, S. C. Will it hurt less if I can control it? A complex answer to a simple question. *Psychological Bulletin,* 1981, *90*(1), 89–101.

Turner, B. F., Tobin, S. S., & Lieberman, M. A. Personality traits as predictors of institutional adaptation among the aged. *Journal of Gerontology,* 1972, *27,*(1), 61–68.

Viederman, M. On the vicissitudes of the need for control in patients confronted with hemodialysis. *Comprehensive Psychiatry,* 1978, *19* (5), 455–466.

Wallston, K. A., & Wallston, B. S. Health locus of control scales. In H. M. Lefcourt (Ed.), *Research with the locus of control construct (Vol. 1): Assessment methods.* New York: Academic Press, 1981.

Weisman, A. D., & Sobel, H. J. Coping with cancer through self- instruction: A hypothesis. *Journal of Human Stress*, 1979, *5*(1), 3–8.

Wiesman, A. D., & Worden, J. W. The existential plight in cancer: Significance of the first 100 days. *International Journal of Psychiatry in Medicine*, 1976, *7*, 1–15.

White, R. W. Motivation reconsidered: The concepts of competence. *Psychological Review*, 1959, *66*, 297–333.

Wilson, C. J., Muzekari, L. H., Schneps, S. A., Wilson, D. M. Time-limited group counseling for chronic home hemodialysis patients. *Journal of Counseling and Clinical Psychology*, 1974, *37*, 376–379.

Windley, P. G., & Scheidt, R. J. Person–environment dialectics: Implications for competent functioning in old age. In L. W. Poon (Ed.), *Aging in the 1980s*. Washington, DC: American Psychological Association, 1980.

Wortman, C. B. Causal attributions and personal control. In J. H. Harvey, W. J. Ickles, & R. F. Kidd (Eds.), *New directions in attribution research* (Vol. 1). Hillsdale, NJ: Erlbaum, 1976.

Wortman, C. B., & Brehm, J. W. Responses to uncontrollable outcomes: An integration of reactance theory and the learned helplessness model. In L. Berkowitz (Ed.), *Advances in experimental social psychology* (Vol. 8). New York: Academic Press, 1975.

Wortman, C. B., & Dintzer, L. Is an attributional analysis of the learned helplessness phenomenon viable? A critique of the Abramson-Seligman-Teasdale reformulation. *Journal of Abnormal Psychology*, 1978, *87*, 75–90.

7

Herbert M. Lefcourt

EPILOGUE

On looking backward at the contributions in this and the preceding volumes, we can conclude that there is reason both to doubt the pervasive utility of the locus of control construct and yet to be encouraged by the fruitful results that are attainable when locus of control is used thoughtfully and imaginatively.

As is true of many personality constructs, adherents and enthusiastic investigators often misapply the locus of control variable and expect it to account for more variance than it is ever wise to hope for. As a consequence, disappointment is commonly experienced and premature withdrawal from further investigation may result. However, when investigators have sought to understand when and where the construct might be more profitably employed, encouraging results have often been obtained.

Even when results have been positive, however, rarely has the locus of control accounted for a large share of the variance from given criterion measures. Rather than considering such a fact as reason for discouragement, it should be regarded as a challenge; not to be concerned with improving the predictive power of locus of control per se but with finding those conditions or other personal characteristics that may interact with locus of control in predicting given criteria.

In a recent chapter and article (Lefcourt, Martin & Ebers, 1981a, 1981b) we attempted to describe a model appropriate for a future clinical psychology. Briefly, we suggested that an appropriate target for clinicians is to assess the occurrence of specific life stresses clients are

RESEARCH WITH THE LOCUS
OF CONTROL CONSTRUCT (Vol. 3.)
Extensions and Limitations

likely to have undergone. In this manner, situations are taken into account in the predictive formulae. If these stresses are construed as negative, we can anticipate symptomatic behaviors. However, at the same time, not everyone succumbs to the influence of negative events, and it is incumbent on the clinician to ascertain which assets the client lacks—social supports, humor, perceived control, or a sense of commitment or responsiveness to challenge? Each of these facets is a component of hardiness (Kobasa, 1982) or of the mature personality (Allport, 1961). Using variables such as locus of control in interaction with situational variables and other personality characteristics that may act in similar fashion should help us to understand clients better and to increase the power of our predictions of criteria such as health and morale.

However, the lessons provided by some of the chapters in this volume should lead us to be humble even with regard to the more interactive models we may employ. For we never can be sure how particular circumstances will affect certain persons. Passivity and acceptance may be better tools for suffering certain inevitabilities than striving and effort. Similarly, limitations of our predictive power may inhere in the fact that locus of control is not always a unified expectancy. Under failure conditions our attributions may serve a different function than under conditions of success, for example.

There is obvious complexity in this research. However, whenever confusion develops and my interest begins to wane, new contributions draw me and other investigators back to the pursuit of exploring the ramifications of the locus of control construct. It is my hope that the contents of these volumes will serve to encourage and stimulate others to continue in their explorations with this provocative construct, and that models such as those proposed by my colleagues and I (Lefcourt et al., 1981a,b) will not prove to be singular and eventually forgotten.

References

Allport, G. W. *Pattern and growth in personality.* New York: Holt, Rinehart & Winston, 1961.

Kobasa, S. C. The hardy personality: Toward a social psychology of stress and health. In J. Suls & G. Sanders (Eds.), *Social psychology of health and illness.* Hillsdale, N.J.: Erlbaum, 1982.

Lefcourt, H. M., Martin, R. A., & Ebers, K. Toward a renewed integration of personality research and clinical practice. In I. Silverman (Ed.), *New directions for methodology of social and behavioral science* (No. 8). San Francisco: Jossey-Bass, 1981. (a)

Lefcourt, H. M., Martin, R. A., & Ebers, K. Coping with stress: A model for clinical psychology. *Academic Psychology Bulletin,* 1981, *3,* 355–364. (b)

AUTHOR INDEX

The numerals in italics indicate pages on which the complete references appear.

A

Abdel-Halim, A. A., 39, 44, *65*
Abrahamson, D., 61, *65*, 234, 235, *291*
Abramowitz, S. I., 253, *291*
Abramson, L. Y., 150, *195*
Achterberg, J., 171, *195*
Adams, J., 314, *357*
Adelson, J., 289, *294*
Adinolfi, A., 280, *291*
Aggarwal, Y. P., 262, 279, *291*
Alain, M., 290, *291*
Albert, M., 189, *195*
Alexander, A. A., 94, *196*
Alker, H. A., 239, *303, 322, 359*
Allen, J. K., 170, *196*
Allison, S. N., 11, *72*
Allport, G. W., 392, *392*
Altman, A., 345, *359*
Alvarez, C. M., 216, 217, *291*
Ames, R. E., 216, 217, 240, *296*
Anastasiades, P., 81, *196*
Anderson, C. R., 2, *4*, 22, 34, 35, 36, *65*, 184, *196*
Anderson, D. E., 109, 137, 144, 151, *198, 206*
Andreasen, A. G., 89, 103, *197*
Andreassi, J. L., 79, 80, *196*
Andrisani, P. J., 15, 16, 46, 47, 50, *65*
Annis, R. C., 2, *4*
Applebaum, E., 15, *65*
Arabian, J. M., 81, *199*

Arkin, R. M., *386*
Arnold, H. J., 11, *65*
Ash, D. D. G., 380, *386*
Atkinson, T., 43, 44, *68*
Audette, R., 154, *207*
Averill, J. R., 80, 84, 86, 92, 94, 108, 174, 182, *196, 201,* 314, 315, *357, 358,* 362, 367, 370, 386
Aviram, A., 222, 268, *291*

B

Back, K. W., 280, *297*
Baer, P. E., 129, 135, *199*
Bakan, P., 116, 118, *201*
Baker, E. K., 164, 167, *196*
Baltes, M. M., 363, 365, *386*
Bandura, A., 136, *196, 331, 357,* 370, *386*
Barker, R. G., 380, *386*
Barling, J., 220, 230, 268, *291*
Barnes, T., 102, 153, *199*
Bar-Tal, D., 222, 259, 261, 278, *291*
Bartel, N. R., 278, *291*
Barton, E. M., 363, 365, *386*
Bar-Zohar, Y., 222, 259, 261, 278, *291*
Bateman, D. E., 86, *202*
Batlis, N. C., *65*
Battle, E., 214, 215, 278, *291*
Baum, J. F., 215, 259, 268, *296*
Beattie, M., 3, *4,* 16, 50, 61, *67,* 229, 234, 238, 239, 247, 252, 255, 263, *296,* 322, *357*

393

SUBJECT INDEX